TRUE FACES OF GANDHI AND AMBEDKAR

Foreword by
Justice Chandrashekhar Dharmadhikari

Sheshrao Chavan

ATLANTIC
PUBLISHERS & DISTRIBUTORS (P) LTD

ATLANTIC
PUBLISHERS & DISTRIBUTORS (P) LTD
7/22, Ansari Road, Darya Ganj, New Delhi
Tel.: +91-11-4077 5252, 2327 3880
E-mail: orders@atlanticbooks.com
Web: www.atlanticbooks.com

Reprint 2026

Published by Atlantic Publishers & Distributors (P) Ltd.

Printed & bound in India by Atlantic Print Services

Foreword

I have immense pleasure in writing a Foreword to this informative and analytical book, written by Shri Sheshrao Chavan. It is said that "to be great is to be misunderstood". I hope this book will help in resolving any misunderstanding about the relationship between these two great personalities, that is, Mahatma Gandhi and Dr. Babasaheb Ambedkar.

The Nagpur airport has been rechristened as Dr. Ambedkar International Airport. We must hail and thank the Indian government and its Civil Aviation Minister for such splendid work. One is reminded of the fact that in one of the parliamentary elections, Dr. Ambedkar was defeated from Bhandara district in Vidharbha. People like me always had a feeling of deep hurt on that count. Today, that very district has gone through an act of atonement. We also believe that a few people should be elected unopposed as members of our parliament and that too even unanimously. That alone would give our parliament an Indian character. This is also essential for upholding the dignity and majesty of our democracy. But Babasaheb was never given that honour, though in terms of qualifications for it, he could have certainly topped the list in that category. That speaks volumes for the kind of power politics that is going on in our country. It is our misfortune that the nation and its interests come last in our considerations.

In this context it is a very welcome step on the part of the government of India to have renamed the Nagpur airport after Babasaheb. Now all those who want not only to go to Nagpur—the land of enlightenment of Babasaheb, but also to Wardha—Gandhi's land of action, or Paunar—Vinoba's land of God-consciousness, would have to pass through the newly renamed Dr. Ambedkar International Airport. The real purpose behind associating something with the name of a great person is that people should continue to seek inspiration for their lives and times for generations to come.

We have imbibed a bad habit of making our great men stand and fight against each other. We do not have to go far to seek such illustrative examples. Various attempts have been made to posit leaders like Tilak and Agarkar, Tilak and Gandhi and even Gandhi and Ambedkar against each other. I have an instinctive feeling that these imaginary and self-created conflicts between such great leaders work as acts of entertainment for their respective followers. Maybe, these are also needed for the very existence of their followers and their organizations. On such occasions, one could easily recall the words of George Bernard Shaw who said that when God could not easily decide the fate and what kind of punishment to be given to the great men, he decided to create the tradition of disciples (*shishya paramapara*) for them. A disciple may or may not be the true successor to his *guru*, but certainly he is entitled to perform his last rites and rituals. It seems that all the *gurus* collectively assemble at the top point of a triangle, but the disciples stand separately on its two lower points. Since they could never reach the height of their *gurus*, they are ever engaged in bringing down their *gurus* to their own levels and are involved in a proxy war on behalf of their *gurus*. It is not surprising that Maharashtra being one of the most enlightened and progressive states also stands on the top of such a list!

Gandhiji always held Dr. Ambedkar in high esteem. They did differ on ideological grounds, but they never lost mutual respect for each other. Their paths may have been different, but the final destination was the same. Both of them were striving hard to build a new society, free from all kinds of domination and exploitation. In other words, both wanted to bring about revolutionary changes in the basic structure of Indian society. It is evident from what Gandhiji wrote about Mahad Satyagraha launched by Dr. Ambedkar. He said:

"For, it should be remembered that it was not the drinking of water at the tank which had brought together the 'touchables' to the temple, but the false report that the untouchables were wanting to enter the temple. But one can hardly expect sanity to exist side by side with unreason. Untouchability itself has no reason behind it. It is an inhuman institution. It is tottering and it is sought to be supported by the so-called orthodox party by sheer brute force.

The so-called untouchables have brought the question a step nearer to solution by their exemplary self-restraint under most provoking circumstances. Had they retaliated, it would have been perhaps difficult to distribute the blame. As it is, the blame is all on the side of the 'touchables'. Brute force will not sustain untouchability. It will bring about a revulsion of feeling in favour of the suppressed classes. It is a sign of the times that there were at least some 'touchables' who tried to defend the poor untouchables. One could wish that there were many more in Mahad. Silent sympathy on such occasions is not of much use. Every Hindu, who considers the removal of untouchability to be of paramount importance, should on such occasions prove his support by publicly defending the suppressed classes and having his own head broken in defending the helpless and the downtrodden.

I cannot help thinking that Dr. Ambedkar was fully justified in putting to test the resolutions of the Bombay Legislative Council and the Mahad Municipality by advising the so-called untouchables to go to the tank to quench their thirst. No incident of this character should pass by unnoticed on the part of associations like the Hindu Mahasabha interested in this reform. Let them investigate the statements made by my correspondent and if they can be substantiated, let them condemn the action of the 'touchables'. There is nothing like the growth of enlightened public opinion for eradicating everything evil, which untouchability undoubtedly is" (*Young India*, 28-4-1927).

At another occasion, Gandhiji spoke highly of Dr. Ambedkar. Speaking at a meeting in Oxford in October 1931, Gandhi stated that he had the highest regard for Dr. Ambedkar: "He has every right to be bitter. That he does not break our heads is an act of self-restraint on his part." Writing to an English friend two years later, he said: "I find nothing unnatural in Ambedkar's hostility to the Congress and its supporters. He has not only witnessed the inhuman wrongs done to the social pariahs of Hinduism, "but in spite of all his culture, all the honours that he has received, he has, when he is in India, still to suffer many insults to which untouchables are exposed". In June 1936 Gandhiji pointed out once again that Dr. Ambedkar "has had to suffer humiliations and insults which should make any one of us bitter and resentful". Had I been in his place, he remarked, "I would have been as angry".

Referring to Dr. Ambedkar's intent to leave Hinduism and embrace some other religion, Gandhiji remarked:

"Dr. Ambedkar is a challenge to Hinduism. Brought up as a Hindu, educated by a Hindu potentate, he has become so disgusted with the so-called Savarna Hindus or the treatment that he and his people have received at their hands that he proposes to leave not only them but the very religion that is his and their common heritage."

But despite all this, of late, some people have tried to present the picture as if Gandhiji and Dr. Ambedkar were hostile to each other. They forget that in spite of Ambedkar's outstanding, intellectual abilities and academic qualifications, the country could have denied him his due and deserving place in the national life. Let us recall that on the eve of Independence when the Constitution for the country was to be framed, there was a proposal to bring foreign experts for the job. It was on Gandhiji's initiative and insistence that Dr. Ambedkar was assigned the job. This is how the man who had earlier burnt *Manusmriti* succeeded in creating a new *Bhimsmriti*. He also became the Law Minister of India. On every count, he was equal to the task assigned. In the process, he drafted the Hindu Code Bill and thus rendered a great service to the Indian society in general and the Hindu community in particular.

Dr. Ambedkar also had great respect for Gandhiji. In the wake of a bomb attack on Gandhiji during 1934, Dr. Ambedkar chose to preside over the meeting which was held to condemn such sinful and nefarious act. He used very strong words to condemn such a cowardly act and wished a long and purposeful life for Gandhiji.

He even suggested that by fixing some tax on salt, an independent fund should be created and that should be used for extending financial help to the needy and deserving Dalits. He wanted that fund to be called Gandhi Fund. He also asserted that Gandhiji had done tremendous good work for Dalits.

It is a puzzle to me whose selfish interests are being served by creating a situation of conflict between these two great sons of India? The fact of the matter is that through service to harijans, Gandhiji tried to eliminate the sin and scourge of untouchability from the hearts and minds of the upper castes of India. On the other hand, Dr. Ambedkar rendered a great service to the entire society by leading a movement for Dalit liberation. Both these movements were complimentary and supplementary to each other. All this ultimately led to the abolition of untouchability under Article 17 of the Indian Constitution. According to Dr. Ambedkar, many of the sages and saints of India have expressed deep concern and compassion for the Dalits of India. But most of them did not actually stand by the Dalits in their suffering and humiliation. Nor did they openly defy and oppose those sections of the upper castes of India who were perpetrating all kinds of injustices against the Dalits. But the only saint who not only sympathized with them but also launched relentless battle on their behalf was no other than Mahatma Gandhi. That is my humble opinion. And ignoring all this, anti-Gandhi tirade is being spread by a section of our own people. I am more than sure that all this is being done only to promote their own petty selfish interests.

Now even the use of the word 'harijan' is being opposed. An attempt is on to replace it by another word 'Dalit'. One need not have much objection to such campaign but let us not forget that it was Narsi Mehta, the Gujarati poet-saint, who had first used the word 'harijan' in his writings. He was a Nagar Brahmin but was very close to harijans. According to Shailendra Mahato, the leader of Jharkhand Mukti Morcha, the word 'harijan' was for the first time used by Maharshi Valmiki who himself was some kind of an untouchable. Now some Dalit leaders are raising the question that if the Dalits are the children of God (harijan), then should others be taken as the children of Satan? Even today, those who are polluting the environment carry greater social prestige than 'Valmikis' who help in keeping it neat and clean. This is a question deserving serious thought on the part of every section of our society. Moving beyond the politics of caste and religion, all of us must join hands towards building up a society based on equality and unity. It is for that reason that Gandhiji made 'broomstick' as the symbol of revolution along with *charkha*.

Making a reference to the low status of the Dalits in the Indian society, Gandhiji said:

"I do not want to be reborn. But if I have to be reborn, I should be born an untouchable, so that I may share their sorrows, sufferings, and the affronts leveled at them, in order that I may endeavour to free myself and them from that miserable condition. I, therefore, prayed that, if I should be born again, I should do so not as a Brahmin, Kshatriya, Vaishya or Shudra, but as an Atishudra." (*Young India*, 4-5-1921)

I am constantly reminded of the glowing terms in which my father Dada Dharmadhikari had spoken about Dr. Ambedkar. Dada was also a member of the Constituent Assembly of India. It was during those days that I happened to meet Dr. Ambedkar both at Delhi and also at Nagpur. I could never forget those moments of my life. They are ever stored in my memory. Dada said: "Dr. Ambedkar is one of those great men of India about whom the people of India would continue to take pride for generations to come. They would always aspire to emulate him. He would remain a shining symbol not only of Dalit identity but that of India. His name would stay in Indian history forever. He used every ounce of his talent and energy for the cause of Dalits, so that they could lead a life of dignity and self-respect, while remaining in the broad framework of Hindu society. Mahad and Kalaram Temple satyagrahis became the source and symbol of inspiration for all those who wanted to work for the liberation of Dalits. But towards the end of his life he came to the firm conclusion that the Dalits could not lead a life of dignity and self-respect, while living within the fold of Hinduism. Consequently, he along with his large number of followers embraced Buddhism during 1956 in Nagpur. Even while taking such a bold and momentous step, he refused to go against the national interest and major ethical and spiritual ethos of India. He opted for Buddhism which has non-violence as its main message. That was also the primary faith of Gandhiji."

The names of Buddha and Gandhi would together go down in Indian history who stood for and represented the best moral and ethical values of the Indian tradition. It was with such an understanding that I had gone to Nasik to attend the centenary celebrations of Dadasaheb Gaikwad—one of the closest associates of Dr. Ambedkar. The convenor of the Committee had handed over a copy of the letter that he had addressed to the Chief Minister of Maharashtra. In that letter he had fervently pleaded that a joint statue of Gandhi and Ambedkar should be installed at Pune. Many people feel that such an initiative should also take place in Nagpur. Nagpur is not only a place at the centre of India but it is also its cultural centre. But statue installation may not be the main issue. The real challenge is to change our mindset for a new social order. We should not forget that during Mahad Satyagraha, a photograph of Mahatma Gandhi was put on the dais. It is an auspicious and welcome initiative taken by the central government that the road to Sevagram would start from Dr. Ambedkar International Airport. This is a doubly welcome step. All that we can say is: Let God bless all of us with good intention and resolve!

Shri Sheshrao Chavan has done a yeoman service in placing before the readers the ground realities about the relationship of two great leaders of this country.

I welcome this book and wish it all success.

Justice Chandrashekhar Dharmadhikari

Preface

I have often wondered as to why I should have undertaken this study. Men better equipped than myself in wisdom could have done fuller justice to the issues I have dealt with. The best justification for my attempt is provided by Edmund Burke, who said: "There are occasions when any, even the slightest chance of doing good, must be laid hold on even by the most inconsiderable person."

I have tried my utmost to place before the readers, thoughts, views and feelings of Mahatma Gandhi and Dr. Babasaheb Ambedkar in their own words quoted verbatim. My only passion has been to be dispassionate about controversies on their relationship. My aim is to help the readers by placing before them all the material, relevant and important, and they will find that I have not sought to impose my views on them. I have placed before them both sides of the issues dealt with in the book and have left them to form their own opinion. While doing so, I have followed historian Jadunath Sarkar and *Rajtarangini* of Kalahana.

I am sure that to a discerning reader, the book will serve as a window not just to the life of Gandhi and Ambedkar, but also to the most significant epoch in the pre-Independence and post-Independence history of India that changed the whole complexion of the Indian subcontinent. In fact, by reading this book, readers can, by and large, acquaint themselves with the story of India's Independence struggle from the British. The book will spur the reader to know more about the history of the tumultuous period.

In preparing this book, I have taken great pains and have come out with a very valuable and authentic information, which will feed readers with a correct and unbiased history. I have not dealt with the matter in a stereotyped manner but have delved deep into the record of these historic events and focused on them without fear or favour. I think that this book should create fresh awareness of a very significant period of India's history and will help readers to form their own opinion as to who was really right and wrong between the two, Gandhi and Ambedkar.

I have made objective assessment of Gandhi and Ambedkar in the chapter, "True Faces of Gandhi and Ambedkar" without any attachment, without any prejudice and kept it completely unbiased. I leave it to the readers to sit on their own judgment. However, I strongly feel that these are the things of the past. As these two leaders will never be erased from the memory of the masses of India, the differences whatsoever, between the two should be given a grand burial and their sterling qualities should be hammered on the minds of the younger generation, so that they can keep both of them as their idol to build India of Mahatma Gandhi's dream and Dr. Ambedkar's conception.

Sheshrao Chavan

Contents

Chapter 1

The First Meeting of Gandhi and Ambedkar

Beginning of Differences

The very first meeting between Mahatma Gandhi and Dr. B.R. Ambedkar took place on 14th August 1931 at Mani Bhavan in Mumbai, which is today known as Mani Bhavan Gandhi Sanghralaya. It was here that Gandhi stayed in Mumbai. This meeting was just a day before Ambedkar's departure to London for the Second Round Table Conference.

Gandhi, probably sensing that Ambedkar was on his way of becoming a force to reckon with in British India requested him vide his letter of 6th August 1931 to meet him.

The following conversation took place between the two.

Gandhi: Well Doctor what have you to say in the matter?

Ambedkar: You called me to hear your views. Please tell me what you have to say or you may ask me some questions and I shall answer.

Gandhi: I understand that you have some grievances against me and the Congress. I may tell you that I have been thinking over the problem of untouchables ever since my school days when you were not even born. You may perhaps be knowing what enormous amount of efforts I had put in to incorporate this problem in the program of the Congress and make it a plank of the Congress platform. The Congress leaders opposed it on the plea that it was a religious and social question and as such it should not be mixed with political one. This is not all. The Congress has spent not less than ₹ Twenty lakhs on the uplift of the untouchables. And it is really surprising that men like you should offer opposition to me and to the Congress. If you have to say anything to justify your stand, you are free to do so.

Ambedkar: It is true. Mahatmaji, that you started to think about the problem of untouchables before I was born. All old and elderly persons always like to emphasise the point of age. It is also true that because of you the Congress party gave recognition to this problem. You say that the Congress spent more than ₹ Twenty lakhs on the uplift of untouchables. I say that it was all waste. With such a backing, I could have effected an outstanding change in the outlook and economic conditions of my people. And in that event it would have been imperative for you to see me long before. But I tell you that the Congress is not sincere about its profession. Had it been sincere, it would have surely made the removal of untouchability a condition, like the wearing of khaddar for becoming a member of the Congress. No person who did not employ untouchable women or men in his house, or rear up an untouchable student or take food at home with an untouchable student at least once a week should have been allowed to be a member of the Congress. Had there been such a condition, you could have avoided the ridiculous sight where the President of the District Congress Committee was seen opposing the temple entry of the untouchables. You might say that the Congress wanted strength and therefore it was unwise to lay down such a condition. Then my point is that the Congress care more for strength than principles. This is my charge against you and the Congress. You say that the British Government does not show a change of heart. I also say that the Hindus have not shown a change of heart in regard to our problems and so long they remained adamant we would believe neither the Congress nor the Hindus. We believe in self-help and self-respect. We are not prepared to have faith in great leaders and Mahatmas. Let me be brutally frank about it. History tells that Mahatmas, like fleeting phantoms, raise dust, but raise no level. Why should the Congress men oppose our movement and dub me a traitor. Mr. Gandhi, I have no homeland.

Gandhi: You have got a homeland, and from the reports that have reached me of your work at the Round Table Conference, I know that you are a patriot of sterling worth.

Ambedkar: You say that I have got a homeland, but still I repeat that I am without it. How can I call this land my homeland and this religion my own wherein we are treated worse than cats and dogs, wherein we cannot get water to drink? No self-respecting untouchable, worth the name will be proud of this land. The injustice and the sufferings inflicted upon us by this land are so enormous that if knowingly or unknowingly we fall a prey to disloyalty to this country, the responsibility for that act would be solely ours. I do not feel sorry for being branded as a traitor; for the responsibility for our action lie with the land that dubs me a traitor. If at all I have rendered any national service as you say, helpful, or beneficial, to the patriotic cause of this country, it is due to my unsullied conscience and not due to any patriotic feelings in me. If in my endeavor to secure human rights for my people, who have been trampled upon in this country for ages, if I do any disservice to this country, it would not be a sin, and if any harm does not come to this country through my action, it may be due to my conscience, owing to the prompting of my conscience, I have been striving to win human rights for my people without meaning or doing any harm to this country. Everybody knows that the Muslims and Sikhs are socially, politically and economically more advanced than the untouchables. The first Round Table Conference has given political recognition to the Muslim demands and has recommended political safeguards for them. The Congress has agreed to their demands. The Conference has also given recognition to the political rights of the Depressed Classes and has recommended for them political safeguards and adequate representation. According to us that is beneficial to the Depressed Classes. What is your opinion?

Gandhi: I am against political separation of the untouchables from the Hindus. That would be absolutely suicidal.

Ambedkar: I thank you for your frank opinion; it is good that I know now where we stand as regards this vital problem.

Ambedkar felt that he had been treated rudely. Gandhi later told that he had not known that Ambedkar was an untouchable. Gandhi was under the impression that Ambedkar was a radical Brahamin, who took keen interest in the cause of Harijans and therefore talked intemperately.

The very next day of the conversation, Ambedkar left for London on 15th August 1931 by SS Multan to attend the Second Round Table Conference. On Boardship, he came across Sir Prabhashankar Pattani, who asked him about the outcome of his conversation with Gandhi. Sir Pattani told Ambedkar that as he had left the hall in the middle of the talk, he was not in the know of its outcome or end. Ambedkar asked Pattani why he had left the hall in the middle of the talk, Pattani said that according to the Hindu scriptures a gentleman should quit the place where a detractor reviled a good man, if the hearer could not cut out the tongue of the detractor on the spot. Ambedkar without loosing his temper asked Pattani as to what punishment was prescribed by Hindu scriptures for a rank hypocrite and an abject flatterer. Pattani got wild and asked Ambedkar what did he mean by such a brutal attack? Ambedkar replied that Gandhi should be freed from the grip of the flatterers like him.

Chapter 2

First Round Table Conference

In the Government of India Act 1919, there was a provision which had imposed an obligation on His Majesty's Government to appoint at the end of ten years a Royal Commission to investigate into the working of the constitution and report upon such changes as may be found necessary. Accordingly, in 1928, a Royal Commission was appointed under the chairmanship of Sir John Simon. Indians expected the Commission to be mixed in its composition of personnel. But Lord Birkenhead, who was then Secretary of State for India was opposed to the inclusion of Indians and insisted on making it a purely Parliamentary Commission. At this, the Congress and the Liberals took serious objection and treated it as an insult. They boycotted the Commission and launched a great agitation against it. To assuage this feeling of opposition, it was announced by His Majesty's Government that after the work of the Commission was completed, representative Indians would be invited for discussion before the new constitution for India was settled. In accordance with this announcement, representative Indians were called to London at a Round Table Conference with the representatives of Parliament and His Majesty's Government.

Invitation to Ambedkar and Diwan Bahadur R. Srinivasan to attend the first Round Table Conference as delegates was an epoch-making event in the history of untouchables. For, it was at this conference that they were being invested along with other Indians with the right to be consulted in the framing of the constitution for India. Their voice was to echo for the first time in the history of 2000 years and more so in the governance of their motherland.

The conference was attended by 87 delegates, 57 of whom were from British India. The Princely States had 16 members, while the British Government and the opposition in the two Houses of Parliament were represented by the remaining number.

The conference was inaugurated in London on 12th November 1930 by His Majesty King George V. It was presided over by Prime Minister Ramsay McDonald. The absence of the Congress was conspicuous.

As the journalist Malcom Muggeridge acidly put it: "The invitation of so many delegates ensured that everything under the Sun represented except the 25000 in jail, and 30,000,000 cultivating their small patches of over-worked soil."

In the fifth sitting of the conference on 20th November 1930, Ambedkar said:

"Mr. Chairman, my purpose in rising to address this conference is principally to place before it the point of view of the depressed classes, whom I and my colleague, Rao Bahadur Srinivasan, have the honor to represent. Regarding the question of constitutional reform, it is a point of view of 43,000,000 people, or one-fifth of the total population of British India. The depressed classes form a group by themselves which is distinct and separate from the Muhammadans and, although they are included among the Hindus, they in no sense form an integral part of that community. Not only they have a separate existence, but they have also assigned to them a status which is invidiously distinct from the status occupied by any other community in India. There are communities in India which occupy a lower and subordinate position; but the position assigned to the depressed classes is totally different. It is one which is mid-way between that of the serf and the slave, and which may, for convenience, be called servile with this difference, that the serf and the slave were permitted to have physical contact, from which the depressed classes are debarred. What is worse that this enforced servility and bar to human intercourse, due to their untouchability, involves, not merely the possibility of discrimination in public life, but actually works out a positive denial of all equality of opportunity and the denial of those most elementary of civic rights on which all human existence depends. I am sure that the point of view of such a community, as large as the population of England or of France, and so heavily handicapped in the struggle for existence, cannot but have some bearing on the right sort of solution of the political problem, and I am anxious that this conference should be placed in possession of that point of view at the very start."

Ambedkar further said: "The bureaucratic form of Government in India should be replaced by a Government which will be a Government of the people, by the people and for the people. This statement of the view of the depressed classes, I am sure will be received with some surprise in some quarters. The tie that bounds the depressed classes to the British has been of a unique character. The depressed classes welcomed the British as their deliverers from age-long tyranny and oppression by the orthodox Hindus. They fought their battles against the Hindus, the Mussalmans and the Sikhs and won for them this great empire of India. The British on their side, assumed the role of trustees for the depressed classes. In view of such an intimate relationship between the parties, this change in the attitude of the depressed classes towards British Rule in India is undoubtedly a most momentous phenomenon. But the reasons for this change of attitude are not far to seek. We have not taken this decision simply because we wish to throw in our lot with the majority. Indeed, as you know, there is not much love lost between the majority and the particular minority I represent. Ours is an independent decision. We have judged the existing administration solely in the light of our own circumstances and we have found it wanting in some of the most essential elements of a good Government. When we compare our present position with the one which it was our lot to bear in Indian society of the pre-British days, we find that, instead of marching on, we are only marking time. Before the British, we were in the loathsome condition due to our untouchability. Has the British Government done anything to remove it? Before the British, we could not enter the temple. Can we enter now? Before the British, we were denied entry into the Police Force. Does the British Government admit us in the Force? Before the British, we were not allowed to serve in the Military. Is that career now open to us? To none of these questions can we give an affirmative answer. That the British, who have held so large a sway over us for such a long time, have done some good we cheerfully acknowledge. But there is no fundamental change in our position. Indeed, so far as we were concerned, the British Government has accepted the social arrangements as it found them, and has preserved them faithfully in the manner of the Chinese tailor who, when given an old coat as a pattern, produced with pride an exact replica, rents, patches and all. Our wrongs have remained as open sores and they have not been righted, although 150 years of British Rule have rolled away.

"We do not accuse the British of indifference or want of sympathy. What we do find is that they are quite incompetent to tackle our problems. If the case was one of indifference only it would have been a matter of small moment, and it would not have made such a profound change in our attitude. But what we have come to realize on the deeper analysis of the situation is that it is not merely a case of indifference, rather it is a case of sheer incompetence to undertake the task. The depressed classes find that the British Government in India suffers from two very serious limitations. There is first of all an internal limitation which arises from the character, motives and interests of those who are in power. It is not because they cannot help us in these things but because it is against their character, motives and interests to do so. The second consideration that limits its authority is the mortal fear that it has of external resistance. The Government of India does realize the necessity of removing the social evils which are eating into the vitals of Indian society and which have blighted the lives of the downtrodden classes for so many years. The Government of India does realize that the landlords are squeezing the masses dry, and the capitalists are not giving the laborers a living wage and decent conditions of work. Yet it is most painful thing that it has not dared to touch any of these evils. Why? Is it because it has no legal powers to remove them? No. The reason why it does not intervene is because it is afraid that its intervention to amend the existing code of social and economic life, will give rise to resistance. Of what good is such a Government to anybody? Under a Government, paralysed between two such limitations, much that goes to make life good must remain held up. We must have a Government in which the men in power will give their undivided allegiance to the best interest of the country. We must have a Government in which men in power, knowing where obedience will end and resistance will begin, will not be afraid to amend the social and economic code of life which the dictates of justice and expediency so urgently call for. This ROLE the British Government will never be able to play. It is only a Government which is of the people, for the people and by the people that will make this possible.

"....We feel that nobody can remove our grievances as well as we can, and we cannot remove them unless we get political power in our own hands. No share of this political power can evidently come to us so long as the British Government remains as it is. It is only in Swaraj Constitution that we stand any chance of getting the political power into our own hands, without which we cannot bring salvation to our people."

While standing for the Dominion Status with safeguards, Ambedkar said: "The depressed classes feel that they will get no share of political power unless the political machinery for the new constitution is of a special make. In the construction of that machine certain hard facts of Indian social life must not be lost sight of. It must be recognized that Indian society is a gradation of Castes forming an ascending scale of reverence and a descending scale of contempt—a system which gives no scope for the growth of that sentiment of equality and fraternity so essential for a democratic form of Government. It must also be recognized that while the intelligentsia is a very important part of Indian society, it is drawn from its upper strata and although it speaks in the name of the country and leads the political movement, it has not shed the narrow particularism of the class from which it is drawn. In other words what the depressed classes wish to urge is that the political mechanism must take account of and must have a definite relation to the psychology of the society for which it is devised. Otherwise you are likely to produce a constitution which, however symmetrical, will be truncated one and a total misfit to the society for which it is designed."

Ambedkar reiterated: "We hold that the problem of the depressed classes will never be solved unless they get political power in their own hands. The problem of depressed classes is eminently a political problem and must be treated as such. We know that political power is passing from the British into the hands of those who wield such tremendous economic, social and religious sway over our existence. We are willing that it may happen, though the idea of Swaraj recalls to the mind of many of us the tyrannies, oppressions and injustices practiced upon us in the past and fear of their recurrence under Swaraj. We are prepared to take the inevitable risk of the situation in the hope that we shall be installed, in adequate proportion, of the political sovereigns of the country along with our fellow countrymen. But we will consent to that on one condition and that is that the settlement is not left to time. The depressed classes have waited too long for time to work its miracle. At every successive step taken by the British Government to widen the scope of representative Government the depressed classes have been systematically left out. No thought has been given to their claim for political power. We will not stand this any longer. The settlement of our problem must be a part of the general political settlement and must not be left over to the shifting sands of the sympathy and goodwill of the rulers of the future. The reasons why the depressed classes insist upon it are obvious. Every one of us knows that the man in possession is more powerful than the man who is out of possession. Every one of us also knows that those in possession of power seldom abdicate in favor of those who are out of it. We cannot therefore hope for the effectuation of the settlement of our social problem. If we allow power to slip into the hands of those who stand to lose by settlement unless we are to have another revolution to dethrone those, whom we today help to ascend the throne of power and prestige. We prefer being despised for too anxious apprehensions, than ruined by too confident a security. It would be just and proper for us to insist that the best guarantee for the settlement of our problem is the adjustment of the political machine itself so as to give us a hold on it, and not the will of those who are contriving to be left in unfettered control of that machine.... Although we want responsible Government, we do not want a Government that will only mean a change of masters. Let the Legislature be fully and really representative, if your Executive is going to be fully responsible."

Feeling sorry to speak in such plain words, Ambedkar said: "The Government all along used the depressed classes only as an excuse for its continued existence. The Hindus claim them only to deny them or, better still, to appropriate rights. The Muhammadans refuse to recognize their separate existence, because they fear that their privileges may be curtailed by the admission of a rival. Depressed by the Government, suppressed by the Hindu and disregarded by the Muslim, we are left in a most intolerable position of utter helplessness to which there is no parallel and to which I was bound to call attention."

In conclusion of his speech, Ambedkar warned: "It is not sufficiently realized that in the present temper of the country, no constitution will be workable which is not acceptable to the majority of the people. The time when you were to choose and India was to accept is gone, never to return. Let the consent of the people and not the accident of logic be the touchstone of your new constitution, if you desire that it should be worked" (Dr. Babasaheb Ambedkar: *Writings and Speeches*, Vol. 2, pp. 503-09).

In the second sitting of the Minorities Committee held on 31st December 1930, Ambedkar and Rao Bahadur Srinivasan submitted a written memorandum giving in clear-cut language what the depressed classes desire by way of political safeguards in the future constitution of India. Summarizing the memorandum, Ambedkar said:

"Although there are various minority communities in India which require political recognition, it has to be understood that the minorities are not on the same plane, that they differ from each other. They differ in the social standing which each minority occupies vis-à-vis the majority community. We have, for instance, the Parsee community, which is the smallest community in India, and yet, vis-à-vis its social standing with the majority community, it is probably highest in order of precedence.

"On the other hand, if you take the depressed classes, they are a minority which comes next to the great Muslim minority in India, and yet their social standard is lower than the social standard of ordinary human beings.

"Again, if you take the minorities and classify them on the basis of social and political rights, you will find that there are certain minorities which are in enjoyment of social and political rights, and the fact that they are in a minority does not necessarily stand in the way of their full and free enjoyment of those civic rights. But if you take the case of depressed classes, the position is totally different. They have in certain matters no rights, and, where they have any, the majority community will not permit them to enjoy them.

"The committee should realize that although, the minorities are all in the same boat, yet the most important fact to remember is that they are not all in the same class in the same boat; some are traveling in "A" class, some in "B" class and some in "C" class, and so on. The depressed classes, though they are a minority and are to that extent in the same boat as other minorities, are not even in "C" or "D" class but are actually in the hold.

"The depressed classes, along with the other minorities, fear that under any future constitution of India by which majority rule will be established and there can be no shadow of doubt that that majority rule will be the rule of the orthodox Hindus—there is great danger of that majority with its orthodox Hindu beliefs and prejudices contravening the dictates of justice, equality and good conscience, there is a great danger that the minorities may be discriminated against either in legislation or administration or in the other public rights of the citizenship, and therefore, it is necessary to safeguard the position of the minorities in such a manner that the discrimination which is feared shall not take place."

Ambedkar proposed the following safeguards for the depressed classes:

"Fundamental Right should be enacted in the constitution which will declare "untouchability" to be illegal for all public purposes; this fundamental right must also invalidate and nullify all such disabilities and all such discriminations as may have been made hitherto; legislation against the social persecution should be enacted."

Ambedkar concluded his speech thus: "...The whole question of minority representation is really the crux of the whole situation, and if the majority community desire that all minorities should associate with them in having or in claiming, a constitution which will give India Dominion Status, or what we prefer to call Government of the people, for the people and in the name of the people, then the majority community must see to it that all fears of the minorities are set at rest. Otherwise, it may not be possible for us to take what I do not conceal from myself is the risk that most of us are taking in claiming Dominion Status" (Dr. Babasaheb Ambedkar: *Writings and Speeches*, Vol. 2, pp. 529-34).

In the Plenary Session held on 19th January 1931, Ambedkar submitted to the Chancellor a statement containing his views on the future constitution for Federal India. In his statement he said:

".... Indeed, if I were given a choice between the existing system and cross-bred by the committee, I would prefer the existing one. But, Sir, if the constitution for the Central Government contained in the Report of the Committee satisfies Sir, T.B. Sapru, who has been the friend, guide and the philosopher of the Conference, if it is agreeable to Mr. Jayakar, who proclaimed himself the representative of the Youth of India, and if it pleases Sir A.P. Patro, who speaks, as he says, in the name of Non-Brahmins of India, it is not for me to oppose. My attitude, therefore, is that of one who does not approve but also who does not obstruct. I will leave it to those who bless it to carry it through.

"This attitude is all the more agreeable to me because I have no mandate from those whom I represent regarding the form of Government. But I have a mandate and that is, while not opposing responsible Government, to see that no responsible

Government was established unless it was at the same time accompanied by a truly representative Government. It is when I look at the achievement at the conference to find out how it has dealt with the question of representative Government that I feel most disappointed.

"When I came to this conference I thought that so far as the question of Franchise was concerned the battle had already been won. But in the Franchise Committee I was completely disillusioned. I found to my great surprise that all those who had signed the Nehru Report had done so with mental reservation, so much so that it was difficult to persuade even the Indian Liberals to consent to Franchise 25 per cent of the population for Provincial Legislatures. The Franchise for Central Legislature is no doubt an unknown quantity. But I have no hope that it will be such as to make the Central Legislature more representative of the people than the Provincial Legislatures are going to be. A Franchise so limited must necessarily make the future Government of India a Government of the masses by the classes."

Regarding the question of the distribution of seats among the majority and the various minority committees, Ambedkar said:

"We all know that there is a deadlock. The deadlock is largely due to the mischief done in the past. If the authorities in India had acted in the past on the principle of justice to all and favour to none, the problem would not have become so difficult of solution. The British Government set different values on different communities according to the political use they made of them and gave to many communities an extraordinary share of political power by denying it to the depressed classes in a measure which was their rightful due. In this matter the most aggrieved community is the depressed classes, and I was hoping that this conference would proceed on the principle that what is wrongly settled is never settled, and give to the depressed classes their rightful quota of seats by a revaluation of the old values. But this has not happened.... The claims of the depressed classes may be whitted down to satisfy the ever-increasing scramble by other communities who are maneuvering not so much for protection as for power."

Making his attitude perfectly plain, Ambedkar said: "As the rights of the depressed classes in the future constitution are not defined, any announcement that might be made on behalf of His Majesty's Government regarding the introduction of responsibility in the Centre as well as in the Provinces should make it clear that any advance in that direction must be on condition and subject to an agreement between the communities which would provide effective safeguards for the rights and interests of the depressed classes. No announcement will be acceptable to us unless the position is made perfectly clear in this behalf, and that failing this I and my colleague will be unable to accept the responsibility of participating in the further work of the conference, and will be compelled to disassociate ourselves from it."

Ambedkar further said: "The British Parliament and those who speak for it, have always stated that they are trustees for the depressed classes and I am sure that what they have been saying is not one of those conventional lies of civilization which we all are led to utter to keep human relations as pleasant as possible. It is the bounden duty of any Government to see that that trust is not betrayed and let me tell you, Mr. Prime Minister, that the depressed classes would regard it as the greatest betrayal on the part of His Majesty's Government if it were to leave us to the mercy of those who have taken no interest in our welfare and whose prosperity and greatness is founded on our ruination and degradation." For saying so I will be called communalist by the nationalists and patriots of India. I am not afraid of that. India is a peculiar country and her nationalists and patriots are a peculiar people. A patriot and a nationalist in India is one who sees with open eyes as his fellowmen treated as being less than men. But his humanity does not rise in protest. He knows that men and women for no cause are denied their human rights. But it does not prick his civic sense to helpful action. He finds whole class of people shut out from public employment. But it does not rouse his sense of justice and fair play. Hundreds of evil practices that injure man and society are perceived by him. But they do not sicken him with disgust. The patriot's one cry is power and more power for him and for his class. I am glad that I do not belong to that class of patriots. I belong to that class which takes its stand on democracy and which seeks to destroy monopoly in a very shape and form. Our aim is to realize in practice our ideal of one man one value in all walks of life, political, economic and social. It is because representative Government is one to that end that the depressed classes attach to it as great a value as it is because of its value to us that I have urged upon you the necessity of making your declarations subject to its fulfillment. You may tell me that the depressed classes have your sympathy. My reply is, for a stricken people what is wanted is something more concrete, something more defined. You may despise me for being unduly apprehensive. My reply is it is better to be despised for too anxious apprehensions rather than be ruined by too confident a security" (Dr. Babasaheb Ambedkar: *Writings and Speeches*, Vol. 2, pp. 597-99).

Ambedkar's study, great industry and intellectual height created tremendous impact upon the delegates and the British Statesmen. The views expressed by him in and outside the Round Table Conference enabled the world know for the first time that the fate of the untouchables in India was worse than those of the Negroes in America.

The *Sunday Chronicle* said: "At heart a true nationalist, he had to put up a stern fight against the persuasive coquetry of the British diehards who are anxious to win him over to their side and at the same time his task was made more difficult by his anxiety to retain his brother delegate Rao Bahadur Srinivasan, within the nationalist fold."

The *Indian Daily Mail* observed: "Ambedkar pointed out that he had a mandate to see that no responsible Government was established, unless it was at the same time, accompanied by a truly representative Government. He voiced a fear that the proposed form of Government would be one of the masses by the classes and his protest found echoing sympathy in the Labour and Liberal parties of Great Britain."

The first Round Table Conference adjourned sine die on the 19th January 1931. In his farewell address, Ramsay MacDonald expressed the hope that the Congress would participate in the next session of the conference.

At the first Round Table Conference, there was no Congress representative. What were the privileges which Ambedkar was able to obtain for the scheduled castes from the pro-British and anti-Congress body? Only the obscure reference in para 8 of the Report of the Minorities Committee. The discussion made it evident that the demand which remained as the only one which would be generally acceptable was separate electorates. The general objection to this scheme has been subject to much previous discussion in India. It involves what is a very difficult problem for solution viz. What should be the amount of communal representation in the various provinces and the centre; that if the whole, or practically the whole, of the seats in a legislature are to be assigned to communities, there will be room for the growth of independent political opinion or of true political parties, and this problem received serious complication by the demand of the representatives of the Depressed Classes that they should be deducted from the Hindu population and be regarded for electoral purposes as a separate community. In para 19, it was merely noted without comment that the Minorities and the Depressed Classes were definite in their assertion that they could not assent to any self-governing constitution for India unless their demands were met in a reasonable manner.

It is obvious that in the absence of the Congress Dr. Ambedkar did not pull much weight and could not cash any of his bills.

It may be recollected that the Congress had refused to attend the conference and when it met the Salt Satyagraha was in full swing. Thousands of Congress workers were in jail. The members of the conference were chosen for their hostility to the Congress. Another object in making the nominations was to magnify the differences in the social structure as a justification for British domination. Dr. Ambedkar's eminence was initially due to his hostility towards the Congress, and the idea had gripped him that it can last only so long as this hostility lasts and so long as the British Government backs him. How his hostility and with it British backing have grown together is evident from his elevation to the position of a Member of the Viceroy's Executive Council (K. Santhanam: *Ambedkar's Attack*, pp. 25-26).

Sapru and Sastri gave the first-hand information of the Round Table Conference to the Congress leaders. Gandhi was not impressed by the achievements of the conference, nor did he feel optimistic about the possibilities of an understanding with the Government. Nevertheless, he wrote to Lord Irwin and asked him for an interview. His argument was that as a Satyagrahi, he has a moral obligation to make a response to the Viceroy's gesture in releasing the Congress Working Committee.

Chapter 3

Second Round Table Conference

On 27 February 1931, Gandhi and Lord Irwin met in Delhi. They had several meetings which resulted in the Gandhi-Irwin Pact announced on 5 March 1931. The first three paras of the pact run as follows:

Consequent on the conversations that have taken place between His Excellency the Viceroy and Mr. Gandhi, it has been agreed that the civil disobedience movement be discontinued, and that, with the approval of His Majesty's Government, certain action be taken by the Government of India and Local Governments.

As regards constitutional questions, the scope of future discussion is stated, with the assent of His Majesty's Government, to be with the object of considering further the scheme for the constitutional Government of India discussed at the Round Table Conference. Of the scheme there outlined, Federation is an essential part; so also are Indian responsibility and reservations or safeguards in the interests of India, for such matters, as for instance, defence; external affairs; the position of minorities; the financial credit of India, and discharge of obligations.

In pursuance of the statement made by the Prime Minister in his announcement of 19 January 1931, steps will be taken for the participation of the representatives of the Congress in the future discussions that are to take place on the scheme of constitutional reform.

The Pact also stipulated that the people who lived in coastal areas were free to pick and manufacture salt. Peaceful picketing was not banned. All political prisoners were to be released and their confiscated properties restored. Further, the Pact allowed Congressmen freedom to advocate complete independence, Poorna Swaraj.

Jawaharlal took the pact as surrender and opposed it. Gandhi, therefore said that he would not insist on the acceptance of the pact if the Working Committee of the Congress so decided. He had so far committed only himself. With some difficulty Jawaharlal withdrew his opposition. Afterwards, he admitted that the pact enhanced the prestige of the Congress even among those who were against it.

The Gandhi-Irwin Pact was considered at the annual session of the Congress held in Karachi on 29 March 1931. At this session, the Congress adopted a resolution on Fundamental Rights of which the following were of great importance to the scheduled castes:

1. All citizens are equal before the law irrespective of caste, creed or sex.
2. All citizens have equal rights and duties in regard to wells, tanks, roads, schools and places of public resort, maintained out of State of local funds or dedicated by private persons for the use of the public.
3. The franchise shall be on the basis of the universal adult suffrage.
4. The State shall provide for free and compulsory primary education.

It shall be seen that except in the matter of separate electorates, the Congress was ready to concede all the demands made on behalf of the scheduled castes.

Gandhi's speech delivered at the Karachi Session gave a peep into the working of his mind. He said:

"I have often wondered myself what we are going to do at the conference when we know that there is such a gulf between what we want and what has been as yet offered at the conference. But considerations of a satyagraha decided me. There comes a stage when he may no longer refuse to negotiate with his opponent.

His object is always to convert his opponent by love. The stage of negotiation arrived when the working committee was released after the Premier's declaration. The Viceroy also made an appeal to us to lay down arms and to indicate what we want."

To the suggestion that there was no need for a truce with the government when the Congress was in a position to continue civil disobedience for at least another one year, Gandhi's answer was: "Well, for that matter we might be capable of carrying on struggle for twenty years and a true satyagrahi fights to the last, even if the rest are tired into submission. But the truce was made not because it was imperative. He who will fight on because he can fight on is no satyagrahi, but a conceited person guilty before God."

Gandhi left Bombay in the afternoon of 29th August 1931 by S.S. Rajputana to attend the second Round Table Conference as the sole representative of the Congress.

"There is every chance of my returning empty handed," he said on embarking.

Gandhi had in his party, his two secretaries Mahadev Desai and Pyarelal, his son Devadas, Dr. Sushila Nayyar, G.D. Birla and Miss Slade, who had made India as her permanent home and Gandhi her spiritual father. Gandhi had given instructions that he and his party shall travel by the lowest class.

Reuter's special correspondent, who was on the same boat with Gandhi, sought an interview with him and asked him about his programme in London. This interview is significant. It gives an idea of Gandhi's conception of free India. He said: "I shall strive for a constitution which will release India from all thralldom and patronage and give her, if need be, the right to sin. I shall work for an India in which the poorest shall feel that it is their country in whose making they have an effective voice; an India in which there shall be no high class and no low class of people; an India in which all communities shall live in harmony. There can be no room in such an India for the curse of untouchability or intoxicating drinks or drugs. Women will enjoy the same rights as men. Since we shall be at peace with the rest of the world, neither exploiting nor being exploited, we should have the smallest army imaginable. All interests not in conflict with the interest of dumb millions will be scrupulously respected, whether foreign or indigenous. I hate the distinction between foreign and indigenous. This is the India of my dreams, for which I shall struggle at the Round Table Conference."

At Eden, the Indian community presented him an address. Messages of good wishes came from Madam Zaglul Pasha and from leaders of the Wafd Party.

Egyptians resentful of Europeans hegemony turned up at Suez and Port Said but were not allowed to meet Gandhi as he was considered as Empire's chief rebel. The poet Ahmed Shauqui had exhorted Egyptians that as Gandhi passed by, they should stop to welcome him from close quarters sitting in boats and also from a distance in whatever way possible. He is a guide and pathfinder like Confucious. He has inspired in Hindus and Muslims the spirit of mutual love and with his spiritual powers brought the two swords in one sheath. He is a great powerhouse which generates the power to tame predators.

At Marseilles, Gandhi was greeted by Madelein Rolland, the sister of the French Savant and was given a warm welcome by French students, who hailed him as the Spiritual Ambassador of India.

Gandhi took a train for Calais on the channel coast, hundreds including scores of journalists, mobbed him and on 12th September about 5000 including many Indians greeted him in Folkestone on the English side of the channel.

Gandhi arrived in London on 12th September and remained in England up to 5th December. He stayed in an East End settlement House called Kingsley Hall as the guest of Muriel Lester, who had visited Gandhi in India in 1926. Kingsley Hall was five miles away from the centre of the city and from St. James Palace where the Round Table Conference met.

He would come home to Kingsley Hall every evening very late. Because he said he enjoyed living among his own kind, the poor people.

Questioned by a reporter about his dress, Gandhi said: "You people were plus-four, mine are minus four."

Winston Churchill remarked: "It is alarming and also nauseating to see Mr. Gandhi, a seditious Middle Temple lawyer, now posing as a Fakir of a type well known in the East, striding half-naked of the steps of the Viceregal palace, while he is still organizing and conducting a defiant campaign of civil disobedience, to parley on equal terms with the representative of the King Emperor."

The conference consisted of 112 delegates: 20 representing the Government of the U.K.; 23 from Princely India—Rajas, Maharajas, Nawabs and their subordinates; 64 from British India. The Viceroy appointed the Princes, and with the exception of Gandhi, Mrs Sarojini Naidu and a few others, he appointed the visitors from British India.

The main work of the conference was done by two large committees namely Federal Structure Committee and Minorities Committee. Gandhi was a member of both and pressed for the acceptance of the Congress demand. He claimed that the Congress was a national and not merely a party organization. It represented, he said, all the communal minorities, and in support of this claim pointed out that there were four Muslims among the fifteen members of the Working Committee and thousands of Muslims in the rank and file. The Congress also represented the Indian States, for it served the Princes' interests on two occasions by refraining from any interference in their domestic affairs. Gandhi even claimed that the Congress not only represented all India but was its only proper representative, since the non-Congress Indian delegates had not been chosen by the people but nominated by the Government. He stuck to the Karachi resolution. He demanded that responsible Government must be established immediately and in full, both at the Centre and in the Provinces, including complete control over the finance, army, defence, and external relations. Safeguards were not needed and therefore no special powers should be given to the Governor-General. The new status of India, he said, would give her freedom to secede from the British Commonwealth, but would not necessarily mean secession.

The outstanding feature of the conference was the unending discussion of the communal problem. Though several meetings of the Minorities Committee were held, and Gandhi himself carried on informal negotiations in order to reach agreements between the various interests affected, it unfortunately proved impossible to devise any scheme which all the parties were willing to accept. Gandhi himself tabled a scheme which was more or less the scheme adopted in the Nehru Report, but it was not accepted.

In his speech made in the Federal Structure Committee held on 15th September 1931, Gandhi said: "The Congress has, from its very commencement, taken up the cause of the so-called untouchables. There was time when the Congress had at every annual session as its adjunct the Social Conference, to which the late Ranade dedicated his energies among his many other activities. Headed by him, you will find in the programme of the Social Conference, reform in connection with the untouchables taking a prominent place. But in 1920 the Congress considered the Hindu-Muslim unity, thereby meaning unity amongst all the classes to be an indispensable condition for the attainment of full freedom. The position the Congress took up in 1920, remains the same today and so you will see that the Congress has attempted from its very beginning to be what it described itself to be, namely, national in every sense of the term."

Commenting on the speech of Gandhi, Ambedkar said: "Any one who has perused how the Congress has failed to carry out the 1922 program for the uplift of untouchables, which was included in Bardoli Program, and how it left it to the Hindu Mahasabha, could have no hesitation in saying that what Mr. Gandhi said was untrue. The speech, however, gave no indication as to what line Mr. Gandhi was going to take on the demands presented by the untouchables, although I could see the drift of it. But he did not leave people long in imagining what his position was going to be. The meeting of the Federal Structure Committee held on 17th September 1931, provided him the necessary occasion. The agenda of the meeting included the question of election of members of the Federal legislature."

Expressing his views on the subject, Mr. Gandhi made the following statement:

"I come to sub-head (v) representation by special constituencies of special interests. The Congress has reconciled itself to special treatment of the Hindu-Muslim-Sikh tangle. There are sound historical reasons for it but the Congress will not extend that doctrine in any shape or form to the untouchables. So far as the untouchables are concerned, I have not quite yet grasped what Dr. Ambedkar has to say, but the Congress will share the honour with Dr. Ambedkar, of representing the interests of the untouchables.

"They are as clear to the Congress as the interests of any other body or of any other individual throughout the length and breadth of India. Therefore I would most strongly resist any further special representation."

In reaction to Gandhi's statement, Ambedkar said: "This is nothing but a declaration of war by Mr. Gandhi and the Congress against the untouchables. In any case it resulted in a war between the two. With this declaration by Mr. Gandhi, I know what Mr. Gandhi would do in the Minorities Committee which was the main forum for the discussion of this question.

"Mr. Gandhi was making his plans to bypass the untouchables and to close the communal problem by bringing about a settlement between the three parties, the Hindus, the Muslims and the Sikhs. He had been carrying on negotiations privately with the Muslims before the Minorities Committee met, but evidently they had not been concluded. Consequently, when the Minorities Committee met on the 28th September 1931, I got up and spoke as follows:

"I should like to say one word before we adjourn. So far as the Depress Classes are concerned, we have already presented our case to the Minorities sub-committee last time. The only thing that remains for me to do is to put before this committee a short statement suggesting the quantum of representation which we want in different legislatures. Those who are negotiating ought to understand that they are not plenipotentiaries appointed by the committee to negotiate a settlement; that whatever may be the representative character of Mr. Gandhi or of the other parties to bind us—certainly not. I say that most emphatically in this meeting."

In the seventh sitting of the Minorities Committee held on 28 September 1931, Ambedkar further said: "....Any negotiations which take place between one minority on the one hand and the Congress or any other people for that matter on the other hand, without taking into consideration the claims which have been put forward by the other minorities can have no chance of success as far as I am concerned. I want to make that absolutely plain. I have no quarrel with the question whether any particular community should get weightage or not, but I do want to say most emphatically that who ever claims weightage and whoever is willing to get that weightage he must not get it—he cannot give it—out of my share. I want to make that absolutely plain."

No settlement was evidently arrived at between the three parties during the adjournment. Consequently when the Minorities Committee met on 1st October 1931, Gandhi told the Prime Minister: "After consultation with His Highness the Agha Khan and other Muslim friends last night, we came to the conclusion that the purpose for which we meet here would be better served if a week's adjournment was asked for. I have not had the opportunity of consulting my other colleagues, but I have no doubt that they will also agree in the proposal I am making. I have been having with my Muslim friends anxious conversations, and I had the pleasure of meeting some other friends also last afternoon belonging to the different groups or classes. We were not able to make much headway, but they too felt that the time at our disposal was too short even for exchanging views. I may say for myself that beyond this week's adjournment I would not press for any further adjournment, but I would report to this committee what has been the result of the endeavour I shall be making during the week."

Gandhi further said: "I am an irrepressible optimist, and often in my life-time when the horizon appeared to be the blackest, some turn has taken place which has given ground for hope. Whatever it may be, so far as human endeavour is possible, all that endeavour will be made."

In reply to Gandhi's proposal for adjournment Ambedkar said: "I do not wish to create any difficulty in our making every possible attempt to arrive at some solution of the problem with which this committee has to deal, and if a solution can be arrived at by the means suggested by Mahatma Gandhi, I, for one, will have no objection to that proposal. But there is just this one difficulty with which I, as representing the depressed classes, am faced. I do not know what sort of committee Mahatma Gandhi proposes to appoint to consider this question during the period of adjournment, but I suppose that the depressed classes will be represented on this committee."

Gandhi's instant reply was: "Without doubt."

Thanking Gandhi, Ambedkar continued: "I do not know whether in the position in which I am today, it would be of any use for me or my colleague to work on the proposed committee. And for this reason, Mahatma Gandhi told us on the first day that he spoke in the Federal Structure Committee that as a representative of the Indian National Congress, he was not prepared to give political recognition to any community other than the Muhammadans and the Sikhs. He was not prepared to recognize Anglo-Indians, the depressed classes and the Indian Christians. I do not think that I am doing any violence to etiquette by stating in this Committee that when I had the pleasure of meeting Mahatma Gandhi a week ago and discussing the question of the depressed classes with him, and when we, as the members of the other minorities, had the chance of talking with him yesterday in his office, he told us in quite plain terms that the attitude that he had taken in the Federal Structure Committee was his full and well considered attitude. What I would like to say is that unless at the outset I know that the depressed classes are going to be recognized as a community entitled to political recognition in the future constitution of India, I do not know whether it will serve any purpose for me to join the particular committee that is proposed by Mahatma Gandhi to be constituted to go into this matter. Unless, therefore, I have an assurance that this committee will start with the assumption that all those communities which the Minorities sub-Committee last year recommended as fit for recognition of India will be included, I do not know that I can whole-heartedly support the proposal for adjournment or that I can whole-heartedly cooperate with the committee that is going to be nominated. That is all that I wish to be clear about."

Making his position further clear, Ambedkar said:

"There has been a certain misunderstanding regarding what I said. It is not that I object to adjournment; it is not that I object to serving on any committee that might be appointed to consider the question. What I would like to know before I enter upon this committee, if they give me the privilege of serving on it, is: What is the thing that this committee is going to consider? Is it only going to consider the question of the Muhammadans vis-à-vis the Hindus? Is it going to consider the question of the Muhammadans vis-à-vis the Sikhs in the Punjab? Or is it going to consider the question of the Sikhs vis-à-vis the Hindus? Is it going to consider the question of the Christians, Anglo-Indians and the Depressed Classes?

"If we understand perfectly well before we start that this committee will not merely concern itself with the question of the Hindus and the Muhammadans, of the Hindus and the Sikhs, but will also take upon itself the responsibility of considering the Depressed Classes, the Anglo-Indians and the Christians. I am perfectly willing to allow this adjournment resolution to be passed without any objection. But I do want to say this, if I am to be left out in the cold, and if this interval is going to be utilized for the purpose of solving the Hindu-Muslim question and the Hindu-Sikh question, I would press that the Minorities Committee should itself grapple with the question and consider it, rather than allow the question to be dealt with by some other informal committee for arriving at solution of the communal question in respect of some minorities only."

In short Ambedkar's attitude was that he would oppose the adjournment, if the private negotiations were to be only regarding Hindu, Muslim, Sikh representation.

Gandhi made the position clear thus: "There is some kind of misunderstanding with reference to the scope of the work that some of us have set before ourselves. I fear that Dr. Ambedkar, Colonel Gidney and other friends are unnecessarily nervous about what is going to happen. Who am I to deny political status to any single interest or class or even individual in India? As a representative of the Congress, I should be unworthy of the trust that has been reposed in me by the Congress, if I were guilty of sacrificing a single national interest. I have undoubtedly given expression to my own views on these points. I must confess that I hold to those views also. But there are ways and ways of guaranteeing protection to every single interest. It will be for those of us who will be putting our heads together to try to evolve a scheme. Nobody would be hampered in pressing his own views on the members of these very informal conference or meeting. I have no authority to convene any committee or to bring into being a committee. I can only act as a humble messenger of peace, try to get together representatives of different interests and groups, and see whether by being closeted in one room and by heart-to-heart conversation, we may not be able to remove cobwebs of misunderstanding and see our way clear to the goal that lies so hazily before us today."

Gandhi further said: "I do not think, therefore, that anybody need be afraid as to being able to express his opinion or carrying his opinion also. Mine will be there equal to that of every one of us; it will carry no greater weight; I have no authority behind me to carry my opinion against the opinion of anybody. I have simply given expression to my views in the national interest, and I shall give expression to these views whenever they are opportune. It will be for you, it is for you to reject or accept these opinions. Therefore, please disabuse your minds, every one of us, of the idea that there is going to be any steamrolling in the conference and the informal meetings that I have adumbrated. But if you think that this is one way of coming closer together than by sitting stiffly at this table, you will not only carry this adjournment motion, but will give your whole-hearted cooperation to the proposal that I have made in connection with these informal meetings."

Ambedkar said: "It is necessary for me to recite what happened at the informal meeting held after adjournment. It was a complete failure, if not a fiasco. The meeting was presided over by Mr. Gandhi. He began with the most difficult part of the communal question, namely the dispute between the Sikhs and the Muslims in the Punjab. This problem at one stage appeared to be near solution when the parties agreed to abide by the decision of an Arbitrator. The Sikhs, however, refused to proceed further in the matter until they knew who the Arbitrator was? As the Musalmans were not prepared to have the name of the Arbitrator disclosed, the matter fell through. Mr. Gandhi was not interested in the problem of the other minorities, such as the untouchables although he enacted the farce of calling upon the representatives of the other minorities to present a catalogue of their demands. He heard them but took no notice of them much. Did he place them before the meeting for its consideration? As soon as the Sikh-Muslim settlement broke up, Mr. Gandhi dissolved the meeting."

Dr. Ambedkar tried to make out that Gandhiji wanted to appease the Muslims at the expense of the untouchables. The negotiations took place in October 1931 soon after Gandhiji reached London. The Muslim draft did not contain any proposals about other minorities. So far as the Muslim representatives were concerned, they were willing to settle with Gandhiji without bothering about the untouchables and other communities. But the negotiations broke down on the demand for a majority of one in the Punjab and Bengal. After this failure, the Muslim delegates conspired with Dr. Ambedkar and others and produced a minorities pact, which was presented to the Minorities Committee at its sitting on 13th November 1931. The boot was on the other leg. The conspiracy was made not by Gandhiji but against him and the Congress by communalists nominated by the British Government for exaggerating the communal claims. It was obvious to the signatories to that pact that it would not be accepted by the people of India.

It may be pointed that Dr. Ambedkar makes the baseless assertion that Gandhiji signed the requisition to Ramsay MacDonald to arbitrate on the communal question. Only some of the members were agreeable to giving the British Premier general authority to arbitrate. Some delegates wanted to give him an award on the Hindu-Muslim question alone. Dr. Ambedkar would have published the requisition and the signatures if it supported his case (K. Santhanam: *Ambedkar's Attack*, pp. 30-31).

After a week of adjournment, the Minorities Committee met on 8th October 1931. The Prime Minister called upon Gandhi to speak first. Gandhi in his speech said: “Prime Minister and friends, it is with deep sorrow and deeper humiliation that I have to announce utter failure on my part to secure an agreed solution of the communal question through informal conversation among and with the representatives of different groups. I apologize to you, Mr. Prime Minister, and the other colleagues for the waste of precious week. My only consolation lies in the fact that when I accepted the burden of carrying on these talks I knew that there was much hope of success and still more in the fact that I am not aware of having spared any effort to reach a solution.

“But, to say that the conversations have to our utter shame failed is not to say the whole truth. Causes of failure were inherent in the composition of the Indian delegation. We are almost all not elected representatives of the parties or groups whom we are presumed to represent; we are here by nomination of the Government. Nor are those whose presence was absolutely necessary for an agreed solution to be found here. Further, you will allow me to say that this was hardly the time to summon the Minorities Committee. It lacks the sense of reality in that way we do not know what it is that we are going to get. If we know in a definite manner that we were going to get the thing we want, we should hesitate fifty times before we threw it away in a sinful wrangle as it would be if we are told the getting of it would depend upon the ability of the present delegation to produce an agreed solution of the communal tangle. The solution can be the crown of the Swaraj constitution, not its foundation—if only because our differences have hardened, if they have not arisen, by reason of the foreign domination. I have not a shadow of doubt that the ice-bag of communal differences will melt under the warmth of the sun of freedom.

“I, therefore, venture to suggest that the Minorities Committee be adjourned sine die and that the fundamentals of the constitution be hammered into shape as quickly as may be. Meanwhile, the informal work of discovering a true solution of the communal problem will and must continue; only it must not baulk or be allowed to block the progress of constitution-building. Attention must be diverted from it and concentrated on the main part of the structure.

"Lastly, in as much as the only reason for my appearance at these deliberations is that I represent the Indian National Congress. I must clearly set forth its position. In spite of appearances to the contrary, especially in England, the Congress claims to represent the whole nation, and most decidedly the dumb millions, among whom are included the numberless untouchables, who are more suppressed than depressed, as also in a way the more unfortunate and neglected classes known as Backward Races.

"It seems to have been represented that I am opposed to any representation of the untouchables on the Legislature. This is a travesty of the truth. What I have said, and what I must repeat, is that I am opposed to their special representation. I am convinced that it can do them no good, and may do much harm; but the Congress is wedded to adult franchise. Therefore millions of them can be placed on the Voters' Roll. It is impossible to conceive that with untouchability fast disappearing, nominees of these voters can be boycotted by the others; but what these people need more than election to Legislatures is protection from social and religious persecution. Custom which is often more powerful than law, has brought them to a degradation of which every thinking Hindu has need to feel ashamed and to do penance. I should, therefore, have the most drastic legislation rendering criminal all the special persecution to which these fellow-countrymen of mine are subjected by the so-called superior classes. Thank God, that the conscience of Hindus has been stirred, and untouchability will soon be a relic of our sinful past."

Ambedkar had his own causes, which were responsible for the failure of the informal committee. He said: "What disturbs me after hearing Gandhi is that instead of confining himself to his proposition, namely, that the Minorities Committee should adjourn sine die he started casting certain reflections upon the representatives of the different communities who are sitting round this table. He said that the delegates were nominees of the Government, and that they did not represent the views of their respective communities for whom they stood. We cannot deny the allegation that we are nominees of the Government, but, speaking for myself, I have not the slightest doubt that even if the depressed classes of India were given the chance of electing their representative to this conference, I would, all the same, find a place here. I say therefore that, whether I am a nominee or not, I fully represent the claims of my community. Let no man be under any mistaken impression as regards that.

"Mahatma has been always claiming that the Congress stands for the depressed classes, and that the Congress represents the depressed classes more than I or my colleague can do. To that claim I can only say that it is one of the many false claims which irresponsible people keep on making, although the person concerned with regard to those claims have been invariably denying them."

With regard to Gandhi's proposition that the committee should be adjourned sine die, Ambedkar said: "I, for one, cannot consent to this proposition. It seems to me that there are only two alternatives—either that this Minorities Committee should go on tackling the problem and trying to arrive at some satisfactory solution, if that is possible, and then, if that is not possible, the British Government should undertake the solution of the problem. We cannot consent to leave this to the arbitration of third parties whose sense of responsibility may not be the same as must be the sense of responsibility of the British Government."

With the permission of the Prime Minister, Ambedkar made it clear: "The depressed classes are not anxious, they are not clamorous, they have not started any movement for claiming that there shall be an immediate transfer of power from the British to the Indian people. They have their particular grievances against the British people and I think I have voiced them sufficiently to make it clear that we feel those grievances most genuinely. But, to be true to facts, the position is that the depressed classes are not clamouring for transfer of political power. Their position, to put it plainly, is that we are not anxious for the transfer of power; but if the British Government is unable to resist the forces that have been set up in the country which do clamour for the transference of political power and we know that the depressed classes in the present circumstances are not in a position to resist that—then our submission is that if you make that transfer, that transfer will be accompanied by such conditions and by such provisions that the power shall not fall into the hands of a clique, into the hands of an oligarchy, or into the hands of a group of people, whether Muhammadans or Hindus; but that that solution shall be shared by all communities in their respective proportions. Taking that view, I do not see how I, for one, can take any serious part in the deliberations of the Federal Structure Committee unless I know where I and my community stand."

After hearing Ambedkar, Gandhi said: "One word more as to the so-called untouchables. I can understand the claims advanced by other minorities, but the claims advanced on behalf of the untouchables, that to me is the unkindest cut of all. It means the perpetual bar-sinister. I would not seal the vital interests of the untouchables even for the sake of winning the freedom of India. I claim myself in my own person to represent the vast mass of the untouchables. Here I speak not merely on behalf of the Congress, but I speak on my own behalf, and I claim that I would get, if there was a referendum of the untouchables, their vote, and that I would top the poll. And I would work from one end of India to the other to tell the untouchables that separate electorate and separate reservation is not the way to remove this bar-sinister, which is the shame, not of them but of orthodox Hindus.

"Let this committee and the whole world know that today there is a body of Hindu reformers who are pledged to remove this blot of untouchability. We do not want on our register and on our census untouchables classified as separate class. Sikhs may remain as such in perpetuity, so may Muhammadans, so may Europeans. Will untouchables remain untouchables in perpetuity? I would far rather that Hinduism died than that untouchability lived. Therefore, with all my regard for Dr. Ambedkar, and for his desire to see the untouchables uplifted, with all my regard for his ability, I must say in all humility that here the great wrong under which he has laboured and perhaps the bitter experiences that he has undergone have for the moment warped his judgment. It hurts me to have to say this, but I would be untrue to the cause of untouchables, which is as dear to me as life itself, if I did not say it. I will not bargain away their rights for the kingdom of the whole world. I am speaking with a due sense of responsibility, and I say that it is not a proper claim which is registered by Dr. Ambedkar when he seeks to speak for the whole of the untouchables of India. It will create a division in Hinduism which I cannot possibly look forward to with any satisfaction whatsoever. I do not mind untouchables, if they so desire, being converted to Islam or Christianity. I should tolerate that, but I cannot possibly tolerate what is in store for Hinduism if there are two divisions set forth in the villages. Those who speak of the political rights of the untouchables do not know their India, do not know how Indian society is today constructed, and therefore I want to say with all the emphasis that I can command that if I was the only person to resist this thing I would resist it with my life."

In conclusion Gandhi said: "I hardly need point out to the committee that my failure does not mean the end of all hope of arriving at an agreed solution. My failure does not even mean my utter defeat; there is no such word in the dictionary. My confession merely means failure of special effort for which I asked for a week's adjournment which you so generously gave.

"I propose to use the failure as a stepping stone to success and I invite you all to do likewise, but should all efforts at agreement fail, even when the Round Table Conference reaches the end of its labours, I would suggest the addition of a clause to the expected constitution appointing a judicial tribunal that would examine all claims and give its final decision on all points that may be left unsettled" (Dr. Babasaheb Ambedkar: *Writings and Speeches*, Vol. 2, pp. 654-63).

The representatives of the Muslims, Depressed Classes, Anglo-Indians, a section of the Indian Christians and the European Commercial community intimated that they had reached an agreement inter se, which they formally presented for the consideration of the committee. But the course of the discussion on 13th November made it clear that the agreement in question was not regarded as acceptable by the Hindu or Sikh representatives, and that there seemed no prospect of a solution of the communal question as the result of negotiation between the parties concerned.

Ramsay McDonald, held that inability to solve the communal question was hampering the progress of constitution-making. In the course of discussions, suggestions were made that the British Government should settle the dispute on its own authority. These suggestions, however, were accompanied by such important reservations that there was little prospect of any one of them securing the necessary harmony in working. Gandhi also offered to accept the arbitration by the Premier, provided it related only to the Muslims and Sikhs. He would not be a party to the separate representation of other communities. The Premier asked a plain question on this subject: "Will you, each of you, every member of the committee, sign a request to me, to settle the communal question and pledge yourself to accept my decision? That, I think is a very fair offer."

Most of the members, but not all, signed such a request. When the Premier finally announced his decision in June, 1932, it was a moot point to decide whether it was an award binding upon all, or merely a proposal of the Government. It was contended that all the members did not sign, it could not be looked upon as an award, which all parties were bound to accept, but only as a proposal.

The whole history of the Round Table Conference and the part played by different parties in it are revealed in a striking manner by a confidential circular issued by the representatives of the European community who attended the Second Round Table Conference.

It clearly showed that they worked with a set purpose to block any real constitutional progress in India beyond what was conceded by the Simon Commission. As a mark of their success they triumphantly pointed out that Gandhi "landed in India with empty hands. They also gloated over the facts that Gandhi undertook to settle the communal problem and failed before all the world." The following passage in the circular throws some light on the cause of Gandhi's failure.

"The Muslims were a solid and enthusiastic team: Ali Imam, the Nationalist Muslim, caused no division. They played their cards with great skill throughout; they promised us support and they gave it in full measure. In return they asked us that we should not forget their economic plight in Bengal and we should without pampering them do what we can to find places for them in the European firms, so that they may have a chance to improve their material; position and the general standing of their community." As regards the general policy, the following para is very revealing:

"On the whole, there was one policy of the British Nation and the British community in India, and that was to make up our minds on a national policy and to stick to it. But after the general elections, the right wing of the Government made up its mind to break up the Conference and to fight the Congress. The Muslims, who do not want responsibility at the Centre, were delighted. The Government undoubtedly changed their policy and tried to get away with provincial autonomy, with a promise of Central reforms. We had made up our minds that the fight with the Congress was inevitable; we felt and said that the sooner it came the better, but we made up our minds that for a crushing success we should have all possible friends on our side. The Muslims were all right; the Minorities Pact and Government's general attitude ensured that. So were the Princes and the Minorities.

"The important thing to us seemed to be to carry the Hindus in the street as represented by such people as Sapru, Jayakar, Patro and others. If we could not get them to fight the Congress, we could at least ensure that they would not back the Congress, and that, by the simple method of leaving no doubt in their minds that there was to be no going back on the Federal Scheme which broadly was also the accepted policy of the European Community, and we acted accordingly. So we joined with strange companions;...and the Conference, instead of breaking up in disorder with 100 per cent of Hindu political India against us, ended in promises of cooperation by 99 per cent of the Conference, including even such people as Malaviya, while Gandhi himself was indisposed to join the Standing Committee.

"The Muslims have become firm allies of the Europeans. They are very satisfied with their own position and are prepared to work with us" (R.C. Majumdar: *Struggle for Freedom,* pp. 493-96).

In his style Churchill attacked the Round Table Conference on 14 December: "Day by day, inch by inch, we see the

R.T.C. crawling towards its destruction." He further observed: "We seem to be riding steadily towards an un-climbable fence" (V.B. Kulkarni: *M.R. Jayakar,* pp. 200-04, 209, 216).

The chorus of discordant voices only tended to show that India was not a nation but a conglomeration of different, and often conflicting, nationalities and religious groups. This is exactly what the conservatives were manoeuvring to show up. There was another straw in the wind. The British politicians did not seem inclined to concede anything beyond what the Simon Commission had recommended. The Labour Party itself did not seem to be willing to go far enough. To hark back to the Simon Commission at that stage when the Round Table Conference had generated as much hope and the expectation was like putting the cloak back (S.K. Bose: *Tej Bahadur Sapru,* p. 85).

Failure of Conference

Ambedkar held Gandhi responsible for the failure of the Round Table Conference. In his own words:

"If the conference failed the fault is entirely of Mr. Gandhi. A more ignorant and more tactless representative could not have been sent to a conference which was convened to forge a constitution which was to reconcile the diverse interests of India. Mr. Gandhi was thoroughly ignorant of the constitutional law or finance. He does not believe in intellectual equipment. Indeed, he has a supreme contempt for it and his contributions to the solutions of the many difficulties is therefore nil. He was tactless because he annoyed almost all the delegates by constantly telling them that they were non-entities and he was the only man who counted and who could deliver the goods. At the first Round Table Conference, the delegates did not agree upon a solution of the communal problem. But it is equally true that they were very near agreeing to it and when they departed they did not give up hope of agreeing. But at the end of second Round Table Conference, so much bad blood was created by Mr. Gandhi that there was no chance of reconciliation left and there was no way except arbitration.

"Apart from this discourtesy to fellow-delegates, did Mr. Gandhi stand for the cause he came to champion? He did not.

His conduct of affairs was ignominious. Instead of standing and fighting he began to yield on issues on which he ought never to have ceased fire. He yielded to the Princes and agreed that their representatives in the Federal Legislature should be nominated by them and not elected, as demanded by their subjects. He yielded to the conservatives and consented to be content with provincial autonomy and not to insist upon central responsibility for which many lakhs of Indians went to jail. The only people to whom he would not yield were the minorities—the only party to whom he could have yielded with honour to himself and advantage to the country. Nothing has helped so much to shatter the prestige of Mr. Gandhi and going to the Round Table Conference. The spectacle of Mr. Gandhi at the Round Table Conference must have been painful to many of his friends. He was not fit to play the role he undertook to play. No country ever sent a delegate to take part in the framing of the constitution who was so completely unequipped in training and study. Gandhi went to the Round Table Conference with the song of Narsi Mehta on his tongue. It would have been better for him and better for his country if he had taken in his armpit a volume on comparatively constitutional law. Devoid of any knowledge of the subject he was called upon to deal with, he was quite powerless to destroy the proposals put forth by the British or to meet them with his alternatives. No wonder Mr. Gandhi, taken out of the circle of his devotees and places among politicians, was at sea. At every turn he bungled and finding that he could not even muddle through, he gave up the game and returned to India.

"Everybody expected that Mr. Gandhi would be more interested in seeing that the constitution that was likely to emerge from these deliberations and negotiations was a constitution which gave India Poorna Swaraj, i.e., complete independence, and he would not interest himself in so unimportant a subject as the allocation of seats among the different minorities. But events completely falsified these hopes. Mr. Gandhi completely gave up his fight against British imperialism altogether. He forgot that he had come with a mandate to secure a constitution which contained Poorna Swaraj. He left that issue and started fighting the minorities and, what is strange, he concentrated all his fire upon the representatives of the untouchables for daring to put forth the claim for special representation. Mr. Gandhi opposed tooth and nail the representatives of the depressed classes. He was not prepared even to look at their claim. He was annoyed at their impudence and the whole conference was astonished by his opposition. They could not understand how a man like Mr. Gandhi who posed himself as the friend of the untouchables could in fact be so great an enemy of their interests. His friends were completely baffled. Mr. Gandhi was prepared to recognize a similar right claimed by the Musalmans and the Sikhs, although he was not prepared to recognize a similar claim by Christians, Europeans and Anglo-Indians, he was not going to oppose their claim.

"Mr. Gandhi's friends could not understand how he could deny similar right to the untouchables. The Muhammadans, Sikhs, Christians, European and Anglo-Indians were far better placed. The untouchables were poorest of the poor. The former were educationally advanced, the latter were educationally most backward. The former were socially well respected, the latter were socially despised. The former enjoyed a position of free citizens, the latter were suffering from certain disabilities. The former were not subjected to social tyranny and social boycott but social tyranny and social boycott were the every day lot of the latter. Having regard to this difference in the status there could never be any doubt that if there was any section of the Indian people whose case called forth special protection, they were the untouchables."

"Having failed to demolish the justice of the claim of the depressed classes, Mr. Gandhi decided to isolate the representatives of the depressed classes, to see that they get no support from any other quarter. He planned to break a possible compact between the depressed classes and the Muslims. A part of the plan was to win over the Musalmans to his side and for that purpose he offered to enter into a pact with them.

"This is the agreement, which Mr. Gandhi was prepared to enter with the Musalmans. By this agreement, he was prepared to give to the Musalmans the 14 points they had been demanding. In return, he wanted the Musalmans among other things to agree to continue the benefit of the principle of special representation to Hindus, Muslims and Sikhs.

"There was no support for these 14 points of the Musalmans from any quarter whatsoever. Gandhi agreed for 14 points with the object of buying the Musalmans so that with their help he could more effectively resist the demand of the other minorities and the depressed classes. It was not an agreement with the Musalmans. It was a plot against the depressed classes. It was worse, it was a stab in the back.

"Mr. Bernard Shaw has said that the British do everything on principle. Similarly, Mr. Gandhi says that he does everything on the principle of morality and good faith. Can the acts of Mr. Gandhi be justified by test of justice and good faith" (Dr. Babasaheb Ambedkar: *Writings and Speeches*, Vol. 5, pp. 288-328).

In the opinion of Jawaharlal Nehru:

"The British Government had, no intention of falling with our wishes in the matter. Their policy was to postpone the consideration of fundamental questions and to make the conference exhaust itself, more or less, on minor and immaterial matters. Even when major matters were considered, the Government held its hand, refused to commit itself, and promised to express its opinion after mature consideration later on. Their trump card was, of course, the communal issue and they played it for all it was worth. It dominated the conference.

"The great majority of the Indian members of the conference fell in, most of them willingly, some unwillingly, with this official manoeuvring. They were a motley assembly. Few of them represented any but themselves. Some were able and respected; of many others this could not be said. As a whole they represented, politically and socially, the most reactionary elements in India. So backward and reactionary were they that the Indian Liberals, so very moderate and cautious in India, shone as progressive in their company. They represented groups of vested interests in India who were tied up with British imperialism, and looked to it for advancement or protection. The most prominent representation came from various Minority and Majority groups on the communal issue. This consisted of a number of upper class irreconcilables who, it was notorious, could never agree among themselves. Politically they were thorough reactionaries, and their sole interest seemed to be to gain a communal advantage even though that might involve a surrender of political advance. Indeed, they proclaimed that they would not agree to having any greater measure of political freedom unless and until their communal demands were satisfied. That was an extraordinary sight, and it revealed with painful clarity the depths to which a subject people could fall and how they could be made pawns in the imperialist game. It was true that the Indian people could not be said to be represented by that crowd of highness, lords, knights and other high degree. The members of the Round Table Conference had been nominated by he British Government, and from its own point of view, the Government had chosen well.

"It was fitting that in this assembly of vested interests—imperialist, feudal, industrial, religious, communal—the leadership of the British Indian delegation should usually fall to the Agha Khan, who in his own person happened to combining all these interests in some degree. Closely associated as he has been with British imperialism and the British ruling class for over a generation, residing chiefly in England, he could thoroughly appreciate and represent our rulers' interests and viewpoint. He would have been an able representative of Imperialist England at the Round Table Conference. The irony of it was that he was supposed to represent India.

"The scales were terribly loaded against us at that conference and, little as we expected from it, we watched its proceedings with amazement and ever-growing disgust. We saw the pitiful and absurdly inadequate attempts to scratch the surface of national and economic problems, the pacts and intrigues and manoeuvres, the joining of hands of some of our own countrymen with the most reactionary elements of the British Conservative Party, the endless talk over petty issues, the deliberate shelving of all that really mattered, the continuous playing in the hands of the big vested interests and especially British imperialism, the mutual squabbles, varied by feasting and mutual admiration. It was all jobbery—big jobs, little jobs, and seats for the Hindus, for the

Muslims, for the Sikhs, for the Anglo-Indians, for the Europeans, but all jobs for the upper classes, the masses had no look—in-opportunism was rampant, and different groups seemed to prowl about like hungry wolves waiting for their prey—the spoils under the new constitution. The very conception of freedom had taken the form of large-scale jobbery. Indianization it was called-more jobs for the Indians in the army, in the civil services, etc. No one thought in terms of independence, of real freedom, of a transfer of power to a democratic India, of the solution of any of the vital and urgent economic problems facing the Indian people.

"In that gilded and crowded hall Gandhiji sat, a very lonely figure. His dress, or absence of it, distinguished him from all others, but there was an even vaster difference between his thought and outlook and that of the well dressed folk around him. His was an extraordinary position in that conference and we wondered from after how he could tolerate it. But with amazing patience, he carried on, and made attempt after attempt to find some basis of agreement. One characteristic gesture he made, which suddenly showed up how communalism covered political reaction. He did not like many of the communal demands put forward on behalf of the Muslim delegates to the conference. He thought, and his own Muslim Nationalist colleagues thought so, that some of these demands were a bar to freedom and democracy. But still he offered to accept the whole lot of them, without question or argument, if the Muslim delegates there join forces with him and the Congress on the political issue, that is, on independence.

"The offer, however, was not accepted, and indeed, it is a little difficult to imagine the Agha Khan standing for Indian independence. This demonstrated that the real trouble was not communal, although the communal issue loomed large before the conference. It was political reaction that barred all progress and sheltered itself behind the communal issue. By careful selection of its nominees for the conference, the British Government had collected these reactionary elements, and by controlling the procedure, they had made the communal issue the major issue, and an issue on which no agreement was possible between the irreconcilables gathered there.

"The British Government succeeded in its endeavour, and thereby demonstrated that it still has not only the physical strength to uphold the Empire, but also the cunning and statecraft to carry on the imperial tradition for a while longer. The people of India failed, although the Round Table Conference neither represented them nor was it a measure of their strength. They failed because they had no ideological background of what they were striving for and could be easily misled and side-tracked. They failed because they did not feel themselves strong enough to discard the vested interests that encumbered their progress. They failed because of an excess religiosity, and the ease with which the communal feelings could be roused. They failed, in short, because they were not advanced enough and strong enough to succeed.

"The previous conference, the first of its kind, had attracted very little attention in India. The nominees of the British Government who went to the conference went with black flags and uncomplimentary slogans. But in 1931, all was different because Gandhiji went as the sole representative of the Congress, and as a leader whom millions followed. This gave prestige to the conference, and India followed its career with far greater interest; and any failure, whatever the cause, rebounded to the desecration of India. We understood why the British Government attached so much importance to Gandhiji's participation in it.

"The conference itself, with all its scheming and opportunism and futile meandering, was no failure for India. It was constituted so as to fail, and the people of India could hardly be made responsible for its failing. But it succeeded in diverting world attention from real issues in India, and in India itself, it produced disillusion and depression and a sense of humiliation. It gave a handle to reactionary forces to raise their heads again.

"Success or failure was to come to the people of the country by events in India itself. The powerful nationalist movement could not fade away, because of distant manoeuvring in London. Nationalism represented a real and immediate need of the middle classes and peasantry, and by its means they sought to solve their problems. The movement could thus either succeed, fulfill its function, and give place to some other movement, which would carry the people further on to progress and freedom, or else it could be forcibly suppressed for the time being. The struggle was to come in India soon after, and was to result in temporary disablement. The second Round Table Conference could not affect this struggle much, but it did create an atmosphere somewhat unfavorable to it" (*Mahatma Gandhi: Jawaharlal Nehru*, pp. 78-84).

This is what Mr. Ewer, who was closely associated with Mr. Gandhi during the Round Table Conference, wrote about the role Mr. Gandhi played at the Round Table Conference in London.

"Gandhi in the St. James' Palace has not fulfilled the unwise expectation of those who saw him bestriding the Conference like a colossus

...He was out of his elements."

"His first speech, with its sentimental appeal, its over-stressing of humility, its reiteration of single-minded concern for the dumb suffering millions, was a failure. No one questioned its sincerity. But somehow it rang false. It was the right thing, perhaps, but it was in the wrong place. Nor were his later interventions on the whole more successful. A rather querulous complaint that the British Government had not produced a plan for the new Indian Constitution shocked some of Gandhi's colleagues, who had hardly expected to see the representative of the National Congress appealing to British Ministers for guidance and initiative. The protest against the pegging of the rupee to the pound was astonishingly ineffective. The contributions to the discussions on franchise and kindred matters were of little importance. Behind the scenes he was active enough in the Hindu-Moslem negotiations, but here, too, results were intangible. Not for a moment did Gandhi take the lead or materially influence the course of committee work. He sat there, sometimes speaking, sometimes silent, while the work went on, much as it would have gone on without him."

This is what Bolton has to say about Mr. Gandhi's achievement at the Round Table Conference.

How did Mr. Gandhi fare as a statesman and a politician?

At the close of the first session of the Round Table Conference there were three questions which had not been settled. The question of minorities, the question of the Federal structure and the question of the status of India in the Empire, were the three outstanding problems which were the subject matter of controversy. Their solution demanded great statesmanship. Many said that these questions were not settled because the wisdom and authority of the Congress was not represented at the Round Table Conference. At the second session, Mr. Gandhi came and made good the deficiency. Did Mr. Gandhi settle any of these unsettled problems? I think it is not unfair to say that Mr. Gandhi created fresh disunity in the Conference. He began the childish game of ridiculing every Indian delegate. He questioned their honesty, he questioned their representative character. He taunted the liberals as arm-chair politicians and as leaders without any followers. To the Muslims he said that he represented the Muslim masses better than they did. He claimed that the Depressed Class delegates did not represent the Depressed Classes and that he did. This was the refrain which he repeated *ad nauseum* at the end of every speech. The non-Congress delegates deserve the thanks of all honest people for their having tolerated this nonsense and arrogance of Mr. Gandhi and collaborated with him to save him and to save the country from his mistake. Apart from this discourtesy to fellow-delegates, did Mr. Gandhi stand up for the cause he came to champion? He did not. His conduct of affairs was ignominious. Instead of standing up and fighting he began to yield on issues on which he ought never to have ceased fire. He yielded to the Princes and agreed that their representatives in the Federal legislature should be nominated by them and not elected, as demanded by their subjects. He yielded to the conservatives and consented to be content with provincial autonomy and not to insist upon central responsibility for which many lakhs of Indians went to gaol. The only people to whom he would not yield were the minorities—the only party to whom he could have yielded with honour to himself and advantage to the country (Dr. Babasaheb Ambedkar: *Writings and Speeches*, Vol. 5, pp. 287-89).

When Gandhi returned to India, the whole country was afire. The failure of Gandhi to achieve any success brings out in relief the inconsistency and un-wisdom of the Congress in refusing to accept the first and accepting the invitation to the second Round Table Conference. The conditions on which the Congress agreed to attend the second Round Table Conference would have been easily secured on the occasion of the first. By joining it from the very beginning in sufficient strength the Congress could influence its outlook and general approach. As it is, Gandhiji was confronted with a communalism structure which had been allowed to grow up freely without let or hindrance. Besides, with Irwin as Viceroy and the Labour Party in power, there was a far greater chance of gaining substantial reforms than in the second conference, when Lord Willingdon was the Viceroy and the Conservatives had come into power.

The failure of the conference was mainly due to the lack of harmony among Indian delegates and the obstinate reluctance of the Conservatives to part with real power in India. But the tactics, or the lack of tactics, on the part of Gandhiji was also responsible for it to a large extent. The saint had no place in the meeting of the die-hard politicians. Gandhiji's idealism made no impression on them, his frank gesture for peace and cooperation at any price was taken as a sign of weakness. His lack of diplomacy in putting all his cards on the table was fully exploited by the astute British politicians and the measure they made of his power and ability by actual contact was far lower than their previous estimate based on reports of his leadership in India. Gandhiji had realized from the very beginning that the importance of the Indian National Congress which he represented was deliberately minimized, if not totally ignored, and it was treated as merely one out of many parties represented at the conference. And he made only piteous appeals to the conference in such words, 'For heaven's sake give me, a frail man of sixty-two, a little bit of chance. Find a little corner for him and the organization that he represents.' Things might have been different, however, if instead, he took a bold stand on the inherent strength of the institution he represented, and made a defiant gesture of leaving the conference if it failed to give due recognition to the Congress which would legitimately claim, as the only All-India organization, to speak in the name of political India as opposed to the rest which as best represented communal, sectional, or vested interests. Gandhiji's Christian meekness and humility fell flat on the followers of Christ who only understood the language of strength or force. His conduct in the conference added one more illustration of his utter inability to carry on negotiations with trained politicians (R.C. Majumdar (ed.): *The History and Culture of Indian People*, Vol. II, Bharatiya Vidya Bhavan, pp. 493-97).

Gandhiji was the sole representative of the Congress at the Round Table Conference. The British press and the politicians made out that Gandhi, however, eminent as an individual, was only one of the Indian delegates, and the Congress was just one of the numerous parties of which a cross-section had been brought together at the conference. All the delegates were the nominees of the Government; they had a sprinkling of able individuals, but the majority of them were drawn from the princely order, the landlords, the titled gentry, the leaders of communal groups and vested interests, big and small. Many delegates were only too willing to become pawns in the political intrigues, the looking for position, the scramble for jobs and seats in legislatures and services, to which the conference gradually reduced itself.

The conference side-tracked its energies into secondary issues particularly the communal problems. Gandhi saw through this game and did some plain thinking in public as well as in private. Surely, he asked, the British Government had not invited the Indian delegates from 6000 miles to London to settle the communal question. He pointed out that the various communities had been led to place an undue emphasis on the communal question as a condition precedent to constitutional advance; this had turned them virtually into hungry wolves prowling about for prey under the new constitution. The problem had been presented to the conference in an inverted way; it had been called upon to divide a cake the size of which was not known. Let us know what we are going to get, Gandhiji asked, so on that basis I might endeavourer to bring unity even in the present ill-assorted group. I could tell them that they are dashing a precious thing to pieces.

Gandhiji pleaded for an honorable and equal partnership between Britain and India, held not by force but by the silken cord of love. The Congress had accepted the principle of federation, as also the principle that there should be safeguards, but the safeguards had to be devised in the interest of India and not to reduce self-Government to a mockery. If all the safeguards which were being proposed were incorporated in the new constitution, the responsible Government which India would enjoy could be no better than the responsible Government prisoners have in their cells; the prisoners too have complete independence immediately after the cell door is locked up.

The Round Table Conference was worse than a failure. By intensifying the religious divisions of India, it exercised sinister, tragic influence on the failure. The British Government advocated a Federation of Princely India, which was roughly a third of India, with British India. This would have introduced the weight of the autocratic princes, British puppets, all into the Government of India. Thus what seemed like the unification of the two Indias was calculated to strengthen feudal, medieval reaction and reinforce British rule.

The delegation from British India included the Agha Khan and others like him. It included British, merchants, Anglo-Indians, Christians, Hindus, Muslims, untouchables, Parsis, landlords, and each of these groups demanded a separate electorate for itself. In other words, a number of seats in the legislative assemblies would be reserved for Englishmen resident in India, for landlords, for Muslims, etc. and the Englishmen would be elected only by the votes of the Englishmen of India; the landlords would be elected by landlords; the Muslims could vote only for Muslim candidates and so on. Every divisive tendency in India was encouraged.

The conference set up a Minorities Committee comprising six Englishmen from England, thirteen Muslims, ten Hindus, two untouchables, two laborites, two Sikhs, one Parsi, two Indian Christians, one Anglo-Indian, two Englishmen domiciled in India and four women. Only the women did not ask for a separate electorate. Of the thirteen Muslims in the committee, only one was a nationalist Muslim, who was an Indian politically and a follower of the Prophet religiously. The remaining twelve mingled Church and State and put the political interests of their religious community above the welfare of India as a whole.

Gandhi told the conference that he rejected all separate electorates. In an independent India, he said, Indians would vote as Indians for Indians. The virtue of Indian nationalism and its appeal to outsiders was not that it would create new national barriers—there were already too many—but rather that it would rid England and the world of the incubus of imperialism and take religion out of politics in India. Instead, the Round Table Conference, under British management intensified old and attempted to introduce new fissiparous influences. Divide and Rule, is the law of empire; the more the rule is threatened, the more diligently that law is applied.

The solution for India would have been to banish religious considerations from politics. But with all its 20th century vitality, Indian nationalism still lacked the strength to unite that which religious, provincial loyalties and economic differences separated. The Indian national movement was faced with the task of liberation before the Indians had been welded into a nation.

The caste system was a further divisive influence which weakened nationalism. The Harijans or untouchables feared and often hated the Hindus, who had harnessed so many brutal disabilities upon them. They, too, through their gifted and ambitious representative at the conference, Dr. Bhimrao Ramji Ambedkar, a lawyer who studied at Columbia University of New York under a scholarship from the Maharaja of Baroda, demanded a separate electorate or at least a right to a specified number of Hindu seats in the legislative assemblies.

Mahatma Gandhi, a supremely devout Hindu was incapable of discriminating against any one on account of religion, race, caste, color, or anything. His contribution to the equality of untouchables and to the education of a new generation which was Indian instead of Hindu or Muslim or Parsi or Christian has world significance. But at the time of the Round Table Conference of 1931, and especially with the British Government pulling in the opposite direction, his arm lacked the power to draw the Hindu, Muslim and Harijan communities together into an Indian unity which could have commanded the British Raj to go home.

At the plenary sitting of the conference James Ramsay MacDonald referred to Gandhi as a Hindu. "Not Hindu," Gandhi exclaimed.

To his God Gandhi was a Hindu. To the British Prime Minister and in politics, he was an Indian. But there were few such Indians at the Round Table Conference and too few in India.

That was the upshot of the Round Table Conference. It was completely abortive. It made the situation in India worse. Gandhi left England with a heart-ache for though he had charmed and convinced many English people, he had failed to bridge or even to narrow the gulf that separated Hindus from Muslims and the British Government was holding on to India (Loius Fischer: *The Life of Mahatma Gandhi*, Bharatiya Vidya Bhavan, 1995, pp. 368-72).

A mammoth crowd cheered Gandhi on his arrival in the morning of 28th December 1931 at Bombay. "I have come empty handed," he told them, "but I have not compromised the honor of my country."

Subhash Chandra Bose remarked: "Gandhi had returned with his integrity; he had not stepped down from the role of half-naked Fakir who parleyed as an equal with the mighty British Empire."

"How was Mr. Gandhi received when he landed on the Indian soil? When the S.S. Pilsner of the Lloyd Triestino entered the harbour of Bombay at 8 a.m. in the morning of the 28th December 1931 there came to receive him an enthusiastic crowd of men, women and children who had assembled at the Pier in tens of thousands to greet him, to welcome him back and to have his Durshan. The following extracts from the *Times of India* and the *Evening News of Bombay* will serve to give a vivid idea of the grandeur of this reception.

"The Pilsner was escorted into the harbour by Desh Sevikas (women volunteers of the Congress) in saffron coloured sarees who went out in launches some distance from the pier.

"The Congress Committee had asked the Bombay Flying Club to fly an Aeroplane or two over the Pilsner and drop garlands as she came alongside the pier, but the Flying Club, sanely preferring to keep out of politics, refused to grant the Congress demand.

"The spacious Central Hall at Ballard Pier was decorated with festoons and Congress flags and a large dais was put up at the centre with chairs placed on all sides for representatives of various organizations, local and upcountry, who were given passes for admission.

"Both the approaches to the reception hall from the wharf and from the city were lined by Desh Sevikas waving national flags and the duty of guarding the dais and of regulating and directing the assembly inside the hall was also entrusted to the women volunteers.

"Mr. Gandhi reached the dais escorted by the Congress leaders and received an ovation. Hardly had he stepped on the dais when he began to be flooded with telegraph messages (presumably of welcome) which arrived one after another.

"Standing on the dais he was garlanded in turn by representatives of the public bodies who had assembled and whose names were called out from a long printed list of which copies were previously distributed.

"The proceedings inside the reception hall terminated with the garlanding.

"A procession was then formed in four, in place of the carriage which was intended to be the conveyance for Mr. Gandhi. He was seated in a gaily decorated motor car, with Mr. Vallabhbhai Patel to his left and Mr. Vitthalbhai Patel to his right and Mr. K.F. Nariman, President of the Bombay Provincial Congress Committee, on the front seat.

"Preceded by a pilot car and followed by others containing the Congress Working Committee members, the procession passed through the Ballard Pier Road, Hornby Road and Kalbadevi which had been decorated by the citizens at the instance of the Congress Committee and lined on either side by cheering crowds, five to ten deep till the party reached "Mani Bhavan, Gamdevi".

The official historian of the Congress describes this reception given to Mr. Gandhi in the following terms:

"There were gathered in Bombay representatives of all parts and Provinces in India to accord a fitting welcome to the Tribune of the people. Gandhi greeted the friends that went on board the steamer to welcome him, patting many, thumping a few and pulling the venerable Abbas Tyabji by his beard. There was a formal welcome in one of the Halls of Customs House and then a procession in the streets of Bombay which kings might envy in their own country" (Pattabhi Sitaramayya: *History of Congress*, p. 857).

"On reading this account one is reminded of the Irish Sein Fein Delegates who in 1921, just 10 years before, had gone to London at the invitation of Mr. Lloyd George for the settlement of the Irish Home Rule question. As is well known the Irish Delegates secured from the British Cabinet a treaty which was signed on the 8th December 1921. The Treaty was subsequently submitted for approval to the Dail, the Parliament of the Sein Fein Party which met from 14th December 1921 to 7th January 1922. On the 7th January a division was taken. There were 64 votes for ratifying the treaty and 57 against. And what was the reception given to the Irish delegates who secured this treaty? Arthur Griffith—who was the head of the Irish Delegation and Michael Collins who was his most prominent colleague, were both of them shot by the anti-treaty Sein Feiners, the former on the 12th and the latter on the 22nd August 1922. The reason for sending them to such cruel death was that the treaty which they signed did not secure the inclusion of Ulster and a republic for Ireland. It is true the treaty did not grant this. But if it is remembered that negotiations were opened on the express understanding on the part of both sides that these two questions were outside the scope of negotiations it will be granted that if the treaty did not include these it was no fault of the Irish Delegates. The fury and ferocity of the anti treaty Sein Feiners against the Irish Delegates had no moral foundation and the fate that befell Arthur Griffith and Michael Collins can by no stretch of imagination be said to be one which they deserved.

"Be that as it may, this welcome to Mr. Gandhi will be regarded as a very strange event. Both went to win Swaraj, Griffith and Collins for Ireland, Gandhi for India, Griffith and

Collins succeeded, almost triumphed; Gandhi failed and returned with nothing but defeat and humiliation. Yet Collins and Griffith were shot and Gandhi was given a reception which kings could have envied!! What a glaring and a cruel contrast between the fate that awaited Collins and Griffith and the reception arranged for Gandhi? Did the masses render this welcome out of blind devotion or were they kept in darkness of the failure of Mr. Gandhi by a mercenary Press? This is more than I can answer."

Ambedkar further said:

While this great welcome was being accorded to Mr. Gandhi the Untouchables of Bombay had come to the Pier to repudiate Mr. Gandhi. Referring to this demonstration, the newspaper reports said:

"Just outside the gate of Ballard Pier, the scene was most exciting. On one side were drawn up Depressed Class volunteers in uniform, weaving black flags to the accompaniment of derisive shouts against Mr. Gandhi and laudatory cries in praise of their leader, while on the other side Congress follower kept up a din of counter shouts."

This Untouchable demonstration included men and women. The demonstrators numbered thousands, all waving Black Flags as a mark of repudiation of Mr. Gandhi. They were a determined crowd and, despite intimidation by the superior forces of the Congress assembled there to welcome Mr. Gandhi, were bent on showing that they repudiated Mr. Gandhi. This led to a clash and blood was split. There were forty casualties on each side.

For the first time Mr. Gandhi was made aware that there could be black flags even against him. This must have come to him as a shock. When he was asked about it later in the day, he said he was not angry, the Untouchables being the flesh of his flesh and bone of his done. This is of course the Mahatmaic way of concealing the truth. One would not mind this convenient and conventional lie if there were behind it a realization that the crowd could not always be trusted to be loyal to its hero. Congressmen in India sadly lack the realism of a man like

Cromwell. It is related that when Cromwell returned after a great battle, an enormous crowd came out to greet him, a friend sought to impress upon him the immensity of the crowd. But Cromwell dismissed the subject with the laconic remark, "Oh yes, I know many more will come to see me hanged!!" No congress leader feels the realism of Cromwell. Either he believes that the day will never come when he will be hanged and he believes that the Indian crowd will never become a thinking crowd. That part of the Indian crowd does think was shown by the representatives of the Untouchables who assembled on the 28th to greet Mr. Gandhi with black flags.

Why did the Untouchabels repudiate Mr. Gandhi? The answer to this question will be found in a statement issued by the organizers of these demonstrations which was printed and circulated on that day. The following are extracts from it.

"Our Charge sheet against Gandhiji and Congress."

"Enough of patronizing attitude and lip sympathy. We ask for justice and fair play."

In spite of the fact that the removal of untouchability has been included in the constructive programme of the Congress, practically nothing has so far been done by that body to achieve that object, and in our fights against untouchability at Mahad and Nasik most of the local Congress leaders have been our bitter opponents.

The attitude of Gandhiji at the Round Table Conference in London with regard to the demands of the Depressed Classes as put forward by their accredited and trusted leader Dr. Ambedkar, was most unreasonable, obstinate and inexplicable.

Gandhiji was prepared to concede on behalf of the Congress the special claims of the Mohamedans and the Sikhs including their demand for separate representation on "historic grounds", but he was not willing even to concede reserved seats in general electorates to the Depressed Classes, although he knew, or should have known, what sort of treatment they would get, should they be thrown upon at the mercy on caste Hindus.

Gandhiji has said in opposing the claims of the Depressed Classes for separate representation that he does not want the Hindu community to be subjected to vivisection or dissection. But the Congress is now dissecting the community of Untouchables by playing one section against another. Gandhiji and the Congress are not playing the fair game. Open enemies are far better than treacherous friends.

Attempts are being made to show that Gandhiji and the Congress alone represent the Depressed Classes by presenting address through a handful of hirelings and dupes. Is it not our duty to demonstrate the fact by coming out in thousands and proclaiming the truth? This is our charge sheet against Gandhiji and the Congress.

Let those who are not blind hero worshippers and blind partisans judge and give their verdict.

General Secretary,
Depressed Classes Institute

On the chargesheet Ambedkar:

Is this charge sheet true? Mr. Gandhi is known to the world not merely as the Political leader of India, but also as the Champion of the Untouchables. It is perhaps true that the outside world takes more interest in Mr. Gandhi because he is the champion of the Untouchables than because he is a political leader. For instance the *Manchester Guardian* very recently devoted an editorial to the work of Mr. Gandhi for the Untouchables.

In the face of this, the charge appears to be quite unfounded. For, has not Mr. Gandhi made the Congress pledge itself to remove untouchability? The Congress before it came into the hands of Mr. Gandhi had refused to allow any social problem to be placed before it for consideration. A clear-cut distinction was made between political and social question, and scrupulous attempt was made to confine the deliberations and activities of the Congress to purely political questions. The old Congress refused to take notice of the Untouchables. It was with great difficulty that the Congress in 1917 for the first time allowed the question of the Untouchables to be placed before it and condescended to pass the following resolution:

"The Congress urges upon the people of India the necessity, justice and righteousness of removing all disabilities imposed by custom upon the Depressed Classes, the disabilities being of a most vexatious and oppressive character, subjecting those classes to considerable hardship and inconvenience" (Dr. Babasaheb Ambedkar: *Writings and Speeches*, Vol. 5, pp. 289-94).

Chapter 4

Communal Award

The communal question was the rock on which the Indian Round Table Conference suffered a shipwreck. The Conference broke up as there could be no agreement between the majority and minority communities. Dr. Ambedkar insisted that the position of minorities under Swaraj should be safeguarded by allowing them special representation in the legislatures. Gandhiji was not prepared to recognize such a claim except in the case of the Muslims and the Sikhs.

There was a complete deadlock. As there was no possibility of an agreement, the hope lay in arbitration. On this everybody was agreed except Dr. Ambedkar, and it was left to Mr. Ramsay MacDonald, the Prime Minister, to decide upon the issue.

On his return to India from Round Table Conference Gandhiji was put behind bars and lodged in Yerwada Jail by the British Government. Gandhiji took the earliest opportunity to be in communication with the British government.

On 11 March 1932, he addressed the following letter to Sir Samuel Hoare, the then Secretary of State for India:

"You will perhaps recollect that at the end of my speech at the Round Table Conference when the minorities claim was presented, I had said that I should resist with my life the grant of separate electorates to the depressed classes. This was not said in the heat of the moment nor by way of rhetoric. It was meant to be a serious statement, I had hoped on my return to India to mobilize public opinion against separate electorates, any rate, for depressed classes, but it was not to be.

"From the newspapers I am permitted to read, I observe that at any moment, His Majesty's government may declare their decision. At first I had thought, if the decision was found to create separate electorates for the depressed classes, I should take such steps as I might then consider necessary to give effect to my vow. But I feel it would be unfair to the British government or me to act without giving previous notice. Naturally, they could not attach the significance I give to my statement.

"I need hardly reiterate all the objections I have to the creation of separate electorates for the depressed classes. I feel as if I was one of them. Their case stands on a wholly different footing from that of others. I am not against their representation in the legislatures. I should favor every one of their adults, male and female, being registered as voters irrespective of education of property qualification, even though the franchise test may be stricter for others. But I hold that separate electorate is harmful for them and for Hinduism, whatever it may be from the purely political standpoint. To appreciate the harm that separate electorates would do them one has to know how they are distributed amongst the so-called Caste Hindus and how dependent they are on the latter. So far as Hinduism is concerned, separate electorates would simply vivisect and disrupt it.

"For me the question of these classes is predominantly moral and religious. The political aspect, important though it is, dwindles into significance compared to the moral and religious issue.

"You will have to appreciate my feelings in this matter by remembering that I have been interested in the condition of these classes from my boyhood and have more than once staked my all for their sake. I say this not to pride myself in anyway. For, I feel that no penance that the Hindus may do can in any way compensate for the calculated degradation to which they have consigned the depressed classes for centuries.

"But I know that separate electorate is neither a penance nor any for the crushing degradation they have groaned under. I, therefore, respectfully inform His Majesty's government, that in the event of their decision creating separate electorate for the depressed classes, I must fast unto death.

"I am painfully conscious of the fact that such a step, whilst I am a prisoner, must cause grave embarrassment to His Majesty's government, and that it will be regarded by many as highly improper on the part of one holding my position to introduce into the political field methods which they would describe as hysterical if not much worse. All I can urge in defence is that for me the contemplated step is not method, it is part of my being. It is the call of conscience which I dare not disobey, even though it may cost whatever reputation for sanity I may possess. So far as I can see now, my discharge from imprisonment would not make the duty of fasting any the less imperative. I am hoping, however, all my fears are wholly unjustified and the British government have no intention whatever of creating separate electorate for the depressed classes."

Sir Samuel Hoare sent the following reply to Gandhiji vide his letter dated 13 April 1932: "I write this in answer to your letter of 11 March, and I say at once I realize fully the strength of your feeling upon the question of separate electorates for the depressed classes. I can only say that we intend to give any decision that may be necessary solely and only upon the merits of the case. As you are aware, Lord Lothian's Committee has not yet completed its tour and it must be some weeks before we can receive any conclusions at which it may have arrived. When we receive that report we shall have to give most careful consideration to its recommendations, and we shall not give a decision until we have taken into account, in addition to the view expressed by the committee, the views that you and those who think with you have so forcibly expressed. I feel sure if you were in our position you would be taking exactly the same action we intend to take. You would await the Committee's report, you would then give it your fullest consideration, and before arriving at a final decision you would take into account the views that have been expressed on both sides of the controversy. More than this I cannot say. Indeed I do not imagine you would expect me to say more."

Communal Award

The Prime Minister's decision on the communal question was announced on 17 August 1932. The terms of the decision in so far as they related to the untouchables were as follows:

"In the statement made by the Prime Minister on the 1st December last on behalf of His Majesty's Government at the close of the second session of the Round Table Conference, which was immediately afterwards endorsed by both Houses of Parliament, it was made plain that if the communities in India were unable to reach a settlement acceptable to all parties on the communal questions which the Conference had failed to solve, His Majesty's Government were determined that India's constitutional advance should not on that account be frustrated, and that they would remove this obstacle by devising and applying themselves a provisional scheme.

"On the 19th of March last His Majesty's Government, having been informed that the continued failure of the communities to reach agreement was blocking the progress of the plans for the framing of a new Constitution, stated that they were engaged upon a careful re-examination of the difficult and controversial question which arose. They are now satisfied that without a decision of at least some aspects of the problems connected with the position of minorities under the new Constitution, no further progress can be made with the framing of the Constitution.

"His Majesty's Government have accordingly decided that they will include provisions to give effect to the scheme set out below in the proposals relating to the Indian Constitution to be laid in due course before Parliament. The scope of this scheme is purposely confined to the arrangements to be laid in due course before parliament. The scope of this scheme is purposely confined to the arrangements to be made for the representation of the British Indian communities in the Provincial Legislatures, consideration of representation in the Legislature at the Centre being deferred. The decision to limit the scope of the scheme implies no failure to realize that the framing of the Constitution will necessitate the decision of a number of other problems of great importance to minorities, but has been taken in the hope that once a pronouncement has been made upon the question of method and proportions of representation the communities themselves may find it possible to arrive at modus vivendi on other communal problems, which have not received the examination they require.

"His Majesty's Government wish it to be most clearly understood that they themselves can be no parties to any negotiations which may be initiated with a view to the revision of their decision, and will not be prepared to give consideration to any representation aimed at securing the modification of it which is not supported by all the parties affected. But they are most desirous to close no door to an agreed settlement should such happily be forthcoming. If, therefore, before a new Government of India Act has passed into law, they are satisfied that the communities who are concerned are mutually agreed upon a practicable alternative scheme, either in respect of anyone or more of the governor's Provinces or in respect of the whole of the British India, they will be prepared to recommend to Parliament that alternative should be substituted for the provisions now outlined.

"Members of the "depressed classes" qualified to vote will vote in a general constituency. In view of the fact that for a considerable period these classes would be unlikely, by this means alone, to secure any adequate representation in the legislature, a number of special seats will be assigned to them. These seats will be filled by election from special constituencies in which only members of the "depressed classes" electorally qualified will be entitled to vote. Any person voting in such a special constituency will, as stated above, be also entitled to vote in a general constituency. It is intended that these constituencies should be formed in selected areas where the depressed classes are most numerous, and that, except in Madras, they should not cover the whole area of the Province.

"In Bengal it seems possible that in some general constituencies a majority of the voters will belong to the depressed classes. Accordingly pending further investigation no number has been fixed for the members to be returned from the special depressed class constituencies in that Province. It is intended to secure that the depressed classes should obtain not less than 10 seats in the Bengal Legislature.

"The precise definition in each province of those who (if electorally qualified) will be entitled to vote in the special depressed class constituencies has not yet been finally determined. It will be based as a rule on the general principles advocated in the Franchise necessary in some Provinces in Northern India where the application of the general criteria of untouchability might result in a definition unsuitable in some respects to the special conditions of the Province.

"His Majesty's Government do not consider that these special depressed classes constituencies will be required for more than the limited time. They intend that the Constitution shall provide that they shall come to an end after 20 years if they have not previously been abolished under the general powers of electoral revision."

The Prime Minister's Communal Award was announced simultaneously from London and Simla. As a background to it, a government communiqué stated as follows:

"The minorities committee had failed to solve the communal problem at the Second Round Table Conference. The Premier had offered to give an award himself, but this was not unanimously acceptable to the members. In the final plenary session, therefore, he declared that, in view of the R.T.C. members continued failure to bring about a communal settlement, the government might have to frame and provide one." This was the rationale for the Award according to the communiqué.

"The substance of the Communal Award was fractionalize the entire electorate by giving separate recognition to the number of minorities including the depressed classes and assigning separate electorates to them. It was a clever way of demonstrating that Indian unity was a myth. It was indeed a great blow to the conception of Indian nationhood which had grown up and had been nurtured through a common struggle and common suffering for about a century past. But if the British wanted to break this national unity or prove that it was non-existent, some sections of the people themselves played no less part in strengthening the hands of the rulers by placing their sectional interests above those of the common motherland.

The British government's attempt to cause disarray in Indian ranks in order to weaken the demand for national freedom were best illustrated by British Prime Minister, Ramsay MacDonald's so-called Communal Award. It was a revealing document which fully confirmed the widely-held belief that the Indian separatists and dissidents could always get more than what they wanted by cooperating with the Raj in its campaign against the nationalists. The Award accepted the principle of separate electorates for the Muslim, Sikh, Indian Christian, Anglo-Indian and European communities, besides confirming the traditional policy of weightage for the minorities.

When the terms of the Communal Award were announced Gandhiji found that his letter to Samuel Hoare had failed to have any effect. He first tried to get terms of the Communal Award revised. He wrote a letter to the Prime Minister.

Yerwada Central Prison,
August 18, 1932

Dear friend,

"There can be no doubt that Sir Samuel Hoare has shown you and the Cabinet my letter to him of 11th March on the question of the representation of the depressed classes. That letter should be treated as part of this letter and be read together with this.

"I have read the British government's decision on the representation of the Minorities and had slept over it. In pursuance of my letter to Sir Samuel Hoare and my declaration at the meeting of the Minorities Committee of the Round Table Conference on 13 November 1931, at St. James Palace, I have to resist your declaration by a perpetual fast unto death from food of any kind save water and or without salt and soda. This fast will cease if during its progress the British Government, of its own motion or under pressure of public opinion, revise their decision and withdraw their scheme of communal electorates for the depressed classes, whose representatives should be elected by the general electorate under the common franchise, no matter how wide it is.

"The proposed fast will come into operation in the next ordinary course from the noon of 20th September next, unless the said decision is in the meanwhile revised in the manner suggested above.

"I am asking the authorities here to cable the text of this letter to you so as to give you ample notice. But in any case I am leaving sufficient time for this letter to reach you in time by the slowest route.

"I also ask that this letter and my letter to Sir Samuel Hoare already referred to be published at the earliest possible moment. On my part, I have scrupulously observed the rule of the jail and have communicated my desire or the contents of the two letters to no one, save my two companions, Sardar Vallabhbhai Patel and Mr. Mahadev Desai. But I want, if you make it possible, public opinion to be affected by my letters. Hence my request for their early publication.

"I regret the decision I have taken. But as a man of religion that I hold myself to be, I have no other course left open to me. As I have said in my letter to Sir Samuel Hoare, even if His Majesty's government decided to release me in order to save themselves from embarrassment, my fast will have to continue. For, I cannot now hope to resist the decision by my other means; and I have no desire whatsoever to compass my release by my means other than honorable.

"It may be that my judgment is warped and that I am wholly in error in regarding separate electorates for depressed classes as harmful to them or to Hinduism. If so, I am not likely to be in the right with reference to other parts of my philosophy of life. In that case my death by fasting will be at once a penance for my error and a lifting of a weight from off these numberless men and women who have childlike faith in my wisdom. Whereas if my judgment is right as I have little doubt it is, the contemplated step is but due to the fulfillment of the scheme of life which I have tried for more than a quarter of a century, apparently not without considerable success."

Your faithful friend
M.K. Gandhi

M.R. Jayakar declared in a statement issued by him on 21 August: "The so-called Award is deplorably reactionary.

It bears the clearest indication that the Prime Minister had to yield to Tory pressure. It strengthens the communal virus and extends its mischievous operation to regions which had so far remained free." He appealed to the rulers of states to ensure that the communal poison was not introduced into territories which had so far remained constitutionally free from its deadly effects.

The Home Department sent a secret note to all provincial governments on 27 August 1932 in which it was emphasized that "the government of India attaches the greatest importance to prompt and vigorous counter propaganda particularly in the districts, the point that it is not a question between Gandhi and His Majesty's government; but between Gandhi and the depressed classes".

The note further informed the provincial authorities to emphasize that the government had announced the award only because the Indian parties had not been able to come to an agreement, that the announcement of the Award itself indicated that, even though the Award had been announced, should all the Indian parties concerned come to an agreement, the government would readily substitute the Award by the terms of that agreement. "If therefore, your faithful friend, M.K. Gandhi: Really decides to make the provisions of the Award regarding the depressed classes the occasion for a 'hunger strike', His Majesty's government will bear no share whatever of the responsibility for the probable outcome of this course of action."

The note asked the provincial authorities to explain that the solution of the matter will lie in Indian hands only. Supposing the depressed classes, out of sympathy for Mr. Gandhi, or for some other reason, were to decide in agreement with the caste Hindus to forego the system of special constituencies in certain areas which His Majesty's government were prepared to grant them, the latter would be quite willing to recommend to parliament the abolition of this particular feature of the Award, provided this did not prejudice the position of the other communities under the new constitution. If, however, the depressed classes should decide that the disabilities to which they had been subjected in the past necessitate their being afforded temporary protection, under a democratic constitution, by the means afforded by His Majesty's government, and if Mr. Gandhi should persist in starving himself to death as a protest against this, the responsibility of the consequences would be his alone.

It is surely a matter for astonishment, the note further stated, that a man like Mr. Gandhi, who unquestionably had the welfare of the downtrodden and oppressed much at heart, should make the introduction of measures designed for their protection the occasion for so drastic and extra-ordinary a protest.

The note asked the provincial authorities to emphasize two points: (i) A large section of untouchables did not accept Gandhiji's view that they would receive fair treatment at the hands of the higher castes in a general electorate. (ii) It was generally accepted in civilized society that the most equitable and wisest method of settling disputes and differences of opinion when they arose was by discussion and argument and an appeal to reason. In this particular instance, however, Mr. Gandhi proposed to convert those who disagreed with him to his own way of thinking by the exercise of force. That it would be a moral rather than physical force which did not render the distinction any the less valid. The essence of Mr. Gandhi's plan clearly was, by a sedulous fostering of popular compassion for him in his suffering, to overwhelm a group of people who had not been able to accept his views regarding a matter which primarily affected them.

The note ended by saying that Mr. Gandhi himself was not of the depressed classes but a caste Hindu, and it was the depressed classes alone who were best entitled to determine where their own interests in this matter lay.

Gandhiji sent a telegram to the Viceroy in Simla, in which he said: "To avoid unnecessary trouble and unnecessary public expense also unnecessary worry to myself I would ask government not to disturb me for I will be unable to confirm to any conditions as to movement from place to place or otherwise that may be attached to foreshadowed release."

The other leaders of the depressed classes, in particular M.C. Rajah, denounced the Award. They proclaimed that it was an attempt to divide Hindu society and in any case what it was given to the depressed classes by way of reserved seats was much, much less than had been recommended under earlier proposals.

The Prime Minister sent the following reply to Gandhiji:

10, Downing Street,
September 8, 1932

Dear Mr. Gandhi,

"I have received your letter with much surprise and, let me add, with very sincere regret. Moreover, I cannot help thinking that you have written it under a misunderstanding as to what the decision of His Majesty's government as regards the depressed classes really implies. We have always understood you were irrevocably opposed to the permanent segregation of the depressed classes from the Hindu community. You made your position very clear in the Minorities Committee of the Round Table Conference and you expressed it again in the letter you wrote to Sir Samuel Hoare on 11 March. We also knew your view was shared by the great body of opinion, and we, therefore, took it into most careful account when we were considering the question of representation of the depressed classes.

"Whilst, in view of the numerous appeals we have received from depressed class organizations and the generally admitted social disabilities under which they labor and which you have often recognized, we felt it our duty to safeguard what we believed to be the right of the depressed classes to a fair proportion of representation in the legislatures, we were equally careful to do nothing that would split off their community from the Hindu world. You yourself stated in your letter of March 11, that you were not against their representation in the legislatures.

"Under the government scheme the depressed classes will remain part of the Hindu community and will vote with the Hindu electorate on an equal footing, but for the first twenty years, while still remaining electorally part of the Hindu community, they will receive through a limited number of special constituencies, means of safeguarding their rights and interests that, we are convinced, is necessary under present conditions.

"Where these constituencies are created, members of the depressed classes will not be deprived of their votes in the general Hindu constituencies, but will have two votes in order that their membership of the Hindu community should remain unimpaired.

"We have deliberately decided against the creation of what you describe as a communal electorate for the depressed classes and included all depressed class voters in the general or Hindu constituencies so that the higher caste candidates should have to solicit the votes or depressed class candidates should have to solicit the votes of the higher castes at elections. Thus in every way was the unity of Hindu society preserved.

"We felt, however, that during the early period of responsible government when power in the Provinces would pass to whoever possessed a majority in the legislatures, it was essential that the depressed classes, whom you have yourself described in your letter to Sir Samuel Hoare as having consigned by Caste Hindus to calculated degradation for centuries, should return a certain number of members of their own choosing to legislatures of seven of the nine Provinces to voice their grievances and their ideals and prevent decisions going against them without the legislature and the government listening to their case—in a word, to place them in a position to speak themselves which every fair-minded person must agree to be necessary. We did not consider the method of electing special representatives by reservations of seats in the existing conditions, under any system of franchise which is practicable, members who could genuinely represent them and be responsible for them, because in practicably all cases, such members would be elected by a majority consisting of higher caste Hindus.

"The special advantage initially given under our scheme to the depressed classes by means of a limited number of special constituencies in addition to their normal electoral rights in the general Hindu constituencies is wholly different in conception and effect from the method of representation adopted for a minority such as the Moslems by means of separate communal electorates. For example, a Moslem cannot vote or be a candidate in a general constituency, whereas any electorally qualified member of the depressed classes can vote in and stand for the general constituency.

"The number of territorial seats allotted to Moslems is naturally conditioned by the fact that it is impossible for them to gain any further territorial seats and in most provinces they enjoy weightage in excess of their population ratio; the number of special seats to be filled from special depressed classes constituencies will be seen to be small and has been fixed not to provide a quota numerically appropriate for the total representation of the whole of the depressed class population, but solely to secure a minimum number of spokesman for the depressed classes in the legislature who are chosen exclusively by the depressed classes. The proportion to their seats is everywhere much below the population percentage of the depressed classes.

"As I understand your attitude, you propose to adopt the extreme course of starving yourself to death not in order to secure that the depressed classes should have joint electorates with other Hindus, because that is already provided, not to maintain the unity of Hindus, which is also provided, but solely to prevent the depressed classes, who admittedly suffer from terrible disabilities today, from being able to secure a limited number of representatives of their own choosing to speak on their behalf in the legislatures which will have a dominating influence over their future.

"In the light of these very fair and cautious proposals, I am quite unable to understand the reason of the decision you have taken and can only think you have made it under a misapprehension of the actual facts.

"In response to very general request from Indians after they had failed to produce a settlement themselves the government much against its will, undertook to give a decision on the minorities question. They have now given it, and they cannot be expected to alter it except on the condition they have stated. I am afraid, therefore, that my answer to you must be that the government's decision stands and that only agreement of the communities themselves can substitute other electoral arrangements for those that government have devised in a sincere endeavour to weigh the conflicting claims on their just merits.

"You ask that this correspondence, including your letter to Sir Samuel Hoare of March 11th should be published. As it would seem to me unfair if your present internment were to deprive you of the opportunity of explaining to the public the reason why you intend to fast, I readily accede to the request if on reconsideration you repeat it. Let me, however, once again urge you to consider the actual details of the government's decision and ask yourself seriously the question whether it really justifies you in taking the action you contemplate."

Yours very sincerely,
J. Ramsay MacDonald

Finding that the Prime Minister would not yield, Gandhiji sent him the following letter:

Yerwada Central Prison
September 9, 1932

Dear friend,

"I have to thank you for your frank and full letter telegraphed and received this day. I am sorry, however, that you put upon the contemplated step an interpretation that never crossed my mind. I have claimed to speak on behalf of the very class, to sacrifice whose interests you impute to me a desire to fast myself to death. I had hoped that the extreme step itself would effectively prevent any such selfish interpretation. Without arguing, I affirm that for me this matter is one of pure religion. The mere fact of the depressed classes having double votes does not protect them or Hindu society in general from being disrupted. In the establishment of separate electorate at all for the depressed classes I sense the injection of poison that is calculated to destroy Hinduism and do no good whatever to the depressed classes. You will please permit me to say that no matter how sympathetic you may be, you cannot come to a correct decision on a matter of such vital and religious importance to the parties concerned.

"I should not be against even over-representation of the depressed classes. What I am against is their statutory separation even in a limited form, from the Hindu fold, so long as they choose to belong to it. Do you realize that if your decision stands and the constitution comes into being, you arrest the marvelous growth of the work of Hindu reformers who have dedicated themselves to the uplift of their suppressed brethren in every walk of life?

"I have, therefore, been compelled reluctantly to adhere to the decision conveyed to you.

"As your letter may give to a misunderstanding, I wish to state that the fact of my having isolated for special treatment the depressed classes question from other parts of your decision does not in any way mean that I approve of or reconciled to other parts of the decision. In my opinion, many other parts are open to very grave objection. Only I do not consider them to be any warrant for calling from me such self-immolation as my conscience has prompted me to, in the matter of the depressed classes."

I remain,

Your faithful friend,
M.K. Gandhi

On September 13, 1932, newspapers all over India carried a sensational announcement: Gandhiji still a prisoner in Yerwada Jail, has decided to fast to death from September 20th, as protest against the grant of separate electorates to the depressed (untouchable) classes in the new constitution.

Jawaharlal Nehru, who was in jail said: "Our peaceful and monotonous routine in jail was suddenly upset in the middle of September 1932 by a bombshell. News came that Gandhiji had decided to 'Fast Unto Death' in disapproval of the separate electorates given by Mr. Ramsay MacDonald communal award to the depressed classes.

"I felt angry with him at his religious and sentimental approach to a political question, and his frequent references to God in connection with it. He even seemed to suggest that God had indicated the very date of the fast. What a terrible example to set.

"And then a strange thing happened to me. I had quite an emotional crises and at the end of it I felt calmer, and the future seemed not so dark. Bapu had a curious knack of doing the right thing at the psychological moment, and it might be that his action would lead to great results not only in the narrow field in which it was confirmed, but in the wider aspects of our national struggle.

"Then came news of the tremendous upheaval all over the country, a magic wave of enthusiasm running through Hindu Society, and untouchability appeared to be doomed. What a magician, I thought, was this little man, sitting in Yerwada Prison, and how well he knew how to pull the strings that move people's hearts."

The British Premier and his advisors were unable to appreciate Gandhiji's deeply emotional and religious approach to the problem. Their first impulse was to scent a political motive in the fast: "Gandhiji was trying a stunt to recover the prestige he had lost through the decline of civil disobedience. If the British Ministers failed to fathom the depth of Gandhiji's feeling on this subject they were even less able to see the ethics of fasting for the solution of what was to them a political problem. Fasting struck them as a thinly-disguised method of coercion." The British reaction to Gandhiji's fast was well exemplified in Low's cartoon as a Prophecy for 1933, in which Lord Willingdon was shown on hunger strike at the instance of 10, Downing Street to force Mr. Gandhi to admit the new constituents as touchable.

P.N. Rajbhoj sought Gandhiji's views on the Award and his fast. In reply Gandhiji informed Rajbhog: "My fast has reference only to separate electorate. As soon as that is withdrawn the letter of the vow will be satisfied and I would be bound to call off the fast. But a very heavy responsibility will then lie upon me of having a substitute that is infinitely superior to separate electorate."

Rajbhoj also asked Gandhiji about the formula which leaders like Rajah and others had been favoring, that is, joint electorates with statutory reservations for the depressed classes. Gandhiji said, "Looking at the matter in this light (that is, as a person who though a 'touchable' by birth was an 'untouchable' by choice) I must say that I am not in love with the idea of statutory reservation. Whilst it is not open to the same objection that separate electorate is, I have not a shadow of a doubt that it will prevent the natural growth of the suppressed classes and will remove the incentive to honorable amends from the suppressers. What I am aiming at is a heart understanding between the two, the greatest opportunity of repentance and the reparation on the part of the suppressors. I am certain that the movement is ripe for the change of the heart among them. I would therefore favor widest possible franchise for the suppressed and establish a convention between the two sections for securing proper election of representatives of the suppressed."

Gandhiji made it clear to Rajbhoj, "Nothing will satisfy me till the last vestige of untouchability is gone. I would therefore, insist on a statutory declaration that all public places of worship, wells, schools, etc. should be open to the suppressed precisely on the same terms as the suppressors. This is roughly my idea. If, however, the representatives of suppressed classes will not look at my idea, they are at liberty to have statutory reservation of seats. I should not fast against it but you will not expect me to bless any such scheme. Nor is my blessing essential to its acceptance by the government. If I get the opportunity, I should certainly try to create public opinion among the suppressed against statutory reservation."

Gandhiji further said to Rajbhoj that if the position he had set out was not clear or not satisfactory, he would be delighted to meet him, Dr. Ambedkar and Mr. Rajah.

Gandhiji pinpointed his ultimate goal in yet another letter he wrote that day to an associate who had remonstrated with him that his decision to fast was contrary to both reason and Dharma. Gandhiji wrote, "My Step has not been dictated by reason; it was inspired by my inner voice. My reason, however, told me: 'Hundreds of persons like you will probably have to die in order to remove the blot of untouchability.' Fasting is a very common practice in Hinduism. I have always loved it. My decision is the cry of my heart. The Prime Minister's decision was only the immediate cause. It provided me with an opportunity to undertake the fast. However, the aim of my fast is not merely to get the decision changed but to bring about the awakening and self-purification which are bound to result from the effort to get the decision changed. In other words, this was an opportunity to strike at the very root of untouchability."

Gandhiji also had a talk with Sardar Vallabhbhai Patel in which he said: "The possible consequence of separate electorates for all other communities will still leave room for me to deal with them, but I have no other means to deal with untouchables. These poor fellows will ask why I who claim to be their friend should offer fast unto death simply because they were granted some privileges. They do not realize that the separate electorates will create division among Hindus so much that it would lead to bloodshed. Untouchable hooligans will make common cause with Muslim hooligans and kill caste Hindus."

As a sharp reaction to Gandhiji's ultimatum to fast unto death, Dr. Ambedkar declared: "I do not care for these political stunts. This threat of Mr. Gandhi to starve himself to death is not a moral fight, but only a political move. I can understand a person trying to negotiate with his political opponent on equal terms by giving credit for honesty, but I will never be moved by these methods. My decision stands and if Mr. Gandhi wants to fight with his life for his interests of the Hindu community, the depressed classes will be forced to fight with their lives to safeguard their interests."

Other depressed class leaders were incensed at Ambedkar's attitude, and many spoke up. Ignore his views altogether, declared one. No one has done more for helping lift us up than Mahatma, said others, his life must be saved at all costs, it is he who can and will persuade caste Hindus to change their attitude. Seize the moment, and secure substantial representation for ourselves in the joint electorate, said still others.

The Times of India representative in Ahmedabad reported on 15 September: "The news of Mr. Gandhi's resolve to fast unto death has caused a stir among local depressed classes over whom Mr. Gandhi has a strong hold by championing their cause for the last 15 years and founding a labor union for the mill hands, most of whom are drawn from the depressed classes. The men have joined the union in large numbers. Some of the prominent leaders met last night and sent a deputation to Bombay in order to interview Dr. Ambedkar and request him to come to terms with Mr. Gandhi so that he may give up his decision to fast. They have also requested Mr. A.V. Thakkar, a member of the Servants of India Society, who is believed to have some influence over Dr. Ambedkar, to proceed to Bombay in order to interview Dr. Ambedkar with the same purpose...."

In Calcutta a meeting of eleven different organizations of the depressed classes was held that very day. It passed a resolution disapproving the grant of separate electorates to the depressed classes, saying that while these did not secure sufficient representation for the depressed classes, they brought about a statutory separation of these classes from the rest of the Hindu society—this in turn would disrupt Hindu society on the one hand, and perpetuate the humiliations that were heaped on the depressed classes on the other. It appealed to Gandhiji to give up or at least postpone his decision to fast, and to the British government to withdraw this provision of the Award and leave the matter entirely to the affected classes to settle among themselves.

On 16 September Gandhiji sent another statement from the jail to the Bombay government with the request that it be released to the press. Reiterating the reasons which had led him to decide on a fast-unto-death, he emphasized that his real target was untouchability itself, that the withdrawal of separate electorates would just be the first step towards this goal.

The gist of Gandhiji's statement is as follows: "The fast is intended to sting Hindu conscience into right religious action. The contemplated fast is not mere appeal to emotion. By the fast I want to throw the whole of my weight in the scales of justice pure and simple. Therefore, there need be no undue haste or feverish anxiety to save my life.... The separate electorate is merely the last straw. No patched-up agreement between caste Hindu leaders and rival 'depressed' class leaders will answer the purpose. The agreement to be valid must be real. If the Hindu mass mind is not yet prepared to banish untouchability root and branch, it must sacrifice me without the slightest hesitation. No compromise which does not ensure the fullest freedom to the 'depressed classes' inside the Hindu fold can be an adequate substitute for the contemplated separation. Any betrayal of the trust can merely postpone the day of the immolation for me and henceforth for those who think with me. The problem before responsible Hindus is to consider whether in the vent of social, civil or political persecution of the 'depressed classes' they are prepared to face Satyagraha in the shape of perpetual fast, not by one reformer like me, but an increasing army of reformers whom I believe to exist today in India and who will count their lives of no cost to achieve the liberation of these classes and there through (rid) Hinduism of an age-long superstition. Since there appears to be a misunderstanding as to the application of my fast", Gandhiji concluded, "I may repeat that it is aimed at a statutory separate electorate, in any shape or form, for the 'depressed' classes. Immediately that threat is removed once and for all, my fast will end. I hold strong views about reservation of seats, as also about the most proper method of dealing with the whole question. But I consider myself unfit as a prisoner to set forth my proposals. I should however abide by an agreement on the basis of joint electorate that may be arrived at between the responsible leaders of caste Hindus and the depressed classes and which has been accepted by mass meetings of all Hindus."

Far away in Shantiniketan at Calcutta, Rabindranath Tagore, dressed in black clothes, addressed a large gathering on the significance of Gandhiji's fast and the urgency of fighting an age-old evil. In his address, Tagore said: "A shadow is darkening today over India like a shadow cast by an eclipsed sun. The people of a whole country are suffering from a poignant pain of anxiety, the universality of which carries in it a great dignity of consolation. Mahatmaji, who through his life of dedication has made India his own in truth, has commenced his vow of extreme self-sacrifice.

"Each country has its own inner geography where her spirit dwells, and where physical force can never conquer even an inch of ground. Those rulers who come from outside the gate, and directly they are called away from the cloud-topping tower of their foreign possessions, the stupendous fabric of unreality vanishes in the void. But the great soul, who achieves victory through the power of truth, continues his dominion even when he is physically no longer present. And we all know such achievement belongs to Mahatmaji. The fact that he has staked his life to a further and final realization of his hope fills up with awe and makes us think.

"Our leaders have requested us to observe fasting for this day, and there is no harm. But here is the risk of some unthinking people putting it in the same category with the fasting that Mahatmaji has begun to observe. Nothing can be more disastrous for us than the utter lessening of the value of a heroic expression of truth by paying it the homage of a mere ceremonial expression of feeling by people emotionally inclined. The penance which Mahatmaji has taken upon himself is not a ritual but a message to all India and to the world. If we must make that message our own, we should accept it in the right manner through a proper process of realization. The gift of sacrifice has to be received in a spirit of sacrifice.

"Mahatmaji has repeatedly pointed out the danger of those divisions in our country that are permanent insults to humanity, but our attention has not been drawn to the importance of its ratification with the same force as it has been to the importance of Khaddar. The social iniquities upon which all our enemies found their principal support have our time-honored loyalty, making it for us to uproot them. Against that deep-seated moral weakness in our society Mahatmaji has pronounced his ultimatum, and though it may be our misfortune to lose him in the battlefield, the fight will be passed on every one of us to be carried on the final end. It is the gift of the fight which he is going to offer to us, and if we do not know how to accept it humbly and yet with proud determination, if we cheaply dismiss it with some ceremonials to which we are accustomed and allow the noble life to be wasted with its great meaning missed, then our people will passively roll down the slope of degradation to the blankness of utter futilely.

"We have observed that the English people are puzzled at the step that Mahatmaji has been compelled to take. They confess that they fail to understand it. I believe that the reason of their failure is mainly owing to the fact that the language of Mahatmaji is fundamentally different from their own. His method of protest is not in accord with the method which they usually follow in cases of grave political crises. I ask them to remember the terrible days of atrocities that reddened in blood at their door when dismemberment was being forced between Ireland and the rest of Great Britain. Those Englishmen, who imagined it to be disastrous to the integrity of their Empire, did not scruple to kill and be killed, even to tear into shreds the decency of civilized codes of honor. The West is accustomed to such violent outbursts in times of desperation and, therefore, such a procedure did not seem strange to them, though to some of them it must have appeared wrong.

"Equally, the dismemberment of a large portion of Hindu society is certainly fatal to its wholeness, and when all our appeals are stubbornly dismissed the reason should not be incomprehensible to other people as to why Mahatmaji is voicing the extreme form of protest on behalf of India. I ask them to imagine what would have happened when the Roman Catholic community of England suffered from a forcible deprivation of its common rights, if some foreign power had come and with efficient benevolence alienated them from the rest of the nation. Very likely the people would like to resort to the method of protest which they consider as honorable in its red fury, of violence. In our case the feeling may be similar, though Mahatmaji has made use of its expression which is his own. The message of non-violence, so often expressed by him in words and in deeds, finds today its final exposition in a great language which should be easiest to understand."

The Hindu Leaders Conference met at Bombay on 19 September. The leaders, included Madan Mohan Malaviya, Tej Bahadur Sapru, M.R. Jayakar, Rajagopalachari, N.C. Kelkar, Rajendra Prasad and Moonje. They were anxious for a quick solution. They had to carry with them, however, the leaders of the depressed classes, particularly Dr. Ambedkar, who was not only a stubborn advocate of separate electorates but fully conscious of his pivotal position. No solution to which he did not agree was likely to commend itself to the government. Ambedkar bargained hard; he was reluctant to give up separate electorates, which the Communal Award gave to his community, unless he received some counter-balancing advantages.

On the eve of the conference, Dr. Ambedkar issued the following statement to the press: "I need hardly say that I was astounded to read the correspondence between Mahatma Gandhi, Sir Samuel Hoare and the Prime Minister Ramsay MacDonald, which were published recently in the papers, in which he has expressed his determination to starve himself unto death till the British government of its own accord or under pressure of public opinion revise opinion and withdraw their scheme of communal representation for the depressed classes. The unenviable position in which I have been placed by the Mahatma's vow of self-immolation, can easily be imagined.

"It passes my comprehension why Mr. Gandhi should stake his life on the issue arising out of the communal question which he, at the Round Table Conference, said was one of comparatively small importance. Indeed, to adopt the language of those of Mr. Gandhi's way of thinking, the communal question was only an appendix to the book of India's constitution and not the main chapter. It would have been justifiable, if Mr. Gandhi had resorted to this extreme step for obtaining independence for the country on which he was so insistent all through the Round Table Conference debates. It is also a painful surprise that Mr. Gandhi should single out the special representation for the depressed classes in the Communal Award as an excuse for his self-immolation. Separate electorates are granted not only to the depressed classes, but to the Indian Christians, Anglo-Indians, Europeans, as well as to the Muhammedans and the Sikhs. Also separate electorates are granted to landlords, laborers and traders. Mr. Gandhi had declared his opposition to the special representation of every other class and creed except the Muhammedans and the Sikhs. All the same, Mr. Gandhi chooses to let everybody else except the depressed classes retain the special electorates given to them.

"The fears expressed by Mr. Gandhi about the consequences of the arrangements for the representation of the depressed classes are, in my opinion, purely imaginary. If the nation is not going to be split up by the separate electorates to the Muhammedans and the Sikhs, the Hindu society cannot be said to be split up if the

depressed classes are given separate electorates. His conscience is not aroused if the nation is split by the arrangements of Special Electorates for classes and communities other than the depressed classes.

"I am sure many have felt that if there was any class which deserved to be given special political rights in order to protect itself against the tyranny of the majority under the swaraj constitution it was the depressed classes. Here is a class which undoubtedly is not in a position to sustain itself in the struggle for existence. The religion to which they are tied, instead of providing for them an honorable place, brands them as lepers, not fit for ordinary intercourse. Economically, it is a class entirely dependent on the high-caste Hindus for earning its daily bread with no independent way of living open to it. Nor are all ways closed by reason of the social prejudices of the Hindus but there is a definite attempt all throughout the Hindu society to bolt every possible door so as not to allow the depressed classes any opportunity to rise in the scale of the life. Indeed, it would not be an exaggeration to say that in every village the caste Hindus, however, divided among themselves, are always in a standing conspiracy to put down in a merciless manner any attempt on the part of the depressed classes who form a small and scattered body of an ordinary Indian citizen.

"In this circumstances, it would be granted by all fair-minded persons that as the only path for a community so handicapped to succeed in the struggle for life against organized tyranny, some share of political power in order that it may protect itself as a paramount necessity.

"I should have thought that a well-wisher of the depressed classes would have fought tooth and nail for securing to them as much political power as might be possible in the new constitution, but Mahatma's ways of thinking are strange and are certainly beyond my comprehension. He not only does not endeavor to augment the scanty political power which the depressed classes have got under the Communal Award, but on the contrary he has staked his very life in order to deprive them of what little they have got. This is not the first attempt on the part of the Mahatma to completely dish the depressed classes out of the political existence. Long before, there was the minorities pact. The Mahatma tried to enter into an agreement with the Muslims and the Congress. He offered to the Muslims all the 14 claims and in return asked them to join with him in resisting the claims for special representation made by me on behalf of the depressed classes.

"It must be said to the credit of the Muslim delegates, that they refused to be a party to such a black act, and saved the Depressed Classes from what might as well have developed into a calamity for them as a result of the combined opposition of the Muhammedans and Mr. Gandhi.

"I am unable to understand the ground of hostility of Mahatma Gandhi to the Communal Award. He says that the Communal Award has separated the depressed classes from the Hindu community. On the other hand, Dr. Moonje, a much stronger protagonist of the Hindu case and a militant advocate of its interests, takes a totally different view of matter. In the speeches which he has been delivering since his arrival from London, Dr. Moonje has been insisting that the Communal Award does not create any separation between the depressed classes and the Hindus. Indeed, he has been boasting that he has defeated me in my attempt to politically separate the depressed classes from the Hindus. I am sure that Dr. Moonje is right in his interpretation of the Communal Award, although I am not sure that the credit of it can legitimately go to Dr. Moonje. It is, therefore, surprising that Mahatma Gandhi, who is nationalist and not known to be a communalist should read the Communal Award in so far as it relates to the depressed classes in a manner quite contrary to that of communalist like Dr. Moonje. If Dr. Moonje does not sense any separation of the depressed classes from the Hindus in the Communal Award the Mahatma ought to feel quite satisfied on that score.

"In my opinion, that Communal Award should not only satisfy the Hindus, but also satisfy those individuals among the depressed classes such as Rao Bahadur Rajah, Mr. Baloo or Mr. Gavai, who are in favor of Joint Electorates. Mr. Rajah's fulmination's in the Assembly have amused me considerably. An intense supporter of Separate Electorates and the bitterest and the most vehement critic of caste Hindu tyranny, now professes faith in the Joint Electorates and love for the Hindus! How much of that is oblivion in which he was cast by his being kept out of the Round Table Conference and how much of it is to his honest change of faith, I do not propose to discuss.

"I do not know what Mr. Gandhi wants. It is assumed that although Mahatma Gandhiji is opposed to the system of separate electorates, he is not opposed to the system of Joint Electorates and Reserved Seats. That is gross error. Whatever his views are today, while in London he was totally opposed to any system of special representation for the depressed classes whether by Joint Electorates or by Separate Electorates. Beyond the right to vote in a general electorate based upon adult suffrage, he was not prepared to concede anything to the depressed classes by way of securing their representation in the legislatures. This was the position he had taken at first. Towards the end of the Round Table Conference, he suggested to me a scheme, which he said, he was prepared to consider. The scheme was purely conventional without any constitutional sanction behind it and without any single seat being reserved for the depressed classes in the electoral law. The scheme was as follows:

'Depressed Class candidates might stand in the general
electorate as against other high caste Hindu Candidates. If an
depressed class candidate was defeated in the election, he shoul
file an election petition and obtain the verdict that he was defeat
because he was an untouchable. If such a decision was obtain
the Mahatma said, he would undertake to induce some Hi
member to resign and thus create a vacancy. There would be
another election in which the defeated depressed class candi
or any other depressed class candidate might again try his
as against the Hindu candidates. Should he be defeated aga
should get similar verdict that he was defeated because he
untouchable and so on ad infinitum.' I am disclosing the
as some people are even now under the impression that
electorates and the reserved seats would satisfy the c
of the Mahatma. This will show why I insist tha
no use of discussing the question until the actual pr
Mr. Gandhi are put forth.

"I must, however, point out that I cannot accept the assurances of the Mahatma that he and his Congress will do the needful. I cannot leave so important a question as the protection of my people to conventions and misunderstandings. The Mahatma is not an immortal person, and the congress, assuming it is not a malevolent force, does not have an abiding existence. There have been many Mahatmas in India whose sole object was to remove untouchability and to elevate and absorb the depressed classes, but every one of them has failed in his mission. Mahatmas have come and Mahatmas have gone, but the untouchables have remained as untouchables.

"I have enough experience of the pace of Reform and the faith of Hindu Reformers in the conflicts that have taken place at Mahad and Nasik, to say that no well-wisher of the depressed classes to rest upon such treacherous shoulders. Reformers who ·n moments of crises prefer to sacrifice their principles rather ·an hurt the feelings of their kindred can be of no use to the ·ressed classes.

·I am therefore bound to insist upon a statutory guarantee ·protection of my people. If Mr. Gandhi wishes to have ·mmunal award altered, it is for him to put forth his ·and to prove that they give a better guarantee than ·ven to us under the Award.

·hat Mr. Gandhi will desist from carrying out the ·ontemplated by him. We mean no harm to the ·hen we demand separate electorates, we do so ·total dependence on the sweet will of the caste ·f affecting our destiny. Like the Mahatma we ·to error and we expect him not to deprive ·etermination to fast himself unto death is ·I could have understood the propriety of ·ing such extreme step for stopping riots ·ammedans or between the depressed ·ny other national cause. It certainly ·he depressed classes. Whether he ·'s act will result in nothing but ·t the depressed classes all over

"Coercion of this sort will not win the depressed classes to the Hindu fold if they are determined to go out. And if the Mahatma chooses to ask the depressed classes to make a choice between Hindu faith and the possession of political power, I am quite sure that the depressed classes will choose political power and save the Mahatma from self-immolation. If Mr. Gandhi coolly reflects on the consequences of his act, I very much doubt whether he will find this victory worth having. It is still more important to note that the Mahatma is releasing reactionary and uncontrollable forces, and is fostering the spirit of hatred between Hindu community and depressed classes by resorting to this method and thereby widening the existing gulf between the two. When I opposed Mr. Gandhi at the Round Table Conference there was a hue and cry against me in the country and there was a conspiracy in the nationalist press to represent me as a traitor to the so-called nationalist cause, to suppress correspondence coming from my side and to boost propaganda against my party by publishing exaggerated reports of meetings and conferences many of which were never held. 'Silver bullets' were freely used for creating division in the ranks of the depressed classes. There have been also a few clashes ending in violence.

"If the Mahatma does not want all this to be repeated on a large scale, let him, for God's sake, reconsider his decision and avert disastrous consequences. I believe the Mahatma does not want this. But if he does not desist, in spite of his wishes these consequences are sure to follow as night follows the day.

"Before concluding this statement, I desire to assure the public that although I am entitled to say that I regard the matter as closed, I am prepared to consider the proposals of the Mahatma. I, however, trust the Mahatma will not drive me to the necessity of making a choice between his life and the rights of my people. For I can never consent to deliver my people bound hand and foot to caste Hindus for generations to come."

Rajen Babu, Rajaji and other Congress leaders who were not yet in jail appealed to the Hindus to open their temples to the untouchables and to work vigorously for the removal of this stigma from Hindu society.

Soon things started moving. Hundreds of temples in Allahabad, Banaras, Calcutta and some places in the Indian states were thrown open to the untouchables. Caste Hindus fraternized with the untouchables at public functions and dined with them. Thousands of messages reached the prison assuring Gandhiji that discrimination against the untouchables would be removed. The politicians conferred with the government to find a solution. Rajen Babu and Sapru went to Poona and stayed there to be able to contact Gandhiji at all stages of their negotiations with the authorities.

However, on the other side, threats to murder Dr. Ambedkar began to be extended. Scores of letters written in blood started pouring in his office, threatening to do away with him if he persisted in his demand and did not yield to the will of Gandhiji. Ambedkar himself said: "I have been getting letters threatening my life. They are not-paid. I have been telling my Secretary that in law when we hang a man we do not inflict a fine on him. Why should these assassins fine me by sending not-paid letters in addition to taking my life."

He declared: "I have not yet shown my full teeth. Do not imagine that we are staging a mock show at Poona. It is only a beginning of the struggle that would grow grimmer and fiercer day by day ultimately rocking the entire country." Giving a sample of this armory, he observed, "For instance, I and my people might fast unto death. A hundred thousand satyagrahis were ready to march to Poona, if the Premier of Bombay promised necessary rations. The struggle would take an All India shape shortly. Poona showed but a glimpse into the tremendous potentialities of this people. I would myself participate in the satyagraha at opportune moment. At the present juncture the 'General Staff' of the movement consisted only of a small nucleus of Commanders."

Justifying his stand Ambedkar said: "We are fighting for our liberty, for our very existence. We have been denied elementary justice for decades. We have been maltreated, our just demands brushed aside with contempt. No chord of sympathy has been touched for many quarters. What we ask is justice and fair play.

Let us have it or by God the consequences would be terrible as none could picture."

It may be recollected what M.C. Rajah said in his speech delivered by him on an adjournment motion moved in the Central Legislature on 13 September 1932 relating to Gandhiji's fast: "Never in the annals of the history of India has the issue of the depressed classes assumed importance as it has today, and for this we the depressed classes must forever be grateful to Mahatma Gandhi. He has told the world, in words which cannot be mistaken, that our regeneration is the fundamental aim of his life. If world conscience cannot be roused even now to realization of the position of the depressed classes, then we can only conclude that all instincts of humanity are dead in the world today.

"The question before the House is the situation created by Mahatma Gandhi opposing the grant of communal electorates to the depressed classes. I am sure there is no honorable member in this House who will not regret that the circumstances should have forced such a great personality to take a vow to play on his life, but sir, the correspondence shows that government had enough warning. If they did not attach full importance to our considered views expressed in our conferences and in the Rajah-Moonje Pact I had signed with the President of Hindu Mahasabha, they should have taken at least the grave warning given by Mahatma Gandhi and desisted from the course of creating separate electorates.

"Indeed, this is my chief attack on the premier's letter to Mahatma Gandhi. He tells us that he has given separate electorates for twenty years to enable us to get the minimum number of seats to place our views before the government and legislature of the day. I contend that this privilege we have already enjoyed under the Montford reforms which have enabled us to get representation in numerous local bodies and in legislatures both provincial and central. We are sufficiently organized for that purpose and do not need either special pleading or special succor. In future what we do need as real remedy for our uplift is definite power to elect our representatives from the general constituencies and hold them responsible to us for their actions.

I do not know why the Prime Minister calls the scheme of joint electorates with reservation of seats as impracticable. It is already in force in local bodies in Madras and some other provinces and has worked very satisfactorily. I contend, sir, that the scheme enunciated in the communal decision involves segregation and makes us politically untouchables. I am surprised at the argument of the Prime Minister that there is no segregation because we can vote for caste Hindus who will have to solicit our votes. But, sir, how can we bring about common ideal of citizenship when depressed class representatives are not to solicit votes of higher castes?

"The sufferings which my community has undergone at the hands of caste Hindus have been acknowledged by caste Hindus themselves and I am prepared to admit that there are a large number of reformers among them who are doing everything possible to improve our status and position. I am convinced that there is a change of heart and a change in the angle of vision of caste Hindus. We, depressed classes, feel ourselves as true Hindus as any caste Hindu can be, and we feel that the moral conscience of the Hindus had been roused to the extent that our salvation lies in bringing about a change from within the main body of Hindu society and not segregating ourselves from them. The course adopted by the government would certainly arrest the progress of this most audible movement. I must say, sir, that the Prime Minister's letter in its entire conception, and expression has disappointed me.

"The crisis that faces us today is very grave. There hangs in the balance the life of the greatest Indian of our time, and there hangs in the balance the future of millions of downtrodden people of this country. Is the government going to take the responsibility for killing the one and reducing the other to perpetual servitude? Let it make its choice well and wisely."

The Times of India in its issue of 14th September carried the statement of M.C. Rajah from Simla in which he said: "Those like him who had been disappointed with the turn which events had taken at the Round Table Conference, and who had felt after the Communal Award that our cause was lost beyond repair, and that we, who had been made socially untouchable by caste Hindus, were condemned by the British government to be politically untouchable."

The decision of Gandhiji to starve himself to death on the question had given a world platform to the matter. He reiterated that the solution lay in joint electorates with reservation for the Depressed Classes. He pointed out that Gandhiji's letter showed that he was willing to agree to such an arrangement. There had been no hue and cry against this solution when it had been proposed earlier. It was the unholy Minorities Pact which had poisoned everything. "Everyone should be grateful to Gandhiji for focusing world attention on the matter, and that everyone will pray and contribute to finding the solution which would save Gandhiji's life."

"Let me end with warning", Rajah said "that the responsibility on those who may play a mischievous role is great, for they will be playing with the life of the greatest Indian of our time, and the greatest benefactor of the poor and downtrodden classes."

Rajah reiterated the points the next day in telegrams he sent to the leaders of the depressed classes all over the country. He stressed that the thing to do was to secure the best terms for the depressed classes through joint electorates. One thing had to be admitted, he told his colleagues, namely, that Gandhiji had roused the consciousness of caste Hindus and had given the greatest impetus to the movement for the uplift of the depressed classes, that it is up to the latter not to let such a benefactor die, or at least not to have the responsibility fall on their shoulders.

Chapter 5

Epic Fast

The historic fast commenced in the Yeravada jail on 20 September 1932, creating a heart-breaking situation. The entire nation was in agony. A most precious life was at stake.

The news shook the country like an earthquake. Those who believed in untouchability woke up to the realization that they would have to offer penance for the great sin they and their forefathers had perpetrated.

Gandhiji rose early in the small hours of the morning as usual and had his favorite 'Vaishnava Jana' sung at the morning prayer. He had his usual meal of milk and fruit in the morning. From 6.30 a.m. to 8 a.m. he had his last meal of lemon-juice and honey with hot water. The fateful hour approached. The little group prepared themselves for the ordeal by singing a beautiful song by Smt. Rehana Tyabji, the eldest daughter of Justice Abbas Tyabji.

On the same day, i.e. 20 September, Gandhiji received a telegram from Rabindranath Tagore saying, "It is worth sacrificing precious life for the sake of India's unity and her social integrity. Though we cannot anticipate what effect it may have upon our rulers who may not understand its immense importance for our people we feel certain that the supreme appeal of such self-offering to the conscience of our own countrymen will not be in vain. I fervently hope that we will not callously allow such national tragedy to reach its extreme length. Our sorrowing hearts will follow your sublime penance with reverence and love."

In reply Gandhiji sent a telegram to Tagore in which he said, "have always experienced God's mercy. Very early this morning I wrote seeking your blessing if you could approve action and behold I have it in abundance in your message just received. Thank you."

Gandhiji sent a telegram to Pandit Jawaharlal Nehru, who was in jail in which he said, "During all these days of agony you have been before mind's eye I am most anxious to know your opinion. You know how I value your opinion" (*Mahatma Gandhi: Jawaharlal Nehru*, p. 87).

On 21 September, a delegation on behalf of the depressed classes consisting of P.N. Rajbhoj, S.M. Mate and Limaye called on Gandhiji in jail. Gandhiji told the delegation: "If I had my way I would insist on temple-entry and the like being included in any pact that may be concluded and I would invite all reformers and untouchables to do so. I am aware that temple-entry is a difficult thing to accomplish in the very limited time that my life can hold out against the fast, but all parties to the pact should pledge themselves to realize this elementary right of human beings as the earliest opportunity. At the same time I do not want this fast to be used for coercing orthodoxy. The fast is certainly intended to sting even orthodoxy into thinking. But if they cannot get on to this elementary truth about human rights we must have patience. But temples and the like are the property not of orthodoxy but of all Hindus. Therefore this idea of excluding a section of Hindus from the use of public utilities is itself a species of violence and, therefore, the support of legislation has got to be invoked in order to protect this fundamental right. I recognize, however, that if the majority of the Hindus are against the exercise of this right by the so-called untouchables, mere legislation will be wholly ineffective. But my opinion is that the mind of the majority is for this reform if it comes stealthily. Therefore, reforms should prepare the ground now ceaselessly and vigilantly to convert the passive attitude towards the reform into active approval thereof. This rising tide of opinion in favor of the reform will convince orthodox that it is inevitable. The work, therefore, must be free of all violence, even mental."

Gandhiji reiterated his belief that the first and primary requirement was the missionary work of Hindu reformers and that what he was really after was social and religious reform of Hindu society. Of course, the immediate task was to ensure that the separation of depressed classes from the rest of Hindu society which the separate electorates were going to bring about was prevented, and while he retained serious misgivings about reservations of seats under joint electorates as a solution, if this is what the others agreed to in the circumstances, Gandhiji said, he would go along, though "with utmost reluctance".

Gandhiji further told the delegation: "Legislation in a free State always represents the will of the majority. All legislation in advance of general opinion argues bankruptcy of missionary effort. My reliance, therefore, always has been on missionary enterprises. Therefore, for the pact to be a living pact, it is absolutely necessary that it should be a condition precedent to an acceptance of the political part of it, that the caste Hindus party to the pact will not only endorse it but actively move in matter. My own opinion is quite clear. I would accept any pact that has not a tinge of separate electorate about it. I would, with the utmost reluctance, tolerate reservation of seats under a joint electorate scheme. But I should insist upon what is to me the vital part of the pact, the social and religious reform. And, therefore, whilst if a settlement is arrived at on the joint scheme and separate electorate is withdrawn by the British government, I will break my fast, I will immediately give notice to the millions of Hindus, who have flocked round me at the innumerable meetings from one end of India to the other, that if within, say, six months the social reform is not demonstrably achieved, the fast will be taken up again. For, if I do not do so I would be guilty of betraying God in whose name I have taken this great fast and the interest of untouchables for whose sake it has been taken."

By the evening of the 21st of September there had been a visible deterioration in Gandhiji's condition. He had been on fast for only 36 hours as yet, but clearly had been drained by the interminable discussions.

The next day also the discussions continued—Pyarelal's *The Epic Fast* gives a day-by-day account of these discussions and the formulae that were being weighed.

Rajbhoj strongly criticized the formulae Ambedkar was insisting on. He said that these proposals were no different from separate electorates and more important, these demands that Ambedkar was pushing were "based upon the interests of a small section of the depressed classes as a whole in India". He said that while Gandhiji continued to have doubts about joint electorates with reservation of seats for the depressed classes, he would accept a settlement which the leaders might reach on this basis. The letter of his fast having been fulfilled by the withdrawal of separate electorates, he would end his fast. Leaders should therefore strive for a solution on this. By the 24th September, Gandhiji's condition had deteriorated to such an extent that the government of Bombay informed the Viceroy and the Secretary of State in Clear Line wire.

"Clear Line Medical authorities report that Gandhi has now reached a stage when two days or so more might see complete collapse both physical and mental and that he is not likely to be able to continue negotiations for much longer. It is just possible that settlement between caste Hindus and depressed class leaders may be reached and agreed to by Gandhiji tonight. If reached it will be communicated to Government at once. Meanwhile in view of Gandhiji's condition we are preparing to move him, if necessary to suitable residence near Poona. Gandhiji's present intention is to continue fasting until orders on settlement are received from His Majesty's government, but his friends hope to prevail upon him to break his fast pending the receipt of these orders."

There was a flurry of hectic activity among the top leadership. Their anxious concern was to devise some solution so that Gandhiji's life could be saved. Madan Mohan Malaviya appealed to both the Hindu and the depressed class leaders to bury their differences and come to a settlement which would be acceptable to Gandhiji. Sapru and Jayakar, immediately bestirred themselves and carried on behind the scene conciliatory moves.

A deputation with Sapru among others met Gandhiji more than once to discuss a new scheme based on joint electorates with adequate safeguards to the depressed classes. For a time Yeravada Prison became a venue of hurried consultations. Sapru, Jayakar Birla, Rajendra Prasad, and Rajagopalachari explained the new scheme to Gandhiji. There was a prolonged conference in the jail among Hindu and depressed class leaders with Sapru playing a key role (S.K. Bose: *Tej Bahadur Sapru*, p. 94).

Both the caste Hindu and the depressed class leaders rose to their fullest stature by coming to an agreement, and the terms were reported to Gandhiji. He accorded his approval. Sapru drafted a cable to the Prime Minister to that effect, urging him to withdraw the separate electorates for the depressed classes.

The agreement was signed by Pandit Madan Mohan Malaviya, M.R. Jayakar, Tej Bahadur Sapru, Chunilal Mehta, B.R. Ambedkar, M.C. Rajah, P.G. Solanki, Rajagopalachari, G.D. Birla and twenty others. Rajaji and Ambedkar exchanged the pens with which they had signed the agreement.

Dr. Ambedkar, after meeting Gandhiji, stated: "The situation is hopeful. Differences of crucial character are few, and there are chances of agreement. Gandhiji is feeling weak owing to the fast, but carried on the conversation with us for over fifteen minutes."

He further stated: "I must confess that I was immensely surprised when I met Mahatma Gandhi in the Yeravada Jail—that there was so much common between him and me I think, in the Poona negotiations a large part of the credit must be attributed to Mahatma Gandhi himself. I was astounded to see that the man who held such a divergent view from mine at the Round Table Conference came to my rescue rather than to the rescue of the other side." I am very grateful to Mahatma Gandhi for having extricated from what might have been a very difficult situation.

"My only regret is, why did not Mahatma take this attitude at the Round Table Conference? If he had shown the same consideration to my point of view, it would not have been necessary for him to go through this ordeal. However, these are things of the past. I am, glad that I am here now to support this resolution."

In support of the resolution confirming the Poona Pact, Dr. Ambedkar declared, "I believe it is no exaggeration for me to say that no man a few days ago was placed in a greater dilemma than I was. There was placed before me a difficult situation in which I had to make a choice between two difficult alternatives. There was the life of the greatest man in India to be saved. There was also before me the problem to try and safeguard the interests of the community which I was in my humble way trying to do at the Round Table Conference according to my light. I am happy to be able to say that it has become possible through the cooperation of all of us to find a solution so as to save the life of the Mahatma and at the same time consistent with such protection as is necessary for the interest of the depressed classes in the future. I think in all these negotiations a large part of the credit must be attributed to Mahatma Gandhi himself" (Dr. Babasaheb Ambedkar: *Writings and Speeches*, Vol. 9, p. 88).

Chapter 6

Poona Pact

The agreement to which the leaders affixed their signatures was as follows:

1. There shall be seats reserved for the depressed classes out of the general electorate seats in the Provincial Legislatures as follows: Madras 30: Bombay with Sind 15; Punjab 8; Bihar and Orissa 18; Central Province 20; Assam 7; Bengal 30; the United Provinces 20; Total 148 (The number of 148 seats was, however, raised to 151 in making adjustments on seats of Bihar and Orissa). These figures are based on the total strength of the Provincial Councils announced in the Prime Minister's decision.
2. Election to these seats shall be by joint electorates, however, to the following procedure. All members of the depressed classes registered in the general electoral roll of a constituency will form an Electoral College which will elect a panel of four candidates belonging to the depressed classes for each of such reserved seats by the method of the single vote, and four persons getting the highest number of votes in such primary election shall be candidates for election by the general electorate.
3. Representation of the depressed classes in the Central Legislature shall likewise be on the principle of joint electorates and reserved seats by the method of primary election in the manner provided for in Clause two above for their representation in the Provincial Legislatures.

4. In the Central Legislature 18 per cent of the seats allotted to the general electorate for British India in the said Legislature shall be reserved for the depressed classes.
5. The System of primary election to a panel of candidates for election to the Central and Provincial Legislatures as here-in-before mentioned shall come to an end after the first ten years unless terminated sooner by mutual agreement under the provisions of Clause 6 below.
6. The system of representation of depressed classes by reserved seats in the Provincial and Central Legislatures as provided for in Clauses 1 and 4 shall continue until determined by mutual agreement between the communities concerned in this settlement.
7. The franchise for the Central and Provincial Legislatures for the depressed classes shall be as indicated in the Lothian Committee Report.
8. There shall be no disabilities attaching to anyone on the ground of his being a member of the depressed classes in regard to any elections to local bodies or appointment to the public services. Every endeavor shall be made to secure a fair representation of the depressed classes in these respects subject to such educational qualifications as may be laid down for appointment to the public services.
9. In every province out of the educational grant an adequate sum be earmarked for providing educational facilities for the members of the depressed classes. The agreement came to be known as POONA PACT (Dr. Babasaheb Ambedkar: *Writings and Speeches*, Vol. 5, pp. 341-42).

The Poona Pact was signed on 24 September 1932. On 25 September 1932, a public meeting of the Hindus was held under the presidentship of Madan Mohan Malaviya in Bombay at the Indian Merchants Chamber Hall to ratify the agreement. At that meeting the following resolutions were passed:

I. "This Conference confirms the Poona agreement arrived at between the leaders of the Caste Hindus and depressed classes on September 24, 1932, and trusts that the British government will withdraw its decision creating separate electorates within Hindu community and accept the agreement in full. The Conference urges that immediate action to be taken by government so as to enable Mahatma Gandhi to break his fast within the terms of his vow and before it becomes too late. The Conference appeals to the leaders of the communities concerned to realize the implications of the agreement and of this resolution and to make earnest endeavor to fulfill them.

II. This Conference resolves that henceforth, amongst Hindus, no one shall be regarded as an untouchable by reason of his birth and that those who have been so regarded hitherto will have the same rights as the other Hindus in regard to the use of public wells, public roads and other institutions. This right shall have statutory recognition at the first opportunity and shall be one of the earliest acts of the Swaraj Parliament, if it shall not have received such recognition before that time.

III. It shall be the duty of all Hindu leaders to secure, by every legitimate and peaceful means, an early removal of all social disabilities now imposed by custom upon the so-called untouchable classes including the bar in respect of admission to temples.

Gandhiji once again made it clear that the British government must accept the Agreement unconditionally, that the separate electorates must be withdrawn completely. He also kept emphasizing that the scrapping of the separate electorates would be but a step, that he would not rest till untouchability had been banished. His concerns at that hour are well reflected in the message which he dictated to V.K. Krishna Menon and Ellen Wilkinson who met him on behalf of the India League on September 25. They had asked him for message for Great Britain.

He said: "Every day of the fast seems to me conclusive evidence of the hand of God in it. Even I with my boundless faith in God and His mercy was not prepared for this great wave of awakening against untouchability. That some of the great temples should have spontaneously admitted the untouchables without restriction is to me a modern miracle. They have only now admitted God. Hitherto, the images which the custodians, falsely and in their pride, thought had God within were Godless.

"The Cabinet decision was to me a timely warning from God that I was asleep when He was knocking at the door and waking me up. The settlement arrived at is to me but the beginning of the work of purification. The agony of the soul is not going to end until every trace of untouchability is gone. I do not want the British Cabinet to come to any hasty decision. I do not want them for saving my life or for appearing to be right with the world to accept it in a niggardly spirit. If they have not realized the true inwardness of the Agreement, they must summarily reject it, but if they have, they will not alter one word or comma of it, but they will implement every condition that is implied in the great settlement which that so-called untouchables and the so-called touchables have arrived at with God as their witness.

"I hope that they and the world will realize that this settlement is, if I may say so in all humility, far superior to the Cabinet decision. There is no pride about it. The Cabinet composed of foreigners, knowing nothing first-hand of the Indian conditions or what untouchability could mean, were laboring under a heavy handicap, and even though some Indians had referred this matter to them, they should have declined the responsibility to which they were unequal. I am not saying this from my penitential bed in any carping spirit or spirit of irritation. "I claim to be a true friend of the British nation and also of the Cabinet, and I would be untrue to them, to myself and to my call, if at this moment I suppressed my relevant opinion. I would like finally to assure Britain that so long as life lasts in me, I shall undergo as many fasts as are necessary in order to purify Hinduism of this unbearable taint. Thank God there is not only one man in this movement but, I believe, there are several thousands who will lay down their lives in order to achieve this reform in its fullness" (*Collected Works of Mahatma Gandhi*, Vol. LI, pp. 140-41).

Gandhiji also dictated a statement for the press, lest anyone be left in any doubt about what he was aiming at. In the statement he said: "If the Premier accepts the settlement, I would be bound to break the fast. The settlement, as far as the political part of it is concerned, merely removes the tremendous obstacle that the cabinet's decision put in the way of reform. The real part of the settlement is now to come and whilst, if the Premier accepts in to the settlement cabled to him, my fast must end, the real struggle for me only begins. As a matter of fact, if the Cabinet had published the correspondence in time I would have been in honor-bound to insist on the due fulfillment of the duty that lies on the so-called caste Hindus.

"I should be guilty of betrayal of trust if I did not ensure that, but as they had no notice worth the name of my intention to fast; I could not expect them all of a sudden to revolutionize Hindu thought.

"They must, therefore, have breathing time for the work, and so I have told fellow-workers that if this fast is broken in virtue of the Cabinets satisfactory answer it would be put in suspension, but sure as fate, it will be taken up again if the part to be performed by the caste Hindus is not well played during the coming months.

"The tremendous awakening that has been placed in the country during the five days fills me with hope that orthodoxy will surpass itself and rid Hinduism of the canker of untouchability which is eating into its vitals" (*Collected Works of Mahatma Gandhi*, Vol. LI, p. 141).

On September 25, the Poona Pact was ratified and on the 26 it was simultaneously announced in London and Delhi. "The whole of the 26th was passed in anxiety and waiting in Yeravada," Pyarelal wrote. "The poet (Tagore) who had made a hurried dash to Poona from Calcutta visited Gandhiji at noon. The meeting was a most touching one. Without a word, he approached Gandhiji's prostrate form and burying his face in the clothes of Gandhiji's breast remained in that position for several minutes overcome with feeling. He had heard the news that the Cabinet had accepted the Agreement. 'I have come floating on the tide of good news. I am so glad that I have come and that I have come in time', he said to Gandhiji as he recovered his voice. Then they talked intimately of several things. The poet told Gandhiji that so far as the social side of the question of untouchability was concerned he could always be depended upon to do his bit to relieve Gandhiji's burden. He then left his bedside as the strain of conversation was proving too much for Gandhiji" (Pyarelal: *The Epic Fast,* p. 77).

The message from London came eventually. It was decided that Gandhiji would break the fast at 5.30 that evening. Pyarelal describes the scene in that prison yard: "The yard was freshly sprinkled over with water. Gandhiji lay on his cot surrounded by the Poet, Shrimati Sarojini Naidu, Shrimati Vasanti Devi, Ambalal Sarabhai and his family, Gandhiji's two companions, Sardar Vallabhbhai Patel and *Sjt.* Mahadev Desai. Before him were assembled a number of inmates of the Sabarmati Ashram and others, in all about 200 persons. The poet led the prayer by singing a Bengali hymn from *Gitanjali*....

"Jeevan jakhan shukaya jaye, karuna-dharaye aisho
Sakal madhuri laukaye jaye, geet-sudharse aisho....

"This was followed by the reciting of some Sanskrit verses by Parchure Shastri, a fellow prisoner from the leper yard of the Yeravada Prison. Then was sung, all joining, Gandhiji's favorite hymn, Vaishnava Jana. When it was finished, Shrimati Kasturbha handed him the orange juice and Gandhiji broke his fast..." (Pyarelal: *The Epic Fast,* pp. 79-80).

Agony Ended

Gandhiji issued a statement for the press in which he said: "The fast undertaken in the name of God was broken in the presence of Gurudev, and Parchure Shastri, the leper prisoner, and a learned pandit, seated opposite each, and in the company of loving and loved ones who had gathered round me. The breaking of fast was preceded from the Upanishads by Parchure Shastri, and then my favorite hymn, Vaishnava Jana.

"The hand of God has been visible in the glorious manifestation throughout the length and breadth of India during the past seven days. He had been sustained by the expression of support which had poured in from many parts of the world.

"The sacrificial fire, once lit, shall not be put out as long as there is the slightest trace of untouchability still left in Hinduism.

If it is God's will that it does not end with my life, I have the confidence that there are several thousands of earnest reformers who will lay down their lives in order to purify Hinduism of this awful curse.

"What has been agreed to is but a step. The settlement is but the beginning of the end. The political part of it, very important though it no doubt is, occupies but a small space in the vast field of reform that has to be tackled by caste Hindus during the coming days, namely, the complete removal of social and religious disabilities under which a large part of the Hindu population has been groaning. I should be guilty of a breach of trust if I did not warn fellow-reformers and caste Hindus in general that the breaking of the fast carried with it a sure promise of a resumption of it if this reform is not relentlessly pursued and achieved within a measurable period. I had thought of laying down a period, but I feel that I may not do so without a definite call from within.

"The settlement arrived at is, so far as I can see, a generous gesture on all sides. It is a meeting of hearts, and my Hindu gratitude is due to Dr. Ambedkar, Rao Bahadur Srinivasan and their party on the one hand and Rao Bahadur M.C. Rajah on the other. They could have taken up an uncompromising and defiant attitude by way of punishment to the so-called caste Hindus for the sins of generations. If they had done so I at least could not have resented their attitude and my death would have been but a trifling price exacted for the tortures that the outcastes of Hinduism have been going through for unknown generations. But they chose a nobler path and have thus shown that they have followed the precept of forgivingness enjoyed by all religions. Let me hope that the caste Hindus will prove themselves worthy of this forgiveness and carry out to the letter and spirit every clause of the settlement with all its implications" (*Collected Works of Mahatma Gandhi*, Vol. LI, pp. 143-45).

Rabindranath Tagore was still in Poona. As Gandhiji's birthday approached, he delivered a speech on 27 September, in which he said: "Mahatmaji's birthday appears today before us in an awful majesty of death which has just left him victorious.

It is our great good fortune today that such a man has indeed come to us, and what is still rarer, that we have not repudiated him, as we have so often done with messengers of Freedom and Truth. His inspiration is actively at work all through India and even beyond its boundaries. It has awakened our consciousness to a truth which goes far beyond the limits of our self-interest. His life itself is a constant call to us to emancipation in service and self-dedication.

"Today is the day of our national acknowledgement of Mahatma as the great brother, who, in the present age, is the central bond of our brotherhood in our motherland. I hope we shall be earnestly solemn in our expression of it and never cheapen the meaning of this occasion by merely indulging in emotional pride. Let us be worthy of the call of this age and accept from Mahatmaji's hand the responsibility which he has accepted for himself.

"We know that, in the Upanishads, the God whoever dwells in the hearts of all men has been mentioned as Mahatma. The epithet is rightly given to the Man of God whom we are honoring today, for his dwelling is not within a narrow enclosure of individual consciousness. His dwelling is in the heart of untold multitude who are born today in India and who are yet to come, and this greatness of his soul, which has power to comprehend other souls, has made possible what never has yet happened in our history, when even masses have been roused to the great fact that India is not merely a geographical entity but is a living truth in which they live and more and have their being.

"Today in our determined effort let us join Mahatmaji in his noble task of removing the burden of ages, the burden of disrespect upon the bent back of those who have been stigmatized for the accident of their birth, and the sin of willful denial, to a large body of our countrymen, of sympathy which is the birthright of all human beings. We are not only casting off the chain of India's moral enslavement but indicating the path for all humanity. We are challenging the victimization, wherever and in whatever form it may exist, to stand the test of relentless questioning of the conscience which Mahatmaji has brought to bear upon our day.

"When Mahatmaji began his penance there were cynics in our country and abroad who mocked and jeered at him, and yet before our very eyes the wonder has happened. Hard rocks of tradition have been blasted. Irrational prohibitions, cramping our national life, are already showing signs of tottering. Great has been the achievement due to his penance, but it will be a greater glory to him and to us if we can fulfill his vow by fighting to finish the evils of untouchability of intolerance, of all that hinders the comradeship of man and man and obstructs our path to freedom and righteousness.

"My friends, I appeal to you, do not betray your Great Man and your own humanity by any deviation of your initiative from the pursuit of justice and love towards your fellow men who have suffered humiliation for ages and remained dumb in a pathetic apathy of resignation, never even blaming Providence and their own cruel destiny. But the angry voice has at last come from the Divine Guide of our history with its warning message that they cut at the root of freedom who, in their unreasoning pride, obstruct the freedom of social communication among own kindred's" (Pyarelal: *The Epic Fast,* pp. 92-94).

Jawaharlal Nehru sent the following telegram to Gandhiji: "Your telegram and brief news that some settlement reached filled me with relief and joy. First news of your decision to fast caused mental agony and confusion, but ultimately optimism triumphed and I regained peace of mind. No sacrifice is too great for depressed downtrodden classes. Freedom must be judged by freedom of the lowest but feel danger of other issues obscuring only goal. I am unable to judge from a religious viewpoint by others but how can I presume, to advise a magician Love" (*Mahatma Gandhi: Jawaharlal Nehru*, p. 87).

J.B. Kripalani said: "Gandhiji's success in this matter raised the sagging morale of the people and infused new hope in them. Out of this crises, India emerged morally superior to her opponents." Prof. N.B. Ranga said: "Ambedkar's attack upon Gandhiji's insistence upon keeping Harijans within the fold of Hindus, i.e., within the joint electorates, was intemperate, unkind and unjust. His insistence upon his pound of flesh, during Gandhiji's Poona fast against Ramsay MacDonald's Award in favor of separate electorates for scheduled castes, hurt the feelings of the nationalists although it forced the orthodox leaders of Hindus to yield to his demands for protection of scheduled castes through reservation of seats within joint electorates. In the end, he won the generous approval of Gandhiji and political admiration of Rajaji, to whom he presented the pen with which he signed the famous Poona Pact. I had quite a painful time in defending his basic stand to my political fellows in Vellore Jail. In the end Gandhiji's life was saved and joint electorates were accepted. All were pleased with that powerful champion of the Harijans."

Rajagopalachari in his article entitled, "The Revolution is Over," wrote, "Untouchability is not yet gone. But the revolution is really over and what remains is but the removal of debris" (B.R. Nanda: *Mahatma Gandhi*, p. 193).

Srinivas Sastri sent a telegram in which he said: "Millions of homes rejoice and bless your superb service performed in your superb style. I trembled in doubt but the result vindicates and establishes you as indisputably the foremost untouchable."

Sir Chimanlal Setalvad, however, in his speech at the meeting of the Western India Liberal Association held on 14 October 1932 in Bombay said: "Had Gandhiji been half as accommodating at the Round Table Conference as he was in Poona, the country would not have had to concede what it had to in those anxious days. For once Gandhiji had announced his intention to fast, and specially once he had begun his fast, the sole consideration in the minds of all nationalists became to save him somehow. The very Ambedkar whose representative capacity Gandhiji had questioned at the Round Table Conference was made into a virtual dictator, and so the latter could afford to be as stubborn as he wanted to be, as unmindful of the opinion of other leaders of untouchables, not because he commanded a large following but because a settlement was necessary to save Gandhiji's life and the veto to that settlement lay in Ambedkar's hand. Gandhiji's fast was intended to prevent the separation of the untouchables from Hindu society. But what were the primary elections now going to do? They would require that the untouchables be listed on a separate register. Had Gandhiji accepted joint electorates with reservations of seats at the Round Table Conference no separate register would have been necessary."

"Whether one agrees with Mahatma Gandhi or not about the efficacy of fasting unto death as a weapon to bring about social change, his most skeptical critic will not doubt that the fast has done incalculable good to the Hindu community as a whole, or to the federation of Hindu communities as Dr. Ambedkar recently described it in Bombay. It has done immense good to both parties who were signatories to the historic Poona Agreement of Saturday, the 24 of September, 1932. It has awakened the conscience of the slow moving and conservative Hindu community in a way in which it could not have been done otherwise. The famous temple of Jagannath at Puri, one of the famous impregnable citadels of Hindu orthodoxy, has been thrown open to the erstwhile untouchables. Progressive sons of orthodox Hindu fathers are dining publicly with so-called depressed classes, including Bhangis, who have been considered the lowest of the low, in cosmopolitan Bombay as well as in conservative Benares, in open challenge to their elders and the whole Hindu community, as if to say that they have begun the revolt against the very institution of caste. Scores of temples and public wells are being thrown open to the heretofore suppressed social workers. Men and women are giving pledges to devote themselves exclusively to the uplift work of their depressed brethren. And to crown all, Mahatma Gandhi himself has threatened to go to another fast, before his fast one was broken—we hope not a 'fast unto death'—unless the caste Hindus change their hearts completely and lift up their downtrodden brethren.

"But let us consider the Agreement arrived at in its political aspect. The Communal award of 4th August gave the depressed classes in the eight provinces (all except N.W.F.P.) 71 seats in provincial councils in their own separate constituencies together with the right of contesting further seats in the Hindu or so-called 'general' constituencies. This latter right would have proved shadowy, frankly speaking. We use the word shadowy

deliberately, without meaning any offence to the caste Hindus. In place of these 71 seats, plus a few more doubtful seats, the depressed classes get under the Agreement 148 seats reserved for them. This is a great service that Dr. Ambedkar has done to his own section of the Hindu community, and let us add, to the whole Hindu community. If the 123 seats that Dr. Ambedkar could have fairly demanded on the population basis, i.e., in the ratio of depressed population to total Hindu population, it is but a poor recompense for the disabilities that have been imposed upon the oppressed classes for centuries past. If the whip of the Mahatma's fast has made the comparatively advanced sections of the Hindu community give away a few more seats in councils, provincial as well as central, to the depressed classes, and stirred them to undertake the collection and expenditure of a fund of 25 lakhs of rupees for their uplift, as the venerable pandit Malaviya proclaimed in the Hindu leaders conference in Bombay on Sunday last, we cannot say that they have an over-generous act, but only an act that ought to have been done years ago. But it is better late than never.

"Some people are likely to enquire why the proportion of depressed classes seats to Hindu seats in the Central Legislature was fixed by the Poona Agreement, when it did not form part of the Premier's Award, which was sought to be modified. It may also be asked why franchise matters were discussed and agreed upon, before anything in that direction was decided by the R.T.C. or the British government. The wisdom of going generally into other questions of representation in local bodies and in services, as well as of educational grants, may be questioned by others. The reply is that, once the questions were raised by Ambedkar, it would have been very impolitic on the part of Hindu leaders to refuse to consider these questions on the merely technical ground that they were outside the scope of the Premier's award. The caste Hindus, in order to show their bona fides and their perfect good faith, had to consider them and meet the wishes of the depressed classes. This has been done, and the British government has taken note of these clauses (8 and 9) as definite pledges of the intention of the caste Hindus towards the depressed classes. This is as it should be.

"The Premier has now ratified the Poona Agreement and has agreed to substitute relevant parts of it for similar parts in his own Award. The Mahatma's fast has been broken, and the whole community-suppressing and suppressed sections together—is overjoyed at the result achieved so far. Let us in all humilities put in a word of warning. The Mahatma is not a man to be easily satisfied with small results obtained at a moment of national crises and threatened disaster. He will exact strenuous and thorough work of a constructive nature from the Hindu reformers. 'There is more in common between Mahatma Gandhi and me than with any of you gathered here', was said on two occasions by Dr. Ambedkar while addressing the Hindu leaders at Bombay and Poona in recent conference. This is so true. The Hindu community will now be put on trial, and a very crucial trial, by the man of whom Mr. Sastri said at Coimbatore only on Saturday last: 'His life, it would be presumptuous to say, is lived as few lived in history or fable have been lived'" (*The Servant of India*, September 29, 1932).

U Turn

Dr. Ambedkar, however, subsequently changed his mind and said that signing the Poona Pact was a sentimental blunder and he can never forgive himself for this blunder. He described his feelings in the following words: "The terms of the Poona Pact were accepted by Mr. Gandhi and given effect to by government by embodying them in the government of India Act. The Poona Pact had produced different reactions. The untouchables were sad. They had every reasons to be. There are, however, people who do not accept this. They never fail to point out that the Poona Pact gave the untouchables larger number of seats than what was given to them by the Prime Minister in his Communal Award. It is true that the Poona Pact gave the untouchables 148 seats, while the Award had only given them 78. But to conclude from this that the Poona Pact gave them more than what was given by the Award is to ignore what the Award had in fact given to the untouchables.

"The increase in the number of seats for the untouchables is no increase at all and was no recompense for the loss of separate electorate and the double vote. The Hindus, although they did not celebrate the Poona Pact, did not like it. Throughout their commotion to save Mr. Gandhi's life there was a definite current of conscious feeling that the cost of saving his life may be great. Therefore, when they saw the terms of the Pact they very definitely disliked it, although they had not the courage to reject it. Disliked by the Hindus and disfavored by the untouchables, the Poona Pact was given recognition by both parties and was embodied in the Government of India Act.

The signing of the Poona Pact was followed by the appointment of the Hammond Committee to demarcate constituencies, to fix the number of seats for each constituency and settle the system of voting for the legislatures to be set up under the new constitution.

In carrying out its functions, the Hammond Committee had to take into account the terms of the Poona Pact and the special sort of electoral plan agreed upon to meet the needs of the untouchables.

Dr. Ambedkar says:

"Unfortunately, the Poona Pact having been concluded in a hurry had left many things undefined. Of the things that were left undefined the most important were two, namely:

1. Does the panel of four to be elected at the primary election imply four as a maximum or a minimum?
2. What was intended to be the method of voting in the final election?

It was contended on behalf of the Hindus that the panel of four was intended to be minimum. If four candidates are not forthcoming there could be no primary election and therefore there can be no election for the reserved seats, which they said must remain vacant and the untouchables should go without representation. On behalf of the untouchables, I was called to state the interpretation of the disputed points. I contended that four in the Poona Pact meant "not more than four". It did not mean "less than four". On the question of voting the Hindus contended that the compulsory distributive vote was most appropriate. On behalf of the untouchables I contended that the cumulative system of voting was the proper system to be introduced.... The object which the Hindus had in demanding four candidates as a minimum for a valid primary election was to place the Hindus in a position to capture the seat for an election of such a representative of the untouchable candidate, who would be their nominee and who would be most willing to be the tool of the Hindus. To get such an untouchable elected in the final election he must first come in the panel, and he can come in the panel only if the panel is a large panel. As the election to the panel is by separate electorates consisting exclusive of untouchable voters, it is obvious that if there is only one candidate in the panel then he would be the staunchest representative of the untouchables and worst from the standpoint of the Hindus. If there are two, the second will be less staunch than the first and therefore good from the standpoint of the Hindus. If there are three, the third will be less staunch than the second and therefore better from the standpoint of the Hindus. If there be four the fourth will be less staunch than the third and therefore best from the point of view of the Hindus. The panel of four could therefore give to the Hindus the best chance of getting into the panel such representatives of the untouchables as is most suitable to the Hindus. That is why they insisted before the Hammond Committee that for a valid panel the minimum number must be four.

"The object of insisting upon the system of compulsory distributive vote was the same namely to enable the Hindus to capture the seats reserved for the untouchables. Under the cumulative vote the elector has as many votes as there are seats. He may give them all to one candidate or he may distribute them over two or more candidates as he may desire. Under the distributive system of voting the elector has also as many votes as there are seats, but he can give only one vote to anyone candidate. Although the two look different yet in effect there may be no difference, because even under the cumulative vote a voter is not prevented from distributing his votes. He is free to give one vote to one candidate. But the Hindus did not want to take any chance. Their main object was to flood election to the seat reserved for the untouchables in the joint electorate by using the surplus votes of the Hindus in favour of the untouchable candidate, who happens to be their nominee. The object was to outnumber the untouchable voters and prevent them from electing their own nominee. This cannot be done unless the surplus votes of the Hindu voters were diverted from the Hindu candidate towards the untouchable candidates. There is a greater chance of the diversion of these surplus votes under the distributive system than there is under the cumulative system. Under the former the Hindu voter can give only one vote to the Hindu candidate. The other vote not being of use to the Hindu candidate is usable only for an untouchable candidate. The distributive system thus had the possibility of flooding the election to the seat reserved for the untouchables and this is why the Hindus preferred it to the system of cumulative voting. But they did not want to leave it to chance. For, even the distributive system from their point of view was not foolproof. Under the distributive system there was no compulsion upon the voter to use all his votes. He may vote one vote for the caste Hindu candidate and may not at all use the balance of his votes. If this happened the purpose of getting in their untouchable nominee would be defeated. Not to leave things to chance, the Hindus wanted that the distributive system of voting should be made compulsory so that a caste Hindu voter whether he wants it or not can have no option but to vote for the untouchable candidate who may be the nominee of the Hindus, and thus make his election sure and certain.

"In the light of these considerations, it cannot but appear that the Poona Pact was only the first blow inflicted upon the untouchables and that the Hindus who disliked it were bent on inflicting on it other blows as and when circumstances gave them an occasion to do so. The two contentions, which the Hindus raised before the Hammond Committee, furnish the best evidence of the existence of a conspiracy by the Hindus the object of which was to make the Poona Pact, as it could not be repudiated, of no benefit to the untouchables. The story of how the Congress dealt with the political demands of the untouchables cannot be left here for the simple reason that it does not end here. The subsequent parts of it are more instructive than those that have gone before.

"Continuing the story, the next part of it relates to the election that took place in February 1937 to the Provincial Legislatures, as reconstituted under the Government of India Act 1935. This was the first occasion in its lifetime that the Congress came down to fight an election. It was also the first time that the untouchables got the privilege to elect their own representatives. Some leaders of the untouchables, who were siding with the Congress when the Poona Pact was being forged—such as the late Dewan Bahadur M.C. Raja—cherished the fond hope that the Congress will not inter-meddle in the elections of the untouchables to the seats reserved for them. But this hope was dashed to pieces. The Congress had a double purpose to play its part in the election to the reserved seats of the untouchables. In the first place, it was out to capture in order to build up its majority which was essential for enabling it to form a Government. In the second place, it had to prove the statement of Mr. Gandhi that the Congress represented the untouchables and that the untouchables believed in the Congress. The Congress, therefore, did not hesitate to play a full, mighty and, I may say so, a malevolent part in the election of the untouchables by putting up untouchable candidates on Congress ticket pledged to Congress programme for seats reserved for the untouchables. With the financial resources of the Congress it made a distinct gain."

The total number of seats allotted to the untouchables under the Government of India Act, 1935 are 151. The Congress got just about fifty-nine per cent of the seats reserved for the untouchables.

The Congress in capturing 78 seats left only 73 seats to be filled by true and independent representatives of the untouchables. The untouchables were worse off under the Poona Pact than they would have been under the Prime Minister's Award. In point of effective representation, the untouchables got less than what the Prime Minister had given them. The Congress on the other hand gained by the Poona Pact. Although under the Poona Pact it gave 151 to the untouchables it took back 78 and thereby made a handsome profit on its political transaction.

This is by no means the sum total of the losses which the Congress inflicted on the untouchables in the election of 1937. There was another and a greater blow which the Congress inflicted on the untouchables. It deprived them of any share in the Executive.

From the very beginning, I had been pressing in the discussions in the Round Table Conference that the untouchables must not only have the right to be represented in the legislature, they must also have the right to be represented in the Cabinet. The woes of the untouchables are not due so much to bad laws as to the hostility of the administration, which is controlled by the Hindus who import into administration their age-old prejudices against the untouchables. The untouchables can never hope to get protection from the police, justice from the judiciary or the benefit of a statutory law from the administration, so long as the Public Services continued to be manned by the Hindus. The only hope of making the Public Services less malevolent and more responsible to the needs of the untouchables is to have members of the untouchables in the higher Executive. For these reasons, I had at the Round Table Conference pressed the claim of the untouchables for the recognition of their right to representation in the Cabinet with the same emphasis as I had done for the recognition of their right to representation in the Legislature. The Round Table Conference accepted the validity of the claim and considered ways and means of giving effect to it. There were two ways of giving effect to this proposal. One was to have a statutory provision in the Government of India Act so as to make it a binding obligation which it would be impossible to evade or escape; the other way was not to have a statutory provision but to leave it to a gentleman's agreement—to a convention—as is the case in the English constitution. I and the representatives of the other minorities although we did not insist upon the first in deference to the wishes of some leading Indians not to show such distrust in our own countrymen were not prepared to accept second alternative as there was no enforceable sanction behind it. A via media was agreed upon. It was to introduce a clause in the Instrument of Instructions to the Governors imposing an obligation upon them to see that in the formation of the Cabinet representatives of the Minorities were included. This clause ran as follows:

"In making appointments to the Council of Ministers our Governor shall use his best endeavours to select his Ministers in the following manner, that is to say, to appoint in consultation with the person who in his judgment is most likely to command a stable majority in the Legislature those persons (including so far as practicable members of important minority communities) who will best be in a position collectively to command the confidence of the Legislature. In so acting, he shall bear constantly in mind the need for fostering a sense of joint responsibility among his Ministers."

The Congress declared that they were not prepared to accept the Government of India Act 1935. It was obvious to all and even to many Congressmen that there was no sincerity behind this declaration. It had no other motive but to enhance the prestige of the Congress in the eyes of the public by making it appear that the Congress was a radical and revolutionary body which was out to destroy and bury British Imperialism which is a legend, the Congress has all along tried to create. It was a mere matter of tactics. The Congress wanted to take the powers which the Governors had been given under the constitution to intervene whenever matters which were his special responsibilities were involved. The Congress did not mind, making the declaration rejecting the constitution because it thought that as it was the only body which could run the new Parliamentary system the British Government would be obliged to come to terms with it. The British Government threatened to bypass the Congress. It not only appointed 1st April 1937 as the date of the inauguration of the Provincial part of the constitution but actually went to the length of appointing an interim Ministry of non-Congressmen. Congressmen, who were hungering for power and who constitute a most jealous crowd of politicians, were shaken and felt that they were going to be deprived of the fruits of their labours. Negotiations were started between His Majesty's Government and the Congress High Command. The Congress High Command demanded that if an undertaking was given by His Majesty's Government that the Governors will not use their powers given to them under the Special Responsibility Clauses in the constitution by interfering in the day-to-day administration of the Provinces, the Congress which was most anxious that the new constitution should begin to operate with the goodwill of the majority, agreed to give the undertaking demanded. The surprising part of it is that the Congress High Command enlarged the scope of this undertaking so as to include in the undertaking the non-exercise by the Governors of the Provinces of the powers given to them under the Instruments of Instructions to see that the representatives of the minorities were included in the Provincial Ministries. The Governors who gave full accommodation to the Congress surrendered their authority and allowed the Congress to ride rough shod through a very important part of the constitution with the result that the untouchables and other minorities were deprived of their right to representation in the Cabinet by the Congress with impunity and with alacrity.

The deprivation of the untouchables by the Congress of their right to representation in the Cabinet has the appearance of malice aforethought. One of the grounds, urged by the Congress for the non-inclusion of representatives of the minorities in their Cabinets, was that a Cabinet must be a party Cabinet if it is to take collective responsibility and that the Congress was quite ready to include the members of the minority communities in its Cabinet provided they were prepared to join the Congress and sign the Congress pledge. Whatever may be the value of such argument against other minorities, it had absolutely no value against the untouchables. The Congress could not use it to defend its conduct in excluding the untouchables from the Cabinet for two reasons. In the first place, the Congress was bound by the terms of the Poona Pact to give representation to the untouchables in the Cabinet. In the second place, the Congress could not say that there were no untouchables in the Legislatures who were not the members of the Congress party. On the contrary, there were as many as 78 untouchables returned on the Congress ticket and pledged to the Congress policy. Why then did the Congress not include them in the Cabinet? The only answer is that it was a part of the Congress policy not to admit the right of the untouchables to be represented in the Cabinet and that this policy had the support of Mr. Gandhi. Those who may have any doubt as to the correctness of this statement may well consider the evidence set out below:

The first piece of evidence lies imbedded in the story of the expulsion of the Hon'ble Dr. Khare from the Congress. As is well-known, Dr. Khare was the Prime Minister in the Congress Ministry in the Central Provinces. Owing to internal quarrels among the members of his Cabinet, Dr. Khare to get rid of those that were inconvenient adopted the perfectly normal course of tendering his own resignation and that of the other ministers to the Governor with a view to form a new Cabinet. Thereafter, the Governor in full conformity with constitutional practice recalled Dr. Khare and asked him to form another Cabinet with himself as the Premier. Dr. Khare accepted the invitation and formed a new Cabinet dropping old and inconvenient hands and taking in some new ones. Dr. Khare's new cabinet was different from the old in one important respect namely, that it included Mr. Agnibhoj, an untouchable, who was a member of the Central Provinces, who belonged to the Congress party and who by his education well qualified to be a minister. On the 26th July 1938, the Congress Working Committee met in Wardha and passed a resolution condemning Dr. Khare on the ground that in tendering the resignation of his colleagues in the old ministry, he was guilty of a grave error of judgment and that in forming a new ministry, he was guilty of indiscipline. In explaining what was behind this charge of indiscipline in forming a new ministry, Dr. Khare openly said that Mr. Gandhi told him that it was wrong on his part to have raised such aspirations and ambitions in the untouchables and it was such an act of bad judgment that he would never forgive him. This statement was repeatedly made by Dr. Khare from platforms. Mr. Gandhi has never contradicted it.

There is, however, more direct evidence on this point. In 1942, there was held All-India Conference of the untouchables. In that conference the resolutions setting out the political demands of the untouchables were passed. An untouchable of the Congress party who attended the conference went to Mr. Gandhi to ascertain what Mr. Gandhi had to say about these demands and put him the following five questions:

1. What will be the position of the Harijans in the future constitution to be framed?
2. Will you advise the Government and the Congress to agree to fix the five seats from a Panchayat Board upwards to the State Council on population basis?
3. Will you advise the Congress and the leaders of the various majority parties in the legislatures in the provinces to nominate the Cabinet members from among the scheduled caste legislators who enjoy the confidence of the majority of scheduled caste members?
4. In view of the backwardness of the Harijans, will you advise the Government to make a provision in the act that Executive posts in the Local Boards and Municipal Councils be held on communal rotation, so as to enable the Harijans to become Presidents and Chairmen?
5. Why do you not fix some percentage of seats for Harijans from District Congress Committee upwards to the Working Committee of the Congress?

Mr. Gandhi gave his answers in the issue of *Harijan* dated 2nd August 1942. This is what Mr. Gandhi said:

1. The constitution, which I could influence, would contain a provision making the observance of untouchability in any shape or form an offence. The so-called untouchables would have seats reserved for them in all elected bodies according to their population within the elected area concerned.
2. You will see that the answer is covered by the foregoing.
3. I cannot. The principle is dangerous. Protection of its neglected classes should not be carried to an extent which will harm them and harm the country. A Cabinet minister should be a topmost man commanding universal confidence. A person after he has secured a seat in an elected body should depend upon his intrinsic merit and popularity to secure coveted position.

4. In the first place, I am not interested in the present Act which is as good as dead. But I am opposed to your proposal on the ground already mentioned.
5. I am opposed for the reasons mentioned. But I should like to compel large elective Congress organizations to ensure the election of Harijan members in proportions to their numbers on the Congress register. If Harijans are not interested enough in Congress to become 4 anna members, they may not expect to find their names in elective bodies. But I would strongly advise Congress workers to see that they approach Harijans and induce them to become members of the Congress.

Is there any doubt that Mr. Gandhi and the Congress were determined on principle not to recognize the right of the untouchables to be represented in the Cabinet? As to the question of qualifications, there would have been some sense if Mr. Gandhi had that limiting condition applicable to all minorities. Dare Mr. Gandhi say that about the Muslim demand? What is the use in shutting it out in the case of the untouchables only? Nobody has claimed that an unqualified untouchable should be made a minister. It only confirms the inner feeling of opposition that lies locked in the heart of Mr. Gandhi.

In the series of acts which the Congress perpetrated in order to nullify the Poona Pact there remains two more to mention. First relates to the policy adopted by the Congress Parliamentary Board in selecting candidates for election. Communal principle played a very great part in it. In a constituency where there were two candidates to choose from, the Congress did not feel it necessary to choose the one from worthy. It chose one who belonged to a caste which was more numerous. Considerations of wealth also played their part. A wealthier candidate was often preferred to a poor and better qualified candidate. These considerations were unjustifiable. But they could be understood as the object was to adopt a safe candidate who will pull through. But there were other principles followed which reveal a deep-seated plot. Different classes of qualifications were set down for different classes of candidates. From candidates who came from high caste Hindus as Brahmins and the allied communities those with the highest qualifications were selected. In the case of the non-Brahmins those with low qualifications were preferred to those with higher qualifications. And in the case of the untouchables those with little or no qualifications were selected in preference of those who had. There seems to be deep laid game behind it. It is designed to allow none but the Brahmins and the allied castes to form the main part of the ministry and to secure for them the support of a docile unintelligent crowd of non-Brahmins and untouchables who by their intellectual attainments could never dream of becoming rivals of the minister-folk but would be content to follow the lead for no other consideration except that of having been raised to the status of the members of Legislatures. Mr. Gandhi did not see this aspect of the case when he said that to be a minister the untouchable aspiring for it must be a qualified person. Otherwise, he would have seen that if there were no qualified persons among the untouchable Congressmen, it was because the Congress Parliamentary Board did choose well-qualified candidates from the untouchables.

If the present system of election continues the Congress can always prevent educated untouchables from becoming members of the Legislature which is the stepping-stone for becoming a member of the Cabinet. The scheme of selecting candidates adopted by the Congress dealt the untouchables a severe blow by depriving them of executive power under the cover of there being no qualified men to hold it which it created for itself by such clandestine and subterranean means.

The second misdeed of the Congress was to subject the untouchable Congressmen to the rigours of party discipline. They were completely under the control of the Congress Party Executive. They could not ask a question which it did not like. They could not move a resolution which it did not permit. They could not bring in legislation to which it objected. They could not vote as they chose and could not speak what they felt. They were there as dumb driven cattle. One of the objects of obtaining representation in the Legislature for the untouchables is to enable them to ventilate their grievances and to obtain redress for their wrongs. The Congress successfully and effectively prevented this wrong happening.

Dr. Ambedkar ended by saying: "The Congress sucked the juice out of the Poona Pact and threw the rind in the face of the untouchables."

In reply to what Dr. Ambedkar said, K. Santhanam, in his book, *Ambedkar's Attack* wrote:

Dr. Ambedkar refers to some disputes he had with some unnamed persons regarding the application of the Poona Pact with reference to the election of the preliminary panel and the method of voting. He has represented this as the attempt of the Hindus to nullify the Poona Pact. As he does not give references or names it is difficult to verify his statements. It was open to any individual to send any representation to the Hammond Committee, and it is, to say the least, most unfair to take up some obscure points raised by unnamed persons, magnify them into a conspiracy of the Hindus, and indirectly suggest that the authors of the Poona Pact were responsible for them. If any body argued that the panel of four should be a minimum and if the number was not forthcoming the reservations must lapse, it was manifestly absurd. But as regards the dispute about cumulative and compulsory distributive vote, Dr. Ambedkar is confused and conflicting. He makes a great ado about the loss of the double vote as a result of the Poona Pact. The compulsory distributive vote would have preserved this feature of the original award by making it obligatory for each scheduled caste voter to vote for a caste Hindu candidate and thereby forced the Hindu candidates to seek scheduled caste votes. Dr. Ambedkar himself complains that the Congress voluntarily adopted the distributive system while non-Congress caste Hindu voters cumulated their votes for caste Hindu candidates. I admit that the cumulative voting system had also some advantages as it would enable constituencies where the scheduled caste votes were considerable to return scheduled caste candidates against the opposition of caste Hindus. The arguments are almost even on the two sides and Dr. Ambedkar only makes himself ridiculous by suggesting that this proposal was put forward maliciously. I have already said that the Congress had no part or lot in all these discussions. As the learned Doctor gained both these points, he should be content, but when one is resolved to be dissatisfied one is led to all kinds of perversities. He had secured 151 seats, at the time of the separation of Orissa three more seats being added to the number agreed to in the Poona Pact; he had gained the cumulative vote and the maximum panel of four. But then he found that the 151 seats secured by the Poona Pact did not belong to him but to the scheduled castes of India and the later did not owe undivided allegiance to him. This shocking discovery has filled his soul with gall and wormwood.

In 1937 elections, the Congress captured 26 out of 30 scheduled caste seats in Madras, 16 out of 20 seats in the U.P., and 11 out of 15 seats in Bihar. On the whole it secured 78 out of 151 seats. This it did by setting up scheduled caste candidates and securing scheduled caste votes. Any fair commentator would have appreciated this political success of the Congress which is a non-communal organization and which is, therefore, bound to contest all seats if it can. Dr. Ambedkar explains in chagrin: "The Congress in capturing 78 seats left only 73 seats to be filled by true and independent representatives of the untouchables." I wonder if Dr. Ambedkar knew that he wrote truer than he meant. The scheduled caste candidate who stood and got elected on the Congress did to a large extent cease to be an untouchable. He became a member of the Congress party in the various legislatures: he sat with them, and discussed all issues as an equal and a comrade, and was feasted and garlanded by women and children of the highest castes just like the other Congress members. If untouchability deserved to be cherished as a precious possession, Dr. Ambedkar is certainly justified in counting out the Congress scheduled caste members. It is not, however, true that the scheduled castes were obliged by the Poona Pact to return representatives whom they did not like. In Bombay, the followers of Dr. Ambedkar secured 11 out of 15 members. He does not explain why similar results were not secured in Madras, Bihar and U.P. Only two explanations are possible. Either, Dr. Ambedkar had no colleagues in these provinces who could organize the scheduled castes in the same way as he had done in Bombay, or the Congress was able to persuade the scheduled castes that they had more to gain by throwing in their lot with the national organization. Perhaps both causes produced the results.

Dr. Ambedkar wants to have his cake and eat it too. He wants to show that the result of the elections of 1937 demonstrated that the Congress did not secure a majority of the scheduled caste seats. If this is correct, a system which confirms the case of the author cannot be wrong. At the same time, he would like the reader to believe that in so far as the scheduled castes returned Congressmen, the system was at fault. He assumes that if the original award had been retained, the Congress could not have captured a large number of scheduled caste seats. This assumption is entirely unwarranted. Many of the Indian Christian seats were captured by the Congress in spite of separate electorates. Naturally, the Congress is in favour of joint electorate as it wants to eliminate communalism and separatism from politics, but even under separate electorates it cannot be prevented from contesting and winning seats.

Dr. Ambedkar intended to show that though the Congress got candidates elected, it was largely through caste Hindu votes and that a majority of the scheduled caste voters were against the Congress. It is inevitable under joint electorates that the representative finally elected is acceptable to the electorate as a whole. It may happen in some instances that a scheduled caste candidate may be defeated by another who may be less acceptable to the scheduled castes but more acceptable to the joint electorate. As the final voting is in common ballot boxes, it is altogether impossible to find out how many votes of a successful candidate were from caste Hindus and how many from the scheduled castes. All that can be known is the total number of votes polled from each of the two sections. Faced with this arithmetical impossibility, Dr. Ambedkar has resorted to a simple stratagem. He has assumed that all the votes obtained by a scheduled caste candidate not belonging to the Congress must have been scheduled caste votes. Deducting these votes from the total scheduled caste votes polled, he has obtained what he thinks must be the scheduled caste votes obtained by the Congress candidate. This is obviously absurd. In Madras for instance, caste Hindu voters of the Justice Party concentrated in some places on defeating the Congress Harijan candidate by voting for his non-Congress rival as they felt that it would not be possible to get their own caste Hindu candidates elected. Dr. Ambedkar's assumption has led to curious absurdities. For example, in the contested constituency of Malapuram, Madras, the successful Congress scheduled caste candidate is presumed to have secured no caste Hindu votes at all. This is an impossibility as it was the uniform directive of the Congress that all Congress votes should be distributed. As the total scheduled caste votes polled were 10,148 and the non-Congress scheduled caste candidate got only 2,606 votes, the Doctor had to attribute all the 7,154 votes polled by the Congress candidate, to scheduled caste voters. Unfortunately for him, even this allotment leaves 388 votes unexplained. It is easy to imagine what must have happened. As each voter had two votes (assuming this was a two member constituency) the total scheduled caste voters must have been 5,074. Of these 1,303 persons must have given their votes to the non-Congress candidate. The other 3,771 scheduled caste voters must have distributed their votes between the two Congress candidates. The reverse kind of absurdity is shown in his analysis of the voting in Sattur. Here the total scheduled caste votes were 6,980. The unsuccessful scheduled caste candidate got 11,894. It is obvious that he must have secured a large number of caste Hindu votes. In this constituency the Justice Party was once strong and the adherents of that party must have voted for this candidate. Dr. Ambedkar assumes that all the scheduled caste votes must have gone to the non-Congress candidate and not a single vote went to make the majority of the Congress scheduled caste candidate who got 18,514 votes. Presumably, the Congress candidate himself—he must be voter as otherwise he could not have contested himself—his relations and friends voted for the opponent.

Dr. Ambedkar angrily asks why the Congress did not include scheduled caste members in the ministries. He has repeated this false statement in more than one place. Yet he shows that scheduled caste ministers were included in the ministries in Madras and Bihar and there were Parliamentary Secretaries belonging to them in the U.P., Madras and Bihar. If it is remembered that the scheduled castes had come into the legislatures in any strength for the first time, these facts do not indicate want of sympathy or lack of recognition of their claims.

Dr. Ambedkar has stated that Gandhiji opposed Dr. Khare's second ministry on the ground of Dr. Khare's taking Mr. Agnibhoj, a scheduled caste member, as one of the ministers. This is as grotesque as it is false. Dr. Khare quarreled with his colleagues and tried to form a second ministry over their heads without consulting the Congress Parliamentary Board. It is not known what authority Dr. Ambedkar has for asserting that Dr. Khare "openly said that according to Mr. Gandhi the act of indiscipline consisted in the inclusion of the untouchable in the ministry". As no reference has been given, it is not right to charge Dr. Khare with this falsehood. If Dr. Ambedkar had followed the usual canons of propriety in such matters, he should have referred this allegation to Gandhiji.

Dr. Ambedkar further asked why Gandhiji disapproved of the appointment of Mr. Agnibhoj as minister by Dr. Khare. The answer is that Gandhiji did not disapprove of the appointment but, he disapproved of Dr. Khare's other actions as Prime Minister and as this disapproval was shared by the Congress Working Committee Dr. Khare had to resign. The question of Mr. Agnibhoj's appointment did not arise at all.

As this is not the only instance of irresponsible and damaging statements being made without any justification or enquiry, it may be concluded that Dr. Ambedkar has throughout acted on the principle that the ends justify the means (K. Santhanam: *Ambedkar's Attack*, pp. 33-40).

With regard to Ambedkar's question as to why Gandhiji did not keep up the gentleman's agreement of the Poona Pact and instruct the Congress High Command to include representatives of the scheduled castes in Congress ministries, K. Santhanam said: "There was no gentleman's agreement about ministries in the Poona Pact and as a matter of fact, representatives of the scheduled castes were included as ministers and parliamentary secretaries in many Congress governments. The ministries were formed by the local legislative parties according to the circumstances of each province, and the Congress High Command interfered only when there were disputes, it is not the habit of Gandhiji to give instructions to the Congress High Command on any matter. He has consistently played the role of adviser when consulted."

Santhanam further says: "It gives the clue to Dr. Ambedkar's fury." I quote it in full: "After having accepted the Poona Pact, why did not Mr. Gandhi keep faith with the Untouchables by telling the Congress not to despoil the politics of the Untouchables by contesting the seats reserved for the Untouchables, by getting such Untouchables elected as were prepared to become the tools of the Hindus?" Every clause of this question is a perversion. The Poona Pact was never meant to segregate the Harijans from the Congress. If it was it would have been the greatest disservice to the Harijans as well as to the country as a whole. The Congress as a national organization, would have stultified itself if it did not seek the support of the Harijans as of every other community. It is a foul accusation that Harijan representatives elected on the Congress ticket were tools of the Hindus. For the first time, they established their claim of absolute equality with the highest of the caste Hindus and the claim was cheerfully conceded. If Dr. Ambedkar thought that because of the Poona Pact, the Harijans would be left out of the national movement and allowed to be exploited by those who worked against the freedom of the country, he was living in a world of self-delusion for which he has to blame only himself. Even if there had been no Poona Pact, the Congress would have attempted to capture the Harijan seats and there is no doubt that the number of non-Congress Harijans in the various legislatures would have been less than in 1937 (K. Santhanam: *Dr. Ambedkar's Attack,* pp. 187-89).

Result of Poona Pact

The "question, however, is what advantage the untouchables have got by entering into the Poona Pact. To understand this one must examine the results of the elections to the Legislatures. The Government of India Act came into operation on 1 April

1937. In February 1937 the elections to the new legislatures as defined in the Act took place. So far as the untouchables are concerned the elections which took place in February 1937 were elections in accordance with the Poona Pact. The following is the analysis of the results of that election to the seats reserved for the untouchables in the different Provincial Assemblies.

"The analysis reveals certain facts which make one ask whether the untouchables have got anything of any value by entering into the Poona Pact and saving the life of Mr. Gandhi and whether the Poona Pact has not made the untouchables the Bondsmen of the Caste Hindus.

"This analysis reveals that a large majority of them have been elected as Congressmen. It is my firm conviction that for the untouchables to merge in the Congress or for the matter of that in any large political party cannot but be fatal for them.

"The untouchables need a movement if they are to remain conscious of their wrongs and if the spirit of revolt is kept alive amongst them. They need a movement because the Caste Hindus have to be told that what is tragedy of the untouchables is their crime. The Congress may not be a red-blooded Hindu body as far as the Musalmans are concerned. But it is certainly a full-blooded and blue-blooded Hindu body in as much as it consists of Caste Hindus. A movement of the untouchables must mean an open war upon the Caste Hindus. A movement of the untouchables within the Congress is quite impossible. It must mean an internecine within the party. The Congress for its own safety cannot allow it.

"The Congress has strictly forbidden the untouchables who have joined the Congress to carry on any independent movement of the untouchables not approved of by the High Command. The result is that in those Provinces where the untouchables have joined the Congress the movement of the untouchables as such is dead.

"The untouchables must retain their freedom of speech and freedom of action on the floor of the Legislature if they are to ventilate their grievances and obtain redress of their wrongs by political action. But this freedom of speech and action has been lost by the representatives of the untouchables who have joined the Congress. They cannot vote as they like, they cannot speak what they think. They cannot ask a question, they cannot move a resolution and they cannot bring in a Bill. They are completely under the control of the Congress Party Executive. They have only such freedom as the Congress Executive may choose to allow them. The result is that though the tale of woes of the untouchables is ever-increasing, the untouchable members of the legislature are unable even to ask questions about them. So pitiable has their condition become that the Congress party sometimes requires them to vote against a measure that may in the opinion of the untouchable members of the legislature be beneficial to the untouchables.

"A recent instance of this occurred in Madras. Rao Bahadur Rajah, a member of the Madras Legislature, brought in a Bill to secure the entry of the untouchables into Hindu Temples in the Madras Presidency. The Congress government had promised to support it at first. Subsequently the Congress government in Madras changed its opinion and opposed the measure. It was a dilemma for the untouchable members of the Madras Legislature. But they had no choice. The whip was applied and they in a body voted against the measure. The representatives of the untouchables were supposed to be the watchdogs of the untouchables. But by reason of having joined the Congress they are muzzled dogs. Far from biting they are not even able to bark. This loss of freedom of speech and action by these untouchable members is entirely due to their having joined the Congress lies in their being unable to secure any real benefit to the untouchables. This is due to two reasons. First of all the Congress is not a radical party.

"The Congress has the reputation of being a revolutionary organization. Its idea of complete independence, the movement of civil disobedience and non-payment of land revenue which the Congress once launched have undoubtedly given that reputation. But many people forget that a revolutionary party is not necessarily a radical party. Whether a revolutionary party is also a radical party must depend upon the social and emotional realities which bring on or induce the revolutionary activity. The Barons of England who under Simon de Mandfort rose against king John in 1215 and compelled him to sign the Magna Charta must be classed as revolutionaries along with the Peasants of England who in 1381 rose in rebellion under War Tyler against their masters and who were all hanged for their rebellious acts. But who can say that the Barons because they were revolutionaries were also radical? The Barons rebelled because they wanted the rights of their class against the King and the peasants established. The Barons revolt was fed by the social emotion of those who were frustrated of power. The emotions behind the peasants revolt were those who were oppressed and who hungering for food and freedom and that is why the peasants were both revolutionary as well as radical. The revolt of the Congress is more like the revolt of the peasants. The Congress under Gandhi is as radical as the Barons were under Simon de Mandfort. Just as the Barons revolt was fed by the social emotions of those who were frustrated of power and not by the emotions of those who were toiling and hungering so was the Congress revolt against the British. It is true that the Congress fathered a large following from the masses but that was by appealing to their anti-British feeling which is natural to all Indians. It is also true that emotions of these were those who were frustrated of food and freedom. But their emotions were in conflict of those socially advanced and the propertied classes. And the latter had all along been the governing class in the Congress. Their emotions are of those only revolutionary body and has not been a radical party. The truth of this can be seen by any one who cares to examine the record of the Congress Governments. Their achievement since they have taken over are just a miscellaneous collection of trifling trinkets. They have shot down the workers more readily than the British and have released criminals sentenced by the High Courts on no other ground than that they have the authority to do it. It is a surprise to me that the Congress has so soon shown that it is just a counterpart of the Tories in England. The governing class in the Congress has lost all its fervor for revolution, for driving the British out. Having now got a field to exploit the masses they want to stick on the power and authority to do the job thoroughly and do not wish to be disturbed by any thought of anti-imperialism at all.

"Not being a radical party the Congress cannot be trusted to undertake a radical programme of social and economic reconstruction without which the untouchables can never succeed in improving their lot. For the untouchables to join such a party is a futile and senseless thing. The Congress will not do anything for them but will only use them as they have done.

"The Congress might do something for the untouchables, if it was compelled to do by force of circumstances. There is only one circumstance in which the Congress would feel such a compulsion—that is when the Congress finds itself dependent upon the representatives of the untouchables for its majority in the legislature. Then the untouchables would be in a position to dictate their terms to the Congress and the Congress would be bound to accept them. In such a contingency it would be worth the while of the untouchables to join the Congress in a coalition. It would be a real bargain. But today the Congress has everywhere such large majorities that in the legislatures it is its own master. It is not dependent on any outside support. The untouchables who are in it are at the end of the tail and the tail so lengthened that it cannot wag. This is the second reason why joining the Congress can be of no benefit to the untouchables.

"Such are the disadvantages that have arisen from the untouchables having joined the Congress. They are not merely disadvantages. I call them dire consequences. All social movement has become dead. All political power has become migratory. It is an understatement to say that under the new Constitution the untouchables are marking time. The fact is that they have been put in chains.

"But the question will undoubtedly be asked and it is this. If such are the consequence of joining the Congress why did these untouchables join it? Why did they not fight their elections independently and in opposition to the Congress? Some of the untouchables who stood on the Congress ticket were just career men on the make who wanted to climb into the legislature so as to be within call when the places of office or profit come for distribution. They did not care by whose ladder they climbed. The Congress being the biggest party and its path the surest way of being admitted into the legislature these careerists felt that to join the Congress was the easiest way of electoral success. They did not want to take any chance. This however explains their object. It does not explain the cause which forced them to join the Congress. I am sure even these careerists would not have joined the Congress if it was possible for them to have got themselves elected independently of the Congress. They have joined the Congress only because they found that course was impossible. Why were they compelled to join the Congress? The answer is that it was due to the system of joint electorates which caused the mischief which was introduced by the Poona Pact.

"A joint electorate for a small minority and a vast majority is bound to result in a disaster to the minority. A candidate put up by the minority cannot be successful even if the whole of the minority were solidly behind him. The fact that a seat is reserved for a minority merely gives a security that minority candidate will be declared elected. But it cannot guarantee that the minority candidate declared elected will be a person of its choice if the election is to be by a joint electorate. Even if a seat is reserved for a minority, a majority can always pick up person belonging to the minority and put him up as a candidate for the reserved seat as against a candidate put up by the minority and get him elected by helping its nominee with the superfluous voting strength which is at its command. The result is that the representative of the minority elected to the reserved seat instead of being a champion of the minority is really the slave of the majority" (Dr. Babasaheb Ambedkar: *Writings and Speeches*, Vol. 5, pp. 343-47).

Ambedkar further said: "Not withstanding the political disaster which has overtaken the untouchables and which is the result of the Poona Pact, there are not wanting friends of Mr. Gandhi, who hold out the Poona Pact as a great boon to the untouchables.

"Firstly it is alleged that the Poona Pact gave the untouchables larger number of seats than was given to them by the Communal Award. It is true that the Poona Pact gave the untouchables 151 seats while the Award had only given them 78. But to conclude from this that the Poona Pact gave them more than what was given by the Award is to ignore what the Award had in fact given to the untouchables. The second argument in favor of the Poona Pact is that in abolishing separate electorates it saved the untouchables from being eternally branded as untouchables".

In one of his speeches delivered in London Mr. Gandhi said: "Muslims and Sikhs are all well organized. The untouchables are not. There is very little political consciousness among them and they are so horribly treated that I want to save them against themselves. If they had separate electorates their lives would be miserable in villages which are the strongholds of Hindu orthodoxy. It is the superior class of Hindus who have to do penance of having neglected the untouchables of ages. That penance can be done by active social reform and by making the lot of the untouchables more bearable by acts of service, but not by asking for separate electorates for them. By giving them separate electorates you will throw the apple of discord between the untouchables and the orthodox. You must understand I can tolerate the proposal for special representation of the Musalmans and the Sikhs only as a necessary evil. It would be a positive danger for the untouchables. I am certain that the question of separate electorates for the 'untouchables' is modern manufacture of government. The only thing needed is to put them on the voters list, and provide for fundamental rights for them in the constitution. In case they are unjustly treated and their representative is deliberately excluded, they would have the right to special election tribunal which would give them complete protection. It should be open to these tribunals to order the unseating of an elected candidate and the election of the excluded man."

Mr. Gandhi further said: "Separate electorates to the untouchables will ensure them bondage in perpetuity. The Musalmans will never cease to be Musalmans by having separate electorates. Do you want the untouchables to remain untouchables for ever? Well, the separate electorates would perpetuate the stigma. What is needed is destruction of untouchability, and when you have done it, the bar sinister which has been imposed by an insolent 'superior' class upon an 'inferior' class will be destroyed. When you have destroyed the bar sinister, to whom will you give the separate electorates? Look at the history of Europe. Have you got separate electorates for the working classes or women? With adult franchise, you give the 'untouchables' complete security. Even the orthodox would have to approach them for votes."

Mr. Gandhiji questioned: "How then, does Dr. Ambedkar, insist on separate electorates for them? I have the highest regard for Dr. Ambedkar. He has every right to be bitter. That he does not break our heads is an act of self-restraint on his part. He is today so much saturated with suspicion that he cannot see anything else. He sees in every Hindu a determined opponent of the untouchables, and it is quite natural. The same thing happened to me in my early days in South Africa, where I was bounded out by Europeans wherever I went. It is quite natural for him to vent his wrath. But the separate electorates that he seeks will not give him social reform. He may himself mount to power and position but nothing good will accrue to the untouchables. I can say all this with authority, having lived with the untouchables and having shared their joys and sorrows all these years."

In reply to Gandhiji's views Ambedkar said: "...But that this argument is silly, there can be no doubt about it. To put a man in a separate category from other is not necessarily an evil. Whether the affixing of a label is good or bad depends upon the underlying purpose. If the object is to deprive him of rights then such a labeling would no doubt be a grievous wrong. But if the purpose is to mark off as a recipient of a privilege then far from being a wrong it would be a most beneficial measure. To enroll an untouchable in a separate electoral roll would be objectionable if the object was to deprive him of the right of the franchise. To enroll him in a separate electoral roll for giving him the benefit of special representation would certainly be an advantage to him. Looked at from the point of view of ultimate purpose it is difficult to see how any person who claims to be the friend of the untouchables could object to separate electorates for them. Not only the argument of Gandhi against separate electorate was silly it was also insincere. Gandhi objected to separate electorates because it involved labeling of the untouchables. But how is this labeling avoided in joint electorates it is difficult to understand. The reservation of a seat for the untouchables in a joint electorate must and does involve such labeling, for the candidate claiming the benefit of the reserved seat must in law declare that he is an untouchable. To that extent there is certainly a labeling involving in the joint Electorate and Mr. Gandhi should have objected to joint electorates as violently as he did to separate electorates. Either Mr. Gandhi was insincere or that he did not know what he was talking about.

"Friends of Mr. Gandhi do not stop to consider how far under the Poona Pact the untouchables have been able to send independent men to represent them in the Legislature and whether these representatives have been putting up any fight and how well they are succeeding. If they stopped to do it they would be ashamed to sing the praises of the joint electorates and the Poona Pact. The Congress and the Hindus have shamefully abused their power and their resources as majority community. Not only have they prevented the untouchables from electing persons of their choice, not only have they got their own nominees elected by the use of their surplus votes, they have done something for which any decent party in any part of the world would be ashamed of itself. The selection of the candidates from the untouchables made by the Congress to fill the seats reserved for the untouchables was a most cowardly and a blackguardly act.

"It was open to the Congress—which is simply a political surname for Hindus—to allow the untouchables the benefits of more seats than those fixed for them by the Poona Pact. They could have done that by adopting untouchable candidates to contest general seats. There was nothing in law to prevent them from doing so. The Congress did nothing of the kind. This shows that if no seat had been reserved to the untouchables, the Hindus would never have cared to see that an untouchable was returned to the legislature. On the other hand, when seats were reserved, the Hindus came forward to spoil the effect of the reservation by seeing to it that the seats went to such untouchables as agreed to be their slaves.

"Thus there has been a tragic end to this fight of the untouchables for political rights. I have no hesitation in saying that Mr. Gandhi is solely responsible for this tragedy.

"Mr. Gandhi's cry against the Communal Award on the ground that it prescribed separate electorates was absolutely false and if the Hindus had not become maddened by his fast they would have seen that it was so. The communal Award had also a provision for joint electorates in addition to separate electorates. The second vote given to the untouchables was to be exercised in a general electorate in the election of a Caste Hindu candidate. This was undoubtedly a system of joint electorates.

"The difference between the Communal Award and the Poona Pact does lie in the nature of electorates. Both provides joint electorates. The difference lies in this, joint electorate of the Communal Award was intended to enable the untouchables to take part and influence the election of the Caste Hindu candidate while the joint electorate of the Poona Pact is intended to enable the Caste Hindus to take part and influence the election of the untouchable candidates. This is the real difference between the two.

"What would a friend of the untouchables wish? Would he support the joint electorates of the Communal Award or the joint electorates of the Poona Pact? There can be no doubt that the real salvation of the untouchables lies in making the Hindus dependent upon the suffrages of the untouchables. This is what Communal Award did. To make the untouchables depend upon the suffrages of the Hindus is to make them the slaves of the Hindus which they already are. This is what the Poona Pact does. The Communal Award was intended to free the untouchables from the thralldom of the Hindus. The Poona Pact is designed to place them under the domination of the Hindus.

"This Fast unto Death of Mr. Gandhi was described in glorious terms by his friends and admires both in India and outside. It was described as 'second crucifixion', as 'martyrdom' and as 'Triumphal struggle'. An American friend of Mr. Gandhi assured the Americans that in laying down his life Mr. Gandhi was neither a 'trickster' nor a stick demagogue. Another

American in his ecstasy went to the length of describing him as the incarnation of 'one against the world'. Of course I was held out as the villain of the peace. I had of course my own view of Gandhiji's fast. I described it as apolitical stunt. His utterances had to me always the ring of falsity and even of insincerity.

"I had always the feeling that what actuated Mr. Gandhi to fast against the Communal award was not any desire to liberate the untouchables as to save the Hindus from disruption. He was prepared to do that at any cost, even at the cost of political enslavement of the untouchables. His disapproval of the enfranchisement of the Negro by the Southerners after the civil war" (Dr. Babasaheb Ambedkar: *Writings and Speeches*, Vol. 5, pp. 350-56).

About the Epic Fast Ambedkar said: "They story of this fast has been told by Mr. Pyarelal in volume which bears the picturesque and flamboyant title of *The Epic Fast*. In the pages of this lours Boswelliana the curious will find all he wants to know about the happenings in India during these mad days and I need say nothing about it here. The Prime Minister had made it quite clear that the British Cabinet would not withdraw it or alter it of its own but that they are ready to substitute for it a formula that may be agreed upon by the Caste Hindus and the untouchables. As I had the privilege of representing the untouchables at the Round Table Conference it was assumed that the assent of the untouchables would not be valid unless I was a party to it. At the moment my position as the representative of the untouchables of India was not only not questioned but was accepted as a fact. All eyes naturally turned to me as the man or rather as the villain of the peace. Mr. Gandhi's life as he himself said was in my hands.

"It is no exaggeration to say that no man was placed in a greater and graver dilemma than I was then. It was a baffling situation. I had to make a choice between two different alternatives. There was before me the duty which I owed as a part of common humanity to save Gandhiji from sure death. There was before me the problem of saving for the untouchables the political rights which the Prime Minister had given them. I responded to the call of humanity and saved the life of

Mr. Gandhi by agreeing to alter the Communal Award in a manner satisfactory to Mr. Gandhi. (It may be pointed out that this response was combined with hard bargaining and shrewd business.)

Dr. Ambedkar further said: "This fast unto death was a great gamble on the part of Mr. Gandhi. He perhaps felt that the mere threat to fast unto death would make me and other depressed classes who were with me just shiver and yield. But he soon found that he was mistaken and that the untouchables were equally determined to fight to the last for their rights. No one except his own followers were convinced that Mr. Gandhi's fast had any moral basis and if Gandhi got a second lease of life, he owes it entirely to the generosity and goodwill shown towards him by untouchables."

Dr. Ambedkar continued: "Pyarelal has described the fast as an Epic Fast. Why it should be described as an Epic Fast it is not easy to follow. There was nothing heroic about it. It was the opposite of heroic. It was an adventure. It was launched by Mr. Gandhi because he believed that both the untouchables and the British government would quake before his threat of fast unto death, and surrender to his demand. Both were prepared to call off his bluff and as a matter of fact did call it off. All his heroism vanished the moment Mr. Gandhi found that he had overdone the trick. The man who started by saying that he would fast unto death unless the safeguards to the untouchables were completely withdrawn and the untouchables reduced to the condition of utter helplessness without rights and without recognition was plaintively pleading 'My life is in your hands, will you save me?' Mr. Gandhi's over-impatience to sign the Poona Pact—though it did not cancel the Prime Minister's Award as he had demanded but only substituted another and a different system of constituent safeguards—is the strongest evidence that the hero had lost his courage and was anxious to save his face and anyhow save his life.

"There was nothing noble in the fast. It was foul and filthy act. The Fast was not for the benefit of the untouchables. It was against them and was the worst form of coercion against a helpless people to give up the constitutional safeguards of which they had become processed under the Prime Minister's Award and agree to live on the mercy of the Hindus. It was a vile and wicked act. How can the untouchables regard such a man as honest and sincere?

"After having gone on a fast unto death, Mr. Gandhi signed the Poona Pact. People say that Mr. Gandhi sincerely believed that political safeguards were harmful to the untouchables. But how could a honest and sincere man who opposed the political demands of the untouchables who was prepared to use the Muslims to defeat them, who went on a Fast unto Death, in the end accept the very same demands—for there is no difference between the Poona Pact and the Communal Award—when he found that there was no use opposing, as opposition would not succeed? How can an honest and sincere man accept as harmless the demands of the untouchables which once he regarded as harmful?" (Dr. Babasaheb Ambedkar: *Writings and Speeches*, Vol. 9, pp. 259-60).

"Mr. Gandhi's attitude towards Swaraj and the untouchables resembles very much the attitude of President Lincoln towards the two questions of the Negroe and the Union. Mr. Gandhi wants Swaraj as did President Lincoln want Union. But he does not want Swaraj at the cost of disrupting the structure of Hinduism which is what political emancipation of the untouchables means as President Lincoln did not want to free the slaves if it was not necessary to do so for the sake of the Union. There is of course this difference between Mr. Gandhi and President Lincoln. President Lincoln was prepared to emancipate the Negro slaves if it was necessary to preserve the Union. Mr. Gandhi's attitude is in marked contrast. He is not prepared for the political emancipation of the untouchables even if it was essential for winning Swaraj, Mr. Gandhi's attitude is let Swaraj perish if the cost of it is the political freedom of the untouchables.

"Some untouchables are probably under the impression that all this is a matter of the dead past and Mr. Gandhi having accepted the Poona Pact cannot now oppose the political demands of the untouchables for as a party to the Poona Pact. Mr. Gandhi must be assumed to have conceded that the untouchables are a separate element in the national life of India. This is complete misunderstanding. For there are grounds to believe that the Poona Pact has made no difference in Mr. Gandhi's view and he still maintains the same attitude to the untouchables, claim for political safeguards as he did at the Round Table Conference and before the Poona Pact. These grounds have their foundation in the fact that when His Majesty's government declared in 1940 that the untouchables are a separate element in the national life of India and that their consent to the Constitution is necessary, Mr. Gandhi came out with a protest.

When the Viceroy Lord Linlithgow referred to the untouchables as a separate element and said that their consent to the Constitution was necessary, Mr. Gandhi said: "I felt that the putting up by the Viceroy, and then the Secretary of State of want of agreement by the Congress with the Princes, the Muslim League and even the scheduled classes as a barrier to the British recognition of India's right to freedom was more than unjust to the Congress and the people.

"The introduction of the scheduled classes in the controversy has made the unreality of the case of the British government doubly unreal. They know that these are the special care of the Congress, and that the Congress is infinitely more capable of guarding their interests than the British government. Moreover, the scheduled classes are divided into as many castes as the caste Hindu society. No single scheduled classes member could possibly and truthfully represent the innumerable castes.

"The argument advanced by Mr. Gandhi is puerile. It may be pointed out that in the hurry he made in stating his opposition to the position assigned to the scheduled castes by the Viceroy, Mr. Gandhi forgot that if the scheduled castes are divided into many castes and no single caste could represent them all, the case of the Muslims and the Indian Christians is in no way different. The Muslims are divided into three groups: 1. Sunnis, 2. Shias and 3. Momins each of which consists of many castes who interdine but do not intermarry. Indian Christians are divided into 1. Catholics, and 2. Protestants. Catholics are again subdivided into 1. Caste Christians, and 2. Non-Caste Christians. Both

Catholics and Protestants have castes which do not intermarry and caste Christians and Non-caste Christians do not even inter-dine or go to the same church. This shows that Mr. Gandhi notwithstanding his being a party to the Poona Pact is determined not to allow the scheduled castes being given the status of a separate element and that he is prepared to adopt any argument, however, desperate to justify his attitude of opposition.

"In short Mr. Gandhi is still on the warpath so far as the untouchables are concerned. He may start the trouble over again. The time to trust him has not arrived. The untouchables must still hold that the best way to safeguard themselves is to say 'Beware of Mr. Gandhi'" (Dr. Babasaheb Ambedkar: *Writings and Speeches*, Vol. 9, pp. 271-73).

Malignant Factor

Dr. Ambedkar later said: "Mr. Gandhi accepted the Poona Pact not as a gentleman signing an agreement with the intention to honour his word but as a crafty person seeking to find a way out of a difficulty. Mr. Gandhi, notwithstanding the Poona Pact, which saved him from death never gave his true and honest consent to the principle underlying the Poona Pact" (Dr. Babasaheb Ambedkar: *Writings and Speeches*, Vol. 17-(III), pp. 253-54).

Poona Pact is Fraught with Mischief

"The Poona Pact has completely disfranchised the Scheduled Castes in as much as candidates whom they rejected in the primary elections...which is a true index of their will... have been returned in the final election by the votes of the caste Hindus.

The Poona Pact is thus fraught with mischief. It was accepted because of the coercive fast of Mr. Gandhi and because of the assurance given at the time that the Hindus will not interfere in the election of the Scheduled Castes" (Dr. Babasaheb Ambedkar: *Writings and Speeches*, Vol. 1, p. 432).

Poona Pact Created Bondsmen Only

".... It was felt that in the case of the Untouchables mere right to vote would not be enough. It was feared that a member elected on the votes of the Untouchables, if he is himself not an Untouchable, might play false and might take no interest in them. It was held that the grievances of the Untouchables must be ventilated in the Legislature and that the surest way of ensuring it would be to provide that a certain number of seats shall be reserved for them so that the Untouchables shall be represented by Untouchables in the legislatures. It is now evident that this hope has not been fulfilled. The Communal Award no doubt gave fewer seats. But they would have been all of them freemen. The Poona Pact gave more but they are all filled by bondsmen. If to have a platoon of bondsmen is an advantage then the Poona Pact may be said to be advantage" (Dr. Babasaheb Ambedkar: *Writings and Speeches*, Vol. 5, p. 351).

Need to Revise the Poona Pact

"The Poona Pact, which prevented true representatives of the Scheduled Castes from being returned to legislatures, must go. It had resulted in disenfranchising 60,000,000 Untouchables. Even according to international law no treaty was final or sacrosanct, as the Poona pact had now become injurious to their cause, the Scheduled Castes were entitled to fight for its revision" (Dr. Babasaheb Ambedkar: *Writings and Speeches*, Vol. 17-(II), p. 241).

"Many critics have found fault with the agreement on the ground that it offers a far bigger electorate to the depressed classes than even an alien Prime Minister had given them. This had to be so obviously to satisfy the demands of Ambedkar and his followers. Since Gandhi had decided to fight for the cause of submerged section of the society, he apparently had no objection to the weightage being given and agreed to the terms of the agreement" (S.K. Bose: *Tej Bahadur Sapru,* p. 95).

Thakkar Bapa said: "That Mahatma Gandhi's life could be saved is enough justification for the Poona Pact. But even if the facts that this historic fast has forged a new unity between the so-called caste Hindus and untouchables and that the British Prime Minister was forced to change his decision are not taken into consideration, the moral value of this agreement cannot be underestimated. The Poona Pact has shown to Britain and the world at large that social consciousness and cultural oneness are still present in Hinduism."

Thakkar Bapa further said: "The Poona Pact was in itself historic. Any agreement signed by Harijan leaders like Dr. Ambedkar, R. Srinivasan, M.C. Rajah, and P.N. Rajbhoj on the one hand and caste Hindus like Madan Mohan Malaviya, Tej Bahadur Sapru, M.R. Jayakar, C. Rajagopalachari, Rajendra Prasad and Ghansyam Das Birla on the other could not but be historic. Because of the Poona Pact, 24th September came to be known as the Harijan Day" (Viyogi Hari: *Thakkar Bapa,* p. 59).

Mahatma Gandhi's Blunder

Looking to the growing heart-burning between Hindus and Scheduled Castes (Neo-Buddhists) after independence, I am constrained to say that Mahatma Gandhi committed a blunder in going on fast against Communal Award. The Communal Award was the outcome of the insistence of Dr. Ambedkar for separate electorates on the lines of the one provided to Muslims and other minorities.

This is what Dr. Ambedkar said to make out his case for separate electorates:

Untouchables are a separate element.

"The basis of my politics lies in the proposition that the Untouchables are not a subhead or a sub-section of the Hindus, and that they are a separate and a distinct element in the national life of India, as separate and distinct as the Muslims and like the Muslims of India the Untouchables are entitled to separate political right as against the Hindus of India. This is the key-note of my politics.... There was a contest between me and Mr. Gandhi. Mr. Gandhi contested that the Untouchables were a sub-section of the Hindus and consequently if any political power was to devolve from the hands of the British it should pass undivided into the hands of the Hindus who could be trusted to look after the interest of the Untouchables. The position taken up by me was totally different; I contended that the Untouchables formed separate and distinct element in the life of the country. The Hindus who were their hereditary enemies could not be trusted and far from using the political power for raising the Untouchables the fear was that they would use it for perpetuating their subjection, and it was therefore, absolutely necessary that there should be political partition between the Untouchables and the Hindus so that the Untouchables may get political power in their own hands to use it to promote their welfare or to use it to save themselves against the tyranny and oppression of the Hindus."

Importance of the Communal Award

"…. At the Round Table Conference, the Untouchables won and the Mahatma lost. The Communal Award was the result of this contest. Its great virtue lies in the fact that the Untouchables were recognized in the national life of India and entitled to claim separate political rights. That is the importance of the Communal Award…our claim was reassured and sustained by the declaration of the victory made on the 8th August 1940 in which it was made clear that the Muslims and the Untouchables were distinct and separate elements in the national life of India and that the British Government will not enforce a Constitution which has not the support of the Muslims and the Depressed Classes" (Dr. Babasaheb Ambedkar: *Writings and Speeches*, Vol. 17-(III), pp. 250-53).

"…. The Untouchables say that they are a separate element, nobody can accuse them of having invented a new theory for the sake of political advantages. They are merely pointing out what the facts are and how these facts are the heritage of Hinduism itself. The Congress cannot honestly and convincingly use Hinduism as an argument for refusing to recognize the Untouchables as a separate element. If it does, it is only because it is actuated by selfish motives. It knows that the recognition of the Untouchables as an element in the national life of India, as distinct and separate from the Hindus, must result in the apportionment of places in the Executives, the Legislatures and in the Public Services between the untouchables and the Hindus and thus limit the share of the Hindus. The Congress does not like that the Hindus should be deprived of the share of the Untouchables which the Hindus are in the habit of appropriating to themselves. That is the real reason why the Congress refuses to recognize that the Untouchables are a separate element in the national life of India....

".... If there is a real separation between the Hindus and the Untouchables and if there is the danger of discrimination being practiced by the Hindus against the Untouchables then the Untouchables must receive political recognition and must be given political safeguards to protect themselves against the tyranny of the Hindus" (Dr. Babasaheb Ambedkar: *Writings and Speeches*, Vol. 9, pp. 187-88).

Had Gandhiji not undertaken the Epic Fast, the Scheduled Castes would have been provided separate electorates, which might have saved the menace of the reservations the young boys and girls have to face. This has thrown them in utter frustration and disappointment. A number of young boys and girls have ventilated their feelings to me. The gradual but sure result will be the deepening of heart-burning with every passing day. I am afraid that the relations between the Hindus and Scheduled Castes obtaining today in India, may take the two communities back to the past, which may either push the Scheduled Castes to the outskirts of the villages or cause social strife.

Scheduled Castes are distributed evenly in all districts, talukas and villages and form a minority everywhere. Dr. Ambedkar wanted to make them a coherent All India community like the Muslims, Anglo-Indians and Indian Christians. It was then and now too seems to be a social and political impossibility.

It may be recollected what K. Santhanam said in his book, *Ambedkar's Attack* and I quote: "If Harijan leadership were wise, it would make common cause with the fight of the landless labourers for a living wage and land, with the poor peasants for the abolition of landlordism and with factory workers for forming powerful trade unions and for social security. To the extent the Harijans get segregated from the section of Hindus which are close to them in poverty and educational backwardness, their fight for emancipation will be more difficult and more prolonged. If they conceive of their struggle, as stated by Dr. Ambedkar, to be one "against Hindu Raj in which the governing class would be the Bania and the Brahmin with low class Hindus as their policemen, all of whom have been the hereditary enemies of the untouchables," their prospect must be bleak indeed. On the other hand, if they place before themselves the objective of social revolution by which caste and creed will be swept away and give place to the conception and human equality must prevail among all the Hindus and that the so-called "untouchable" is not a whit inferior in theory or fact to any other, they will have time, reason, nationalism, all the great men of India and the good wishes of humanity with them."

Chapter 7

Gandhi and Ambedkar on Caste and Varnashram

Dr. Babasaheb Ambedkar was invited to preside over the conference of the Jat-Pat-Todak Mandal held in 1936 at Lahore. Dr. Ambedkar prepared his presidential address and sent it to Shri Sant Ram, who was a moving spirit and the leading light of the Jat-Pat-Todak Mandal. The Mandal found the address provocative and pinching and therefore requested Dr. Ambedkar to modify the address.

Shri Har Gopal another leading member of the Mandal wrote a letter to Dr. Ambedkar on 22-4-1936 in which he said:

"...You have more than once stated in your address that you had decided to walk out of the fold of Hindus and that was your last address as a Hindu. You have also unnecessarily attacked the morality and unreasonableness of Vedas and other religious books of the Hindus, and have at length dwelt upon the technical side of Hindu religion, which has absolutely no connection with the problem at issue, so much so, that some of the passages have become irrelevant and off the point. We doubt the wisdom of making the address unnecessarily provocative and pinching.

"In fact, we thought that you would give us a lead in the destruction of the caste system, especially when you have studied the subject so thoroughly, strengthen our hands by bringing about a revolution and making yourself as a nucleous in the gigantic effort, but the declaration of the nature made by you when repeated loses its power, and becomes a hackneyed term."

Shri Har Gopal requested Dr. Ambedkar to consider the whole matter and make his address more effective by saying, that he would be glad to take a leading part in the destruction of the caste system, if the Hindus are willing to work in right earnest toward that end, even if they had to forsake their kith and kin and the religious notions.

Shri Har Gopal concluded his letter by saying: "In case, you still insist upon the printing of the address in toto, we very much regret it would not be possible—rather advisable for us to hold the conference, and we would prefer to postpone it sine die."

Dr. Ambedkar informed Shri Har Gopal on 27 April 1936 that he would not alter a cama and also would not allow any censorship over his address and requested to cancel the conference. Dr. Ambedkar printed his address under the title, "Annihilation of Caste". The views expressed by Dr. Ambedkar in his address with regard to Caste, Varnashram, Shashtras and Manu Smriti are summerised below:

Caste

Caste is the monster that crosses your path. You cannot have political reform, you cannot have economic reform unless you kill this monster. It is a pity that Caste even today has its defenders. The defences are many. It is defended on the ground that the Caste System is but another name for division of labour and if division of labour is a necessary feature of every civilized society then it is argued that there is nothing wrong in the Caste System. Now the first thing is to be urged against this view is that Caste System is not merely division of labour, it is also a division of labourers. Civilized society undoubtedly needs division of labour. But in no civilized society is division of labour accompanied by this unnatural division of labourers into water-tight compartments. Caste System is not merely a division of labourers which is quite different from division of labour—it is an hierarchy in which the division of labourers are graded one above the other. In no other country is the division of labour accompanied by this gradation of labourers. There is also a third point of criticism against this view of the Caste System. This division of labour is not spontaneous, it is not based on natural aptitudes. Social and individual efficiency requires us to develop the capacity of an individual to the point of competency to choose and to make his own career. This principle is violated in the Caste System in so far as it involves an attempt to appoint tasks to individuals in advance, selected not on the basis of trained original capacities, but on that of the social status of the parents. Locked at from another point of view this stratification of occupations which is the result of the Caste System is positively pernicious. Industry is never static. It undergoes rapid and abrupt changes. With such changes an individual must be free to change his occupation. Without such freedom to adjust himself to changing circumstances it would be impossible for him to gain his livelihood. Now the Caste System will not allow Hindus to take to occupations where they are wanted if they do not belong to them by heredity. If a Hindu is seen to starve rather than take to new occupations not assigned to his Caste, the reason is to be found in the Caste System. By not permitting readjustment of occupations, caste becomes a direct cause of much of the unemployment we see in the country. As a form of division of labour the Caste System suffers from another serious defect. The division of labour brought about by the Caste System is not a division based on choice. Individual sentiment, individual preference has no place in it. It is based on the dogma of predestination. Considerations of social efficiency would compel us to recognize that the greatest evil in the industrial system is not so much poverty and the suffering that it involves as the fact that so many persons have callings which make no appeal to those who are engaged in them. Such callings constantly provoke one to aversion, ill-will and the desire to evade. There are many occupations in India which on account of the fact that they are regarded as degraded by the Hindus provoke those who are engaged in them to aversion. There is a constant desire to evade an escape from such occupations which arises solely because of the blighting effect which they produce upon those who follow them owing to the slight and stigma of caste upon them by the Hindu religion. What efficiency can there be in a system under which neither men's hearts nor their minds are in their work? As an economic organization Caste is therefore a harmful institution, inasmuch as, it involves the subordination of man's natural powers and inclinations to the exigencies of social rules.

Some have dug a biological trench in defence of the Caste System. It is said that the object of Caste was to preserve purity of race and purity of blood. Now ethnologists are of opinion that men of pure race exist nowhere and that there has been a mixture of all races in all parts of the world. Especially is this the case with the people of India? Mr. D.R. Bhandarkar in his paper on Foreign Elements in the Hindu Population has stated that "There is hardly a class, or Caste in India which has not a foreign strain in it. There is an admixture of alien blood not only among the warrior classes—the Rajputs and the Marathas—but also among the Brahmins who are under the happy delusion that they are free from all foreign elements." The Caste System cannot be said to have grown as a means of preventing the admixtures or as means of maintaining purity of blood. As a matter of fact Caste System came into being long after the different races of India had commingled in blood and culture. To hold that distinctions of Castes or really distinctions of race and to treat different Castes as though they were so many different races is a gross perversion of facts.

Caste System does not demarcate racial division. Caste system is a social division of people of the same race. Assuming it, however, to be a case of racial division one may ask: What harm could there be if a mixture of races and of blood was permitted to take place in India by intermarriages a distinction that science recognizes men and animals as two distinct species. But even scientists who believe in purity of races do not assert that the different races constitute different species of men. They are only varieties of one and the same species. As such they can interbreed and produce an offspring which is capable of breeding and which is not sterile. An immense lot of nonsense is talked about heredity and eugenics in defence of the Caste System. Few would object to the Caste System if it was in accord with the basic principle of eugenics because few can object to the improvement of the race by judicious mating. But one fails to understand how the Caste System secures judicious mating. Caste System is a negative thing. It merely prohibits persons belonging to different Castes from intermarrying. It is not a positive method of selecting which two among a given Caste should marry. If Caste is eugenic in origin the origin of sub-castes must also be eugenic. But can any one seriously maintain that the origin of sub-castes is eugenic? I think it would be absurd to contend for such a proposition and for a very obvious reason. If Caste means race then differences of sub-castes cannot mean differences of race because sub-castes become ex hypothesia subdivisions of one and the same race. Consequently the bar against intermarrying and interdining between sub-castes cannot be for the purpose of maintaining purity of race or of blood. If sub-castes cannot be eugenic in origin there cannot be any substance in the contention that Caste is eugenic in origin. Again if Caste is eugenic in origin one can understand the bar against intermarriage. But what is the purpose of the interdict placed on interdining between Castes and sub-castes alike? Interdining cannot infect blood and therefore cannot be the cause either of the improvement or of deterioration of the race. This shows that Caste has no scientific origin and that those who are attempting to give it an eugenic basis are trying to support by science what is grossly unscientific. Even today eugenics cannot become a practical possibility unless we have definite knowledge regarding the laws of heredity.

Caste does not result in economic efficiency. Caste cannot and has not improved the race. Caste has however done one thing. It has completely disorganized and demoralized the Hindus.

Hindu society as such does not exist. It is only a collection of castes. Each caste is conscious of its existence. Its survival is the be all and end all of its existence. Castes do not even form a federation. A caste has no feeling that it is affiliated to other castes except when there is a Hindu-Muslim riot. On all other occasions each caste endeavours to segregate itself and to distinguish itself from other castes. Each caste not only dines among itself and marries among itself but each caste prescribes its own distinctive dress.

The Caste System prevents common activity and by preventing common activity it has prevented the Hindus from becoming a society with a unified life and a consciousness of its own being.

The literature of the Hindus is full of caste genealogies in which an attempt is made to give a noble origin to one caste and an ignoble origin to other castes. The Sahyadrikhand is a notorious instance of this class of literature. This anti-social spirit is not confined to caste alone. It has gone deeper and has poisoned the mutual relations of the sub-castes as well.

The Hindus, therefore, are not merely an assortment of castes but they are so many warring groups each living for itself and for its selfish ideal. There is another feature of caste which is deplorable.

The present-day non-Brahmins cannot forgive the present-day Brahmins for the insult their ancestors gave to Shivaji. The present-day Kayasthas will not forgive the present-day Brahmins for the infamy cast upon their forefathers by the forefathers of the latter.

The existence of Caste and Caste Consciousness has served to keep the memory of past feuds between castes green and has prevented solidarity.

Hindu's whole life is one anxious effort to preserve his caste. Caste is his precious possession which he must save at any cost. He cannot consent to lose it by establishing contact with the aborigines the remnants of the hateful Anaryas of the Vedic days. Not that a Hindu could not be taught the sense of duty to fallen humanity, but the trouble is that no amount of sense of duty can enable him to overcome his duty to preserve his caste. Caste is, therefore, the real explanation as to why the Hindu has let the savage remain a savage in the midst of his civilization without blushing or without feeling any sense of remorse or repentance. The Hindu has not realized that these aborigines are a source of potential danger. If these savages remain savages they may not do any harm to the Hindus. But if they are reclaimed by non-Hindus and converted to their faiths they will swell the ranks of the enemies of the Hindus. If this happens the Hindu will have to thank himself and his Caste System.

Not only has the Hindu made no effort for the humanitarian cause of civilizing the savages but the higher-caste Hindus have deliberately prevented the lower castes who are within the pale of Hinduism from rising to the cultural level of the higher castes.

I have no hesitation in saying that if the Mohammedan has been cruel the Hindu has been mean and meanness is worse than cruelty.

Unlike the club the membership of caste is not open to all and sundry. The law of caste confines its membership to person born in the caste. Castes are autonomous and there is no authority anywhere to compel a caste to admit a new-comer to its social life. Hindu Society being a collection of castes. And each caste being a close corporation there is no place for a convert. So long as castes remain, Hindu religion cannot be made a missionary religion and shudhi will be both a folly and a futility.

A caste has an unquestioned right to excommunicate any man who is guilty of breaking the rules of the caste and when it is realized that excommunication involves a complete cesser of social intercourse it will be agreed that as a form of punishment there is really little to choose between excommunication and death.

A caste is ever ready to take advantage of the helplessness of a man and insist upon complete conformity to its code in letter and in spirit. A caste can easily organize itself into a conspiracy to make the life of a reformer a hell and if a conspiracy is a crime I do not understand why such a nefarious act as an attempt to excommunicate a person for daring to act contrary to the rules of caste should not be made an offence punishable in law. But as it is, even law gives each caste an autonomy to regulate its membership and punish dissenters with excommunication. Caste in the hands of the orthodox has been a powerful weapon for persecuting the reforms and for killing all reform.

The effect of caste on the ethics of the Hindus is simply deplorable. Caste has killed public spirit. Caste has destroyed the sense of public charity. Caste has made public opinion impossible. A Hindu's public is his caste. His responsibility is only to his caste. His loyalty is restricted only to his caste. Virtue has become caste-ridden and morality has become caste-bound. There is no sympathy to the deserving. There is no appreciation of the meritorious. There is no charity to the needy. Suffering as such calls for no response. There is charity but it begins with the caste and ends with the caste. There is sympathy but not for men of other castes. Would a Hindu acknowledge and follow the leadership of a great and good man? The case of a Mahatma apart, the answer must be that he will follow a leader if he is a man of his caste. A Brahmin will follow a leader only if he is a Brahmin, a Kayastha if he is a Kayastha and so on. The capacity to appreciate merits in a man apart from his caste does not exist in a Hindu. There is appreciation of virtue but only when the man is a fellow caste-man. The whole morality is as bad as tribal morality. My caste-man, right or wrong; my caste-man, good or bad. It is not a case of standing by virtue and not standing by vice. It is a case of standing or not standing by the caste. Have not Hindus committed treason against their country in the interest of their caste?

Caste among Non-Hindus is fundamentally different from caste among Hindus. First, the ties, which consciously make the Hindus hold together, are non-existent, while among Non-Hindus there are many that hold them together. The strength of a society depends upon the presence of points of contact, possibilities of interaction between different groups which exist in it. These are what Carlyle calls "organic filaments" i.e. the elastic threads which held to bring the disintegrating elements together and to reunite them. There is no integrating force among the Hindus to counteract the disintegration caused by caste. While among the Non-Hindus there are plenty of these organic filaments which bind them together. Again it must be borne in mind that although there are castes among Non-Hindus, as there are among Hindus, caste has not the same social significance for Non-Hindus as it has for Hindus. Ask Mohammedan or a Sikh, who he is? He tells you that he is a Mohammedan or a Sikh as the case may be. He does not tell you his caste although he has one and you are satisfied with his answer. When he tells you that he is a Muslim, you do not proceed to ask him whether he is a Shiya or Suni; Sheikh or Saiyad; Khatik or Pinjari. When he tells he is a Sikh, you do not ask him whether he is Jat or Roda; Mazbi or Ramdasi. But you are not satisfied, if a person tells you that he is a Hindu. You feel bound to inquire into his caste. Why? Because so essential is caste in the case of a Hindu that without knowing it you do not feel sure what sort of a being he is. That caste has not the same social significance among Non-Hindus as it has among Hindus is clear if you take into consideration the consequences which follow breach of caste. There may be castes among Sikhs and Mohammedans but the Sikhs and the Mohammedans will not outcast a Sikh or a Mohammedan if he broke his caste. Indeed, the very idea of excommunication is foreign to the Sikhs and the Mohammedans. But with the Hindus the case is entirely different. He is sure to be outcastes if he broke caste. This shows the difference in the social significance of caste to Hindus and Non-Hindus. This is the second point of difference. But there is also a third and a more important one. Caste among the non-Hindus has no religious consecration; but among the Hindus most decidedly it has. Among the Non-Hindus, caste is only a practice, not a sacred institution. They did not originate it. With them it is only a survival. They do not regard caste as a religious dogma. Religion compels the Hindus to treat isolation and segregation of castes as a virtue. Religion does not compel the Non-Hindus to take the same attitude towards caste. If Hindus wish to break caste, their religion will come in their way. But it will not be so in the case of Non-Hindus, without caring to know what place caste occupies in their life and whether there are other "organic filaments", which subordinate the feeling of caste to the feeling of community. The sooner the Hindus are cured of this delusion the better.

There is no doubt, in my opinion, that unless you change your social order you can achieve little by way of progress. You cannot mobilize the community either for defence or for offence. You cannot build anything on the foundations of caste. You cannot build up a nation, you cannot build up a morality. Anything that you will build on the foundations of caste will crack and will never be a whole.

The only question that remains to be considered is—How to bring about the reform of the Hindu social order? How to abolish caste? This is a question of supreme importance. There is a view that in the reform of caste, the first step to take, is to abolish sub-castes. This view is based upon the supposition that there is a greater similarity in manners and status between sub-castes than there is between castes.

The real remedy is inter-marriage. Fusion of blood can alone create the feeling of being kith and kin and unless this feeling of kinship, of being kindred, becomes paramount the separatists feeling—the feeling of being aliens—created by Caste will not vanish.

The real remedy for breaking Caste is inter-marriage. Nothing else will serve as the solvent of Caste.

Why is it that a large majority of Hindus do not inter-dine and do not inter-marry? There can be only one answer to this question and it is that inter-dinning and inter-marriage are repugnant to the beliefs and dogmas which the Hindus regard as sacred. Caste is not a physical object like a wall of bricks or a line of barbed wire which prevents the Hindus from co-mingling and which has, therefore, to be pulled down. Caste is a notion, it is a state of the mind. The destruction of Caste does not therefore mean the destruction of a physical barrier. It means a notional change.

In my view, what is wrong is their religion, which has inculcated this notion of Caste. If this is correct, then obviously the enemy, you must grapple with, is not the people who observe Caste, but the Shastras which teach them this religion of Caste. Criticizing and ridiculing people for not inter-dining or inter-marrying or occasionally holding inter-caste dinners and celebrating inter-caste marriages, is a futile method of achieving the desired end. The real remedy is to destroy the belief in the sanctity of the Shastras.

Reformers working for the removal of untouchability including Mahatma Gandhi, do not seem to realize that the acts of the people are merely the results of their beliefs inculcated upon their minds by the Shastras and that people will not change their conduct until they cease to believe in the sanctity of the Shastras on which their conduct is founded.

To agitate for and to organize inter-caste dinners and inter-caste marriages is like forced feeding brought about by artificial means. Make every man and woman free from the thralldom of the Shastras, cleanse their minds of the pernicious notions founded on the Shastras, and he or she will inter-dine and inter-marry, without your telling him or her to do so.

It is no use seeking refuge in quibbles. It is no use telling people that the Shastras do not say what they are believed to say, grammatically read or logically interpreted. What matters is how the Shastras have been understood by the people. You must take the stand that Buddha took. You must take the stand which Guru Nanak took. You must not only discard the Shastras, you must deny their authority, as did Buddha and Nanak. You must have courage to tell the Hindus, that what is wrong with them is their religion—the religion which has produced in them this notion of the sacredness of Caste. Will you show that courage?

The Hindus hold to the sacredness of the social order. Caste has a divine basis. You must therefore destroy the sacredness and divinity with which Caste has become invested. In the last, analysis, this means you must destroy the authority of the Shastras and the Vedas.

Brahmins form the vanguard of the movement for political reform and in some cases also of economic reform. But they are not to be found even as camp-followers in the army raised to break down the barricades of Caste. Is there any hope of the Brahmins ever taking up a lead in the future in this matter? I say no. You may ask why? You may argue that there is no reason why Brahmins should continue to shun social reform. You may argue that the Brahmins know that the bane of Hindu Society is Caste and as an enlightened class could not be expected to be indifferent to its consequences. You may argue that there are secular Brahmins and priestly Brahmins and if the latter do not take up the cudgels on behalf of those who want to break Caste, the former will. All this of course sounds very plausible. But in all this it is forgotten that the break up of the Caste system is bound to affect adversely the Brahmin Caste. Having regard to this, is it reasonable to expect that the Brahmins will ever consent to lead a movement the ultimate result of which is to destroy the power and prestige of the Brahmin Caste? Is it reasonable to expect the secular Brahmins to take part in a movement directed against the priestly Brahmins? In my judgment, it is useless to make a distinction between the secular Brahmins and priestly Brahmins. Both are kith and kin. They are two arms of the same body and one bound to fight for the existence of the other.

A man who is born a Brahmin has much less desire to become a revolutionary. Indeed, to expect a Brahmin to be a revolutionary in matter of social reform is as idle as to expect the British Parliament, as was said by Leslie Stephen, to pass an Act requiring all blue-eyed babies to be murdered.

Some of you will say that it is a matter of small concern whether the Brahmins come forward to lead the movement against Caste or whether they do not. To take this view is in my judgment to ignore the part played by the intellectual class in the community. Whether you accept the theory of the great man as the maker of history or whether you do not, this much you will have to concede that in every country the intellectual class is the most influential class, if not the governing class. The intellectual class is the class which can foresee, it is the class which can advise and give lead. In no country does the mass of the people live the life of intelligent thought and action. It is largely imitative and follows the intellectual class. There is no exaggeration in saying that the entire destiny of a country depends upon its intellectual class. If the intellectual class is honest, independent and disinterested it can be trusted to take the initiative and give a proper lead when a crisis arises. It is true that intellect by itself is not virtue. It is only a means and the use of means depends upon the ends which an intellectual person pursues. An intellectual man can be a good man but he can easily be a rogue. Similarly an intellectual class may be a band of high-souled persons, ready to help, ready to emancipate erring humanity or it may easily be a gang of crooks or a body of advocates of a narrow clique from which it draws its support. You may think it a pity that the intellectual class in India is simply another name for the Brahmin caste. You may regret that the two are one; that the existence of the intellectual class should be bound with one single caste, that this intellectual class should share the interest of that caste, rather than of the interest of the country. All this may be very regrettable. But the fact remains, that the Brahmins form the intellectual class of the Hindus. It is not only an intellectual class but it is a class which is held in great reverence by the rest of the Hindus. The Hindus are taught that the Brahmins are *Bhudevas* (God on earth) *Varnanam Brahmin guru*. The Hindus are taught the Brahmins alone can be their teacher. Manu says, "If it be asked specially mentioned, the answer is that which Brahmins who are Shishthas propound shall doubtless have legal force."

When such an intellectual class, which holds the rest of the community in its grip, is opposed to the reform of Caste, the chances of success in a movement for the break-up of the Caste system appear to me very, very remote.

The second reason, why I say the task is impossible, will be clear if you will bear in mind that the Caste system has two aspects. In one of its aspects, it divides men into separate communities. In its second aspect, it places these communities in a graded order one above the other in social status. Each caste takes its pride and its consolation in the fact that in the scale of castes it is above some other caste. As an outward mark of this gradation, there is also a gradation of social and religious rights technically spoken of an *Ashtadhikaras* and *Sanskaras*. The higher the grade of a caste, the greater the number of these rights and the lower the grade, the lesser their number. Now this gradation, this scaling of castes, makes it impossible to organize a common front against the Caste System. If a caste claims the right to inter-dine and inter-marry with another caste placed above it, it is frozen, instantly it is told by mischief-mongers, and there are many Brahmins amongst such mischief-mongers, that it will have to concede inter-dining and inter-marriage with castes below it! All are slave of the Caste System. But all the slaves are not equal in status.

Chaturvarnya—Varnashram

In his Presidential address Dr. Babasaheb Ambedkar expressed his views on varnashram as given below:

The protagonists of Chaturvarnya take great care to point out that their Chaturvarnya is based not on birth but on *guna* (worth). At the outset, I must confess that notwithstanding the worth-basis of this Chaturvarnya, it is an ideal to which I cannot reconcile myself. In the first place, if under the Chaturvarnya of the Arya Samajists an individual is to take his place in the Hindu Society according to his worth. I do not understand why the Arya Samajists insist upon labeling men as Brahmin, Kshatriya, Vaishya and Shudra. A learned man would be honoured without his being labeled a Brahmin. A soldier would be respected without his being designated a Kshatriya. If European society honours its soldiers and its servants without giving them permanent labels, why should Hindu Society find it difficult to do so is a question, which Arya Samajists have not cared to consider. There is another objection to the continuance of these labels. All reform consists in a change in the notions, sentiment and mental attitudes of the people towards men and things. It is common experience that certain names become associated with certain notions and sentiments, which determine a person's attitude towards men and things. The names, Brahmin, Kshtriya, Vaishya and Shudra, are names which are associated with a definite and fixed notion in the mind of every Hindu. That notion is that of a hierarchy based on birth. So long as these names continue, Hindus will continue to think of the Brahmin, Kshatriya, Vaishya and Shudra as hierarchical divisions of high and low, based on birth, and act accordingly. The Hindu must be made to unlearn all this. But how can this happen if the old labels remain and continue to recall to his mind old notions. If new notions are to be inculcated in the minds of people it is necessary to give them new names. To continue the old name is to make the reform futile. To allow this Chaturvarnya, based on worth to be designated by such stinking labels of Brahmin, Kshatriya, Vaishya, Shudra, indicative of social division based on birth, is snare.

To me this Chaturvarnya with its old labels is utterly repellent and my whole being rebels against it. But I do not wish to rest my objection to Chaturvarnya on mere grounds of sentiments. There are more solid grounds on which I rely for my opposition to it. A close examination of this ideal has convinced me that as a system of social organization, Chaturvarnya is impracticable, harmful and has turned out to be a miserable failure. From a practical point of view, the system of Chaturvarnya raises several difficulties which its protagonists do not seem to have taken into account. The principle underlying caste is fundamentally different but they are also fundamentally opposed. The former is based on worth. How are you going to compel people who have acquired a higher status based on birth without reference to their worth to vacate that status? How are you going to compel people to recognize the status due to a man in accordance with his worth, who is occupying a lower status based on his birth? For this you must first break up the Caste System, in order to be able to establish the Varna system. How are you going to reduce the four thousand castes; based on birth, to the four Varnas, based on worth? This is the first difficulty which the protagonists of the Chaturvarnya must grapple with. There is a second difficulty which the protagonists of Chaturvarnya must grapple with, if they wish to make the establishment of Chaturvarnya a success. Ram Raj was a Raj based on Chaturvarnya.

Assuming that Chaturvarnya is practicable, I contend that is the most vicious system. That the Brahmins should cultivate knowledge, that the Kshtriya should bear arms, that the Vaishya should trade and that the Shudra should serve sounds as though it was a system of division of labour. Whether the theory was intended to state that the Shudra need not or that whether it was intended to lay down that he must not, is an interesting question. The defenders of Chaturvarnya give it the first meaning. They say, why should the Shudra need trouble to acquire wealth, when the three Varnas are there to support him? Why need the Shudra bother to take to education when there is the Brahmin to whom he can go when the occasion for reading or writing arises? Why need the Shudra worry to arm himself because there is the Kshatriya to protect him? The theory of Chaturvarnya, understood in this sense, may be said to look upon the Shudra as the ward and the three Varnas as his guardians. Thus interpreted, it is a simple, elevating and alluring theory. Assuming this to be the correct views of the underlying conception of Chaturvarnya, it seems to me that the system is neither foolproof nor knave-proof. What is to happen, if the Brahmins, Vaishyas and Kshatriyas fail to pursue knowledge, to engage in economic enterprise and to be efficient soldier which are their respective functions?

The three classes, Brahmins, Kshatriyas and Vaishyas although not very happy in their mutual relationship managed to work by compromise. The Brahmin flattered the Kshatriya and both let the Vaishya live in order to be able to live upon him, but the three agreed to beat down the Shudra. He was not allowed to acquire wealth lest he should be independent of the three Varnas. He was prohibited from acquiring knowledge lest he should keep a steady vigil regarding his interests. He was prohibited from bearing arms lest he should have meant to rebel against their authority. That this is how the Shudras were treated by the Tryavarnikas is evidenced by the Laws of Manu. There is no code of laws more infamous regarding social rights than the Laws of Manu. Any instance from anywhere of social injustice must pale before it. Why have the mass of people tolerated the social evils to which they have been subjected? There have been social revolutions in other countries of the world, why have there not been social revolutions in India is a question which has incessantly troubled me. There is only one answer, which I can give and it is that the lower classes of Hindus have been completely disabled for direct action on account of this wretched system of Chaturvarnya. They could not bear arms and without arms they could not rebel. They were all ploughmen or rather condemned to be ploughmen and they never were all ploughmen or rather condemned to be ploughmen and they never were allowed to convert their ploughshare into swords. They had no bayonets and therefore everyone who chose could and did sit upon them. On account of the Chaturvarnya, they could receive no education. They could not think out or know the way to their salvation. They were condemned to be lowly and not knowing the way of escape and not having the means of escape, they become reconciled to eternal servitude, which they accepted as their inescapable fate.

There cannot be a more degrading system of social organization than the Chaturvarnya. It is the system which deadens, paralyses and cripples the people from helpful activity. This is no exaggeration. History bears ample evidence. There is only one period in Indian history which is a period of freedom, greatness and glory. That is the period of the Mourya Empire.

At all other times the country suffered from defeat and darkness. But the Mourya period was a period when Chaturvarnya was completely annihilated, when the Shudras, who constituted the mass of the people, came into their own and became the rulers of the country. The period of defeat and darkness is the period when Chaturvarnya flourished to the damnation of the greater part of the people of the country.

Chaturvarnya is not new. It is as old as the Vedas. That is one of the reasons why we are asked by the Arya Samajists to consider its claims. Judging from the past as a system of social organization, it has been tried and it has failed. How many times have the Brahmins annihilated the seed of the Kshatriyas! How many times have the Kshatriyas annihilated the Brahmins! The Mahabharata and the Puranas are all full of incidents of the strife between the Brahmins and the Kshatriyas. They even quarreled over such petty question as to who should salute first, as to who should give way first, the Brahmins or the Kshatriyas, when who met in the street. Not only was the Brahmin an eyesore to the Kshatriya and the Kshatriya an eyesore to the Brahmin, it seems that the Kshatriyas had become tyrannical and the masses, disarmed as they were under the system of Chaturvarnya, were praying Almighty God for relief from their tyranny. The Bhagwat tells us very definitely that Krishna had taken Avtar for one sacred purpose and that was to annihilate the Kshatriyas. With these instances of rivalry and enmity between the different Varnas before us, I do not understand how any one can hold out Chaturvarnya as an ideal to be aimed at or as a pattern, on which the Hindu Society should be remodeled.

Manu Smriti

Can you appeal to reason and ask the Hindus to discard Caste as being contrary to reason? That raises the question: is a Hindu free to follow his reason? Manu has laid down three sanctions to which every Hindu must conform in the matter of his behaviour. Here there is no place for reason to play its part. A Hindu must follow either *Veda*, *Smriti* or *Sadachar*. He cannot follow anything else. In the first place how are the texts of the *Vedas* and *Smritis* to be interpreted whenever any doubt arises regarding their meaning? On this important question the view of Manu is quite definite. He says: "According to this rule, rationalism as a canon of interpreting the *Vedas* and *Smritis*, is absolutely condemned. It is regarded to be as wicked as atheism and the punishment provided for it is ex-communication. Thus, where a matter is covered by the *Veda* or the *Smriti*, a Hindu cannot resort to rational thinking. Even when there is a conflict between *Vedas* and *Smritis* on matters on which they have given a positive injunction, the solution is not left to reason. When there is a conflict between two *Shrutis*, both are to be regarded as of equal authority. Either of them may be followed. No attempt is to be made to find out which of the two accords with reason." This is made clear by *Manu*.

Vindication of Caste by Mahatma Gandhi

As a reaction to what Ambedkar said in his address, Mahatma Gandhi wrote two articles in *Harijan* which are reproduced below:

The readers will recall the fact that Dr. Ambedkar was to have presided last May at the annual conference of the Jat-Pat-Todak Mandal of Lahore. But the conference itself was cancelled because Dr. Ambedkar's address was found by the Reception Committee to be unacceptable. How far a Reception Committee is justified in rejecting a President of its choice because of his address that may be objectionable to it is open to question. The Committee knew Dr. Ambedkar's views on caste and the Hindu scriptures. They knew also that he had in unequivocal terms decided to give up Hinduism. Nothing less than the address that Dr. Ambedkar had prepared was to be expected from him. The committee appears to have deprived the public of an opportunity of listening to the original views of a man, who has carved out for himself a unique position in society. Whatever label he wears in future, Dr. Ambedkar is not the man to allow himself to be forgotten.

Dr. Ambedkar was not going to be beaten by the Reception Committee. He has answered their rejection of him by publishing the address at his own expense. He has priced it at 8 annas, I would suggest a reduction to 2 annas or at least 4 annas.

No reformer can ignore the address. The orthodox will gain by reading it. This is not to say that the address is not open to objection. It has to be read only because it is open to serious objection. Dr. Ambedkar is a challenge to Hinduism. Brought up as a Hindu, educated by a Hindu potentate, he has become so disgusted with the so-called Savarna Hindus for the treatment that he and his people have received at their hands that he proposes to leave not only them but the very religion that is his and their common heritage. He has transferred to that religion, his disgust against a part of its professors.

But this is not to be wondered at. After all, one can only judge a system or an institution by the conduct of its representatives. What is more. Dr. Ambedkar found that the vast majority of Savarna Hindus had not only conducted themselves inhumanly against those of their fellow religionists, whom they classed as untouchables, but they had based their conduct on the authority of their scriptures, and when he began to search them he had found ample warrant for their beliefs in untouchability and all its implications. The author of the address has quoted chapter and verse in proof of his three-fold indictment—inhuman conduct itself, the unabashed justification for it on the part of the perpetrators, and the subsequent discovery that the justification was warranted by their scriptures.

No Hindu who prizes his faith above life itself can afford to underrate the importance of this indictment. Dr. Ambedkar is not alone in his disgust. He is its most uncompromising exponent and one of the ablest among them. He is certainly the most irreconcilable among them. Thank God, in the front rank of the leaders, he is singularly alone and as yet but a representative of a very small minority. But what he says is voiced with more or less vehemence by many leaders belonging to the depressed classes. Only the latter, for instance Rao Bahadur M.C. Rajah and Dewan Bahadur Srinivasan, not only do not threaten to give up Hinduism but find enough warmth in it to compensate for the shameful persecution to which the vast mass of Harijans are exposed.

But the fact of many leaders remaining in the Hindu fold is no warrant for disregarding what Dr. Ambedkar has to say. The

Savarnas have to correct their belief and their conduct. Above all those who are by their learning and influence among the Savarnas have to give an authoritative interpretation of the scriptures. The question that Dr. Ambedkar's indictment suggest are:

(1) What are the scriptures?

(2) Are all the printed texts to be regarded as an integral part of them or is any part of them to be rejected as unauthorized interpolations?

(3) What is the answer of such accepted and expurgated scriptures on the question of untouchability, caste, equality of status, inter-dining and intermarriages?

These have been all examined by Dr. Ambedkar in his address.

(*Harijan*, July 11, 1936)

In his second article Gandhi wrote:

The *Vedas*, *Upanishads*, *Smritis* and *Puranas* including Ramayana and Mahabharata are the Hindu Scriptures. Nor is this a finite list. Every age or even generation has added to the list. It follows, therefore, that everything printed or even found handwritten is not scripture. The Smritis for instance contain much that can never be accepted as the word of God. Thus, many of the texts that Dr. Ambedkar quotes from the Smritis cannot be accepted as authentic. The scriptures, properly so-called, can only be concerned with eternal varieties and must appeal to any conscience i.e. any heart whose eyes of understanding are opened. Nothing can be accepted as the word of God which cannot be tested by reason or be capable of being spiritually experienced. And even when you have an expurgated edition of the scriptures, you will need their interpreter? Not learned men surely. Learning there must be. But religion does not live by it. It lives in the experiences of its saints and seers, in their lives and sayings. When all the most learned commentators of the scriptures are utterly forgotten, the accumulated experience of the sages and saints will abide and be an inspiration for ages to come.

Caste has nothing to do with religion. It is a custom whose origin I do not know and do not need to know for the satisfaction of my spiritual hunger. But I do know that it is harmful both to spiritual and national growth. *Varna* and *Ashrama* are institutions which have nothing to do with castes. The law of *Varna* teaches us that we have each one of us to earn our bread by following the ancestral calling. It defines not our rights but our duties. It necessarily has reference to calling that are conducive to the welfare of humanity and to no other. It also follows that there is no calling too low and none too high. All are good, lawful and absolutely equal in status. The callings of a Brahmin—spiritual teacher—and a scavenger are equal, and their due performance carries equal merit before God and at one time seems to have carried identical reward before man. Both were entitled to their livelihood and no more. Indeed one traces even now in the villages the faint lines of this healthy operation of the law. Living in Segaon with its population of 600, I do not find a great disparity between the earnings of different tradesmen including Brahmins. I find too that real Brahmins are to be found even in these degenerate days who are living on alms freely given to them and are giving freely of what they have of spiritual treasures. It would be wrong and improper to judge the law of *Varna* by its caricature in the lives of men who profess to belong to a *Varna*, whilst they openly commit a breach of its only operative rule. Arrogation of a superior status by and of the *Varna* over another is a denial of the law. And there is nothing in the law of *Varna* to warrant a belief in untouchability. (The essence of Hinduism is contained in its enunciation of one and only God as Truth and its bold acceptance of Ahimsa as the law of the human family.)

I am aware that my interpretation of Hinduism will be disputed by many besides Dr. Ambedkar. That does not affect my position. It is an interpretation by which I have lived for nearly half a century and according to which I have endeavored to the best of my ability to regulate my life.

In my opinion the profound mistake that Dr. Ambedkar has made in his address is to pick out the texts of doubtful authenticity and value and the state of degraded Hindus who are not fit specimens of the faith they so woefully misrepresent. Judged by the standard applied by Dr. Ambedkar, every known living faith will probably fail.

In his able address, the learned Doctor has over proved his case. Can a religion that was professed by Chaitanya, Jnyandeo, Tukaram, Tiruvalluvar, Ramkrishna Parmahansa, Raja Ram Mohan Roy, Maharshi Devendranath Tagore, Vivekanand and host of others who might be easily mentioned, so utterly devoid of merit as is made out in Dr. Ambedkar's address? A religion has to be judged not by its worst specimens but by the best it might have produced. For that and that alone can be used as the standard to aspire to, if not to improve upon.

(*Harijan*, July 18, 1936)

Ambedkar's Reply to Gandhi's Articles

I appreciate greatly the honour done me by the Mahatma in taking notice in his *Harijan* of the speech on Caste which I had prepared for the Jat-Pat-Todak Mandal. From a perusal of his review of my speech, it is clear that the Mahatma completely dissents from the views I have expressed on the subject of Caste. I am not in the habit of entering into controversy with my opponents unless there are special reasons which compel me to act otherwise. Had my opponent been some mean and obscure person I would not have pursued him, but my opponent being the Mahatma himself I feel I must attempt to meet the case to the contrary which he has sought to put forth. While I appreciate the honour he has done me, I must confess to a sense of surprise on finding that of all the persons the Mahatma should accuse me of a desire to seek publicity as he seems to do when he suggests that in publishing the undelivered speech my object was to see that I was not "forgotten". Whatever the Mahatma may choose to say my object in publishing the speech was to provoke the Hindus to think and take stock of their position. I have never hankered for publicity and if I may say so, I have more publicity that I wish or need. But supposing it was out of the motive of gaining publicity that I printed the speech who could cast a stone at me? Surely not those, who like the Mahatma live in glass houses.

Motive apart, what has the Mahatma to say on the question raised by me in the speech? First of all any one who reads my speech will realize that the Mahatma has entirely missed the issues raised by me and that the issues he has raised are not the issues that arise out of what he is pleased to all my indictment of the Hindus. The principal points which I have tried to make out in my speech may be catalogued as follows: (1) That caste has ruined the Hindus; (2) That the reorganization of the Hindu society on the basis of Chaturvarnya is impossible because the *Varnavyavastha* is like a leaky pot or like a man running at the nose. It is incapable of sustaining itself by its own virtue and has an inherent tendency to degenerate into a caste system unless there is a legal sanction behind it which can be enforced against every one transgressing his *Verna*; (3) That the reorganization of the Hindu Society on the basis of Chaturvarnya is harmful because the effect of the *Varnavyavastha* is to degrade the masses by denying them the right to be armed; (4) That the Hindu society must be reorganized on a religious basis which would recognize the principles of Liberty, Equality and Fraternity; (5) That in order to achieve this object the sense of religious sanctity behind Caste *Varna* must be destroyed; (6) That the sanctity of Caste and *Varna* can be destroyed only by discarding the divine authority of the Shastras. It will be noticed that the questions raised by the Mahatma are absolutely beside the point and show that main argument of the speech was lost upon him.

Let me examine the substance of the points made by the Mahatma. The first point made by the Mahatma is that the texts cited by me are not authentic. I confess I am no authority on this matter. But I should like to state that the texts cited by me are all taken from the writings of the late Mr. Tilak who was a recognized authority on the Sanskrit language and on the Hindu *Shastras*. His second point is that these *Shastras* should be interpreted not by the learned but the saints and that, as the saints have understood them, the *Shastras* do not support Caste and Untouchability. As regards the first point what I like to ask the Mahatma is what does it avail to any one if the texts are interpolations and if they have been differently interpreted by the saints? The masses do not make any distinction between texts which are genuine and texts which are interpolations. The masses do not know what the texts are. They are too illiterate to know the contents of the *Shastras*. They have believed what they have been told and what they have been told is that the

Shastras do enjoin as a religious duty the observance of Caste and Untouchability.

With regard to the saints, one must admit that howsoever different and elevating their teachings may have been as compared to those of the merely learned have been lamentably ineffective. They have been inffective for two reasons. Firstly, none of the saints ever attacked the Caste System. On the contrary, they were staunch believers in the System of Castes. Most of them lived and died as members of the castes which they respectively belonged. So passionately attached was Jnyandeo to his status as a Brahmin fraternity. And even the saint Eknath who now figures in the film "Dharmatma" as a hero for having shown courage to touch the untouchables and dine with them, did so not because he was opposed to Caste and Untouchability but because he felt that the pollution caused thereby could be washed away by a bath in the sacred waters of the river Ganges. The saints have never according to my study carried on a campaign against Caste and Untouchability. They were not concerned with the struggle between men. They were concerned with the relation between man and God. They did not preach that all men were equal. They preached that all men were equal in the eyes of God—a very different and a very innocuous proposition which nobody can find difficult to preach or dangerous to believe in. The second reason why the teachings of the saints proved inflective was because masses have been taught that a saint might break Caste but the common man must not. A saint therefore never became an example to follow. He always remained a pious man to be honoured. That the masses have remained staunch believers in Caste and Untouchability shows that the pious lives and noble sermons of the saints have had no effect on their life and conduct as against the teachings of the *Shastras*. Thus it can be a matter of no consolation that there were saints or that there is a Mahatma who understands the *Shastras* differently from the learned few or ignorant many. That the masses hold different views of the *Shastras* is fact which should and must be reckoned with. How is that to be dealt with except by denouncing the authority of the *Shastras*, which to continue govern their conduct, is a question which the Mahatma has not considered. But whatever the plan the Mahatma puts forth as an effective means to free the masses from the teachings of the *Shastras*, he must accept that the pious life led by one good Samaritan may be very elevating to himself but in India, with the attitude the common man has to saints and to Mahatmas—to honour but not to follow—one cannot make much out of it.

The third point made by the Mahatma is that a religion professed by Chaitanya, Jnyandeo, Tukaram, Tiruvalluvar, Ramkrishna Parmahansa, etc. cannot be devoid of merit as is made out by me and that a religion has to be judged not by its worst specimens but by the best it might have produced. I agree with every word of this statement. But I do not quite understand what the Mahatma wishes to prove thereby. That religion should be judged not by its worst specimens but by its best is true enough but does it dispose of the matter? I say it does not. The question still remains—why the worst number so many and the best so few? To my mind there are two conceivable answers to this question: (1) That the worst by reason of some original perversity of theirs are morally uneducable and are therefore incapable of making the remotest approach to the religious ideal. Or (2) That the religious ideal is a wholly wrong ideal which has given a wrong moral twist to the lives of the many and that the best have become best in spite of the wrong ideal—in fact by giving to the wrong twist a turn in the right direction. Of these two explanations I am not prepared to accept the first and I am sure that even the Mahatma will not insist upon the contrary. To my mind the second is the only logical and reasonable explanation unless the Mahatma has a third alternative to explain why the worst are so many and the best so few. If the second is the only explanation then obviously the argument of the Mahatma that a religion should be judged by its best followers carries us nowhere except to pity the lot of the many who have gone wrong because they have been made to worship wrong ideals.

The argument of the Mahatma that Hinduism would be tolerable if only many were to follow the example of the saints is fallacious for another reason. By citing the names of such illustrious persons as Chaitanya, etc. what the Mahatma seems to me to suggest in its broadest and simplest form is that

Hindu society can be made tolerable and even happy without any persuaded to follow a high standard of morality in their dealings with the low caste Hindus. I am totally opposed to this kind of ideology. I can respect those of the caste Hindus who try to realize a high social ideal in their life. Without such men India would be an uglier and a less happy place to live in than it is. But nonetheless anyone who relies on an attempt to turn the members of the caste Hindus into better men by improving their personal character is in my judgment wasting his energy and hugging an illusion. Can personal character make the maker of armaments a good man, i.e. a man who will sell shells that will not burst and gas that will not poison? If it cannot, how can you accept personal character to make a man loaded with the consciousness of Caste, a good man, i.e. a man who would treat his fellows as his friends and equals? To be true to himself he must deal with his fellows either as a superior or inferior according as the case may be; at any rate, differently from his own caste fellows. He can never be expected to deal with his fellows as his kinsmen and equals. As a matter of fact, a Hindu does treat all those who are not of his Caste as though they were aliens, who could be discriminated against with impunity and against whom any fraud or trick may be practiced without shame. This is to say that there can be a better or a worse Hindu. But a good Hindu there cannot be. This is so not because there is anything wrong with his personal character. In fact what is wrong is the entire basis of his relationship to his fellows. The best men cannot be moral if the basis of relationship between them and their fellows is fundamentally a wrong relationship. To a slave his master may be better or worse. But there cannot be a good man. The same applies to the relationship between high caste and low caste. To a low caste man a high caste man can be better or worse as compared to other high caste men. A high caste man cannot be a good man in so far as he must have a low caste man to distinguish him as high caste man. It cannot be good to a low caste man to be conscious that there is a high caste man above him. I have argued in my speech that a society based on *Varna* or Caste is a society which is based on a wrong relationship. I had hoped that the Mahatma would attempt to demolish my argument. But instead of doing that he has merely reiterated his belief in Chaturvarnya without disclosing the ground on which it is based.

Does the Mahatma practise what he preaches? One does not like to make personal reference in an argument which is general in its application. But when one preaches a doctrine and holds it as a dogma there is a curiosity to know how far he practises what he preaches. It may be that his failure to practise is due to the innate hypocrisy of the man. In any case he exposes his conduct to examination and I must not be blamed if I asked how far has the Mahatma attempted to realize his ideal in his own case. The Mahatma is a Bania by birth. His ancestors had abandoned trading in favour of ministership which is a calling of the Brahmins. In his own life, before he became a Mahatma, when occasion came for him to chose his career he preferred law to scales. On abandoning law he became half saint and half politician. He has never touched trading which is his ancestral calling. His youngest son—I take one who is a faithful follower of his father—born a Vaishya has married to Brahmin's daughter and has chosen to serve a newspaper magnate. The Mahatma is not known to have condemned him for not following his ancestral calling. It may be wrong and uncharitable to judge an ideal by its worst specimens. But surely the Mahatma as a specimen has no better and if he even fails to realize the ideal then the ideal must be an impossible ideal quite opposed to the practical instincts of man. Students of Carlyle know that he often spoke on a subject before he thought about it. I wonder whether such has not been the case with the Mahatma in regard to the subject matter of Caste. Otherwise certain questions which occur to me would not have escaped him. When can a calling be deemed to have become an ancestral calling so as to make it binding on a man? Must man follow ancestral calling even if it does not suit his capacities, even when it has ceased to be profitable? Must a man live by his ancestral calling even if he finds it to be immoral? If every one must pursue his ancestral calling then it must follow that a man must continue to be a pimp because his grandfather was a pimp and a woman must continue to be a prostitute because her grandmother was a prostitute. Is the Mahatma prepared to accept the logical conclusion of his doctrine? To me his ideal of following one's ancestral calling is not only an impossible and impractical ideal, but it is also morally an indefensible ideal.

The Mahatma sees great virtue in a Brahmin remaining a Brahmin all his life. Leaving aside the fact there are many Brahmins who do not like to remain Brahmins all their lives. What can we say about those Brahmins who have clung to their ancestral calling of priesthood? Do they do so from any faith in the virtue of the principle of ancestral calling or do they do so from motives of filthy lucre? The Mahatma does not seem to concern himself with such queries. He is satisfied that these are "real Brahmins who are living on alms freely given to them and giving freely what they have of spiritual treasures". This is how a hereditary Brahmin priest appears to the Mahatma—a carrier also be drawn. A Brahmin can be a priest to Vishnu—the God of Love. He can be a priest to Shankar—the God of Destruction. He can be a priest at Buddha Gaya worshipping Buddha—the greatest teacher of mankind who taught the noblest doctrine of Love. He also can be a priest to Kali, the Goddess, who must have a daily sacrifice of an animal to satisfy her thirst for blood; He will be a priest of the temple of Rama—the Kshatriya God! He will also be a priest of the Temple of Parshuram, the God who took Avatar to destroy the Kshatriyas! He can be a priest to Brahma, the Creator of the world. He can be a priest to a Pir whose God Allah will not brook the claim of Brahma to share his spiritual domination over the world! No one can say that this is a picture which is not true to life. If this is a true picture one does not know what attributes are so antagonistic that no honest man can be a devotee to all of them. The Hindus rely upon this extraordinary phenomenon as evidence of the greatest virtue of their religion—namely its catholicity, its spirit of toleration. As against this facile views, it can be urged that what is toleration and catholicity may be really nothing more creditable than indifference or flaccid latitudinarianism. These two attitudes are hard to distinguish in their outer seeming. But they are so vitally unlike in their real quality that no one who examines them closely can mistake one for the other. That a man is ready to render homage to many Gods and Goddesses may be cited as evidence of his tolerant spirit. But can it not also be evidence of insincerity born of a desire to serve the times? I am sure that this toleration is merely insincerity. If this view is well founded, one may ask what spiritual treasure can there be with a person who is ready to be a priest and a devotee to any deity which it serves his purpose to worship and to adore? Not only must such a person be deemed to be bankrupt of all spiritual treasures but for him to practice so elevating a profession as that of a priest simply because it is ancestral, without faith, without belief, merely as a mechanical process handed down from father to son, is not a conversation of virtue; it is really the prostitution of a noble profession which is not other than the service of religion.

Why does the Mahatma cling to the theory of every one following his or her ancestral calling? He gives his reasons nowhere. But there must be some reason although he does not care to avow it. Years ago writing on "Caste versus Class" in his *Young India* he argued that Caste System was better than Class System on the ground that caste was the best possible adjustment of social stability. If that be the reason why the Mahatma clings to the theory of every one following his or her ancestral calling, then he is clinging to a false view of social life. Everybody wants social stability and some adjustment must be made in the relationship between individuals and classes in order that stability may be had. But two things, I am sure nobody wants. One thing nobody wants static relationship, something that is unalterable, something that is fixed for all times. Stability is wanted but not at the cost of change when change is imperative. Second thing nobody wants is mere adjustment. Adjustment is wanted but not at the sacrifice of social justice. Can it be said that the adjustment of social relationship on the basis of caste i.e. on the basis of each to his hereditary calling avoids these two evils? I am convinced that it does not. Far from being the best possible adjustment I have no doubt that it is of the worst possible kind inasmuch as it offends against both the canons of social adjustment—namely fluidity and equity.

Some might think that the Mahatma has made much progress inasmuch as he now only believes in *Varna* and does not believe in Caste. It is true that there was a time when the Mahatma was a full-blooded and a blue-blooded Sanatani Hindu. He believed in the *Vedas*, the *Upanishads*, the *Puranas* and all that goes by the name of Hindu scriptures and therefore in avatars and rebirth. He believed in Caste and defended it with the vigour of the orthodox. He condemned the cry for inter-dining, inter-drinking and inter-marrying and argued that restraints about inter-dining to a great extent "helped the cultivation of will-power and the conservation of certain social virtue". It is good that he has repudiated this sanctimonious nonsense and admitted that caste "is harmful both to spiritual and national growth," and may be, his son's marriage outside his caste has had something to do with this change of view. But has the Mahatma really progressed? What is the nature of the *Varna* for which the Mahatma stands? Is it the *Vedic* conception as commonly understood and preached by Swami Dayanand Saraswati and his followers, the Arya Samjists? The essence of the *Vedic* conception of *Varna* is the pursuit of a calling which is appropriate to one's natural aptitude. The essence of the Mahatma's conception of *Varna* is the pursuit of ancestral calling irrespective of natural aptitude. What is the difference between Caste and *Varna* as understood by the Mahatma? I find none. As defined by the Mahatma, *Varna* becomes merely a different name for Caste for the simple reason that it is the same essence—namely pursuit of ancestral calling. Far from making progress the Mahatma has suffered retrogression. By putting this interpretation upon the *Vedic* conception of *Varna* he has really made ridiculous what was sublime. While I reject the *Vedic Varnavyavastha* for reasons given in the speech I must admit that the *Vedic* theory of Varna as interpreted by Swami Dayanand and some others is a sensible and an inoffensive thing. It did not admit birth as determining factor in fixing the place of an individual in society. It only recognized worth. The Mahatma's view of *Varna* not only makes nonsense of the *Vedic Varna* but it makes it an abominable thing. *Varna* and Caste are two very different concepts. It is based on the principle of each according to his worthwhile Caste is based on the principle of each according to his birth. The two are as distinct as chalk is from cheese. In fact there is an antithesis between the two. If the

Mahatma believes as he does in every one following his or her ancestral calling, then most certainly he is advocating the Caste System and that in calling it the *Varna* System he is not only guilty of terminological inexactitude, but he is causing confusion worse confounded. I am sure that all his confusion is due to the fact that the Mahatma has no definite and clear conception as to what is *Varna* and what is Caste and as to the necessity of either for the conservation of Hinduism. He has said and one hoped that he will not find some mystic reason to change his views that caste is not the essence of Hinduism. Does he regard Varna as the essence of Hinduism? One cannot as yet give any categorical answer. Readers of his article on "Dr. Ambedkar's Indictment" will answer "No". In that article he does not say that the dogma of *Varna* is an essential part of the creed of Hinduism. Far from making *Varna* the essence of Hinduism he says "the essence of Hinduism is contained in its enunciation of one and only God as Truth and its bold acceptance of Ahimsa as the law of the human family". But the readers of his article in reply to Mr. Sant Ram will say "Yes". In that article he says "How can a Muslim remain one if he rejects the Quran, or a Christian remain as Christian if he rejects the Bible? If Caste and Varna are convertible terms and if *Varna* is an integral part of the Shastras which define Hinduism I do not know how a person who rejects Caste, i.e. Varna can call himself a Hindu?" Why this prevarication? Why does the Mahatma hedge? Whom does he want to please? Has the saint failed to sense the truth? Or does the politician stand in the way of the Saint? The real reason why the Mahatma is suffering from this confusion is probably to be traced to two sources. The first is the temperament of the Mahatma. He has almost in everything the simplicity of the child with the child's capacity for self-deception. Like a child he can believe in anything he wants to believe. We must therefore wait till such time as it pleases the Mahatma to abandon his faith in *Varna* as it has pleased him to abandon his faith in *Varna* as it has pleased him to abandon his faith in Caste. The second source of confusion is the double role which the Mahatma wants to play—of a Mahatma and a Politician. As a Mahatma he may be trying to spiritualize Politics. Whether he has succeeded in it or not Politics have certainly commercialized him. A politician must know that Society cannot bear the whole truth and that he must not speak the whole truth; if he is speaking the whole truth it is bad for his politics. The reason he is afraid that if he opposed them he will lose his place in politics. Whatever may be source of this confusion the Mahatma must be told that he is deceiving himself and also deceiving the people by preaching Caste under the name of *Varna*.

The Mahatma says that the standards I have applied to test Hindus and Hinduism are too severe and that judged by those standards every known living faith will probably fail. The complaint that my standards are high may be true. But the question is not whether they are high or whether they are low. The question is whether they are the right standards to apply. A people and their Religion must be judged by social standards based on social ethics. No other standards would have any meaning if religion is held to be a necessary good for the well-being of the people. Now I maintain that the standards I have applied to test Hindus and Hinduism are the most appropriate standards and that I know of none that are better. The conclusion that every known religion would fail if tested by my standards may be true. But this fact should not give the Mahatma as the champion of Hindus and Hinduism a ground for comfort any more than the existence of one madman should give comfort to another madman or the existence of one criminal should give comfort to another criminal. I like to assure the Mahatma that it is not the mere failure of the Hindus and Hinduism which has produced in me the feelings of disgust and contempt with which I am charged. I realize that the world is a very imperfect world and any one who wants to live in it must bear with its imperfections. But while I am prepared to bear with the imperfections and shortcomings of the society in which I may be destined to labour, I feel I should not consent to live in a society which cherishes wrong ideals or a society which having right ideals will not consent to bring its social life in conformity with those ideals. If I am disgusted with Hindus and Hinduism it is because I am convinced that they cherish wrong ideals and live a wrong social life. My quarrel with Hindus and Hinduism is not over the imperfections of their social conduct. It is much more fundamental. It is over their ideals.

Hindu society seems to me to stand in need of a moral regeneration which it is dangerous to postpone. And the question is who can determine and control this moral regeneration? Obviously only those who have undergone an intellectual regeneration and those who are honest enough to have the courage of their convictions born of intellectual emancipation. Judged by this standard the Hindu leaders who count are in my opinion quite unfit for the task. It is impossible to say that they have undergone the preliminary intellectual regeneration. If they had undergone an intellectual regeneration they would neither delude themselves in the simple way of the untaught multitude nor would they take advantage of the primitive ignorance of others as one sees them doing. Notwithstanding the crumbling state of Hindu society these leaders will nevertheless unblushingly appeal to ideals of the past which have in every way ceased to have any connection with the present; which however suitable they might have been in the days of their origin have now become a warning rather than a guide. They still have a mystic respect for the earlier forms which make them disinclined—nay opposed to any examination of the foundations of their Society. The Hindu masses are of course incredibly heedless in the formation of their beliefs. But so are the Hindu leaders. And what is worse is that these Hindu leaders become filled with an illicit passion for their beliefs when any one proposes to rob them of their companionship. The Mahatma is no exception. The Mahatma appears not to believe in thinking. He prefers to follow the saints. Like a conservative with his reverence for consecrated notions he is afraid that if he once starts thinking, many ideals and institutions to which he clings will be doomed. One must sympathize with him. For every act of independent thinking puts some portion of apparently stable world in peril. But it is equally true that dependence on saints cannot lead us to know the truth. The saints are after all only human beings and as Lord Balfour said, "the human mind is no more a truth finding apparatus than the snout of a pig". In so far as he does think, to me he really appears to be prostituting his intelligence to find reasons for supporting this archaic social structure of the Hindus. He is the most influential apologiest of it and therefore the worst enemy of the Hindus.

Unlike the Mahatma there are Hindu leaders who are not content merely to believe and follow. They dare to think, and act in accordance with the result of their thinking. But unfortunately they are either a dishonest lot or an indifferent lot when it comes to the question of giving right guidance to the mass of the people. Almost every Brahmin has transgressed the rule of Caste. The number of Brahmins who sell shoes is far greater than those who practise priesthood. Not only have the Brahmins given up their ancestral calling of priesthood for trading but they have entered trades which are prohibited to them by the *Shastra*. Yet how many Brahmins who break Caste every day will preach against Caste and against the *Shastras*? For one honest Brahmin preaching against Caste and Shastras because his practical instinct and moral conscience cannot support a conviction in them, there are hundreds who break Caste and trample upon the Shastras every day but who are the most fanatic upholders of the theory feel that if the masses are emancipated from the yoke of Caste they would be a menace to the power and prestige of the Brahmins as a class. The dishonesty of this intellectual class who would deny the masses the fruits of their thinking is a most disgraceful phenomenon.

The Hindus in the words of Matthew Arnold are "wandering between two worlds, one dead, the other powerless to be born". What are they to do? The Mahatma to whom they appeal for guidance does not believe in thinking and can therefore give no guidance which can be said to stand the test of experience. The intellectual classes to whom the masses look for guidance are either too dishonest or too indifferent to educate them in the right direction. We are indeed witnesses to a great tragedy. In the face of this tragedy all one can do is to lament and say—such be thy Leaders, O! Hindus" (Dr. Babasaheb Ambedkar: *Writings and Speeches*, Vol. 1, pp. 81-96).

Beginning of Caste System

Jawaharlal Nehru, in his *Discovery of India* writes:

The coming of the Aryans into India raised new problems—racial and political. The conquered race, the Dravidians, had a long background of civilization behind them, but there is little doubt that the Aryans considered themselves vastly superior and wide gulf separated the two races. Then there were also the backward aboriginal tribes, nomads or forest-dwellers. Out of this conflict and interaction of races gradually arose the caste system, which, in the course of succeeding centuries, was to affect Indian life so profoundly. Probably caste was neither Aryan nor Dravidian. It was an attempt at the social organization of different races, a rationalization of the facts as they existed at the time. It brought degradation in its train afterwards, and it is still a burden and a curse; but we can hardly judge it from subsequent standards or later developments. It was in keeping with the spirit of the times and some such grading took place in most of the ancient civilizations, though apparently China was free from it. There was a four-fold division in that other branch of the Aryans, the Iranians, during the Sassanian period, but it did not petrify into caste. Many of these old civilizations, including that of Greece, were entirely dependent on mass slavery. There was no such mass or large-scale labour slavery in India, although there were relatively small numbers of domestic slaves. Plato in his *Republic* refers to a division similar to that of the four principal castes. Medieval Catholicism knew this division also.

Caste began with a hard and fast division between Aryans and non-Aryans, the latter again being divided into the Dravidian races and the aboriginal tribes. The Aryans, to begin with, formed one class and there was hardly any specialization. The word *Arya* comes from a root word meaning to till, and the Aryans as a whole were agriculturists and agriculture was considered a noble occupation. The tiller of the soil functioned also as priest, soldier, or trader, and there was no privileged order of priests. The caste divisions, originally intended to separate the Aryans from the non-Aryans, reacted on the Aryans themselves, and as division of functions and specialization increased, the new classes took the form of castes.

Thus at a time when it was customary for the conquerors to exterminate or enslave the conquered races, caste enabled a more peaceful solution which fitted in with the growing specialization of functions. Life was graded and out of the mass of agriculturists evolved the *Vaishyas*, the agriculturists, artisans, and merchants; the *Kshatriyas*, or rulers and warriors; and the *Brahmins*, priests and thinkers who were supposed to guide policy and preserve and maintain the ideals of the nation. Below these three were the *Shudras* or labourers and unskilled workers, other than the agriculturists. Among the indigenous tribes many were gradually assimilated and given a place at the bottom of the social scale, that is among the Shudras. This process of assimilation was a continuous one. These castes must have been in a fluid condition; rigidity came in much later. Probably the ruling class had always great latitude, and any person who by conquest or otherwise assumed power, could, if he so willed, join the hierarchy as Kshatriya, and get the priests to manufacture an appropriate genealogy connecting him with some ancient Aryan hero.

The Aryans not only divided society into four main groups but also divided the individual's life into four parts: the first part consisted of growth and adolescence, the student period of life, acquiring knowledge, developing self-discipline and self-control continence; the second was that of the householder and man of the world; the third was that of the elder statesman, who had attained a certain poise and objectivity, and could devote himself to public work without the selfish desire to profit by it; and last state was that of the recluse, who lived a life largely cut off from the world's activities. In this way also they adjusted the two opposing tendencies which often exist side by side in man—the acceptance of life in its fullness and the rejection of it.

In India, as in China, learning and erudition have always stood high in public esteem, for learning was supposed to imply both superior knowledge and virtue. Before the learned man the ruler and the warrior have always bowed. The old Indian theory was that those who were concerned with the exercise of power could not be completely objective. Their personal interests and inclinations would come into conflict with their public duties. Hence the task of determining values and the preservation of ethical standards was allotted to a class or group of thinkers who were freed from material cares and were, as far as possible, without obligations, so that they could consider life's problems in a spirit of detachment. This class of thinkers or philosophers was thus supposed to be at the top of the social structure, honoured and respected by all. The men of action, the rulers and warriors came after them and, however powerful they might be, did not command the same respect. The possession of wealth was still less entitled to honour and respect. The warrior class, though not at the top, held a high position, and not as in China, where it was looked upon with contempt.

In India the Brahmin class, in addition to supplying the thinkers and the philosophers, became a powerful and entrenched priesthood, intent on preserving its vested interests. Yet this theory in varying degrees has influenced Indian life profoundly, and the ideal has continued to be of a man full of learning and charity, essentially good, self-disciplined, and capable of sacrificing himself for the sake of others.

The Brahmin class has shown all the vices of a privileged and entrenched class in the past, and large numbers of them have possessed neither learning nor virtue. Yet they have largely retained the esteem of the public, not because of temporal power or possession of men of intelligence, and their record of public service and personal sacrifice for the public good has been a notable one. The whole class profited by the example of its leading personalities in every age, and yet the public esteem went to the qualities rather than to any official status. The tradition was one of respecting learning and goodness in any individual who possessed them. There are innumerable examples of non-Brahmins, and even persons belonging to the depressed classes, being so respected and sometimes considered as saints. Official status and military power never commanded the same measure or respect, though it may have been feared.

Even today, in this money age, the influence of this tradition is marked, and because of it Gandhiji (who is not a Brahmin) can become the supreme leader of India and move the hearts of millions without force or compulsion or official position or possession of money. Perhaps this is as good a test as any of a nation's cultural background and its conscious or subconscious objective: to what kind of a leader does it give its allegiance?

Buddha did not attack caste directly, yet in his own order he did not recognize it, and there is no doubt that his whole attitude and activity weakened the caste system. Probably caste was very fluid in his day and for some centuries later.

New castes were formed at the bottom of the scale, and any successful invading element became transformed soon into Kshatriyas or the ruling class. Coins of the period just before and after the beginning of the Christian era show this rapid change in the course of two or three generations. The first ruler has a foreign name. His son or grandson appears with a Sanskrit name and is crowned according to the traditional rites meant for Kshatriyas.

Many of the Rajput Kshatriya clans date back to the Shaka or Scythian invasions which began about the second century BC or from the later invasion of the White Huns. All these accepted the faith and institutions of the country and then tried to affiliate themselves to the famous heroes of the Epics. Thus the Kshatriya group depended on status and occupation rather than on descent, and so it was much easier for foreigners to be incorporated into it.

It is curious and significant that throughout the long span of Indian history there have been repeated warnings given by great men against priest craft and the rigidity of the caste system, and powerful movements have risen against them; yet slowly, imperceptibly, almost, it seems, as if it were the inevitable course of destiny, caste has grown and spread and seized every aspect of Indian life in its strangling grip. Rebels against caste have drawn many followers, and yet in course of time their group has itself become a caste. Jainism, a rebel against the parent religion and in many ways utterly different from it, was yet tolerant to caste and adapted itself to it; and so it survives and continues in India, almost as an offshoot of Hinduism. Buddhism, not adapting itself to caste, and more independent in its thought and outlook, ultimately passes away from India, though it influences India and Hinduism profoundly. Christianity comes here eighteen hundred years ago and settles down and gradually develops its own castes. The Muslim social structure in India, in spite of its vigorous denunciation of all such barriers within the community, is also partly affected.

In our own period numerous movements to break the tyranny of caste have arisen among the middle classes and they have made a difference, but not a vital one, so far as the masses are concerned. Their method was usually one of direct attack. Then Gandhi came and tackled the problem, after the immemorial Indian fashion, in an indirect way, and his eyes were on the masses. He has been direct enough, aggressive enough, persistent enough, but without challenging the original basic functional theory underlying the four main castes. He has attacked the rank undergrowth and overgrowth, knowing well that he was undermining the whole caste structure thereby. He has already shaken the foundations and the masses have been powerfully affected. For them the whole structure holds or breaks altogether. But an even greater power than he is at work: the conditions of modern life—and it seems that at last this hoary and tenacious relic of past times must die.

But while we struggle with caste in India which, in its origin, was based on colour, new and overbearing castes have arisen in the west with doctrines of racial exclusiveness, sometimes clothed in political and economic terms, and even speaking in the language of democracy.

Before the Buddha, seven hundred years before Christ, a great Indian, the sage and lawgiver Yagnavalkya, is reported to have said: 'It is not our religion, still less the colour of our skin, that produces virtue; virtue must be practiced. Therefore, let no one do to others that he would not have done to himself.'

Buddha's Teaching

Behind these political and economic revolutions that were changing the face of India, there was the ferment of Buddhism and its impact on old-established faiths and its quarrels with vested interests in religion. Far more than the debates and arguments, of which India has always been so enamoured, the people and his memory was fresh in their immersed in metaphysical subtleties, captured the imagination of the intellectuals; it went deep down into the hearts of the people. 'Go unto all lands,' had said the

Buddha to his disciples, 'and preach this gospel. Tell them that the poor and the lowly, the rich and the high, are all one, and that all castes unite in this religion as do the rivers in the sea.' His message was one of universal benevolence, of love for all. For 'Never in this world does hatred cease by hatred; hatred ceases by love.' And 'Let a man overcome anger by kindness, evil by good.'

It was an ideal of righteousness and self-discipline. 'One may overcome a thousand men in battle, but he who conquers himself is the greatest victor.' 'Not by birth, but by his conduct alone, does a man become a low-caste or a Brahmin.' Even a sinner is not to be condemned, for 'who would willingly use hard speech to those who have done a sinful deed, strewing salt, as it were, upon the wound of their fault'? Victory itself over another leads to unhappy consequences—'Victory breeds hatred, for the conquered is unhappy.'

The Caste System in the time of the Buddha was flexible and had not developed the rigidity of later periods. More importance was attached to capacity, character, and occupation, than to birth. Buddha himself often used the term Brahmin as equivalent to an able, earnest, and disciplined person. There is a famous story in the Chhandogya Upanishad which shows us how caste and sex relations were viewed then.

This is the story of Satyakama whose mother was Jabala. Satyakama wanted to become a student of the sage Gautama (not the Buddha) and, as he was leaving his home, he asked his mother; 'Of what gotra (family or clan) am I?' His mother said to him: 'I had to move about much as a servant (waiting on the guests in my father's house), I conceived there. I do not know of what family thou art. I was Jabala by name, thou art Satyakama. Say that thou art Satyakama Jabala (that is, Satyakama, the son of Jabala).'

Satyakama then went to Gautama and the sage asked him about his family. He replied in the words of his mother. Thereupon the teacher said: 'no one but a true Brahmin would thus speak out. Go and fetch fuel, friend. I shall initiate you. You have not swerved from the truth.'

Probably at the time of the Buddha the Brahmins were the only more or less rigid caste. The Kshatriyas or the ruling class were proud of their group and family traditions but, as a class, their doors were open for the incorporation of individuals or families who became rulers. For the rest, most people were Vaishyas, the agriculturists, an honoured calling. There were other occupational castes also. The so-called caste-less people, the untouchables, appear to have been very few, probably some forest folk and some whose occupation was the disposal of dead bodies, etc.

The emphasis of Jainism and Buddhism on non-violence led to the tilling of the soil being considered a lowly occupation, for it often resulted in the destruction of animal life. This occupation, which had been the pride of the Indo-Aryans, went down in the scale of values in some parts of the country, in spite of its fundamental importance, and those who actually tilled the land descended in the social scale.

Thus Buddhism, which was revolt against priestcraft and ritualism and against the degradation of any human being and his deprivation of the opportunities of growth and leading a higher life, unconsciously led to the degradation of vast numbers of tillers of the soil. It would be wrong to make Buddhism responsible for this, for it had no such effect elsewhere. There was something inherent in the caste system which took it in this direction. Jainism pushed it along that way because of its passionate attachment to non-violence—Buddhism also inadvertently helped in the process.

The Caste System does not stand by itself; it is a part, and an integral part, of a much larger scheme of social organization. It may be possible to remove some of its obvious abuses and to lessen its rigidity, and yet to leave the system intact. But that is highly unlikely, as the social and economic forces at play are not much concerned with this superstructure; they are attacking it at the base and undermining the other supports which held it up. Indeed, great parts of these are already gone or are rapidly going, and more and more the caste system is left stranded by itself. It has ceased to be a question of whether we like caste or dislike it. Changes are taking place in spite of our likes and dislikes. But it is certainly in our power to mould those changes and direct them, so that we can take full advantage of the character and genius of the Indian people as a whole, which have been so evident in the cohesiveness and stability of the social organization they built up.

Sir George Birdwood has said somewhere: "So long as the Hindus hold to the caste system, India will be India; but from the day they break from it, there will be no more India. That glorious peninsula will be degraded to the position of a bitter 'East End' of the Anglo-Saxon Empire." With caste or without it, we have long been degraded to that position in the British Empire; and, in any event, whatever our future position is likely to be, it will not be confined within the bounds of that empire. But there is some truth in what Sir George Birdwood said, though probably he did not look at it from this point of view. The break-up of a huge and long-standing social organization may well lead to a complete disruption of social life, resulting in absence of cohesion, mass suffering and the development on a vast scale of abnormalities in individual behaviour, unless some other social structure, more suited to the times and to the genius of the people, takes its place. Perhaps disruption is inevitable during the transition period; there is enough of this disruption all over the world today. Perhaps it is only through the pain and suffering that accompany such disruption that a people grow and learn the lessons of life and adapt themselves anew to changing conditions.

Nevertheless, we cannot just disrupt and hope for something better without having some vision of the future we are working for, however vague that vision may be. We cannot just create a vacuum, or else that vacuum will fill itself up in a way that we may have to deplore. In the constructive schemes that we may make, we have to pay attention to the human material we have to deal with, to the background of its thought and urges, and to the environment in which we have to function. To ignore all this and to fashion some idealistic scheme in the air, or merely to think in terms of imitating what others have done elsewhere would be folly. It becomes desirable therefore, to examine and understand the old Indian social structure which has so powerfully influenced our people.

This structure was based on three concepts: the autonomous village community, caste, and the joint family system. In all these three it is the group that counts; the individual has a secondary place. There is nothing very unique about all this separately and it is easy to find something equivalent to any of these three in other countries, especially in medieval times. Like the old Indian republics, there were primitive republics elsewhere. There was also a kind of primitive communism. The old Russian *mir* might be comparable in some way to the Indian village community. Caste has been essentially functional and similar to the medieval trade guilds of Europe. The Chinese family system bears a strong resemblance to the Hindu joint family.

The Theory and Practice of Caste

'In India', says Havell, 'religion is hardly a dogma, but a working hypothesis of human conduct adapted in different stages of spiritual development and different conditions of life.' In the ancient days when Indo-Aryan culture first took shape, religion had to provide for the needs of men who were as far removed from each other in civilization and intellectual and spiritual development as it is possible to conceive. There were primitive forest-dwellers, fetishists, totem-worshipers and believers in every kind of superstition, and there were those who had attained the highest flights of spiritual thought. In between, there was every shade and gradation of belief and practice. While the highest forms of thought were pursued by some, these were wholly beyond the reach of many. As social life grew, certain uniformities of belief spread, but, even so, many differences, cultural and temperamental, remained. The Indo-Aryan approach was to avoid the forcible suppression of any belief or the destruction of any claim. Each group was left free to work out its ideals along the plane of its mental development and understanding. Assimilation was attempted but there was no denial or suppression.

A similar and even more difficult problem had to be faced in social organization. How to combine these utterly different groups in one social system, each group co-operating with the whole and yet retaining its own freedom to live its own life and develop itself. In a sense—though the comparison is farfetched—

this may be compared to the numerous minority problems of today which afflict so many countries minority problems, more or less, by trying to make every citizen a 100 per cent American. They make everyone conform to a certain type. Other countries, with a longer and more complicated past, are not so favourably situated. Even Canada has its strong race, religion and language-conscious French group. In Europe the barriers are higher and deeper. And yet all this applies to Europeans, or those who have spread from Europe; people who have a certain common background and similarity of culture. Where non-Europeans come in, they do not fit this pattern. In the United States, negroes, though they may be 100 per cent American, are a race apart, deprived of many opportunities and privileges, which others have as a matter of course. There are innumerable worse examples elsewhere. Only Soviet Russia is said to have solved its problem of nationalities and minorities by creating what is called a multinational state.

If these difficulties and problems pursue us even today with all our knowledge and progress, how much harder they must have been in the ancient days when the Indo-Aryans were evolving their civilization and social structure in a land full of variety and different types of human beings. The normal way to deal with these problems then and later was to exterminate or enslave the conquered populations. This way was not followed in India, but it is clear that every precaution was taken to perpetuate the superior position of the upper groups. Having ensured that superiority, a kind of multiple-community state was built up, in which, within certain limits and subject to some general rules, freedom was given to each group to follow its avocation and live its own life in accordance with its own customs or desires. The only real restriction was that it must not interfere or come into conflict with another group. This was a flexible and expanding system, for new groups could always be formed either by newcomers or by dissident members of an old group, provided they were numerous enough to do so. Within each group there was equality and democracy and the elected leaders guided it and frequently consulted the entire group whenever any important question arose.

These groups were almost always functional, each specializing in a particular trade or craft. They became thus some kind of trade union or craft-guild. There was a strong sense of solidarity within each, which not only protected the group but sheltered and helped an individual member who got into trouble or was in economic distress. The functions of each group or caste were related to the functions of other castes, and the idea was that if each group functioned successfully within its own framework, then society as a whole worked harmoniously. Over and above this, a strong and fairly successful attempt was made to create a common national bond which would hold all these groups together—the sense of a common culture, common traditions, common heroes and saints, and a common land, to the four corners of which people went on pilgrimage. This national bond was of course very different from present-day nationalism; it was weak politically but, socially and culturally, it was strong. Because of its political lack of cohesiveness it facilitated foreign conquest; because of its social strength it made recovery easy, as well as assimilation of new elements. It had so many heads that they could not be cut off and they survived conquest and disaster.

Thus caste was a group system based on services and functions. It was meant to be an all-inclusive order without any common dogma and allowing the fullest latitude to each group. Within its wide fold there was monogamy, polygamy, and celibacy; they were all tolerated, just as other customs, beliefs, and practices were tolerated. Life was to be maintained at all levels. No minority need submit to a majority, for it could always form a separate autonomous group, the only test being: is it a distinctive group large enough to function as such? Between two groups there could be any amount of variation of race, religion, colour, culture, and intellectual development.

An individual was only considered as a member of a group; he could do anything he liked so long as he did not interfere with the functioning of the group. He had no right to upset that functioning, but if he was strong enough group. If he could not fit in with any group, that meant that he was out of joint so far as the social activities of the world were concerned. He could then become a *sanyasi* who had renounced caste, every group and the world of activity, and could wander about and do what he liked.

It must be remembered that while the Indian social tendency was to subordinate the individual to the claims of the group and society, religious thought and spiritual seeking have always emphasized the individual. Salvation and knowledge of the ultimate truth were open to all, to the member of every caste, high or low. This salvation or enlightenment could not be a group affair; it was highly individualistic. In the search for this salvation also there were no inflexible dogmas and all doors were supposed to lead to it.

Though the group system was dominant in the organization of society, leading to caste, there has always been an individualistic tendency in India. A conflict between the two approaches is often in evidence. Partly that individualism was the result of the religious doctrine which laid emphasis on the individual. Social reformers who criticized or condemned the caste system were usually religious reformers and their main argument was that the divisions of the caste system came in the way of spiritual development and that intense individualism to which religions pointed. Buddhism was a breakaway from the group-caste ideal towards some kind of individualism as well as universalism. But this individualism became associated with a withdrawal from normal social activities. It offered no effective alternative social structure to caste, and so caste continued then and later.

What were the main castes? If we leave out for a moment those who were considered outside the pale of caste, the untouchables, there were Brahmins, the priests, teachers, intellectual; the Kshatriyas or the rulers and warriors; the Vaishyas or merchants, traders, bankers, etc.; and the Shudras, who were the agricultural and other workers. Probably the only closely knit and exclusive caste was that of the Brahmins. The Kshatriyas were frequently adding to their numbers both from foreign incoming elements and other in the country traders and bankers and also engaged in a number of other professions. The main occupations of the Shudras were cultivation and domestic service.

There was always a continuous process of new castes being formed as new occupations developed, and for other reasons the older castes were always trying to get up in the social scale. These processes have continued to our day. Some of the lower castes suddenly take to wearing the sacred thread which is supposed to be reserved for the upper castes. All these really made little difference, as each caste continued to function in its own ambit and pursuit its own trade or occupation. It was merely a question of prestige. Occasionally men of the lower classes, by sheer ability, attained positions of power and authority in the state, but this was very exceptional.

The organization of society being, generally speaking, non-competitive and non-acquisitive, these divisions into castes did not make as much difference as they might otherwise have done. The Brahmin at the top, proud of his intellect and learning and respected by others, seldom had much in the way of worldly possessions. The merchants, prosperous and rich, had not very high standing in society as a whole.

The vast majority of the population consisted of the agriculturists. There was no landlord system, nor was there any peasant proprietorship. It is difficult to say who owned the land in law; there was nothing like the present doctrine of ownership. The cultivator had the right to till his land and the only real question was as to the distribution of the produce of the land. The major share went to the cultivator, the king or the state took a share (usually one-sixth), and every functional group in the village, which served the people in any way, had its share—the Brahmin priest and teacher, the merchant, the blacksmith, the carpenter, the cobbler, the potter, the builder, the barber, the scavenger, etc., thus, in a sense, every group from the state to the scavenger was a shareholder in the produce.

Who were the depressed classes and the untouchables? The 'depressed classes' is a new designation applying rather vaguely to a number of castes near the bottom of the scale. There is no hard and fast line to separate them from the others. The untouchables are more definite. In north India only a very small numbers, engaged in scavenging or unclean work, are considered untouchable. Fa-Hsien tells us that when he came the persons who removed human faeces were untouchable. In south India the numbers are much larger. How they began and grew to such numbers it is difficult to say. Probably those who were engaged in occupations considered unclean were so treated; later landless agricultural labour may have been added.

The idea of ceremonial purity has been extraordinarily strong among the Hindus. This has led to one good consequence and many bad ones. The good one is bodily cleanliness. A daily bath has always been an essential feature of a Hindu's life, including most of the depressed classes. It was from India that this habit spread to England and elsewhere. The average Hindu, and even the poorest peasant, takes some pride in his shining pots and pans. This sense of cleanliness is not scientific and the man who bathes twice a day will unhesitatingly drink water that is unclean and full of germs. Nor is it corporate, at any rate now. The individual will keep his own hut fairly clean but throw all the rubbish in the village street in front of his neighbor's house. The village is usually very dirty and full of garbage heaps. It is also noticeable that cleanliness is not thought of as such but as a consequence of some religious sanction. When that religious sanction goes, there is marked deterioration in the standards of cleanliness.

The evil consequence of ceremonial purity was a growth of exclusiveness, touch-me-not-ism, and of not eating and drinking with people of other castes. This grew to fantastic lengths unknown in any other part of the world. It led also to certain classes being considered untouchable because they had the misfortune to do some kinds of essential work which were considered unclean. The practice of normally feeding with one's own caste people spread to all castes. It became a sign of social status and the lower castes stuck to it even more rigidly than some of the higher ones. This practice is breaking up now among the higher castes but it still continues among the lower castes, including the depressed classes.

If inter-dining was taboo, much more so was inter-marriage between castes. Some mixed marriages inevitably took place but on the whole it is extraordinary how much each caste kept to itself and propagated its own kind. The continuation of racial identity through long ages is an illusion and yet the caste system in India has to some extent managed to preserve distinctive types, especially among the higher castes.

Some groups at the bottom of the scale are sometimes referred to as outside the caste groups. As a matter of fact no group, not even the untouchables, are outside the framework of the caste system. The depressed classes and the untouchables form their own castes and have their *panchayats* or caste councils for setting their own affairs. But many of them have been made to suffer cruelly by being excluded from the common life of the village.

The autonomous village community and the caste system were thus two of the special features of the old Indian social structure. The third was the joint family where all the members were joint sharers in the common property and in heritance went by survivorship. The father or some other elder was the head but he functioned as a manager, and not as the old Roman paterfamilias. A division of property was permitted under certain circumstances and if the parties concerned so desired. The joint property was supposed to provide for the needs of all the members of the family, workers or non-workers. Inevitably this meant a guaranteed minimum for all of them, rather than high rewards for some. It was a kind of insurance for all, including even the subnormal and the physically or mentally deficient. Thus while there was security for all, there was a certain leveling down of the standard of service demanded as well of the recompense given. Emphasis was not laid on personal advantages or ambition but on that of the group, that is the family. The fact of growing up and living in a large family minimized the egocentric attitude of the child and tended to develop an aptitude for socialization.

All this is the very opposite of what happens in the highly individualistic civilization of the West and more especially of America, where personal ambition is encouraged and personal advantage is the almost universal aim, where all the plums go to the bright and pushing, and the weak, timid or second rate go to the wall.

The joint family system is rapidly breaking up in India and individualistic attitudes are developing, leading not only to far-reaching changes in the economic background of life but also to new problems of behavior.

All the three pillars of the Indian social structure were thus based on the group and not on the individual. The aim was social security, stability and continuance of the group, that is of society. Progress was not the aim and progress therefore had to suffer. Within each group, whether this was the village community, the particular caste, or the large joint family, there was a communal life shared together, a sense of equality, and democratic methods. Even now caste *panchayats* function democratically. It surprised me at one time to see the eagerness of a villager, sometimes illiterate, to serve on elected committees for political or other purposes. He soon got into the way of it and was a helpful member whenever any question relating to his life came up, and was not easily subdued. But there was an unfortunate tendency for small groups to split up and quarrel among themselves.

The democratic way was not only well-known but was a common method of functioning in social life, in local government, trade-guilds, religious assemblies, etc. Caste, with all its evils, kept up the democratic habit in each group. There used to be elaborate rules of procedure, election and debate. The Marquis of Zetland has referred to some of these in writing about the early Buddhist assemblies:

And it may come as a surprise to many to learn that in Assemblies of the Buddhists in India 2000 or more years ago are to be found the rudiments of our own parliamentary practice of the present day. The dignity of the assembly was preserved by the appointment of a special officer—the embryo of 'Mr Speaker' in the House of Commons. A second officer was appointed whose duty it was to see that when necessary a quorum was secured—the prototype of the parliamentary chief whip in our own system. A member initiating business did so in the form of a motion which was open to discussion. In some cases this was done once only, in others three times, thus anticipating the practice of parliament in requiring that a Bill be read a third time before it becomes law. If discussion disclosed a difference of opinion the matter was decided by the voice of the majority, the voting being by ballot.

The old Indian social structure had thus some virtues, and indeed it could not have lasted so long without them. Behind it lay the philosophical ideal of Indian culture—the integration of man and stress on goodness, beauty and truth rather than acquisitiveness. An attempt was made to prevent the joining together and concentration of honour, power, and wealth. The duties of the individual and the group were emphasized, not their rights.

The *Smritis* (Hindu religious books) give lists of dharmas, functions and duties of various castes but none of them contains an inventory of rights. Self-sufficiency was aimed at in the group, especially in the village and, in a different sense, in the caste. It was a closed system, allowing a certain adaptability, change, and freedom within its outer framework, but inevitably growing more and more exclusive and rigid. Progressively it lost its power to expand and tap new sources of talent. Powerful vested interests prevented any radical change and kept education from spreading to other classes. The old superstitions, known to be such by many among the upper classes, were preserved and new ones were added to them. Not only the national economy but thought itself became stationary, traditional, rigid, unexpansive and unprogressive.

The conception and practice of caste embodied the aristocratic ideal and was obviously opposed to democratic conceptions. It had its strong sense of *noblesse oblige*, provided people kept to their hereditary stations and did not challenge the established order. India's success and achievements were on the whole confined to the upper classes; those lower down in the scale had very few chances and their opportunities were strictly limited. These upper classes were not small limited groups but large in numbers and there was a diffusion of power, authority and influence. Hence, they carried on successfully for a very long period. But the ultimate weaknesses and failing of the caste system and the Indian social structure were that they degraded a mass of human beings and gave them no opportunities to get out of that condition—educationally, culturally, or economically. That degradation brought deterioration all along the line, including in its scope even the upper classes. It led to the petrifaction which became a dominant feature of India's economy and life. The contrasts between this social structure and those existing elsewhere in the past were not great, but with the changes that have taken place all over the world during the past few generations they have become far more pronounced. In the context of society today, the caste system and much that goes with it are wholly incompatible, reactionary, restrictive, and barriers to progress. There can be no equality in status and opportunity within is framework, nor can there be political democracy and much less economic democracy. Between these two conceptions conflict is inherent and only one of them can survive (Jawaharlal Nehru: *The Discovery of India,* pp. 81-84; 121-23; 129; 185-86; 265-66; 268-77).

Gandhiji believed in the Vedas, the Upanishadas, the Puranas and all that goes by the name of Hindu scriptures. He believed in caste and defended it with the vigour of the orthodox. But later he admitted that caste is harmful both to spiritual and national growth. All the kind words, he ever said about caste system, which are often quoted against him, were about what he believed it to have been in the hoary past and not about what it was in his own time. Closer acquaintance with the Indian social scene convinced him that the system was so flawed by superstition, 'touch-me-not-ism', social inequality and discrimination that it was past-mending. We can see a progressive hardening of Gandhiji's attitude to the caste system. In December 1920, he wrote: "I consider the four divisions alone to be fundamental, natural and essential. The innumerable sub-castes are sometimes a convenience, often a hindrance. The sooner there is fusion, the better. Fifteen years later, he declared that the *Varnashram of the Shastras* is today non-existent in practice. The present caste system is the very anti-thesis of Varnashram. The sooner public opinion abolishes it better. In 1930, Gandhiji denounced any exclusiveness which stemmed from caste or local prejudice. "It must be left to the unfettered choice of the individual," he wrote, "as to where he or she will marry or dine." In 1946, he made the startling announcement that no marriage will be celebrated in his ashram at Sevagram, unless one of the parties was an untouchable by birth.

Gandhiji's reluctance to make a frontal assault on the caste system in the early years may have been a matter of tactics. In a conversation with a Hungarian journalist, Tibor Mende in 1956, Jawaharlal Nehru recalled: "I spoke to Gandhiji repeatedly: Why do not you hit out the caste system directly? He said that he did not believe in the caste system except in some idealized form of occupations and all that; but that the present caste system is thoroughly bad and must go." "I am undermining it completely," he said, "by my tackling untouchability." He had a way of seizing one thing and concentrating on it. "If untouchability goes," he said, "the caste system goes" (B.R. Nanda: *Gandhi and His Critics,* pp. 25-26).

Gandhiji's references to caste have been progressively stronger and more pointed. He made it repeatedly clear that caste as a whole and as it exists must be eliminated. Referring to the Constructive Programme which he placed before the nation, he said: "It has undoubtedly independence, political, social and economic as its aim. It is a moral, non-violent revolution in all the departments of life of a big nation, at the end of which caste and untouchability and such other superstitions must vanish." Again, he said: "The Caste System, as we know, is an anachronism. It must go if both Hinduism and India are to live and grow from day to day."

Gandhi's views on the Caste System were fully elaborated by him in 1921-22 in a Gujarathi Journal called *Nava-Jivan.* In his words:

"1. I believe that if Hindu Society has been able to stand it is because it is founded on the Caste System.

2. The seeds of Swaraj are to be found in the Caste System. Different castes are like different sections of military division. Each division is working for the good of the whole....

3. A community which can create the Caste System must be said to possess unique power of organization.

4. Caste has a ready made means for spreading primary education. Every caste can take the responsibility for the education of the children of the Caste. Caste

has a political basis. It can work as an electorate for a representative body. Caste can perform judicial functions by electing persons to act as judges to decide disputes among members of the same caste. With castes it is easy to raise a defence force by requiring each caste to raise a bridge.

5. I believe that interdining or intermarriage are not necessary for promoting national unity. That dining together creates friendship is contrary to experience. If this was true there would have been no war in Europe.... Taking food is as dirty an act as answering call of nature. The only difference is that after answering call of nature we get peace while after eating food we get discomfort. Just as we perform the act of answering the call of nature in seclusion so also the act of taking food must also be done in seclusion.
6. In India children of brothers do not intermarry. Do they cease to love because they do not intermarry? Among the Vaishnavas many women are so orthodox that they will not eat with the members of the family nor will they drink water from a common water pot. Have they no love? The Caste System cannot be said to be bad because it does not allow interdining or intermarriage between different Castes.
7. Caste is another name for control. Caste puts a limit on enjoyment. Caste does not allow a person to transgress caste limits in pursuit of his enjoyment. That is the meaning of such caste restrictions as interdining and intermarriage.
8. To destroy caste system and adopt Western European social system means that Hindus must give up the principle of hereditary occupation which is the soul of the caste system. Hereditary principle is an enternal principle. To change it is to create disorder. I have no use for a Brahmin if I cannot call him Brahmin for my life. It will be a chaos if every day a Brahmin is to be changed into a Shudra and Shudra is to be changed into a Brahmin.

9. The Caste System is a natural order of society. In India it has been given a religious coating. Other countries not having understood the utility of the Caste System it existed only in a loose condition and consequently those countries have not derived from Caste System the same degree of advantage which India has derived.

These being my views I am opposed to all those who are out to destroy the Caste System."

In 1922, Gandhi was defender of the Caste System. Pursuing the inquiry, one comes across a somewhat critical view of the caste system by Gandhi in the year 1925. This is what Gandhi said on 3rd February 1925:

"I gave support to caste because it stands for restraint, it means limitations. Restraint is glorious and helps to achieve freedom. But limitation is like chain. It binds. There is nothing commendable in castes as they exist today. They are contrary to the tenets of shastras. The number of castes is infinite and there is a bar against intermarriage. This is not a condition of elevation. It is a state of fall."

In reply to the question: What is the way out Gandhi said:

"The best remedy is that small castes should fuse themselves into one big caste. There should be four such big castes so that we may reproduce the old system of four Varnas."

In short, in 1925 Gandhi became an upholder of the Varna system.

Gandhi explained his Varna system in the following terms:

"1. I Believe that the division into Varna is based on birth.

2. There is nothing in the Varna system which stands in the way of the Shudra acquiring learning or studying military art of offence or defence. Contra it is open to a Kshatriya to serve. The Varna system is no bar to him, what learning the Varna system enjoins is that a Shudra will not make way of earning a living. Nor will a Kshatriya adopt service as a way of earning a living. (Similarly a Brahmin may learn the art of war or trade. But he must not make them a way of earning his living.

Contra a Vaishya may acquire learning or may cultivate the art of war. But he must not make them a way of earning his living.)

3. The Varna system is connected with the way of earning a living. There is no harm if a person belonging to one varna acquires the knowledge or science and art specialized in by persons belonging to other varnas. But as far as the way of earning his living is concerned he must follow the occupation of the varna to which he belongs which means he must follow the hereditary profession of his forefathers.
4. The object of the Varna system is to prevent competition and class struggle and class war. I believe in the Varna system because it fixes the duties and occupations of persons.
5. Varna means the determination of man's occupation before he is born.
6. In the Varna system no man has any liberty to choose his occupation. His occupation is determined for him by heredity."

Criticising Gandhi on Caste and Varnas, Ambedkar said:

"The social ideal of Gandhi is either Caste or Varna. For, whether one takes for comparison caste or Varna both are fundamentally opposed to democracy. Mr. Gandhi's defence of the caste system is the most insensible piece of rhetoric one can think of. Gandhi's arguments in support of castes are spacious if not puerile. Even the orthodox may say, "Save us from Mr. Gandhi." It shows that what a deep-dyed Hindu Mr. Gandhi is. He has outdone the most orthodox of orthodox Hindus. It is not enough to say that it is an argument of a cave man. It is really an argument of a mad man.

"Mr. Gandhi has given a new interpretation to Varna system. He has changed it out of recognition. Under the old orthodox interpretation caste connoted hereditary occupation but Varna did not. Mr. Gandhi by his own whim has given a new connotation to the Varna. With Mr. Gandhi Varna is determined by birth and the profession and a profession of a Varna is determined by the principle of heredity so that Varna is merely another name for caste. That Mr. Gandhi changed from caste to Varna does not indicate the growth of any new revolutionary ideology. The genius of Mr. Gandhi is elvish, always and throughout. He has all the precocity of an elf with no little of its outward guise. Like an elf he can never grow up and grow out of the caste ideology."

K. Santhanam in his book *Ambedkar's Attack* says:

"I feel it a great pity that in his anger against the Hindus and eagerness to secure a separate communal status for the scheduled castes, Dr. Ambedkar should have missed the opportunity of a rational exposition of the many far-reaching problems of social and economic reconstruction which he has touched upon in his book (What Congress and Gandhi have done for untouchables). The most important of them is the future of caste. Can Hinduism exist without caste? What will be the consequences of the destruction of the caste system on Hindu society? Though the system is breaking down before our very eyes, Dr. Ambedkar asserts it as an axiom that it cannot go. In an eloquent passage, he says: "The social psychology of the Hindu Communal majority is dominated by the dogma which recognizes not merely inequality as the rule governing the inter-relationship among the various communities. This dogma of graded inequality is absolutely inimical to liberty and fraternity. It cannot be believed that this graded inequality will vanish or that the Hindus will strive to abolish it. That is impossible. This graded inequality is not accidental or incidental. It is the religion of Hindus. It is the official doctrine of Hinduism. It is sacred and no Hindu can think of doing away with it. The Hindu Communal Majority with its religion of graded inequality is not therefore a passing phase. It is a permanent fact and a menace for ever."

In reports Santhanam says:

"If this is so, then it becomes the sacred duty of Dr. Ambedkar to fight this menace and not to make peace with it by accepting a few crumbs of communal representation which will not materially affect the Hindu Communal majority. Fortunately for India and the world, the demon is largely a fiction created by Dr. Ambedkar's imagination. Graded inequality is the universal basis of every medieval society in which the objective conditions for enforcing social equality are lacking. As for its being the religion of the Hindus, it will go the way of many other things which constituted their religion in the past. Orthodox Brahmin families are cheerfully accommodating themselves to low caste and non-caste brides. As I write, it is reported that a high caste Hindu has requested Mahatma Gandhi to find a Harijan bride for him. As caste has no legal basis and the graded inequality rests entirely on individual habits and family custom, it is bound to take time to disappear. But as a doctrine, it is wholly repudiated by the Indian National Congress which is strongly socialist and equalitarian. As a superstitious practice, it has been given a mortal blow by Gandhiji who has just performed a pilgrimage to the ancient and sacred temples of Madura where, surrounded by a party of Harijans, he worshipped the deity and was offered honours which were customarily due only to the most orthodox religious heads. Gandhiji once wrote that if it was a choice between the death of Varnashram Dharma and the maintenance of untouchability, he would unhesitatingly prefer the former. It can be said similarly that if it is a choice between graded inequality and disappearance of Hinduism, all enlightened Hindus will prefer the latter. But through 3000 years of their history, Hinduism and Hindu society have passed through so many phases and shed so many doctrines and practices that they are quite capable of adjusting themselves to the fundamental need of modern times. In fact, the very word "Hindus" and "Hinduism" have been coined for the convenience of separatist religious communities afraid of assimilation in the manner of Buddhism, Jainism, and other protestant and even atheist movements. If Dr. Ambedkar really believes that there is no prospect of equality for the scheduled castes among the Hindus of whom they are an integral and inseparable part, he destroys all hope of emancipation for them, and sooner the scheduled castes free themselves of his leadership, the better will it be for them" (K. Santhanam: *Ambedkar's Attack,* pp. 79-81).

Anyone who has read Gandhiji's *Autobiography* or reflected on his experiments with truth in the various Ashrams he founded in South Africa and India will have no hesitation in admitting that

Gandhiji never observed distinctions of castes, race or religion in his dealings with men and women. The idea of birth as conferring inferiority and superiority has been always abhorrent to him. He almost idealized the sweeper and the bhangi for doing which he is blamed by Dr. Ambedkar as much as for advocating an idealized caste system. Nor have his ideas been rigid in this matter. His views on inter-dining and inter-marriage afford an interesting illustration. It is true that 20 years ago Gandhiji was not inclined to support them. Food and sex being among the chief distractions of man in his spiritual pursuit, any restrictions placed on them serve, in his opinion, to help spiritual growth. The limitation of marriage within the same caste should be considered as a call to look upon the rest of womankind as mothers and sisters. But Gandhiji never thought that prohibition of inter-dining and inter-marriage was essential to the Caste System of his conception. "I do not believe that inter-dining or even inter-marriage necessarily deprives a man of the caste status that birth has given him. The four divisions, Brahmin, Kshatriya, Vaishya, and Shudra define a man's calling; they do not restrict or regulate social intercourse. The divisions define duties; they confer no privileges. It is, I hold, against the genius of Hinduism to arrogate to oneself a higher status or assign to another a lower status. All are born to serve God's creation—a Brahmin with his knowledge, a Kshatriya with his power of protection, a Vaishya with his commercial ability and a Shudra with his bodily labour."

This is Gandhiji's own description of his views at that time. In 25 years, his views have been changing. He has had to admit that caste in India survives more by what he has called its excrescences than by what he thinks are its virtues. He has also said that it is an anachronism and the taboos against inter-dining and inter-marriage should be abandoned. As a matter of fact no other individual in Indian history has been responsible for erasing caste and other social distinctions as Gandhiji has been. His practice in his Ashrams has had more effect than his ideological interpretation of caste. His great movements of Satyagraha have provided opportunities on a grand scale for workers of all castes and creeds to come together inside jails and outside on a plane of absolute social equality and this has led to the abandonment of caste distinctions to a greater extent than could be effected by previous social reform movements. It is no exaggeration to say that as a result the taboo against inter-dining has disappeared except in rural areas where the masses are still illiterate. Inter-caste marriages have become more frequent than before, though it cannot be said that they are numerous enough to bring about any degree of homogeneity in Hindu society.

The issue here is not whether Gandhiji's views are right or wrong. No one will question Dr. Ambedkar's right to oppose and even condemn them. The objection is to the unfair presentation of Gandhiji's views. Having given the reader to understand that Gandhiji's views were static from the time of Hind Swaraj, Dr. Ambedkar had to explain the statement of Gandhiji that caste was an anachronism. I shall simply quote the reaction of Dr. Ambedkar to this radical change and leave the reader to judge for himself: "Those who are carried away by this recantation of Mr. Gandhi, forget two things. In the first place, all that Mr. Gandhi has said is that caste is an anachronism. He does not say it is an evil. He does not say it is an anathema. Mr. Gandhi may be taken to be not in favour of caste. But Mr. Gandhi does not say that he is against the Varna system. And what is Mr. Gandhi's Varna system? It is simply a new name for caste system and retains all the worst features of the caste system."

Really, Gandhiji's views on caste have no relevance to the issue of untouchability. Gandhiji declared war on untouchability and never compromised on it. When the untouchables have become one with the rest of the Hindus, the reform of Hindu society will be speeded up. The entire thesis of Dr. Ambedkar is that the Harijans should be treated as a separate element, and therefore should be politically separated from the rest of the Hindus. It cannot be doubted that this political separation will tend to confirm and strengthen social segregation and, therefore, caste in its worst aspects. Thus while, theoretically, Dr. Ambedkar indulges in diatribes against caste, his practical policy is to support it, while it is exactly the reverse in the case of Gandhiji who, in spite of his theoretical support of Varnashrama Dharma, struck by his campaign against untouchability the greatest blow to the existing structure of Hindu society.

He was the first person to object and the last to any attempt to enforce his ideas of Varnashrama Dharma or economics through force or even legislation. During his tour in South India at the end of 1927, Gandhiji was asked many questions which Dr. Ambedkar has put in his book "What Gandhi and Congress have done to Untouchables". The late Mr. Mahadev Desai has given an interesting resume of these questions and answers in the *Young India* of November 27, 1927. I content myself with three of them.

Q. So long as you do not destroy Varna, untouchability cannot be destroyed.

A. I do not think so. But if Varnashrama goes to the dogs in the removal of untouchability, I shall not shed a tear. But what bearing has Varna as defined by me on untouchability?

Q. But the opponents of reform quote you in support.

A. That is the lot of every reformer. He will be misquoted by interested parties, but you also know that some of them want me to relinquish Hinduism. Others would banish me from the Hindu fold. I have gone nowhere to defend Varnashrama Dharma though for the removal of untouchability I went to Vykom. I am the author of the Congress resolution for propagation of Khadi, establishment of Hindu-Muslim unity, and removal of untouchability, the three pillars of Swaraj. But I have never placed establishment of Varnashrama Dharma as the fourth pillar. You cannot therefore accuse me of placing a wrong emphasis on Varnashrama Dharma.

Q. Do you know that many of your followers distort your teachings?

A. Do I not know it? I know that I have many followers only so-called.

Supreme Court's Judgment in Mandal Case

Writing on the Supreme Court's Judgment in the Mandal Case, Nani Palkhivala, an eminent Constitutional expert said:

Future historians of the Indian republic will regard 1992 as one of the saddest years in the history of our jurisprudence. This is the year in which the Supreme Court, by a majority, continued, virtually in perpetuity, the scourge of casteism.

Over the last thousand years, the greatest curse which had afflicted the Indian nation had been the curse of casteism, as Justice Kuldip Singh has pointed out in his minority judgment. Historians are agreed that the reason why foreign invaders—the Afghans, the Turks, the Moghuls—succeeded in subjugating this country was because casteism divided Indian society and assigned military duties to one caste only.

Dr. B.R. Ambedkar was the Chairman of the Drafting Committee of free India's republican Constitution. He ensured that caste would be anathema to our noble Constitution and strove single-mindedly to bring about the social integration of India.

In Dr. Ambedkar's own words, "Fraternity means a sense of common brotherhood of all Indians—of Indians being one people.... Castes are anti-national: in the first place they bring about separation in social life. They are anti-national also because they generate jealousy and antipathy between caste and caste. But we must overcome all these difficulties if we wish to become a nation in reality. For fraternity can be a fact only when there is a nation. Without fraternity, equality and liberty will be no deeper than coats of paint."

We have impaired Dr. Ambedkar and desecrated his greatest monument—the Constitution of India.

The majority judgments of the Supreme Court held that reservations in government service on the basis of caste are permissible under Article 16(4) of the Constitution, in spite of the face that discrimination against any citizen on the ground of caste in respect of any employment or office under the State is prohibited under Article 16(2).

The minority judgments of Justices Thommen, Kuldip Singh and R.M. Sahai state the correct law. They rule that casteism can never be the basis of reservations or employment under the Government.

It is submitted that the majority judgments in the Mandal case are patently erroneous, and need to be overruled in the public interest and in the long-term interests of the backward castes themselves.

The basic structure of the Constitution envisages a cohesive, unified, casteless society. By breathing new life into casteism the judgment fractures the national and disregards the basic structure of the Constitution. The decision would revitalize casteism, cleave the nation into two—forward and backward—and open up new vistas for internecine conflicts and fissiparous forces, and make backwardness a vested interest. It will undo whatever has been achieved since independence towards creating a unified, integrated nation.

The majority judgments will revive casteism which the Constitution emphatically intended to end; and the pre-independence tragedy would be re-enacted with the roles reversed—the erstwhile underprivileged would now become the privileged. (The desperate tale of the forward caste woman in Kerala who, merely with a view to gaining admission for her son in a medical college, deposed before a magistrate in the presence of her husband that the son was her illegitimate offspring by a harijan, does not seem to have attracted the attention of our unawakened people.) Caste will be given precedence over merit and caliber. Article 16(4) has been virtually rewritten by substituting "caste" for "class". The majority judgment which upheld reservations on the basis of caste, prescribe the following qualifications and conditions without which the reservations cannot be allowed to continue. The judgments enjoin that (a) the "creamy layer" of backward classes should be excluded, because otherwise they would lap up all the benefits of reservations meant for the class; (b) within four months the Government of India should "specify the basis of exclusion—whether on the basis of income, extent of holding or otherwise—of the creamy layer"; (c) the inclusion or exclusion of a caste or a section of a caste would have to be periodically reviewed to take care of changing circumstances; (d) permanent commissions should be appointed within four months by the central government and by the state governments to decide regularly the cases which would arise involving question whether a particular caste or a section of a caste was rightly included or excluded; and all further proceedings in such matters can be taken only in the Supreme Court; (e) it is advisable to have armed forces, and some higher civilian posts to be selected by the government, outside the purviews of caste reservations.

The crucial point is that under the majority judgments of the Supreme Court it is the members belonging to certain caste only, who are eligible to be considered for reservations. When you have removed the creamy layer, what you are left with are still the members of certain castes only. The sections of society which fall outside those designated castes do not qualify for reservations, however socially and educationally backward they may be.

It is undisputed that 45 years of independence have changed the social, educational, and economic landscape beyond recognition. There are crores of backward individuals in forward castes and crores of forward individuals in backward castes. By making caste the essential condition, the majority judgments have (a) included for reservation all members of backward castes who do not belong to the creamy layer, and (b) excluded all members of forward castes, however backward and deserving. Such a classification patently discriminates against those who do not belong to those castes which are listed as backward.

A backward class may be given the benefit of Article 15(4) or Article 16(4), but the class must consist of a homogeneous group—the element of homogeneity should be the backwardness characterizing the class. In other words, the link or the thread holding the class together should be the backwardness of the members. Such a link or thread can never be supplied by caste. Excluding the creamy layer of the caste would not get rid of the vice that the only link or thread binding the benefited class together is caste. In other words, a classification may be justified on the ground that it is a backward "class", but never on the ground that it is a backward "caste" or "a section of a backward caste". This principle was precisely enunciated by the Constitution Bench in *Triloki Nath* [(1969) 1 SCR 103], *Pradip Tandon* [(1975) 2 SCR 761], *Jayashree* [(1977) 1 SCR 194], *Akhil Bhartiya Soshit* [(1981) 2 SCR 185]. These judgments were cited before the Supreme Court and are referred to in the majority judgments without disapproval, but they are inexplicably overlooked.

The majority judgments did not pause to consider the reasons why for all the past decades the Union Government had not made reservations on caste basis in areas of employment, admissions and promotions. The practice of mentioning the caste in service records was discontinued by the Government of India by 1951. The last census records to proceed on caste basis are those of 1931 which, though hopelessly obsolete, were relied upon by the Mandal Commission because they were the latest census records to proceed on the caste basis.

Kaka Kalelkar's own letter forwarding his Report (1955) to the President said, "I am definitely against reservations in government services for any community, for the simple reason that the services are not meant for the servants but they are meant for the service of society as a whole." Kalelkar's Report, which was not accepted by the then government, had listed 2,399 castes as backward. Dealing with this list the Union Government said, "If the entire community, barring a few exceptions, has thus to be regarded as backward, the really needy would be swamped by the multitude and hardly receive any special attention or adequate assistance." This objection would apply a *fortiori* to the Mandal Report which lists (not exhaustively) 3,743 backward castes. Like the expanding universe the list of backward castes is ever expanding. Many more are already waiting in the wings to receive attention.

The last word on the subject may be left with Pandit Jawaharlal Nehru who, in his letter to the Chief Ministers sent on June 27, 1961 said, "I dislike any kind of reservation, more particularly in service. I react strongly against anything which leads to inefficiency and second-rate standards.... The only real way to help a backward group is to give opportunities for a good education.... But if we go in for reservations on communal and caste basis, we swamp the bright and able people and remain second-rate or third-rate.... It has amazed me to learn that even promotions are based sometimes on communal or caste considerations. This way lie not only folly, but disaster. Let us help the backward groups by all means, but never at the cost of efficiency."

Reading Article 16(4) and Article 335 together, it is evident that when efficiency of administration cannot be sacrificed even in favour of the scheduled castes and the scheduled tribes, much less can it be sacrificed to favour less weak sections, viz., the other backward classes. The majority judgments accept this proposition. How will the Government ensure the fulfillment of the condition of "efficiency of administration" or lay down satisfactory criteria to exclude the creamy layer of backward castes in a country where less than one per cent of the population are income-tax payers?

Public opinion needs to be mobilized to make the Government realize what an imponderable responsibility lies on its shoulders. No doubt it is bound by the law as laid down by the majority judgments of the Supreme Court. But it is not bound to continue the policy of reservations. The qualifications and conditions indicated by the majority judgments of the Supreme Court are such that they would necessarily entail unforgivable squandering of the nation's resources, time and energy. The Cabinet would be well advised, and undoubtedly entitled, to say that it is not in the national interest to continue the system of caste quotas on the fulfillment of conditions and qualifications which would involve such colossal waste.

The choice before the government is clear. It can opt for populism, carry on with the policy of reservations and, acting upon what the majority judgments have enjoined, convert this poor country into a paradise for lawyers. Or, it can give up the thoughtless policy of caste reservations.

Mr. V.P. Singh said that after the Supreme Court judgment in the Mandal case he could die in peace. But unfortunately his policy has ensured that the nation will not live in peace. The poisonous weed of casteism has been replanted "where it will trouble us a thousand years, each age will have to reconsider it" (Nani Palkhivala: *We the Nation,* pp. 178-83).

In platform speeches, leaders after leaders, be they of any shade preach against castes, but in practice the very same leaders with hardly any exception strengthen caste feelings. This is nothing short of hypocracy and sooner the people understand the ulterior motives of their leaders, better for them and better for the country.

The vast machinery of protective discrimination for the Scheduled Castes was developed chiefly in the 1930s and 1940s under the British and legitimized psychologically by the Gandhian campaigns of the period. The post-independence Government adopted most of these measures and further refined and extended them. Benefits since accorded to untouchables have included reserved seats in all Legislative bodies, the reservation of Government jobs, and aid to students through the college level, prizes to villages demonstrating equality, gifts, money for marriages, in which one partner is an untouchable, support for housing projects and legal machinery for suits against discriminative practices.

Ambedkar's view that the problem of untouchables is economic, social and political as well as religious, widely prevails in India. The untouchable who enters the modern sector of Indian society as school teacher, factory worker, or Government servant is comparatively free from earlier social disabilities. However, for the majority of untouchables, who are landless villagers, the only open road to higher economic and social status entails leaving the security of their village and some how obtaining education. Gandhi may have softened the Hindu heart, Ambedkar may have awakened self-respect and an interest in politics among untouchables, but economic dependence upon others continues to restrict the upward movement of the untouchables even today.

During the decades, preceding Independence policies and programmes were profoundly affected by the difference in views of Gandhi and Ambedkar on the key questions like: what is the ultimate goal—assimilation of the untouchable minority or the establishment of separate but equal status in a reformed version of the traditional social order? If change is in order, who should change, the untouchable minority or the Hindu majority? Given a commitment to a change, how might it best be implemented? Through voluntary means or Government coercion?

Gandhi's answers to such questions were rooted in his view that caste Hindus were primarily responsible for righting the wrongs done to the untouchables. Meaningful change, therefore, must arise from a change of heart on the part of the majority. Ambedkar, advocated policies resuming marked change on the part of the untouchable minority who he believed must equip themselves with the education and skills, needed to compete effectively in a "modern" society. He assumed also that little fundamental change, could be expected in the Hindus treatment of the untouchables without recourse to Government intervention.

Over five fateful decades have elapsed since Ambedkar's death, but no Harijan leader of his ability and heroic stamp has yet come forth to lead the downtrodden millions of India. This failure raises the question of what becomes of those untouchables who do attain college education and urban employment. Indications are that many of these potential leaders retreat into anonymity? Few of them appear rooted in an urban community. Rather they appear to be isolated by choice or circumstances from their village brethren. Leaders in Buddhist movement are often educated untouchables living in Provincial towns. In such instances the link between the 'modern' man and his village counterpart is reaffirmed in a traditional manner—via an appeal in terms of religion rather than political ideology or class interest.

The availability of political offices to untouchables despite their weak economic base through the provisions of reserved seats in Legislatures, represents a major effort by the Government, the reports show that this policy has not given rise to an effective untouchable party—nor does it appear to have generated leaders of the heroic stamp of Ambedkar.

In a country, where unemployment of the educated is chronic educated untouchables have long felt themselves dependent on Government for employment and have done little to attract private employers to hire them.

The political dominance of congress since independence has also given credence to the belief that it is better to support the party in power, whose major leaders have atleast voiced their concern with untouchables, than to lend support to a militant party committed to untouchables but with little prospect for attaining power.

Untouchable politicians including those elected to reserve seats are beholden to the party that supports them with campaign funds and organizational assistance. Given this and similar considerations, prospects seem most unfavourable for the development of an effective national party dedicated primarily to untouchable interests.

The untouchable leaders of today, whosoever and whatever they are, are after going for alliance with Congress or Rashtrawadi Congress or Bharatiya Janta Party and Shiv Sena. And what for? Only for power, pelf and pleasure. Ambedkar had a dream to see his own people a ruling class before his death. His dream remained to be dream and with the present-day leadership without backbone and enblock backing of their own people will remain a dream.

To ensure faster and abiding progress, not only in promoting the welfare but in abolishing the caste system itself, two important areas need to be explored afresh. One area is the role of Science and Technology in abolishing primitive system, the other the role of education in freeing the minds of India's youths from the fetters of casteism.

Science indeed has an effective answer to untouchability, but unfortunately, because of her poverty, India is still years behind the advanced countries in the matter of application of Science to the needs of daily living.

The second approach is to be found in education that will lead to inter-caste marriages and eventually inter-linguistic and inter-religious. Sooner or later India must become emotionally integrated society. Inter-caste marriages have remained an intractable problem complicated by two major difficulties: The reactionary Hindu law and the tradition of arranged marriages.

No less a person than Dr. S. Radhakrishnan, the distinguished Indian Philosopher, pointed out when he was President of India: "Caste has ceased to be a social evil, but has become a political and administrative evil. We want to get out votes and we set up candidates suited to the people who have to vote.... It is essential that politics should be as far as possible lifted out of this kind of morass."

This has been continued after independence. The example is distribution of tickets for Assembly elections held in five States in 2012. Every party seems to have chosen their candidates on the basis of castes. Take for example the case of the distribution of tickets by Bahujan Samaj Party in U.P. Dalits 88, O.B.Cs. 113, Muslims 85, Caste Hindus 117, Brahmins 74, Kshatriya 33. The distribution of tickets have been done under the garb of "social engineering". The similar pattern seems to have been adopted by almost all political parties.

The million dollar question is with this attitude and approach how castes will be annihilated?

Chapter 8

Gandhi and Ambedkar on Hindus and Hinduism

Gandhiji repeatedly made it clear that if he found Hinduism really countenanced untouchability, he will have no hesitation in renouncing Hinduism itself. For he held that religion, so worthy of the name, must not be inconsistent with the fundamental truths of ethics and morality.

The views expressed by Gandhiji from time to time on Hinduism *vis-à-vis* untouchability are summarized below:

"I feel deeply humiliated as a Hindu to find that untouchability appears in its most hideous form of untouchability is a curse which is eating into the vitals of Hinduism and unless we take due precautions and remove this curse from our midst, Hinduism itself is in danger of destruction. That in this age of reason, in this age of wide travel, in this age of comparative study of religions, there should be found people, some of whom are educated, to uphold the hideous doctrine of treating a single human being as untouchable, because of his birth, passes my comprehension.

"I have regarded untouchability as the greatest blot on Hinduism. I was hardly yet twelve when this idea had dawned on me, a scavenger named UKA, an untouchable, used to attend our house for cleaning latrines. Often I would ask my mother why it was wrong to touch him, why I was forbidden to touch him. I accidentally touched UKA. I was asked to perform ablutions and though I naturally obeyed, it was not without smilingly protesting that untouchability was not sanctioned by religion, that it was impossible that it should be so. I was a very dutiful and obedient child and so far as it was consistent with respect for the parents, I often had tussels with them on this matter. I told my mother that she was entirely wrong in considering physical contact with UKA was sinful.

"While at school, I would often happen to touch the untouchables and as I would never conceal that fact from my parents, my mother would tell me that the shortest cut to purifications after the unholy touch was to cancel the touch by touching any Musalman passing by. And simply out of reverence and regard for my mother I would do so. I do not pretend that this thing had crystallized as a conviction in me at the age of twelve, but I do say that I did then regard untouchability as a sin.

"I have always claimed to be a sanatani Hindu. It is not that I am quite innocent of the scriptures. I am not a profound scholar of Sanskrit. I have read the *Vedas* and the *Upanishads* only on translation. Naturally, therefore, mine is not a scholarly study of them. My knowledge of them is no way profound but I have studied other religions also.

"Untouchability is a hydra-headed monster; it is therefore, necessary each time the monster lifts its head to deal with it. The stories told in *Puranas* are, some of them, most dangerous, if we do not know their bearing on the present conditions. The *shastras* would be death trap if we were to regulate our conduct according to every detail given in them.

"Happily, Hindu reformers have recoiled with horror from this practice. They have come to the conclusion that it has no support in the Hindu *shastras* taken as a whole. Isolated texts torn from their contexts and considered by themselves can no doubt be produced in support of this practice, as of any evil known to mankind. But there is abundant authority in the *shastras* to warrant the summarily rejection as being un-Hindu of anything or any practice that is manifestly, of *ahimsa* or *satya*.

"From all the discussions I had with the *shastris*, I have gathered that there is no warrant whatsoever for untouchability as we know it.

"I have had many discussion with many learned *shastris*. I had occasions also to study the shastras which have any bearing on untouchability, and I came to the definite conclusion that there was no warrant whatsoever in the *shastras* for untouchability as we practise today and that there is no warrant whatsoever for the prohibition of the entry on any single Hindu, be he called untouchable or otherwise into public temples.

"I am certain that we shall be blotted out of the book of life, if we do not completely destroy untouchability while still there is time. I do not know a sin more hideous than that in the whole catalogue of sins for it is practiced in the name of religion. It is another thing altogether to fall and to imagine at the same that we are rising.

"There was time when I was wavering between Hinduism and Christianity. When I recovered my balance of mind, I felt that to me salvation was possible only through the Hindu religion and my faith in the Hinduism grew deeper and more enlightened. But even then I believed that untouchability was no part of Hinduism; and that if it was such Hinduism was not for me.

"Untouchability poisons Hinduism as a drop of arsenic poisons milk. Knowing the quality of milk and the use of milk and knowing the quality of arsenic, we should be inpatient with a man sitting near a pitcher of milk and trying to remove arsenic grain by grain and we should throw the pitcher overboard. The curse of untouchability is rendering the milk of Hinduism altogether poisoned and impure. The patience in a matter of this character is not a virtue, patience with evil is really trifling with evil and with ourselves. We have long neglected our duty to the untouchables and unapproachable, and to this extent we have been false representatives of Hinduism. The advance of every person who comes in defence of untouchability should be summarily rejected. In this age whatever man or group of men or women do/does not remain secret for any length of time and we are being daily weighed and found wanting so long as we nurse untouchability in our bosom. All the great religions of the world are in the melting pot. Let us not hide ostrich-like our present faces and ignore the danger that lies at the back of us. In the great turmoil now that is taking place either untouchability has to die or Hinduism has to disappear. But I do know that Hinduism is not going to die or Hinduism has to die, because I see untouchability is a corpse struggling with its last breath to hold on for a little while.

"For reforms of Hinduism and for its real protection removal of untouchability is the greatest thing. Removal of untouchability is the greatest thing. Removal of untouchability is a spiritual process. If untouchability lives, Hinduism must die. I would far rather that Hinduism died than that untouchability lived. Untouchability in its extreme form has always caused me so much pain, because I consider myself to be a Hindu of Hindus saturated with the spirit of Hinduism. I have failed to find a single warrant for existence of untouchability as we believe and practise it today in all those books which we call Hindu *shastras*. But as I have repeatedly said, if I found that Hinduism really countenanced untouchability, I should have no hesitation in renouncing Hinduism itself. I have never been able to reconcile myself to untouchability, I have always regarded it as an excrescence in Hinduism. It is true that it has been handed down to us from generations but so are many evil practices even to this day.

"The practice of untouchability is intolerable to me. I cannot endure it. The Hindus owe it as duty to make a determined effort to purify Hinduism and eradicate the practice of untouchability. Till Hindu society is purged of this sin, Swaraj is an impossibility. I am more pained of this evil being a part of Hindu religion than the *Antyajas* are by their being treated as untouchables whose Shuddhi I effect, but my own and that of the Hindu religion."

In reply to a question from an *Adi-Dravida* correspondent whether he is really interested in the welfare of Harijans or is he actuated by any ulterior motives so as to show an increase in population of the Hindus, Gandhiji replied, "He should await my death for framing the final judgment. Meanwhile if he is prepared to accept my word, I would assure him that I set no value upon increase in the number of Hindus so-called false professors of a creed not only do no service to it but may kill it. The only motive therefore, that guides me in working for the Harijan cause is to see Hinduism purified of the curse of untouchability.

"Whether in prison or outside prison Harijan service will be always after my heart and will be the breath of life for me, more precious than the daily bread. I cannot live without Harijan service for one single minute. It is my constant prayer to the Almighty that this blot of untouchability may be removed in its entirety from Hinduism and that the millions of caste Hindus may see the sun of Truth which shines upon us if we would only remove the scales from our eyes. My life is dedicated to this cause and I shall consider no penance too great for the vindication of this Truth.

"To remove untouchability is a penance that caste Hindus owe to Hinduism and themselves. The purification required is not for untouchables, but for the so-called superior castes. There is no vice that is special to the untouchables, not even dirt and insanitation. It is our arrogance which blinds us, superior caste, Hindus to our own blemishes and which magnifies those of our downtrodden brethren whom we have suppressed and whom we keep under suppression.

"Untouchability as it is practiced is a sin against God and man and is therefore like a poison slowly eating into the very vitals of Hinduism. It has no sanction whatsoever in the Hindu shastras. It might be difficult for me to establish my point by quoting authorities from the *Bhagavad* or *Manusmriti.* But I claim to have understood the spirit of Hinduism as sinned in giving sanction to untouchability and if we do not get rid of it in time, we will destroy Hinduism. Therefore, the sooner it is ended the better for Hinduism, the better for India and perhaps for mankind in general.

"It is therefore the bounden duty of every Hindu to wake up to a sense of his duty and to wake up his lethargic brethren also to a sense of their duty. If the Savarna Hindus could with one voice express their wish this monster of untouchability would go.

"Untouchability is a snake with a thousand mouths through each of which it shows its poisonous fangs even when you may least expect them to see.

"It is repugnant to our sense of humanity to consider a single human being as untouchable by birth. If we were to examine the scriptures of the world and the conduct of people other than Hindus, you do not find any parallel to the untouchability. The ulcer of untouchability has gone so deep down that it seems to pervade our life. Hence the usual difference. Brahmin and non-Brahmin, provinces and provinces; religions and religions. Why should there be all this poison smelling of untouchability? Why should we not all be children of one Indian family and further of one human family? Are we not like branches of the same tree?

"When untouchability is rooted out, these distinctions will vanish and no one will consider himself superior to another. Naturally, exploitation too will cease and cooperation will be the order of the day.

"Every educated Hindu should constitute himself the untouchable's friend and regard his duty to free him from the tyranny of custom masquerading under the name of religion.

"Hindus should be brave to get rid of their sins. So long as they have not rid themselves of the sin, have not begged forgiveness of untouchables, they will be visited with no end of misfortune. They should know that the practice of untouchability is sin. If they can, by their own voluntary efforts, purge themselves of the evils in them, they will have freedom for the asking.

"Today Brahmins and Kshatriyas, Vaishyas and Shudras are mere labels. I wish that all the Hindus call themselves Shudras. That is the only way to demonstrate the truth of Brahminism.

"In India a Brahmin may be as poor as the untouchable but he will not be ill-treated on that account. Untouchability in India rests upon the idea of superiority of one section of people over another on account of their birth. The untouchable, in spite of his being treated cruelly by the caste Hindus, yet continues to profess the Hindu religion. He worships the same God and Goddess. But he is denied access to the Hindu temples. Also strangely enough, this pernicious system is supposed to be sanctified by Hindu religion. Once the untouchable is allowed entry into Hindu temples the stigma attached to his community will no more be there, being deprived of his so-called religious sanction.

"I claim to be able to speak of Harijans from North to South, the East and the West of India. My only business is if it is at all possible, to lift those who are in mire. I want to do it because I want to lift myself. With their abjectness, I feel myself also abject.

I know that if Hindus are freed from the coil of untouchability you would find that all the corroding distinctions not between Hindus and Hindus only, but also between Hindus and non-Hindus, will disappear as if by a mere touch.

"I would ask you to believe me when I say that there is no political motive behind my Harijan work. The political consequences of the removal of untouchability have no attraction for me. Indeed I believe that if we approached this question with a political motive, we should fail to serve the Harijans and we should damage Hinduism. A duty religiously performed carries with it many other important consequences.

"Seek ye first the kingdom of God; and everything else will be added unto you, is to my mind a scientific truth. I must say that the service of the so-called untouchables does not rank with me in anyway subordinate to any kind of political work. I saw that to a certain extent my social work would be impossible without the help of political work, I took to the latter and only to the extent that it helped the former. The work of social reform of self-purification of this nature is a hundred times dearer to me than what is called purely political work.

"I look to the movement as purely religious, moral or humanitarian. It is to me purely one of desire to expiate for sins that we have been guilty of all these years. Therefore, I cannot think of the movement in the terms of any political end. Not that it will not have political results; but we need not give a moment's thought to the broadest of movements of our times.

"In my opinion, untouchability is a wholly artificial product. It has no connection with moral or intellectual development of people for the simple reason that in Hindu society there are to be seen men described as untouchables who are in every way equal in moral and intellectual development to the highest among the caste Hindus and yet who are treated as untouchables. My picture of a society free from untouchability is one in which no one will consider himself superior to another. It is obvious that in society so composed there will be no unseemly rivalry or quarrelling.

"My effort for the removal of untouchability is an integral part of my life and you cannot isolate it from my other activities.

I would not be a true Hindu unless I live and move and have been trying to rid Hinduism of this curse. We shall be the laughing stock of humanity if we hug this curse, and the religion that nurses it shall stand condemned by the world.

"In my opinion, untouchability in the form in which we practise today is not and ought not to be, an essential part of Hinduism. There is sheer ignorance and cruelty behind it. I look upon it as an excrescence on Hinduism. It does not project religion, but suffocates it. Treating Antyajas as untouchables is a cruel form of boycott. Whatever the justification there may have been for the practice when it started, there is none now. Like tuberculosis, therefore, it is eating into the vitals of Hinduism.

"I see in the continuance of untouchability slow destruction overtaking Hinduism, and I promise that if you study the thing itself as I am doing, you will observe that the low disintegration which Hinduism is going through may become so rapid as to make it impossible for the workers to overcome it.

"I will say even with my last breath that, if we do not wash out the stain of untouchability, Hindus and Hinduism will be wiped out from the face of the earth. I want to uplift Hinduism. I regard the untouchables as an integral part of the Hindu community. I believe in the doctrine of equality as taught by Lord Krishna in the Gita. The Gita teaches us that members of all the four castes should be treated on equal basis. It is therefore our duty to see that the untouchables do not feel that they are despised or looked down upon. Let them not be offered leavings from our plates for their subsistence. I for one would regard the leavings from the kitchen as failed to render him personal assistance when he was in need.

"I can make an appeal to your reason and to your heart. But it is God alone who can arm the word that I speak to you with the power to shoot an arrow and make a lodgment in your heart. If you can believe the word of a man who is perpetually seeking after truth, believe me that throughout my waking hours, and if I can say so, during my sleep also, my one constant prayer to God is that He may give that power to my words so that the Hindu heart can be touched and it may be purged of the virus of untouchability, and Hindus and Hinduism may be saved from this impending doom.

"Please remember that your duty and my duty does not end with merely recognizing the Harijans as blood brothers and blood sisters. That is the beginning of the end. The end is that we should rid ourselves of every form of untouchability that is eating into the vitals of Hindu society. The poison has corrupted the whole of our society. What, therefore, you and I have to do is to forget that there is anybody high or low on this earth. That, being the children of the same creator, the same God no matter to which faith we may belong, no matter what view we may have, we are all equal in the eyes of our maker.

"We shall have to make such a sustained effort to purge ourselves of this terrible sin in that the effort will by itself raise us very high. We might have to pour out our blood like water before the curse is removed and Hinduism becomes purified.

"I have declared times without number from various public platforms that it is the prayer of my heart that if I should fail to obtain Moksha in this very birth I might be born a Bhangi in my next birth. I believe in Varnashrama both according to birth and Moksha. But I do not regard Bhangi as in any sense a low order. On the contrary I know many Bhangis who are worthy of reverence. On the other hand, there are Brahmins going about whom it would be very difficult to regard with any reverence. Holding these views, therefore, if there is a rebirth in store for me, I wish to be reborn a Pariah in the midst of Pariahs, because thereby I would be able to render more effective service to them and also be in a better position to plead with other communities on their behalf."

Yet on another occasion Gandhiji expressed: "I do not want to attain Moksha. I do not want to be reborn. But if I have to be reborn, I should be born an untouchable, so that I may share their sorrows, sufferings, and the affronts levelled at them, and that I may endeavour to free myself and them from that miserable condition. I therefore pray that if I should be born again, I should do so not as a Brahmin, Kshatriya. Vaishya or Shudra, but as an Atishudra. I also pray that if am I of the untouchable unfinished, with my Hinduism unfulfilled, I may be born again amongst the untouchable to bring my Hinduism to its fulfillment.

"I would be worthy of the title of Mahatma which the country has conferred on me—but which I have not accepted—only when Hinduism was purged of the evil of untouchability.

Gandhi's fight on behalf of untouchables was a part of his fight for social justice. He spoke against the practice of untouchability with all his might. He tried to convince people of its unreasonableness. And characteristically he staked his life to bring social equality to them. Gandhi marshalled all his fund of vehemence to bridge the wall of prejudice that guarded the unjust tradition of untouchability. 'I regard untouchability as the greatest blot on Hinduism,' he said. 'A hideous doctrine', he called it, 'a curse that is eating into the vitals of Hinduism.' It was for him, 'a sin,' 'an excrescence to be removed by every effort,' 'a heinous crime against humanity,' 'social leprosy,' 'a hydra headed monster,' poison on Hinduism 'as a drop of arsenic in milk,' and so on. Such language from a man so meek and mild points to the deep feelings Gandhi had against untouchability.

To convince people of the injustice of the untouchability Gandhi had recourse to many ways of persuasion. For instance he repeatedly told people that we have no right to speak against foreign domination till we rid ourselves of the domination of our own people. 'The curse of foreign domination and the attendant exploitation is the just redistribution meted out by God to us for our exploitation of a sixth of our own race and their studied degradation in the sacred name of religion' (*Young India*: 13th October 1921).

He allied this argument with the argument of Swaraj; 'without the removal of the taint Swaraj is a meaningless term. I consider the removal of untouchability as a most powerful factor in the process of attainment of Swaraj.'

He even said it is essential to it. And at another time he declared: 'There seems to be a lurking thought with many of us that we can gain Swaraj and keep untouchability. They do not even see the contradiction inherent in the thought.'

Gandhi put forward the argument from reason, the argument of social equality. Untouchability is repugnant to reason and to their instinct of mercy, pity or love. It is a heinous crime against humanity and ought to be fought on all fronts. And such a fight is a fight for the recognition of human dignity. He could not understand how one could accord differential treatment to any person, be he Brahmin or Bhangi, who worships the same God. So he pleaded for equality in the eye of the law, in the matter of elementary human rights even as, irrespective of caste, race, creed or colour, we have certain things in common, e.g. hunger, thirst, etc.

Defining his aim, he said: "You must have the right to worship in any temple in which the members of other castes are admitted. You must have admission to schools along with the children of other castes without any distinction. You must be eligible to the highest office in the land not excluding even that of the Viceroy's. That is my definition of the removal of untouchability."

Gandhi once said that if he had his own way he would make a Harijan girl the head of the Indian State. She would discharge her high duties with the help of wise ministers. He and the intimates of his Ashram performed all the so-called menial services themselves, including the work of scavenging. The Ashram was a colony where the Communist ideal of "from each according to ability and to each according to need" was fully and literally carried out.

Nowhere is his attitude to the dignity of man better typified than in his struggle to redeem the Hinduism from the canker of untouchability. Here was social emancipation not merely for the unfortunate suppressed and depressed classes, but even for the so-called high-caste Hindus who subjected them to untold misery in the name of time-worn taboos. Gandhi's fight for the emancipation of the untouchables will always be reckoned in history as the most glorious part of his championship of human rights and dignity. The only comparable instance in history is Lincoln's struggle for the emancipation of the Negro slaves in America. But Gandhi's campaign, while it lacked the glamour and heroism of the battlefield, had a power and a halo of its own, unparalleled in man's annals. It possessed the bravery of the soul, it depended on the strength of self-suffering and the triumph of the human spirit. His own life was an epic struggle against the age-old prejudice of untouchability. It grossly offended his sense of human dignity and human justice. In the emancipation of the untouchables, he indeed saw the emancipation of true Hinduism itself.

Political freedom had no meaning to him if it did not apply to the untouchables. In the India of his dreams, he declared: "There will be no untouchability. The untouchables will have the same rights as any other." It is true that merely incorporating in the Constitution a provision by which untouchability is declared illegal or by enacting special legislative measures to secure rights to those denied them is not enough to wipe off an ancient and vicious system of social discrimination. But no man prepared the ground and led us to the road to its abolition more than Gandhi.

Gandhi expressed his views and feelings about untouchables and untouchability through his writings and speeches and columns of the *Harijan* and *Young India* from time to time, which are given below:

Untouchability as it is practiced in Hinduism today is a sin against God, and man and is, therefore, like a poison slowly eating into the very vitals of Hinduism. It has no sanction whatsoever in the Hindu Shastras taken as a whole. The untouchability as we are observing in India is a hideous thing and wears various forms in various provinces, even in districts. It has degraded both the untouchables and the touchables. It has stunted the growth of nearly 40 million human beings. They are denied even the ordinary amenities of life. The sooner, therefore, it is ended, the better for Hinduism, the better for India, and perhaps better for mankind in general (*Harijan*: 11-2-1933).

I have no shadow of doubt that in the great turmoil now taking place either untouchability has to die or Hinduism has to disappear. But I do know that Hinduism is not dying, is not going to die, because I see untouchability is a corps struggling with its last breath to hold on for a little while.

The untouchables are a class apart—a standing reproach to Hinduism. The castes are a handicap, they are no sin. Untouchability is a sin, a grievous crime, and will eat up Hinduism, if the later does not kill the snake in time. Untouchables should no longer be the outcastes of Hinduism. They should be regarded as honoured members of Hindu society (*Young India*: 4.6.1931).

I am certain that we shall be blotted out of the Book of Life, if we do not completely destroy untouchability while still there is time. I do not know of a sin more heinous than that in the whole catalogue of sins, for it is practiced in the name of religion. It is one thing to fall because we are weak; it is another thing altogether to fall and to imagine at the same time that we are rising (*Harijan*: 29.6.1934).

The fact that we addressed God as the 'purifier of the polluted,' and by similar appellations, shows that it is a sin to regard anyone born in Hinduism as polluted or untouchable- that it is satanic to do so. I have hence been never tired of repeating that it is a great sin. I do not pretend that this thing had crystallized as a conviction in me at the age of twelve, but I do say that I did then regard untouchability as a sin.

The Jambusar Municipality in Gujarat had presented an address to Gandhi. The address studiously omitted all references to Gandhi's efforts for the removal of untouchability, but otherwise full of warm praise. In reply to the address Gandhi said:

"My effort for the removal of untouchability is an integral part of my life, and you cannot isolate it from my other activities. I would not be a true Hindu, unless I live and move and have my being in trying to rid Hinduism of this curse. Those, therefore, who believe in untouchability as part of Hinduism, or who are indifferent in the matter cannot give me an address of welcome. I am no official, nor a Sardar, that you should give me a conventional address. Not that any conventional address of welcome can be called one. But I deserve it the least. I am a bhangi, a scavenger, a spinner, a weaver and a laborer, and I want, if at all, to be honored as such. We shall be laughing stock of humanity if we hug this curse, and the religion that nurses it shall stand condemned by the world. You should not therefore have presented to me this address. It will, however, serve as a beacon-light to me. I hope that no association will trouble to present me with an address if it cannot endorse my work for and among the untouchables" (*Young India*: 23.4.1925).

It is my certain conviction that if the Hindu heart is completely purged of the taint of untouchability, the event will have its inevitable influence not only upon all communities in India but on the whole world. This belief is daily becoming stronger. I cannot remove from my heart untouchability regarding several millions of human beings and harbor it towards some other millions. The very fact of the Hindu heart getting rid of distinctions of high and low must cure us of mutual jealousies and distrusts of and among other communities. It is for that reason that I have staked my life on this issue. If we believe that we are all children of one and the same God and that God is Truth and Justice, how can there be untouchability amongst us, His children? God of Truth and Justice can never create distinctions of high and low among His own children. I, therefore, invite all without distinction of race and religion to assist this movement by praying for its complete success, so that we may all live in peace and friendship.

Whatever weaknesses we may notice about untouchables are a reflection of our own weaknesses and sins. They are a direct result of the ill-treatment that we have heaped upon their devoted heads. Their real rise, therefore, depends upon the removing of untouchability root and branch and upon showing a growing purity in our lives.

I have long since counted myself as a 'bhangi' in my speech, in my actions and above all in mind and spirit. Anyone who looks upon them with contempt does the same to me. Indeed, I hold it an honor to be among the despised Harijans and among the 'bhangis'.

The ideal 'bhangi' of my conception would be a Brahmin, par excellence, possibly even excel him. It is possible to envisage the existence of a 'bhangi,' without a Brahmin but without the former, the latter could not be. It is the 'bhangi' that enables the society to live. A 'bhangi' does to the society what a mother does for a baby. A mother washes her baby of direct dirt and ensures his health. Even so a 'bhangi' protects and safeguards the health of the entire community by maintaining sanitation for it. The Brahmin's duty is to look after the sanitation of the soul, the 'bhangi's' that of the body of the society. But there is difference in practice; the Brahmin generally does not live up to his duty, the 'bhangi' does, and willy-nilly, no doubt. Society is sustained by his services. The 'bhangi' constituted the foundation.

The only motive that guides me in working for the Harijan cause is to see Hinduism purified of the curse of untouchability. And if, in so becoming, it is represented only by one Hindu, I would have no repentance but real joy that it was not dead (*Harijan*: 6.4.1934).

Removal of untouchability is a question of double education, that of "touchables" as well as "untouchables". "Touchables" have to be taught to be patiently by precept and example that untouchability is a sin against God and humanity, and the "untouchables" that they should cease to fear the "touchables" and shed untouchability among themselves. I know that that is very easily said. But have found nothing else. Living in the midst of both, I know how hard the work is among both. If Hinduism is to live, the work has to be done, however difficult and even hopeless it may appear to be (*Harijan*: 8.6.1940).

It was I who pushed the item to the forefront of the Congress program, and anyone bent on cavilling at me might say that it was a clever bait held out by me to the untouchables. Let me say at once that that charge is idle. It grew on me very early in life that those who believed themselves to be Hindus must perform the penance in the shape of wiping out this stain before they could be proud of Hinduism, and as the majority of Congressmen were Hindus, and as the program then put before the nation was not one of self-purification, I put it in front of the Congress program, in the conviction that unless the Hindus were prepared to wipe out this stain they could not regard themselves as fit for Swaraj. That conviction has come upon me as a self-evident proposition. If we came into power, with the stain of untouchability unaffected, I am positive that the untouchables would be far worse under that Swaraj than they are now, for the simple reason that our weaknesses and our failings would then be buttressed up by the accession of power. That in brief is my position and I have always held that this self-purification is an indispensable condition of Swaraj. It is not a position that I have arrived at today. It is as old as when I began to think of Swaraj. I know that those to whom only the exciting thing called politics has an exclusive appeal will laugh at this kind of thing. But for me it is nearest and dearest to my heart.

We have not been able to win Swaraj because of the load of sin that we are still carrying on our backs. If all the so-called touchable Hindus did real penance for having wronged their untouchable brethren, Swaraj would be automatically in our hands.

To blame the Harijans for their present condition is like a slave holder blaming his slave for the misery and squalor of latter may be living in. We would ridicule the slave holder, perhaps even accuse him of insincerity, if he made the removal of squalor by the slave as a condition precedent to the grant of freedom.

On God's earth nobody is low and nobody is high. We are all his creatures; and just as in the eyes of parents all their children are absolutely equal, so also in God's eyes all His creatures must be equal.

My mission is to invite Savarna Hindus to wash themselves clean of the guilt of untouchability. And if, during the short period of grace open to Savarna Hindus, they fail to do this duty, I have not the shadow of doubt that Hinduism will perish. If you understand thoroughly the spirit of my message, the change of heart is an incredibly simple performance; and you can see in the twinkling of an eye how, if this change comes about in Savarna Hindu hearts, the economic, social and religious progress of Harijans must follow. It will then be a sign and seal of this change of heart. May God give you strength to do it and save Hinduism from impending doom (*Harijan*: 12.1.1934).

If untouchability is not removed root and branch from Hinduism, Hinduism is bound to perish. I would not have untouchability removed by force or show of force or compulsion of any kind whatsoever. Removal of untouchability is not a matter of law or of compulsion. Removal of untouchability is a matter of change of heart, perfect purification on the part of millions of Hindus. And that can be only brought about by the sacrifice of thousands of workers themselves, and not by causing injury to other people.

It has been my custom to practice what I believe. Hence to come in contact with and touch the 'Antyajas' is with me an object-lesson. It is my request to the Antyajas to keep patience. The Hindu atmosphere is changing, though slowly but steadily. Even the orthodox Hindus have begun to realize the sin of untouchability, and it is very probable that this sin will not last long. The Antyajas should make great efforts to remedy their own shortcomings (*Young India*: 10.9.1919).

The Harijans should realize that the untouchability is dead and gone. Its evil effect will persist for a long time to come. The duration will be the measure of our joint-neglect. Greater by far is the responsibility of the caste Hindus. If they will do their duty and work whole-heartedly, they will certainly succeed in stopping these sacrifices and the habit of carrion-eating. Nothing but the spread of enlightenment is required to rid the community of evil superstition and evil habits (*Harijan*: 18.3.1933).

The object of the movement is to do away with this utterly unnatural division and to secure for Harijans the simple justice to which they are entitled at the hands of Savarna Hindus. Thus the movement is one of repentance and reparation. Hence it is confined, on the one hand, to constructive work among Harijans and, on the other hand, to conversion of Savarnas by persuasion, arguments and, above all, by correct conduct on the part of reformers (*Harijan*: 15.6.1934).

The Harijan Sevak Sangh is performing the double duty of asking the caste Hindus, on the one hand, to repent of the injustice that they have done to the Harijans by spreading education among them and by bringing to their notice the evils that oppression always breeds among the oppressed (*Harijan*: 26.10.1934).

The so-called Hindus are responsible for their failings, and only the inherent strength of Hinduism is responsible for their good points. Hinduism has helped them to retain some of their culture in spite of the oppression they have labored under. They would never have been reduced to their present state if we had regarded them as our own kith and kin (*Young India*: 19.4.1928).

The work of removal of untouchability is not merely a social or economic reform whose extent can be measured by so much social amenities or economic relief provided in so much time. Its goal is to touch the hearts of the millions of Hindus who honestly believe in the present day untouchability as a God-made institution, as old as the human race itself. This it will be admitted, is a task infinitely higher than mere social and economic reform. Its accomplishment undoubtedly includes all these and much more. For it means nothing short of a complete revolution in the Hindu thought and the disappearance of the horrible and terrible doctrine of inborn inequality and high-and-lowness, which has poisoned Hinduism and is slowly undermining its very existence. Such a change can only be brought about by an appeal to the highest in man (*Harijan*: 8.7.1933).

Removal of untouchability is not a popular cause in the sense in which great political movements have been and become popular all over the world. Removal of untouchability is a mighty social reform. But it cannot furnish sensations. It is a plodder's work. And a record of the work of plodders require editorial gifts of a higher order to make it interesting. Plodders can only attract plodding editors. Therefore, the only way before those who are intimately connected with the Harijan movement is to continue to work with an ever increasing faith in the cause and leave the result to take care of itself (*Harijan*: 21.12.1934).

Those who regard untouchability as a sin must be prepared to suffer all the hardships of boycott and the like as a part of the process of purification and penance. In all humility they must learn to dispense with the outward form. Anything done in the name of God and for His sake needs no support from officiating priest, whether it is a death or a marriage or a shraddha. Anybody can unite a couple in marriage by reciting the sacred mantra. God is known not by His thousand names only but by millions of names. Any name which comes from the heart and by which we can recognize Him is as good as any other or, rather the best of all for us. But these things can only be done by those who have the courage of their conviction, faith in themselves, faith in their cause and faith in a living God. This is not a movement in which faint-heartedness can be of any use. Only workers with stout hearts and irreproachable character will be able to infect the villagers with their own strong convictions and enable them to do the right thing in the face of boycott or worse persecution (*Harijan*: 4.3.1933).

I am quite clear in my mind that untouchability is gone. The untouchables will not remain slaves for ever. Thank God, they are being surely, if slowly, awakened. The pace is daily increasing. There are limits even to the patience of God almighty. He gives a long rope to untruth and irreligion. But in the end, only Truth remains and nothing else. Hence Hinduism can only live minus untouchability, which is an untruth (*Harijan*: 22.4.1933).

We Hindus are undergoing a period of probation. Whether we desire it or not, untouchability is going. But if during this period of probation, we repent for the sin, if we reform and purify ourselves, history will record that one act as a supreme act of purification on the part of Hindus. But if, through the working of the time spirit, we are compelled to do the things against our will and Harijans come to their own, it will be no credit to the Hindus or to Hinduism. If we fail in this trial, Hinduism and Hindus will perish.

It is cowardly for anyone to suggest that the Antyajas will be emancipated when the old generation has passed away. Our worth as men consists in doing Tapascharya and awakening in our elders compassion and the present sense of Dharma. That and nothing less is our duty. If we boldly translate our words into action, the task can be accomplished quite soon. It is a mean desire to wish to kill an enemy so that one may rule over his kingdom afterwards. Dharma consists in winning him over to our way of thinking and converting him into friend.

It is the duty of every Congress worker to befriend the untouchable brother and to plead with the Hindus, that Hinduism of the Vedas, the Upanishads, Hinduism of Bhagwat Gita and of Shankara and Ramanuja contains no warrant for treating a single human being, no matter how fallen, as an untouchable. Let every Congressman plead in the gentlest manner possible with orthodox, that the bar sinister is the very negation of ahimsa.

The above were the views expressed by Gandhi about untouchables and untouchability. Any person who has a rational and open mind will believe that Gandhi wanted from the bottom of his heart to remove untouchability and uplift the untouchables through various constructive programs. But Ambedkar never believed in Gandhi and his methods.

And now look at what Ambedkar said about Hindus and Hinduism. In his own words: 'It must be borne in mind that those who like Mr. Gandhi accept the Chaturvarnya as an ideal form of society, either do not know the history of the mutual relations of the four varnas or cherishing an illusions conjuring up of a vision for purpose which they are out to serve. For the fact is that the four varnas never formed a society based on cooperative effort. The four varnas were animated by nothing but a spirit of animosity towards one another. There would not be the slightest exaggeration to say that the social history of the Hindus is a history not merely of class struggle but class war fought with such bitterness that even the Marxist will find it difficult to cite parallel cases to match.

"In Hinduism there is no hope for untouchables. But this is not the only reason why the untouchables wish to quit Hinduism. There is another reason which makes it imperative for them to quit Hinduism. Untouchability is a part of Hinduism. Even those who for the sake of posing as enlightened reformers deny that untouchability is part of Hinduism does not matter. It enhances his sense of superiority by the reason of this consciousness that there are millions of untouchables below him. But what does it mean for an untouchable to say that he believes in Hinduism? It means that he accepts that he is an untouchable and that he is an untouchable is the result of Divine dispensation. For Hinduism is Divine dispensation. An untouchable may not cut the throat of a Hindu but cannot be expected to give an admission that he is an untouchable and rightly so. Which untouchable is there with soul so dead as to give such an admission by adhering to Hinduism? That Hinduism is inconsistent with the self-respect and honour of the untouchables is the strongest ground which justifies the conversion of the untouchables to another and nobler faith.

"The untouchables should bear in mind two things. Firstly, it is futile to expect the Hindu religion to perform the mission of bringing about social justice. Such a task may be performed by Islam, Christianity, or Buddhism. The Hindu religion is itself the embodiment of inequality and injustice to the untouchables. For it, to preach the gospel of justice is to go against its own being. To hope for this is to hope for miracle. Secondly, assuming that this task which Hinduism was fitted to perform, it would be impossible for it to perform. The social barrier between them and the Hindus is much greater than the barrier between them and the Hindus and their men. Religion, however efficacious it may be within a community or a nation, is quite powerless to break these barriers and make them one whole.

"The untouchables can very well ask the protagonists of Hinduism the very question which Lord Balfour asked to positivist. Nay the untouchables can ask many more. They can ask, Does Hinduism recognize their worth as human beings? Does it stand for the equality? Does it at least help to forge the bond of fraternity between them and us Hindus? Does it teach the Hindus that the untouchables are their kindred? Does it say to the Hindus it is a sin to treat the untouchable as being neither man nor beast? Does it inculcate upon the Hindus the virtue of being friendly to them? Does it tell the Hindus to love them, to respect them, and to do them no wrong? Does Hinduism universalize the value of life without distinction?

"In India itself, the whole Brahmin community is educated man, woman, and child. How many Brahmins are free from their belief in untouchability? How many are prepared to stand by the side of the untouchables in their fight against injustice? In short, how many are prepared to make the cause of the untouchables their own cause?

"No Hindu can give an affirmative answer to any of these questions. On the contrary, the wrongs to which the untouchables are subjected by the Hindus are acts which are sanctioned by Hindu religion. They are done in the name of Hinduism and are justified in the name of Hinduism. The spirit and tradition which make the lawful the lawlessness of the Hindu towards the untouchables is founded and supported by the teachings of Hinduism. How can the Hindus ask the untouchables to accept Hinduism and stay in Hinduism? Why should the untouchables adhere to Hinduism which is solely responsible for their degradation? How can the untouchables stay in Hinduism? Untouchability is the lowest depth to which the degradation of human being can be carried. To be poor is bad but not so bad as to be an untouchable. The low can rise above his status, an untouchable cannot. To be suffering is bad but not so bad as to be an untouchable. They shall some day be comforted. An untouchable cannot hope for this. To have to be meek is bad but it is not so bad as to be an untouchable. The meek if they do not inherit the earth may at least be strong. The untouchable cannot hope for that.

"Many Hindus have a vested interest in untouchability. That vested interest may take the shape of feeling of social superiority or it may take the shape of economic exploitation such as forced labour or cheap labour, the fact remains that Hindus have a vested interest in untouchability. It is only natural that vested interest should not yield to the dictates of reason. The untouchables should therefore, know that there are limits to what reason can do.

"The established order is hereditary order both in status as well as in function. Once an untouchable, always untouchable. Once a Brahmin, always a Brahmin. Once a sweeper, always a sweeper. Under it, those who are born high, remain high, those who are born low, remain low. In other words, the established order is based on an inexorable law of Karma or destiny which is fixed once and for all and can never be changed. This destiny has no relation to the merits of the individuals living, under it. An untouchable, however, superior he may, be mentally and morally, is below a touchable in rank, no matter how inferior he may be morally. An untouchable however poor he may be, must always take rank above an untouchable, however rich he may be.

"The Indian village is the very negation of a republic. If it is a republic it is republic of the untouchables, by the untouchables and for the untouchables. It is a kind of colonialism of the Hindus designed to exploit the untouchables. The untouchables have no rights. They are there only to wait, serve and submit. They are there to do or die. They have no rights. They have no rights because they are outside the village republic, and because they are outside the so-called republic they are outside the Hindu fold. This is a vicious circle. But this is a fact which cannot be gainsaid.

"To an average Hindu, the untouchable is not fit even for human association. He is the carrier of evil. He is not a human being. He must be shunned.

"The Hindus are prepared to use every means to suppress untouchables whenever the untouchables try to upset it even in the slightest degree. The ordinary non-violent Hindu will not hesitate to use the most violence against the untouchables. There is no cruelty which he will not praise against them to sustain the established order. Not many will readily believe this. But this is a fact.

"Under the established order, the untouchables have no right to education and certainly have no right to be admitted to the village schools. Those untouchables who have dared to make a breach in these rules of the established order have been severely punished by the Hindus.

"Under the established order the work of lifting and removing dead cattle as well as doing the scavenger's work is beneath the dignity of the Hindus. It must be done by the untouchables. The untouchables have also begun to think that it is derogatory to their status and are refusing to do it. The untouchables, however, are forced by the Hindus to do it against their will.

"The Hindus treat the untouchables as being born to serve the Hindu community. It being his duty to serve, the untouchable cannot refuse to serve the Hindu whenever the latter is called upon to do so. The Hindu hold the belief that they can command the labour of the untouchables.

"If the Hindu observes untouchability it is because his religion enjoins him to do so. If he is ruthless and lawless in putting down the untouchables rising against the established order it is because his religion not only tells him that the established order is divine and therefore sacrosanct but also imposes upon him a duty to see that this established order is maintained by all means possible. If he does not listen to the call of humanity, it is because his religion does not enjoin him to regard the untouchables as human beings. If he does not feel any qualms of atrocities against the untouchable, it is because his religion tells him that nothing is sin which is done in defence of the social order.

"It is incontrovertible that the main cause which is responsible for the fate of the untouchables is the Hindu religion and its teachings. Those who are fond of comparing slavery with untouchability do not realize that they are facing a paradox. Legally the slave was not a free man. Yet, socially he had all the freedom necessary for the growth of his personality.

"This is indeed a very glaring paradox. What is the explanation of this paradox? There is only one explanation of this paradox. It is that while religion was on the side of the slave, religion has been against the untouchables. The Hindu law declared that the untouchable was not a person. As the Hindu law did not regard the untouchable a person, Hinduism refused to regard him as a human being fit for comradeship.

"What has saved the slave is that his personality was recognized by society and what has ruined the untouchable is that Hindu society did not recognize his personality, treated him as one whose personality was unclean which rendered him as unfit for human association and common dealing.

"Hinduism has made the untouchable sub-human. It has made the Hindu inhuman. There is no escape to either from the established order of the sub-human and the inhuman. The untouchables do not belong to the society of Hindus and the Hindu does not feel that he and the untouchables belong to one society. This is the reason why the conduct of the Hindu is marked by a moralistic unconcernedness.

"Not having conscience, the Hindu has no such thing in him as righteous indigestion against the iniquities and injustices from which the untouchable has been suffering. He sees no wrong in these inequities and injustices and refuses to budge. By his absence of conscience the Hindu is a great obstacle in faith of the removal of untouchability.

"The Hindu social order is based on the principle of graded inequality. It may not be an exaggeration to say that not many people understand the significance of this principle. The social system based on inequality stands on a different footing from a social system based on graded inequality. The former is a weak system which is not capable of self-preservation. The latter, on the other hand, is capable of self-preservation. In a social system based on a graded inequality, the low orders can combine to overthrow the system. None of them have any interest to preserve it. In a social system based on a graded inequality possibility of a general common attack by the aggrieved parties is non-existent. In a system of graded inequality, the aggrieved parties are not on a common level.

"Untouchability may be a misfortune to the untouchables. But there is no doubt that it is good fortune to the Hindus. It gives them a class which they can look down upon. The Hindus do not want a system in which nobody will be anybody. They also do not want a system in which everybody may be somebody. They want a system in which they will be somebodies and others will be nobodies. The untouchables are nobodies. This makes the Hindus somebodies. The system of untouchability sustains the natural pride of the Hindus and make them feel as well as look big. This is an additional reason why the Hindus are not likely to give up untouchability particularly those large majority who are small men.

"The discrimination against the untouchables is practiced by the Hinduism on a scale, the extent of which it is impossible for an outsider to imagine. There is no field of life in which the untouchables and the Hindus come into competition and in which the former is not subjected to the discrimination. It is also of the most virulent type.

"In the matter of social relationship, it takes the form of barriers against dancing, bathing, eating, drinking, wrestling, worshipping. It puts a ban on all common cycles of participation.

"In the use of public facilities, the spirit of discrimination manifests itself in the exclusion of untouchables from schools, wells, temples and means of conveyance. Discrimination against untouchables in the matter of securing land, credit, jobs, exist in the most rampant form. It is in service that discrimination shows itself most strongly. Though there are no regulations, there are well recognized rules which govern the entry and promotions of the untouchables in the matter of service. Most often an untouchable will not get any entry. All departments are closed to them. The weaving side of the textile mills—the whole of the Army—is closed to the untouchables. If he did, there is a well set limit beyond which the untouchable may not rise, no matter what his efficiency or length of service is. The principle in general is maintained that the untouchables shall not be placed in the administrative authority over the Hindus. The consequence is that unless some entire branch of service is turned over to the untouchables, there are very few posts of consequence which the untouchables are allowed to fill. The only field of service in which there is no discrimination against the untouchables is scavenging. Here also all supervisory posts which carry higher salary and which do not involve contact with fifth by Hindus. In this situation rights of citizenship cannot mean the rights of the untouchables. The government of the people and for the people cannot mean government for the untouchables. The government of the people and for the people cannot mean government for the untouchables, equal rights for all cannot mean equal rights for the untouchables. This discrimination is the strongest barrier against the untouchables. It prevents them from rising out of it. It has made the life of the untouchable one of the constant fear of one thing or another of unemployment, assault, persecution, etc. It is a life of insecurity.

"There is another form of discrimination which though subtle is nonetheless real. Under it a systematic attempt is made to lower the dignity and status of a meritorious untouchable. A Hindu leader would be described merely as a great Indian leader. No one would describe him as the leader of the Kashmiri Brahmin even though he be one. If a leader happens to be an untouchable he will be described as so and so, the leader of the untouchables.

A Hindu doctor would be described as a great Indian doctor. No one would describe him as an Iyengar even though he be one. If the doctor happens to be an untouchable doctor, he would be referred to as to so and so, the untouchable doctor. A Hindu singer would be described as a great Hindu Indian singer. If the same person happens to be an untouchable he would be described as an untouchable singer. A Hindu wrestler would be described as a great Indian gymnast. If he happens to be an untouchable he would be described as an untouchable gymnast.

"This type of discrimination has its origin in the Hindu view that the untouchables are an inferior people and however qualified. their great men are only great among the untouchables. They can never be greater nor even equal to the greater men among the Hindus. This type of discrimination, though social in character, is no less galling than economic discrimination. Discrimination is merely another name for the absence of freedom. The discrimination against untouchables are merely the reflections of that deep and strong Hindu sentiment which is carried over in law and administration which justifies the distinctions between Hindu and untouchables to disadvantages of the untouchables. Those discriminations have their roots I fear of the Hindu that in free field, the untouchables may rise above the prescribed station in life and become a menace to the Hindu social order, the cardinal principle of which is the maintenance of Hindu superiority and Hindu domination over the untouchables. So long as the Hindu social order lasts, discrimination against the untouchables continue to exist.

"The untouchables have the culture of the Hindu community. They observe the religious rites of the Hindu community. They recognize the sacred as well as the secular laws of the Hindu festivals. But they derive no benefit from this. On the contrary they are segregated and shunned because their physical contact is held by the Hindus to cause pollution. They live on the outskirts of the Hindu not in the midst of it. Segregated from the rest of the Hindu population they are bound to a code of behaviours which is appropriate to a servile state. According to this code an untouchable may not do anything which raises him above his appointed station in life. He would not dress in style superior to that of his status, nor should untouchable woman adorn herself with ornaments after the fashion of the higher class Hindu women. He should not have a house better or bigger than the houses of the rest of the Hindus in the village. In my case he must not have a tiled roof over his house. An untouchable must not sit in the presence of Hindu and must always salute him first. An untouchable must not wear clean clothes, must not use brass or copper post, and must not wear gold or silver ornaments. When someone dies in the family of a Hindu, an untouchable must go miles to convey the message of the death to the relatives of the family, no matter how far away they might be living, because a Hindu in a village feels disgraced in the eyes of his relatives, if he has to communicate such message by postal communication. An untouchable must accompany the womenfolk of the Hindu on their journey from their homes to their parents and vice versa. Their dignity requires that they should have retinue and the untouchable is the only available class from which a retinue can be drawn without any cost. At every ceremony at the house of Hindu, the untouchable must come and do the menial work. An untouchable must not own and cultivate land and lead an independent life. For his livelihood he must depend upon stale remnants of food left over by the Hindu household and upon meat of cattle that die in the village. These remnants of food must collect from door to door. For the most he must go on his begging routine every evening. Similarly, the untouchables must carry the dead animals out of the village. Indeed he alone must carry them because no Hindu will agree to do scavenging. An untouchable should not take to such services as would give him authority and power over caste Hindus. He must be humble and must not ask for more than his lot under this code.

"There does not seem to be much hope for the emancipation of the untouchables, at any rate their emancipation is far more problematic and distant than the emancipation of the primitive tribes. The problem of slaves was one of the denial of political or economic rights. If the problem of the untouchables was one of political and economic rights, it could be solved by legal or constitutional methods. The denial of political and economic rights is the result of the social psychology of the Hindus. The problem for the untouchables arises directly out of the social behaviour of the Hindu. Untouchability will vanish only when Hindus will change their mentality. The problem is how to make the Hindus unlearn the way of life. It is no small matter to make a whole nation give up its accustomed way of life. Besides the way of life the Hindus are accustomed to, in a way which is sanctified by their religion, at any rate they believe it to be so. To change their way of life is almost to change their religion.

"How can this happen? Only when it is realized that what tragedy for the untouchables is the crime of the Hindus. How long shall the untouchables have to wait for this revolution in the religious psychology of the Hindu? Let those who have a gift for prophecy answer", Ambedkar said.

Ambedkar never agreed with Gandhi that the untouchability would be removed by change of heart by Hindus. He held this view as sensible as the view of a person who says to people living in the plague-stricken area not to leave the area, but to wait and not mind the disease till the municipal members repent of their neglect of duties and come forward to make measures to fight the disease. Ambedkar despaired that the change could be brought about within the framework of Hinduism. He reminded that there have been many Mahatmas in India whose sole object was to remove untouchability and to elevate and absorb the depressed classes, but everyone of them failed in this mission. Mahatmas have come and Mahatmas have gone. They raised a lot of dust, but never the level of people. The sooner we rid of them, the better it would be for humanity.

Ambedkar emphatically said: "If the Hindu social order was to be loosened its stronghold, it could happen only under two conditions. First, it must be subjected to constant fire, and, secondly, the untouchables must be independent of the Hindus both in thought and action."

Ambedkar asked the untouchables to rise for the triumph of their cause and through their crusading spirit subdue the hearts of the so-called Savarnas. "The time has come," he said, "when every so-called 'Panchama' must show forth that which will ensure the liberty and equality of the social outcaste and the downtrodden." He repeatedly said that when equality goes out of the country, all prosperity goes, and when prosperity goes, slavery steps in, and when slavery steps in, all the deadly inequities step in.

Believing in the essential equality of all men, Ambedkar's message was one man, one value, equality and casteless society. He said that there will be outcastes so long as there are castes, nothing can emancipate the outcastes except the destruction of the caste system.

Unfortunately, after independence, instead of seeing the destruction of castes, every successive year has seen the strengthening of caste system on one or the other ground.

Chapter 9

Gandhi and Ambedkar on Temples and Temple Entry

The Poona Pact was singed on the 24th of September 1932. On 25th September 1932, a public meeting of the Hindus was held in Bombay to accord to it their support. At that meeting the following resolution was passed:

"This conference confirms the Poona agreement arrived at between the leaders of the caste Hindus and depressed classes on 24th September 1932, and trusts that the British Government will withdraw its decision creating separate electorates within the Hindu community and accept the agreement in full. The Conference urges that immediate action be taken by Government so as to enable Mahatma Gandhi to break his fast within the terms of his vow and before it is too late. The Conference appeals to the leaders of the communities concerned to realize the implications of the agreement and of this resolution and to make earnest endeavour to fulfill them.

"This Conference resolves that henceforth, amongst Hindus, no one shall be regarded as an untouchable by reason of his birth, and that those who have been so regarded hitherto will have the same right as other Hindus in regard to the use of public wells, public schools, public roads, and all other public institutions. This right shall have statutory recognition at the first opportunity, and shall be one of the earliest Acts of the Swaraj Parliament, if it shall not have received such recognition before that time.

"It is further agreed that it shall be the duty of all Hindu leaders to secure, by every legitimate and peaceful means, an early removal of all social disabilities now imposed by custom upon the so-called untouchable classes, including the bar in respect of admission to temples."

The resolution passed at the public meeting held in Bombay on 25 September 1932 was followed by activities on the part of the Hindus to throw open temples to the untouchables. No week passed in which the Harijan a weekly paper started by Mr. Gandhi did not publish a list of temples thrown open, wells thrown open and schools thrown open to the untouchables set out under special column headed "Week to Week" on the first page.

When the owners or trustees of temples were not prepared to throw open their temples to the untouchables, the Hindus actually started satyagraha against them to compel them to fall in line. The satyagraha by Mr. Kelappan for securing entry to the untouchables in the temple at Guruvayur was a part of this agitation. To force the hands of the trustees of the temples who had the courage to stand against the current, many Hindu legislators came forward with Bills requiring the trustees to throw open temples to the untouchables if a referendum showed that the majority of the Hindu worshippers voted in favour. There was a spate of such Bills and a race among legislators to take the first place. There was a Temple Entry Bill by Dr. Subbaroyan of the Madras Legislative Council. There were four Bills introduced in the Central Assembly. One was by Mr. C.S. Ranga Iyer, another by Mr. Harabilas Sarada, a third by Mr. Lalchad Navalrai, and a fourth one by Mr. M.R. Jayakar.

As Gandhiji threw himself in the movement of removal of untouchability, he discovered that the evil was of much greater magnitude than he had thought at first.

Gandhiji directed his time and energy exclusively for the eradication of untouchability. In September 1933, he moved to Wardha and announced his intention to gift the Sabarmati Ashram to the Harijan Sevak Sangh. On 7 November 1933, he commenced his nationwide tour to promote the Harijan cause. In a period of nine months he traveled 12,500 miles penetrating into some of the remotest parts of the country. He called on caste Hindus to purge themselves of prejudice against the Harijans, and at the same time he urged the Harijans to shake off the vices which came in their way for the absorption into the Hindu fold.

He addressed hundreds of public meetings exhorting the Hindus to take to Harijan uplift work in explication of centuries of operation and exploitation of their brethren. He repudiated and ridiculed the idea of the people being high or low, clean or unclean by birth. He urged for all public temples to be opened to the Harijans.

The orthodox Hindus observed the activities of Gandhiji with anger, dismay and even hatred. They organized black flag demonstrations against him. Their active members disturbed his meetings. Controversies were raised in the newspapers. They accused him of heresy. The orthodox Hindus tried their utmost to provoke the workers into violence. To meet all this Gandhiji declared in May 1934 that he would cover the rest of his journey on foot, thus fully exposing himself to the attacks of his opponents. And he did so.

He went to Poona to commence his tour in Maharashtra on 25th June 1934. While he and his party were on the way to the Municipal Hall, a bomb was thrown at him. He was escaped miraculously, but some members of his party were injured. He expressed his deep pity for the bomb thrown and said, "I am not aching for martyrdom, but if comes in my way in the prosecution of what I consider to be the supreme duty on defence of the faith I hold in common with millions of Hindus, I shall have well earned it."

"Temple entry', Gandhiji said, "is the one spiritual act that would constitute the message of freedom to the untouchables and assure them that they are not outcastes". He further said, "It is not a question of Harijans asserting their right of temple entry or claiming it. They may or may not want to enter the temple even if it is declared open to them. But it is the bounden duty of every caste Hindu to secure that opening for Harijans."

Gandhiji strode the country from North to South and made his views clear on the question of temple entry and fervently appealed to the caste Hindus to throw open the public temples to the Harijans.

This is what Gandhiji said from time to time and from place to place: "Temples are to Hindus what churches are to Christians. In my opinion, we are all idolaters; that in Hinduism we have images of stone or metal inside temples makes to me no difference. Thousands of Hindus who visit temples in simple faith derive precisely the same spiritual benefit that Christians visiting churches in simple faith do. Deprive a Hindu of his temple, and you deprive him of the thing he generally prizes most in the life. That superstition and even have grown round many Hindu temples is but too true.

"That, however, is an argument for temple reform, not for lowering their value for Harijans or any Hindu. It is my certain conviction that temples are an integral part of Hinduism.

"It is my firm belief that caste Hindus will not have fulfilled their obligations till they have opened all their temples to Harijans. It is immaterial to me whether Harijans come to worship in those temples or not. It is a matter of sheer justice and penance for caste Hindus. It is repugnant to my sense of justice that Harijans should be excluded from places of worship which are open to other Hindus. I would not consider untouchability as having been eradicated unless and until the bar against Harijans entry into temples is removed altogether.

"It is not for the material benefit of Harijans. It is for the spiritual benefit of the Savarna Hindus, who have to purify themselves and who owe a debt to the Harijans. If untouchability is a sin and if Harijans are as good Hindus as the rest of us, they have as much right to enter the temples as the others. Whether they can get any material benefit from it, or whether they themselves want it or not, is beside the point. The point is whoever cares to go to a temple, provided he observes the rules observed by all other Hindus, ought to have the right to do so. He may be a sinner, but it is precisely because we are all sinners that we would like to go to temples to wash out our sins there. A saint need not go there. The sanatanists may expect him to observe all the rules of outward cleanliness that they themselves observe, but nothing more.

"Untouchability as at present practiced is the greatest blot on Hinduism. It is (with apologies to sanatanists) against the shastras. It is against the fundamental principles of humanity; it is against the dictates of reason that a man should by mere reason of birth, be for ever regarded as an untouchable, even unapproachable and of the thing itself. It is crime for certain men, women and their children to touch, or to approach within stated distances, or to be seen by those who are called caste Hindus. The tragedy is that millions of Hindus believe in this institution as if it was enjoined by the Hindu religion.

"Happily, Hindu reformers have recoiled with horror from this practice. They have come to the conclusion that it has no support in the Hindu shastras taken as a whole Isolated texts torn from their context and considered by themselves can no doubt be produced in support of this practice, as of any evil known to mankind. But there is abundant authority in the shastras to warrant the summary rejection, as being un-Hindu of anything or any practice that is manifestly against the fundamental principles of humanity or morality, or *ahimsa* or *satya*.

"I have had many discussions with many other learned shastris. I had occasion also to study, as far as a layman like myself can do, the shastras which have bearing on untouchability and I came to the definite conclusion that there was no warrant whatsoever in the shastras for untouchability as we practise it today and that there is no warrant whatsoever for the prohibition of the entry of any single Hindu, be he called untouchable or otherwise, into public temples.

"I want to give this absolute assurance on my behalf to those who are opposed to entry by Harijans that there will be no force nor compulsion used against those who are opposed to this Temple entry. You have been kind enough to refer to me as a true and sincere sanatanist. I think in all humility and truthfulness I can accept that description. I have always claimed to be a sanatanist, for the simple reason that from youth up I have endeavoured, to the best of my ability, to live up to the *shastras* as I have understood them; and as such I feel it the duty of a sanatanist to do repentance in connection with untouchability, to purify himself and to get rid of this taint. It is his bounden duty to admit Harijans to the same rights and privileges as he himself possesses. He may not be satisfied till he has endeavoured his best for temple entry for Harijans on the same terms on which he enjoys it. What is more, at Bombay, in the month of September 1932, when that fast was going on, representative of Hindus met in assembly and came to the solemn resolution that Harijans had the same right to temple entry as other Hindus and that, if there was any legal obstacle in the way, means would be adopted to remove that legal obstacle also. Therefore, for a man like me, it becomes a double duty to prosecute the claim of Harijans to temple entry on the same terms as to caste Hindus.

"I have absolutely no desire that the temple should be opened to Harijans, until caste Hindu opinion is ripe for that opening. It is not a question of Harijans asserting their right of temple entry or claiming it. They may or may not want to enter that temple even when it is declared open to them. But it is the bounden duty of every caste Hindu to secure that opening for Harijans. But it cannot be opened because a humble individual like me thinks that it should be opened. It can only be opened when there is a general consensus of opinion on the part of caste Hindus. Difficulty comes in only when a single Hindu says, 'So long as I am opposed the temple should not be opened.' If such an impossible doctrine is to be accepted, we can never think of any progress in Hinduism. We should never be able to deal with any question on those terms.

"I have not a shadow of a doubt that unsophisticated caste Hindu mind today accepts the right of Harijans to enter temples and to enjoy all other rights and privileges that caste Hindus enjoy. Therefore I suggest to those who are opposed to this movement that they should not confuse the issue. If they do not like temple entry, let them leave it alone. Let them give their help and cooperation in many other things.

"Temple entry is a question purely for the caste Hindus to solve. If caste Hindus say as a body that Harijans shall not enter the temple, I shall say it will be unfortunate, it will be marching against the spirit of the times; but so long as that opinion persists, no Harijans will enter any temple. My duty is merely to confine myself to the cultivation of public opinion in that direction. I come to the parting of the ways when I am told that I should not whisper a word about the subject. I cannot do not. For I feel, as a lover of my faith to say that caste Hindus will not be doing their elementary duty so long as they prohibit temple entry to Harijans. I hold it to be impossible for a man who has studied Hindu shastras with an unbiased mind to feel otherwise. When an overwhelming majority favours the entry of Harijans into a particular temple, it should be opened. Wherever I have gone and opened temples to Harijans, I have done so in presence of thousands of caste Hindus and with their consent. The thousands of caste Hindus who were most concerned about the temple entry said, 'We want the temple to be opened.'

"But if you say that no temple should be opened so long as there is one caste, Hindu who says, "No, the temple should not be opened", then, I would say that is coercion with a vengeance.

"I would call it exercise of force when one man says, 'My ideas ought to prevail against the idea of 9,999. The majority should no doubt consist of Hindu who believes in temple, not scoffers.' In naked terms, this is coercion of the worst type, a minority of one bending the will of the majority to its will.

"None but tyrants are reported by history to have succeeded in enforcing their will against all others, and that they did to their own utter destruction. So far as I can speak for the reformers, their position is plain. They do not wish to see a single temple opened to Harijans until there is an overwhelming majority of existing temple-goers in favour of such entry. There is, therefore, no question of compulsion or coercion, unless the enforcement of the will of an overwhelming majority may be so-called. The majority may be, ought to be, expected to be forbearing and accommodating towards a minority. But the minority wants no accommodation, it insists on the present position remaining intact. This would mean stagnation and ultimate death. Hence it is what I have been saying, 'Either we kill untouchability or it will kill us surely as the rising of the sun on morrow.'

"There will be no abolition of untouchability till every public temple is open to every untouchable precisely on the same terms as to the other Hindus. A common place of worship is the surest test of a common faith. No wonder all other efforts appear as insincere to Harijans. But they are not necessarily insincere because they appear so. There are hundreds of workers whose efforts to remove the blot of untouchability are not any the less sincere because they are unable today to have every temple flung open to Harijans. The seed has been sown, never to die. It is bound to bear fruit in its own time. Seeds of hardy trees take long to sprout. Nonetheless they are growing. The reformers will not rest till every public temple to open to Harijans. All ameliorative measures are steps in the direction of temple entry."

But Gandhiji faced two pronged attack. One from the Sanatanists and orthodox Hindus and the other from Dr. Ambedkar. Dr. Ambedkar carried on a campaign against Gandhiji and Hinduism. According to him all that Gandhiji did for the Harijans was suspect and hypocrisy.

This is what Ambedkar said: "Before 1932, Mr. Gandhi was opposed to allow untouchables to enter Hindu temples. To quote his own words Mr. Gandhi said: 'How is it possible that the antyajas (untouchables) should have the right to enter all the existing temples? As long as the law of caste and ashram has the chief place in Hindu religion, to say that every Hindu can enter every temple is a thing that is not possible today.'

"His joining the movement for temple entry must therefore remain a matter of great surprise. Why Mr. Gandhi took this somersault it is difficult to imagine. Was it an honest act of change of heart, due to a conviction that he was in error in opposing the entry of the untouchables in Hindu temples? Was it due to a realization that the political separation between the Hindus and the untouchables brought about by the Poona Pact might lead to a complete severance of the cultural and religious ties and that it was necessary to counteract the tendency by some such measure as temple entry as will bind the two together? Or was his object in joining the temple entry movement to destroy the basis of the claim of the untouchables for political rights by destroying the barrier between them and the Hindus which makes them separate from the Hindus? Or was it because Mr. Gandhi saw before him looming large a possibility of adding to his name and fame and rushed to make the most of it, as is his habit to do? The second or the third explanation may be nearer the truth."

"What was the attitude of the untouchables to this movement for temple entry? I was asked by Mr. Gandhi to lend my support to the movement for temple entry. I declined to do so and issued a statement on the subject to the Press. As it will help the reader know the grounds for my attitude to his question I have thought it well to set it in full. Here it is."

Statement on Temple Entry Bill, 14 February, 1933:

"Although the controversy regarding the question of temple, entry is confined to the Sanatanists and Mahatma Gandhi, the depressed classes have undoubtedly a very important part to play in it, in so far as their position is bound to weigh the scales one way or the other, when the issue comes for finals settlement. It is, therefore, necessary that their viewpoint should be defined and stated so as to leave no ambiguity about it."

Dr. Ambedkar continued: "To the Temple Entry Bill of Mr. Ranga Iyer as drafted, the depressed classes cannot possibly give their support. The principle of the Bill is that if a majority of Municipal and Local Board voters in the vicinity of any particular temple on a Referendum decide by a majority that the depressed shall be allowed to enter the temple, the Trustees or the Manager of that temple shall give effect to that decision. The principle is an ordinary principle of majority rule and there is nothing radical or revolutionary about the Bill, and if the sanatanists were a wise lot, they would accept it without demur.

"The reasons why the depressed classes cannot support a Bill based upon this principle are two. One reason is that the Bill cannot hasten the day of temple entry for the depressed classes any nearer than would otherwise be the case. It is true that under the Bill the minority will not have the right to obtain an injunction against the Trustee or the Manager who throws open the temple to the depressed classes in accordance with the decision of the majority. But before one can draw any satisfaction from this clause and congratulate the author of the Bill, one must first of all feel assured that when the question is put to the vote there will be a majority in favour of the temple entry. If one is not suffering from illusion of any kind, one must accept that the hope of a majority voting in favour of temple entry will be rarely realized, if at all. Without doubt the majority is definitely opposed today—a fact which is conceded by the author of the Bill himself in his correspondence with Shankaracharya.

"What is there in the situation as created after the passing of the Bill, which can lead one to hope that the majority will act differently? I find nothing. I shall, no doubt, be reminded of the results of the Referendum with regard to the Guruvayur temple. But I refuse to accept a referendum so overweighed as it was by the life of Mahatma Gandhi as the normal result. In any such calculations, the life of the Mahatma must necessarily be deducted.

"Secondly, the Bill does not regard untouchability in temple as sinful custom. It regards untouchability merely as a social evil not necessarily worse than social evil of other sorts. For, it does not declare untouchability as such to be illegal. Its binding force is taken away only if a majority decides to do so. Sin and immorality cannot become tolerable because a majority is addicted to them or because the majority chooses to practice them. If untouchability is a sinful and an immoral custom, then in the view of the depressed classes it must be destroyed without any hesitation, even if it was acceptable to the majority. This is the way in which all customs are dealt with by courts of law if they find them to be immoral and against public policy.

"This is exactly what the Bill does not do. The author of the Bill takes no more serious view of the custom of untouchability than does the temperance reformer of the habit of drinking. Indeed, so much is he impressed by the assumed similarity between the two that the method he has adopted is a method which is advocated by temperance reformers to eradicate the evil habit of drinking, namely, by local option. One cannot feel much grateful to a friend of the depressed classes who holds untouchability to be no worse than drinking. If Mr. Ranga Iyer had not forgotten that only a few months ago Mahatma Gandhi had prepared himself to fast unto death if untouchability was not removed, he would have taken more serious view of this curse and proposed almost thoroughgoing reform to ensure its removal lock, stock and barrel. Whatever its shortcomings may be from the standpoint of efficacy, the least that the Depressed Classes could expect is for the Bill to recognize the principle that untouchability is a sin.

"I really cannot understand how the Bill satisfies Mahatma Gandhi who has been insisting that untouchability is a sin. It certainly does not satisfy the depressed classes. The question whether this particular Bill is good or bad, sufficient or insufficient, is a subsidiary question. The main question is, do the depressed classes desire temple entry or do they not? This main question is being viewed by the depressed classes by two points of view. One is the materialistic point of view. Starting from it, the depressed classes think that the surest way for their elevation lies in higher education, higher employment and better ways of earning a living. Once they become well placed in the scale of social life they would become respectable and once they become respectable the religious outlook of the orthodox towards them is sure to undergo change, and even if this did not happen it can do no injury to their material interest. Proceeding on these lines the depressed classes say that they will not spend their resources in such an empty thing as temple entry. There is also another reason why they do not care to fight for it. That argument is the argument of 'self-respect'.

"Not very long ago there used to be boards on club doors and other social resorts maintained by Europeans in India, which said 'Dogs and Indians not allowed'. The temples of the Hindus carry similar boards today, the only difference is that the boards on the Hindu temples practically say 'All Hindus and all animals including dogs are admitted, only untouchables not admitted.' The situation in both cases is on a parity. But the Hindus never begged for admission in those places from which the Europeans in their arrogance had excluded them. Why should an untouchable beg for admission in a place from which he has been excluded by the arrogance of the Hindus? This is the reasoning of the depressed class man who is interested in his material welfare. He is prepared to say to the Hindus, 'To open or not to open your temples is a question for you to consider, and not for me to agitate. If you think, it is bad manners not to respect the sacredness of human personality, open your temples and be a gentleman. If you rather be a Hindu than be a gentleman, then shut the doors and damn yourself, for I don't care to come.'

"I found it necessary to put the argument in this form, because I want to disabuse the minds of men like Pandit Madan Mohan Malaviya of their belief that the depressed classes are looking forward expectantly for their patronage. The second point of view is the spiritual one. As religiously minded people, do the depressed classes desire temple entry or do they not? That is the question. From the spiritual point of view, they are not indifferent to temple entry as they would be, if the material point of view alone were to prevail. But their final answer must depend upon the reply which Mahatma Gandhi and the Hindus give to the following question: 'What is the drive behind this offer of temple entry? Is temple entry to be the final goal of the advancement in the social status of the depressed classes in the Hindu fold? Or is it only the first step and if it is the first step, what is the ultimate goal?' Temple entry as a final goal the depressed classes can never support. Indeed they will not only reject it, but they would then regard themselves as rejected by Hindu society and free to find their own destiny elsewhere. On the other hand, if it is only to be a first step in the direction, they may be inclined to support it. The position would then be analogous to what is happening in the politics of India today. All Indians have claimed dominion status for India. The actual constitution will fall short of dominion status and many Indians will accept it. Why? The answer is that as the goal is defined, it is one jump. But if the British had not accepted the goal of dominion status, no one would have accepted the partial reforms which many are now prepared to accept.

"In the same way, if Mahatma Gandhi and the reformers were to proclaim what the goal which they set before themselves is for the advancement of the social status of the depressed classes in the Hindu fold, it would be easier for the depressed classes to define their attitude towards temple entry. The goal of the depressed classes might as well be stated here for the information and consideration of all concerned. What the depressed classes want is a religion, which will give them equality of social status. To prevent any misunderstanding, I would like to elaborate the point by drawing a distinction between social evils which are the results of secular causes and social evils which are founded upon the doctrines of religion. Social evils can have no justification whatsoever in a civilized society. But nothing can be more odious and vile than that admitted social evils should be sought to be justified on the ground of religion. The depressed classes may not be able to overthrow inequities to which they are being subjected.

"But they have made up their mind not to tolerate a religion that will lend its support to the continuance of these inequities. If the Hindu religion is to be their religion then it must become a religion of social equality. The mere amendment of Hindu religious code by the mere inclusion in it of a provision to permit temple entry for all cannot make it a religion of equality of socials status. All that it can do is to recognize them as nationals and not aliens, if I may use these terms which have become so familiar in politics. But that cannot mean that they would thereby reach a position where they would be free and equal without being above or below any one else, for the simple reason that the Hindu religion does not recognize the principle of equality of social status; on the other hand fosters inequality by insisting upon grading people as Brahmins, Kshatriyas, Vaishyas and Shudras which now stand towards one another in an ascending scale of hatred and descending scale of contempt.

"If the religion is to be a religion of social equality then an amendment of its code to provide temple entry is not enough. What is required is to purge it of the doctrine of Chaturvarna. That is the root cause of all inequality and also the parent of the caste system and untouchability which are merely forms of inequality. Unless it is done not only will the depressed classes reject temple entry they will also reject the Hindu faith. Chaturvarna and the caste system are incompatible with the self-respect of the depressed classes. So long it continues to be the cardinal doctrine, the depressed classes must continue to be looked upon as low. For the depressed classes to say that they are Hindus is to admit their inferiority of status by their own mouth. They can call themselves as Hindus only when the theory of Chaturvarna and caste system is abandoned and expunged from the *shastras*. Do the Mahatma and the Hindu reformers accept this as their goal and will they show the courage to work for it? I shall look forward to their pronouncements on this issue as I have stated it with great concern. But whether Mahatma Gandhi and the Hindus are prepared for this or not, let it be known once and for all that nothing short of this will satisfy the depressed classes and make them accept temple entry. To accept temple entry and be content with it is to temporize with evil and barter away the sacredness of human personality that dwells in them.

"There is, however, one argument which Mahatma Gandhi and the reforming Hindus may advance against the position I have taken. They may say, 'Acceptance by the depressed classes of temple entry now will not prevent them from agitating hereafter for the abolition of Chaturvarna and caste. If that is their goal, I like to meet the argument right at this stage so as to clinch the issue and clear the road for future development. My reply is that it is true that my right to agitate for the abolition of Chaturvarna and caste system will not be lost, if I accept temple entry now. But the question is on what side will Mahatma Gandhi be at the time when the question is put. If he will be in the camp now. If he will be in my camp, he ought to be in it now.'

"But Mr. Gandhi felt otherwise that securing temple entry to the untouchables was a liability of the Hindus which ought to be liquidated first. Accordingly immediately after the Poona Pact he started a campaign among the Hindus for opening the doors of their temples to the untouchables.

"How far has Mr. Gandhi succeeded in this matter is a question that may legitimately be asked. But it is difficult to know the truth. As a result of the fast, many temples were reported to have been thrown open by the Hindus to the untouchables. How far this was true and how far it is a part of lying propaganda which the Congressman is so good at it is difficult to say. That many of the temples that were opened as a sequel to the fast were purified and closed to the untouchables is beyond dispute. Again the opening of a temple may be quite a meaningless act. There are hundreds and thousands of temples in which there is no worship. They are occupied by only donkeys. Instances of such temples can be seen at places of pilgrimage such as Nasik and Wai. If such a temple is declared to be open it is not only a meaningless act but it is an insult to the untouchables. But if it is abandoned by the caste Hindus as a place of worship it cannot be said that it is open in the sense that they are welcomed by the Hindus to it. There is yet another possibility which must be taken into account in arriving at the truth. A temple may be open to the untouchables in the same sense as the Ritz Hotel in London is open to all. We however, know that the Ritz Hotel is not in fact open to all. It is open to those who can afford. In the same way a temple may be open to the untouchables yet in fact it is open only to those untouchables who can afford to enter. If the cost of temple entry is assault or social boycott then the cost will be prohibitive and the temple though nominally open is really closed. Assault and social boycott are a matter of course with the Hindus and it would not be too much to assume that in some cases the Hindus would resort to such means to prohibit the untouchables who dare to enter a temple which is declared to be open to them. If the case is one like this then it is fraud.

"Which of the two classes of cases are more numerous, it is difficult to say accurately. But guess may be made on the basis of certain facts. There are two classes of Hindus now in India—the orthodox Hindus who care more for religion than for politics and the Congress Hindus who care more for politics and less for religion. The former who have no political ends to subserve can be honest, i.e., true to their convictions however wrong they may be. The latter who have to serve political ends cannot always take an honest view but are prone to adopt dishonest ways. The first method of abandonment, though honest, brings discredit upon the Hindu community in the eyes of the world and is therefore politically unsuitable. The second method of opening the temple nominally and closing it really by Hindus is politically highly advantageous. It has the merit of a system which shows to the world that credit is opened and which clandestinely but without the world knowing prevents its being drawn upon by the person in whose favour it is declared to be opened. The Congress Hindus are more numerous than the orthodox Hindus. That being the case I should think that the second classes of cases must be more numerous than the first.

"That genuine cases of opening of temples are very few and that most of the published reports of opening of temples is just false propaganda is clear from the fate of the Temple Entry Bill of Mr. Ranga Iyer brought by him in the Central Legislature in 1934.

"Mr. Gandhi insists that a spiritual awakening has taken place among the Hindus and relies upon the Temple Entry Proclamation of Travancore. I am obliged to deal with this claim. The success of Temple entry cannot be determined by the number of temples opened. It can be determined only by reference to the motive with which it is done. Is the motive spiritual? That can be the only test.

"Now I say that temple entry is not a spiritual act. It is a political maneuver. Is Mr. Gandhi acting from spiritual motive? In appealing to the Hindus he said: 'I have addressed this appeal to you, which proceeds out of my soul's agony. I ask you to share that agony and share with me and cooperate with me, for I have no other end to serve than to see Sanatana Dharma revivified and lived in its reality in the lives of millions who at present seem to me to deny it.'

"This soul's agony was born after the Poona Pact. What did Mr. Gandhi think of the problem of temple entry before the Poona Pact? Before the Poona Pact Mr. Gandhi was of different opinion. That opinion was expressed not very long before the Poona Pact and not long before this appeal was addressed to the Hindus from which I have.... It was expressed in *Gandhiji Shikshan*, Vol. II, p. 132, Mr. Gandhi then held the opinion that separate temples should be built for the use of untouchables.

"It is obvious that temple entry is not original with him and therefore not spiritual. The agony is caused by the grave and sudden provocation brought by the demand of the untouchables for separate electorates. Mr. Gandhi was afraid of the principle underlying separate electorates. He felt that this principle may be extended and may ultimately lead to separation and cessation of the untouchables from the Hindu fold. It was to counter this move that he changed his opinion and started the temple entry move. The motive of Mr. Gandhi is political and there is nothing spiritual about it.

"I do not wish this conclusion to rest merely upon this evidence of change of front on the part of Mr. Gandhi. There is abundance of other evidence in support of it.

"I will refer first to the Guruvayur Temple satyagraha which was started by a caste Hindu by name Kellappan to secure entry into the Guruvayur temple for the untouchables. A few facts regarding this episode may be interesting.

"The point to note is the attitude that Mr. Gandhi finally adopted in this matter when he was challenged by the leaders of the orthodox Hindus. Mr. Gandhi became ready for a compromise with the orthodox. The terms of the compromise were as follows. I give them in Mr. Gandhi's own words as reported in the papers. 'During certain hours of the day the Guruvayur temple should be thrown open to the Harijans and other Hindus, who have no objection to the presence of the Harijans and during certain other hours it should be reserved for those, who have scruples against whatsoever in the acceptance of this suggestion, seeing that in connection with the Krithikai Ekadashi festival in Guruvayur, the Harijans are allowed to enter side by side with the Hindus and then the temple or the idol undergoes purification.'

"Asked if his suggestion was that the temple might undergo purification daily after the entry of the Harijans, Mr. Gandhi replied: 'Personally, I am opposed to purification at all. But if that would satisfy the conscience of the objectors I would personally in this case, raise no objection to purification. If purification has any value, then there are so many possibilities of daily defilement from a variety of causes referred to in various texts that there should be a daily purification, whether the Harijans are allowed to enter or not.'

"This attitude is not spiritual. It is purely commercial. This is almost admitted by Mr. Gandhi. Asked if the compromise suggested by him did not still maintain a distinction between the untouchables and the caste Hindus, Mr. Gandhi is reported to have said: 'The Harijan's attitude should be this, if there is a person who objects to my presence, I would like to respect his objection so long as he (the objector) does not deprive me of the right that belongs to me and so long as I am permitted to have my legitimate share of the days of offering worship side by side with those, who have no objection to my presence, I would be satisfied.'

"I do not know if any self-respecting untouchable would adopt this attitude of Mr. Gandhi. On these terms even dogs and cats are admitted in all temples when there are no human beings present in them. To divide the House of God in time or in space for worship for reconciling the rival claims of two opposing classes is in itself a quaint or grotesque idea. Mr. Gandhi evidently forgot that worshipping in the same temple is quite different from worshipping in common. Temple entry if it is to be spiritual must mean the latter. The former accepts that the presence of one class is repugnant to the other and proceeds to reconcile the interests of the two. The latter presupposes that there is no repugnance between the two classes and that they accept the common denominator of humanity as being present in both.

"This shows that Mr. Gandhi is least motivated by spiritual considerations. He is in a hurry to bring the untouchables within the Hindu stables so as to prevent their running away.

"Another piece of evidence which goes to disprove Mr. Gandhi's claim that he is acting from spiritual consideration is furnished by his conduct with reference to Mr. Rnaga Iyer's 'Temple Entry Bill'. It shows that the soul's agony is only a picturesque phrase and not a fact.

"Since the new constitution came into operation two Acts have been passed in two Provinces by the Congress governments, one in Bombay and another in Madras. There is no substance in the Acts. They do not declare the temples to be open. They permit the trustees of the temples under their management if they desire and as there is nothing to compel the trustees to do so the Acts are just scraps of paper and nothing more. But the Madras Act has a history which is somewhat puzzling. The Madras Prime Minister who got the Act passed is Mr. Rajagopalachari. He occupies a very high place in the Congress, so high indeed that he is called Deputy Mahatma. If one can solve the puzzle the solution will reveal the mind behind all this.

"Let me turn to the Travancore temple entry. This proclamation of 12th November is a gorgeous document. It reads as follows: 'Profoundly convinced of the truth and validity of our religion, believing that it is based on divine guidance and on all comprehending toleration, knowing that in its practice it has throughout the centuries adopted itself to the need of the changing times, solicitous that none of our Hindu subjects should, by reason of birth, caste or community, be denied the consolation and solace of the Hindu faith, we have decided and hereby declare, ordain and command that, subject to such rules and conditions as may be laid down and imposed by us for preserving their proper atmosphere and maintaining their ritual and observances, there should henceforth be no restriction placed on any Hindu by birth or religion on entering or worshipping at temples controlled by us and our government.'

"What spirituality underlies this proclamation? The proclamation was issued by the Maharaja of Travancore in his name. But the real active force behind the scene was the Prime Minister Sir C.P. Ramaswami Iyer. It is his motives that we must understand. In 1933 Sir C.P.R. Iyer was also the Prime Minister of Travancore. In 1933 Mr. Gandhi was fighting to get the Guruvayur Temple opened to all untouchables. Among the many who took part in the controversy over the issue of temple entry was Sir C.P. Ramaswami Iyer. Nobody seems now to remember this fact. But it is important to recall it because it helps us to understand the motives which prompted him to press the Maharaja to issue this proclamation. What attitude did Sir C.P. Ramaswami Iyer have regarding this issue in 1933? It will be clear from the following statement which he issued to the press: 'Personally I do not observe caste rules. I realize there are strong, though not very articulate, feelings in this matter in the minds of men who believe that the present system of temple worship and its details are based on divine ordinances. The problem can be permanently solved only by a process of mutual adjustment and by the awakening of religious and social leaders of Hindu society to the realities of the present situation and to the need for preserving the solidarity of the Hindu community.

"Shock tactics will not answer the purpose and direct action will be even more fatal in this sphere than in the political. I have the misfortune to differ from Mr. Gandhi when he says that 'the problem of temple entry can be divorced from such topics as entertaining and I agree with Dr. Ambedkar that the social and economic uplift of the depressed classed should be our immediate and urgent programme'.

"This question can be answered only if one bears in mind the fact that in 1936 there was held in Travancore a Conference of the Yezawa Community to consider the issue of conversion which was raised by me at Yeola in 1953. The Yezawas are in untouchable community spread over Malabar. It is an educated community and economically quite strong. It is also a vocal community and has been carrying on agitation in the state for social, religious and political rights. The Yezawas form a very large community. The cessation of so large a community would be a deathknell to the Hindus and the Conference had made the danger real as well as immediate. It was this which brought about a change in the attitude of Sir C.P. Ramaswami Iyer. The spiritual considerations are just an excuse. They did not form the motives.

"How far did this Proclamation change facts and how far has it remained a show? It is not possible to get real facts as they exist in Travancore. In the course of the discussion on the Malabar Temple Entry Bill in the Madras Legislative Assembly certain facts relating to Travancore were mentioned by Sir T. Pannirselvam, which if true would show that whole thing is hollow."

"Sir T. Pannirselvam said: 'One of the arguments advanced by the Premier in support of the measure was that temples in Travancore had been thrown open to the Untouchables. A Maharaja vested with autocratic powers did so by an order. But how was it working there? From representations received, he was led to believe that after the first flush of enthusiasm, Harijans had left off going to temples, and people who used to worship previously before Harijans were allowed to enter the temples, had stopped worshipping in temples. He would ask the government to tell them if the measure was really a success in Travancore.'

"On the third reading of the Bill, Sir T. Pannirselvam made a statement which must have come as a surprise to many. He said: 'He wanted to know whether it was a fact that the private temples of the Senior Maharani were excluded from the proclamation. What was the reason for it? Again during the celebration of the marriage of the daughter of the Senior Maharani it was found necessary, so he was told, to perform pacificator ceremony of the temple. If such a purification of temples took place, what happened to the proclamation?'

"These facts were not challenged by the Prime Minister. Evidently they cannot be challenged. If they are incontrovertible then the less said about the Malabar temple entry proclamation as a spiritual testament the better.

"If the plan of temple entry is ultimately to deprive the untouchables of their statutory rights then the movement is not only not spiritual but it is positively mischievous and it would be the duty of all honest people to warn the untouchables, 'Beware of Gandhiji'.

"To the question I put to Mr. Gandhi in my statement he gave a straight reply. He said that though he was against untouchability he was not against caste. If at all, he was in favour of it and that he would not therefore carry his social reform beyond removing untouchability. This was enough for me to settle my attitude. I decided to take no further part in it.

"Mr. Gandhi did not mind any opposition and was indifferent as to whether it came from orthodox Hindus or from the untouchables. He went on in mad pursuit of his object. It is interesting to ask, what happened to this movement?

"To put it briefly, after a short spurt of activity in the direction of removing untouchability by throwing open temples and wells the Hindu mind returned to its original state. The reports appearing in the 'Week to Week' columns of the *Harijan* subsided, became few and far between ultimately vanished. For myself I was not surprised to find that the Hindu heart was so soon stricken with palsy. For I never believed that there was so much milk of human kindness locked up in the Hindu breast as the 'Week to Week' column in the *Harijan* would have the world believe. As a matter of fact a large part of the news that appeared in the 'Week to Week' was fake and was nothing but a lying propaganda engineered by Congressmen to deceive the world that the Hindus were determined to fight untouchability. Few temples if any were really opened and those that were reported to have been opened most of them were dilapidated and deserted temples which were used by none but dogs and donkeys. One of the evil effects of the Congress agitation is that it has made the political-minded Hindus a lying squad which will not hesitate to tell any lie if it can help the Congress. Thus ended the part which the Hindu public played or was made to appear to play in this temple entry movement. The same fate overtook the Guruvayur Temple satyagraha and the legislation for securing temple entry for the untouchables. As these are matters which were pursued by Mr. Gandhi and Congressmen their history might be told in some detail in as much as it reveals the true mentality of Mr. Gandhi and the Congress towards the untouchables.

"Here was a case of retreat from glory! And what an inglorious retreat! How did Mr. Gandhi react to it? In a statement issued on 4th November 1932, Mr. Gandhi said: 'Untouchables in the villages should be made to feel that their shackles have been broken, that they are in no way inferior to their fellow villagers, that they are worshippers of the same God as the other villagers and entitled to the same rights and privileges that the latter enjoy. But if these vital conditions of the Pact are not carried out by caste-Hindus, could I possibly live to face God and man? I ventured even to tell Dr. Ambedkar, Rao Bahadur, M.C. Rajah and other friends belonging to the suppressed group that they should regard me as a hostage for the due fulfillment by caste Hindus of the conditions of the Pact. The fast, if it is to come, will not be for coercion of those who are opponents of reform, but it will be intended to sting into action those who have been my comrades or who have taken pledges for the removal of untouchability. If they belie their pledges or if they never meant to abide by them and their Hinduism was a mere camouflage, I should have no interest left in life.'

"He was never tired of repeating this. Exclusion of the untouchables from the Hindu temples, he described, as the agony of his soul. What did Mr. Gandhi do in this connection?

"The Temple entry, what one is to say of, except to describe it a strange game of political acrobatics! Mr. Gandhi begins as an opponent of temple entry. When the untouchables put forth a demand for political rights, he changes his position and becomes a supporter of temple entry. When the Hindus threaten to defeat the Congress in the election, if it pursues the matter to a conclusion, Mr. Gandhi in order to preserve political power in the hands of the Congress, gives up temple entry! Is this sincerity? Does this show conviction? Was the 'agony of soul' which Mr. Gandhi spoke of more than a phrase?

"Gandhiji in the *Harijan* issue of 28 November, 1936 said: 'If the Travancore proclamation of the religious freedom of Harijans is a matter for great rejoicing, it is also an event calling us to greater humiliation, greater effort and greater purification. It is not the end of untouchability. It is certainly, as C. Rajagopalachari says, an indication of the potentiality that exists in us, if only we seek his aid. It inspires us with hope and faith in our mission. But on no account will it warrant relaxation of effort and vigilance over ourselves. If the mute prayer of the selfless workers of Travancore aided by kindred spirits all over India, rather than the advertised meetings and their resolutions, inspired H.H. the Maharajah and his advisers to issue the Proclamation (it does not matter whether consciously or unconsciously to them), it follows that greater selflessness and devotion of workers must do the rest.

"Let us realize the contents of the rest. We do not yet know how the orthodoxy to Travancore and the Harijans will react to the Proclamation. If it is followed up by suitable response on the part of the public, it can easily become a dead letter. The mere opening of temples will mean nothing, if it does not lead to their purification and that of the priesthood.

"The opening of temples in Travancore must lead to their opening in the sister state Cochin and must also lead to the opening of the sister temple of Guruvaryur. These are of a piece, guided by the same tradition and ceremonial. Then come the great temples of Tamil, Telgu and Canarese India. Kashi Viswanath, Dwarka and Puri temples in the North, West and East still remain closed to the Harijans. Of the big black patches of India Travancore, though a big patch in itself, considered relatively was a small speck. It has, by the grace of God showing itself through the proclamation of H.H. the Maharaja, become suddenly a bright spot radiating its light throughout India.

"And the religious freedom, if it is real in the sense that it comes from the heart of orthodoxy, must be followed by the economic and social betterment of the Harijans all over India. A mere mention of these most important things should be sufficient to chasten us. But it cannot frighten us if we have a living faith in God and our cause.

"For this great and glorious task we want more workers—men and women, boys and girls. We want more money, paper, gold, silver, copper, even handfuls of grain, but these too will surely, as also only, come if the workers whom we already have, are, like Caesar's wife, above suspicion. Are we all pure in heart? Are we faithful to our trust? Have we faith in the purely spiritual nature of our mission? If the answers can be in the affirmative, all is well. But the cases I have somewhat discussed and which I am still following up, make me cautious. How will it fare if I have other black sheep among us? We are none without sin. But if we are not men enough publicly and without any attempt to underestimate it, to own up to our guilt, again I ask, how will it fare with us and the cause we have dared to represent? My rejoicing over the Proclamation is thus tempered by the necessary sadness induced by a vivid knowledge of what is happening in our midst. No cause for gloom, equally no warrant for over-exultation, but the greatest cause for vigilant introspection and a vivid sense of our responsibility rendered greater by the Proclamations."

In the *Harijan* issue of 5.12.1936, Gandhiji further said: It is not possible to criticize the rules in anticipation of their application. As with all rules naturally they lead themselves to an interpretation and application as liberal as the Proclamation itself, and to so narrow an interpretation and application as to make the Proclamation wholly ineffective and thus make things worse than before. There is no warrant whatsoever for fearing any calamitous result. The proclamation, as I believe it, is in response to the Time Spirit by a prince imbued with the spirit of reform. It has behind it the sanction of popular approval, if what appears in the press and what I have learnt from person who should know can be relied upon.

"But as I have said in these columns the brunt of making the working of the reform successful will fall on the shoulders of the reformers of Travancore. It should be possible to create an atmosphere whereby the rules may never need enforcement by authority. Temples are generally visited by sincere devotees or hypocrites. The former are meticulous in their observance of rules prescribed by custom for fear of losing all merit of temple worship, and the latter have to observe rules equally meticulously for fear of their being found out. Framing of rules such as we have now to deal with is a novelty of the modern age though absolutely necessary. When the temple doors are opened by secular proclamation to thousands of people, it becomes necessary also to frame secular rules for its due enforcement. There is no doubt the whole of this great experiment of Travancore requires careful, sympathetic and prayerful handling by all concerned. If the spirit behind is purely religious all will be well. Who can lead in that direction better than the reformers and the Harijans whom they will bring to these temples?"

The following telegram was received at Poona from the Harijan Sevak Sangh, Trivandrum, on the 3rd December 1936: "Actual working (of the) Proclamation most successful. It has disproved all fears entertained (in) certain quarters. No part of (the) temple open to any devotee is barred against Ezhavas and Harijans now. Excepting (the) innermost chamber which has been always used only by (the) officiating priest, all other places including mandaps, enclosures, platforms (and) corridors are as freely used by newly admitted devotees as by caste Hindus. What is of the greatest importance is that waters in sacred tanks attached to temples are also freely used now by Ezhavas and Harijans. (The) sense of horror at (the) approach of Harijans seems completely overcome. Harijan devotees do not seem to excite any special reaction in devotees of other castes who are engaged in worship at the same time. (It is) hardly necessary to say that special hour (has been fixed) or any other distinction (has been) made against new entrants. A hopeful feature is (that) priests and other temple officials (are) genuinely (and) wholeheartedly cooperating. They do not seem to suffer any mental strain. (The) Indian Social Reformer's inferential statement that Trivandrum Ananthapadmanabha temple (is) not covered by the Proclamation (is) incorrect. In fact this temple being near the palace (and) daily attended by (the) Maharajah, (the) Proclamation is given completest effect in it. Forty boys of (the) Harijan hostel, including Pulayas, Parayas, Kuravas had privilege (of) darshan and worship in Ananthapadmanabha temple yesterday. They were permitted to go up to (the) chamber of (the) great image up to the point (that) any devotee of (the) highest caste can go to.

"On second December one of our workers took a hundred and fifty Harijans from (a) village thirty-seven miles off to the same Ananthapadmanabha temple without any notice to us. He came yesterday to our office with his party and reported (that) he had been received very kindly and had been allowed darshan (and) worship without any restriction. He said also in answer (to) particular inquiries that he had darshan from the single slab mandap, the maximum point of approach for all devotees even of (the) highest caste. He and his group were fortunate to have darshan of His Highness near the precincts of the temple. Again a bath of our Harijan students visited the local important Subramaniaswamy temple. They had (a) bath in the sacred tank and had darshan without (the) slightest objection (or) restriction (and) the priests were most sympathetic and kind. In fact it may be said they were enthusiastic and joined (sic) snapshots taken by (a) photographer at the time. President, and Sjt. C. Rajagopalachari were at Varkala on (the) second. They made personal enquiries of priests there and the reports were very satisfactory. It was learnt that number of Ezhavas (and) Harijans were voluntarily going to Janardan temple and enjoying benefit of the Proclamation without any difficulty.

"The proclamations covers 1,526 temples managed or controlled by (the) State. Of these 155 are major temples, including 12 wide-famed shrines of all-India importance, like those of Cape Comorin, Suchindram, Ananthapadmanabha, Janardan of Varkala, Haripad, Ambulapuzha, Vaikom, Aranmula, Chenganoor, Ettumanoor, Neyyattinkara, (and) Kalady. The fact is there are few temples of any importance outside Government control in Travancore. Reports received from mofussil centres show satisfactory peaceful working of (the) Proclamation in the same faithful manner as at Trivandrum. Such reports (have been) already received from Cape Comorin, Suchindram, Neyyattinkara, Quilon, Haripad, Alleppey, Vaikom, Aranmula, Ettumanoor, Ambalapuzha (and) Parur. The reaction among Ezhavas is very satisfactory. Their jubilation is greater than (that of) all others, both among ordinary folk and educated sections. Reports indicate that even Ezhavas who were bitter and skeptical about Hinduism are displaying great enthusiasm and (a) spirit of genuine co-operation. Orthodox people including Nambudris have as groups or individuals displayed no hostility, most of them expressing themselves in terms of full approval of (the) Proclamation. We see no signs whatever of resentment. Their behaviour is such as if nothing extraordinary had happened, which from what we know of previous orthodoxy is an astonishing achievement. The noble Proclamation has been followed up by thorough execution? Changanchery K. Parameswaran Pillai, President, Kerala Harijan Sevak Sangh; M. Govindan, President, Trivandrum District Harijan Sevak Sangh; G. Ramachandran, Secretary, Kerala Harijan Sevak."

Gandhiji said: "When the Temple entry Proclamation was issued, I had misgivings which I could not and would not suppress. Was it a political document with loopholes and reservations? What would be its effect on the caste Hindus, if it was a superimposed thing? What would be its effect on Harijans? Would it not leave them cold?

"Friends took me to task for not sharing their enthusiasm. I could not help it. Not that I had any doubt about the genuine desire of H.H. the Maharanee, or the Maharajah, or the Dewan Sir C.P. Ramaswami Iyer. Indeed I had the privilege of meeting the Maharanee and her young hope, the present Maharajah when I was in Travancore years ago. The Maharanee had even then professed her belief in the reform. I had even jokingly asked the boy, as the Maharajah then was, whether he would remove untouchability and throw open temples when he mounted the gadi to Travancore. He had enthusiastically said 'Of course'. Have I not known Sir C.P. Ramaswami Iyer since 1915 or 1916 as a reformer? My misgivings had a deeper meaning which I had tried to express. It may be that it was my want of faith in the people. There certainly was in the adequacy of the effort the purity of reformers working under the aegis of the Harijan Sevak Sangh.

"But the latest happening described in the foregoing telegram with such wealth of detail has dispelled all doubts. The rules reproduced last week have lost all their formidableness. The actuality has surpassed all expectations. The enthusiasm of the Harijans, the absence of all opposition to their entrance to the farthest limit permissible to the highest caste, and the willing, nay the hearty cooperation of the officiating priests, show the utter genuineness of the great and sweeping reform. What seemed impossible for man has been made possible by God. Royal proclamations cannot convert tens of thousands of people. Here, therefore, is an instance of mass conversion of caste Hindus. It is real because it is spontaneous.

"Only a few year ago in Vaikom the caste Hindus had threatened violence if Harijans crossed even certain roads leading to the Vaikom temple. Now that very temple has been opened to Harijans on absolutely the same terms as to any caste Hindu. And all this without the slightest pressure from anybody. What was quoted to me as the Shankara Smriti has given place to the Maharajah Smriti whose validity is proved by the unequivocal response of the caste Hindus as a whole and the equally unequivocal response in another sense by the Harijans. Truly, God is great, if we would but open the eyes of our understanding. My congratulations to the Maharajah and his good mother and his great Dewan, as also the Hindus of Travancore. Let us hope that all caste distinctions, in so far as they connote high and low grades, are things of the past in Travancore. If we garner the enthusiasm of Travancore, it cannot be long before the whole of India catches the Travancore spirit."

Writing under Travancore Pilgrimage, in the *Harijan* issue of 23-1-1937 Gandhiji said: "I am writing this at the Cape in front of the sea where three waters meet and furnish a sight unequalled in the world. For this is no port of call for vessels. Like the goddess the waters around are virgin. The Cape has no population worth the name. The place is therefore eminently fitted for contemplation. This is the third day of the pilgrimage. Having a mentally and voluntarily become an untouchable and therefore shunned the temples which were barred against fellow untouchables, I feel like them the joy of the removal of the bar, I approached the great temple in Trivandrum with awe and due veneration. Curiosity had given way to the incoming of something that was to fill the void of years. As I write these lines I am reminded of the peace I felt in the Cathedral in Madras to which Bishop Whitehead had taken me now over twenty years ago. In that Cathedral on the particular morning, so far as I remember, we were the only two persons present. In the Trivandrum temple there were thousands awaiting the arrival of my party. But there was no noise, no bustle. Untouchables of yesterday were in the silent concourse in perhaps equal numbers. I could not distinguish between the two. All had almost the same marks on their bodies, all had the same kind of garments. Evidently the custom is to have only seamless wear which need not be more than a lungi, never more than a wrapper added to it. The majority including the persists were bare bodied. In the midst of this vast assemblage, I seemed to enjoy the kind of peace I had felt in the Madras cathedral. And yet two were quite different. The Madras peace had no background. This in Padmanabha temple had. And I would not have experienced it, if the crowd had been boisterous or at all in a non-spiritual mood. All those bare bodies in spotlessly white lungies standing row in perfectly silent and reverent attitude produced an impression upon me which will endure till life lasts. The entry into the very spacious temple crowded with images which the guiding priest in his choice Hindu made almost to speak, was no less soul-stirring. Then we reached the great central image. It was all like a day dream. The knowledge that I was visiting the temple designed specially for the Maharajah of Travancore and that too in the company of the hitherto despised untouchables, heightened the effect which the images and the surroundings had produced upon me. The silence and the attitude of worship have continued at the three temples I visited between Trivandrum and the Cape. And this morning I visited the famous temple at the Cape, dedicated to the Virgin. Accompanied by a large party of Harijans who were singing bhajans, we passed through the street leading to the temple. The street like the temple was forbidden to the untouchables. But now, without any opposition from anywhere, we walked through it and then into the temple as if we had never been prohibited. It is a dream realized in a manner and in a place where the realization seemed almost unthinkable before it was realized elsewhere. You may have temples opened in the North, but you will never succeed in having them opened in Cochin and Travancore—the citadels of orthodoxy, used to be told before. Now one citadel has yielded with rare generosity and grace. The genuineness of the generosity and grace seems to have disarmed all opposition. The legend attached to the acts of the Maharajah of Travancore had perhaps its due share in the conversion of the people. The Maharajahs are called Padmanabhadas, meaning servants of Padmanabha, i.e., God. The Maharajahs are supposed to visit the temple every morning (and I understand they do whilst in Trivandrum) and receive instructions for the day's work from God. The proclamation is therefore an act of God through His servant, the present Maharajah. Whatever may be the cause, the fact of the Proclamation being given effect to by an overwhelming number of Savarnas and being freely availed of by Avarnas stands out as a miracle.

"But the very miracle weighs me down with a sense of responsibility which chastens me and affects my elation. If what is going on today is to be consolidated, there must be continued effort by all true Harijan workers for the education of both Savarnas and Avarnas on the meaning of the Proclamation. But a few months ago it was the fashion on the part of Savarnas to say that Avarnas did not want temple entry. It was equally the fashion on the part of some vocal members among the Avarnas to say that they did not care for temple or want temple entry and that they cared only for economic uplift. Both mistook the meaning of the anti-untouchability campaign. The right of entering temples abolishes untouchability at a stroke—untouchability that prevented a large section of Hindus from sharing with the rest the privilege of worship in the same manner as the latter. Economic uplift was there. But the best among the Avarnas felt the sting of the deprivation. It soured them and angered them against the haughty Savarnas. Now all that has changed. The Avarnas feel the glow of freedom which they had never felt before.

All this marvellous result may easily be nullified if it is to follow out to its logical conclusion. Before Avarnas can forget the past, they must be made conscious of what they have come to. The message of freedom must be carried to the humblest hut. The minds of the Pulayas and the Pariahs could be opened to the implication of the suddenly acquired freedom. This does not need an elaborate programme of literacy. That must come. But what is needed is immediate human contact. For this an army of volunteer workers of the right type is needed. And just as the message of freedom has to be taken to the avarna huts, so has it to be taken to the Savarna homes.

Then there is the question of reform of temples form within. Here I cannot do better than quote from a long letter from a mussalman friend who believes in Hinduism as much as he believes in Islam: 'You will soon be going to Travancore to celebrate the entry of Harijans into the temples thrown open to them. It is indeed a step forward. But what we need most is the restoration of the temples to their pristine purity and sanctity. The ideal lying behind temples is most holy. In the temples of ancient India resided great Rishis who imparted divine wisdom. Today the priest sits there barring the way to those who need instruction and help to solve the problem of life. Alas! the priests of all religions are more in need of instruction than the poor masses.' "These words are true. Never was the need for temple reform more urgent than today. Fortunately in Travancore the vast majority of temples belong to the state and are under special management and addition. They are never empty. They supply a felt want. If the priests had better education and would be custodians of the spirituality of the people, the temples would be houses both of worship and spiritual instruction as they were before."

Regarding the message of the Proclamation, Gandhiji said: "I suppose you can better imagine than I can describe my joy for being a second time in your midst and under such happy auspices as you all know. Only a few years ago one had to struggle hard to get the roads leading to the great temple thrown open to Avarna Hindus. Good Madhavan assisted by Krishnaswami of revered memory and by Kelappan laid the foundation of that struggle. It is a matter of deep sorrow to me, as it must be to you, that neither Madhavan nor Krishnaswami is here to share your rejoicings."

A Call to Purification

Gandhiji said, "Now I am on a pilgrimage, as I have called the present tour of Travancore. Throughout the whole course of my life I do not remember having entered so many temples as have during these few days of pilgrimage, and only an hour more and I shall have privilege of entering the forbidding looking walls as they then were which surround the great temple of this place. And all these good things have come to pass because the Maharajah and the Maharanee resolved to carry out the sacred resolve under the inspiration of Padmanabhaswami. But the Proclamation can be rendered fully ineffective if the Savarnas and Avarnas of Travancore do not make an adequate response to this proclamation. It is not enough that the Savarnas and the Avarnas continue to go to the temples just as they are doing now. Hitherto people have gone to the temples more by way of formality than from conviction. They had not reasoned out for themselves why they needed to go to the temples. Largely throughout India the temples have been popular more with women than men, and they have gone there in order to ask some boon of the God residing in those temples. But now if you have rightly understood the Proclamation and all it means, I expect much more from you than a mere formal going to the temples. In my opinion the Proclamation is a call to purification addressed to every Hindu in Travancore, whether Savarna or

Avarna. It was the Savarnas who for a thousand years, may be several thousand years had deprived their own fellow-religionists of the right of worshipping the same God in the same manner that they worshipped. And in order to justify such an atrocious injustice—no matter for what causes—a whole class of human beings were held as untouchables. Now that the sinful distinction has been abolished by a stroke of the pen, in order that you have got to adopt some measure to let them know that you are no longer the superior beings that you have claimed to be all these years. Therefore I would expect all Savarnas to take the glorious message of liberation to every Avarna home. It can be done very easily and without much effort on your part. Only one condition is indispensable. You should believe from the bottom of our heart in the necessity of the Proclamation, and every Hindu-Savarna and Avarna, man and woman—should make it his other individual work to get hold of some Avarnas, to take to them the message of the Proclamation, and take them to the temples. And since the spiritual regeneration of an individual or a nation must include all the departments of life, economic, religious, social uplift in those departments is bound to follow. You will be vastly mistaken if you labour under the delusion that all these things are going to be done by the Proclamation."

A Historical Fact

Gandhiji said: "I think that the Maharajah's and the Maharanee's task is finished, so far as untouchability is concerned, by issuing this Proclamation. That there would be financial aid by the state for the education of these classes is a foregone conclusion. But that can never bring about the regeneration that I am picturing to myself. That requires a hearty and willing cooperation of the Savarna Hindus as a class. You can therefore understand my sorrow when I heard—I do not know with what truth that some women and even men were hesitating to enter the temple which they used to do regularly. In order to disabuse such doubters, if there are any here, of their doubts I want to quote one historical fact that took place when I was here in connection with Vaikom satyagraha. Some of you may remember that I had more than one serious discussion with the *shastris* who were then residing within the temple precincts, and who were attached, if

I remember rightly to the temple in some shape or other. I am trying to give you as correct a version of that discussion as I can recall at the present moment. In support of the proposition that even roads leading to the temples were barred against Avarna Hindus although they were not barred against non-Hindus, they produced a book called *Shankara Smriti*. I had never heard of such a *Smriti* before I came to Vaikom and heard it quoted. You will be astonished to find that when I had the *Smriti* translated for me, I could not find in it any authority for closing the roads. But I grant that it was enough for them that they believed that the *Shankara Smriti* supported their contention.

"Then, as I was negotiating through the then Commissioner of Police and with the Senior Maharanee, I just asked the question that supposing as a result of the negotiations the Maharanee issued orders to open the roads to the Avarna Hindus, what would be their attitude to them? Then without the slightest hesitation they said: 'Oh! that is a different thing altogether; a Hindu Prince or Princess has every right to issue an order which has the authority of a *Smriti*!' They said that was implied in Hinduism as Hindu kings are repositories of Hindu faith and they have every right to issue orders which are not inconsistent with the *Shruti*. I asked them whether the same thing applied to the opening of the temples. They said, 'Most decidedly'. Let me tell you that these *shastris* were not the only *shastris* that gave this reply. I asked the same question to *shastris* in Cochin and Tamil Nadu and they gave the same answer. As a matter of fact that is the historical evolution of *smritis* and for that matter of the eighteen *Puranas*. They were all produced or inspired in response to the want of those times. They do not always express eternal varieties. The eternal verity is summed up in verse of the *Ishopanishad* as I have been saying. And without fear of contradiction I am here to say that every believer in this verse is wholly a Hindu, and if he acts up to what is taught by this mantra he will find his freedom here and hereafter. I know no other road or better road to happiness than is contained in this first mantra of *Ishopanishad*. And if a Hindu prince in conformity with the implications and teachings of this *mantra*, issued a proclamation such as has been issued by the Maharajah of Travancore, it would carry such authority. And I invite those who know anything of the *Ishopanishad* to tell me whether this Proclamation is in any way inconsistent with this *mantra*. If they will make a prayerful search within and examine it, they will find that the Proclamation is a tardy fulfillment of its requirements. Therefore with all the earnestness that I can command I want to ask every doubter, man and woman, to throw away those doubts and heartily respond to the Proclamation. I shall conclude this part by hoping that the Proclamation will have your hearty, no lukewarm, support and that you will carry it out in letter and spirit."

Gandhiji explained the meaning of temple entry in the *Harijan* issue of 26.1.1934 as follows: "I will not be guilty of being party to the opening of a single temple under coercion. But I do want temples to be opened where public opinion is absolutely and clearly ripe for the opening of those temples. If there is any legal obstruction in the process I want that legal obstruction to be removed. That is the meaning, and the only meaning, of the Temple Entry Bill, and no other. This Bill simply removes the powerlessness that many trustees today feel about opening the temples under their charge because of the legal obstruction. There is not the slightest trace of compulsion or coercion about this Temple Entry Bill or the kindred bill called of Anti-untouchability Bill.

"But I heard a whisper this morning that behind this temple entry agitation there is a nefarious design, if not on my part, on the part of my co-workers, that we should take possession of these temples and own them. I have no hesitation whatsoever in categorically denying this statement. I have certainly no such design whatsoever, and I do not know of a single worker who has any such design. And if there is any such co-worker who has such a design, he has no place whatsoever on this platform. The possession will remain undoubtedly in the hands of those who are today lawfully in possession."

Gandhiji suggested the following four-fold programme for raising Harijans: Great as this Proclamation is and great as is its religious merit, greater skill is the responsibility that His Highness has taken upon his shoulders, and so also his advisers. Whilst without the effort of every Savarna Hindu the Proclamation can undoubtedly be rendered ineffective, I must also say that the Proclamation would not have its full effect unless it is backed in an ample measure by State action. So far as I can see, the Proclamation demands state activities in all departments of life. Of these I propose to take the religion first; because from it must follow activities in all the other departments. Temples have been matters of indifference, except to women, who have no capital save divine faith, and to men who from many mixed motives have been going to them. They have been neglected by what may be called the intelligentsia. The result has been that they have almost ceased to be repositories of Hinduism and have ceased to impart spiritual power to those who have followed the faith. They almost ceased to shed unmistakable spiritual fragrance in and about and around them. Then, I venture to suggest that it is the duty of the state, or of the Maharajah, if there is any distinction between the two, for he is the custodian of the vast majority of Hindu temples, that he should see to it that the temples are renovated spiritually, and have the authority and sanction that they used doubtedly to have at one time. And I believe that it can only the done if they are one time. And I believe that it can only be done if they are in charge of priests who know what they have to do, who know something of the sanctity of them and of the duties to which they are called. In other words, they should not be ignorant people following their calling for livelihood, but they should be men who are proud of their privilege of bringing the message of God to temple goers, showing by their own conduct and their life that these temples are abodes of divinity.

"Then there should be the correct kind of instruction given in these temples. The Harijans will be taken by the hand by someone in charge of temples and they will be told what they are expected to gain by temple worship. This means undoubtedly, according to modern thought, a revolution in the upkeep and conduct of these temples. But the Proclamation itself is nothing short of a revolutionary document, and if that revolution is to touch, as it ought to touch, the lives of all Hindus, naturally temples have to be abodes of the living God, and not abodes of a mere mass of gold or other metals worked into figures. Then I should expect a history of these temples understandable by the common folk, to be distributed freely or at a cheap price to all who want to know what these temples are. That means a training school for training the right kind of teachers who will be entrusted with the religious training of the people. If some such thing does not happen, I fear that the purpose of the Proclamation, viz., to expect and to induce lakhs and lakhs of Harijans to go to these temples in a religious spirit will fail.

"So much for the religious department. Then I take the economic. The economic life of the Harijans has got to be lifted out of its miserable state. I venture to think that by a judicious and thoughtful working out of the programme, it can be prosecuted in a short time and with a limited financial outlay, in such a manner that Harijans may be easily able to hold their own by being taught to turn an honest chakram. Nor can the state now dare neglect the mental training—I mean literary of these people. I know to my cost that today it is very difficult to carry on a connected conversation with Pulayas and Pariahs so that you can get a ready response even about simple facts of life.

"Similarly, the state has to raise the social status of these people. They should be invited to all state occasions and functions, as, for instance durbars. They must not be allowed to feel that these functions are a sealed book to them, and that they should have another agitation before they can attain a social status entitling them to be invited or allowed to take part in those functions. But if the Proclamation bears the meaning I have given to it, then the social uplift of the Harijans has to come as if by magic, as the religious status of going to the temples has come.

"In my humble opinion, in suggesting this fourfold programme of the uplift of the Harijans in the State I have not suggested any programme beyond the capacity or resources of state like Travancore.

"But having addressed these few words to the state in all humility, I want to come back to you. The state may resolve to do all these things, but its resolution will not mean the coming in of manpower in order to carry out all these things. And if, from the few words I have addressed to Their Highnesses and their advisers, you think that after all it is Their Highnesses who have to do everything and you to do nothing, then I am afraid that my labours will have gone in vain. The requisite manpower has got to be supplied by you, and as a man of experience I will tell you that manpower cannot come by offers of money. Thus, for instance, men who are capable of taking the management of temple cannot be had by offering scholarships of hundreds of rupees. For such people have got to be fired by a religious spirit, by love of their own work, and should therefore be ready to work for a bare maintenance. It should be their proud privilege to take this training and to fit themselves for this highest task in life. Similarly, unless the state gets men required for giving Harijans educational training, the state can do nothing.

"After all, there is a world of meaning about the title that the Maharajahs of Travancore have adopted for themselves, viz., Padmanabhadas. They pride themselves in calling themselves servants of God, but that means that they are also servants of their people. So, as I said at one of these meetings, the Maharajahs are not the first lords among the people of Travancore, but they are the first servants among the people who are also servants. But the first servants of the people will fare badly unless they are ably assisted by the people who are their fellow servants. Therefore, the meaning of His Highness the Maharajah going to the temple everyday and taking instruction as to his daily duties from Shri Padmanabhaswami means nothing less than that he should be assisted by his people for their own good-spiritual, religious, social, economic."

With regard to the economic and educational uplift of untouchables Gandhiji said: "The economic and educational uplift is no doubt an essential part of true repentance by caste Hindus. It is a test of the sincerity of their professions. But the uplift will not be complete without the throwing open of temples. The throwing open of temples will be an admission of the religious equality of Harijans. It will be the surest sign of their ceasing to be the outcastes of Hinduism, which they are today.

"It is beside the point that tens of thousands of Harijans do not want to enter temples. If it properly probed, the fact would be found to be quite otherwise. Thousands of Harijans do want to enter temples. Only they have been so accustomed to the prohibition that the very hope of entering temples has dried up in them. They believe that admission to temples on a par with the other Hindus is an impossibility.

"But whether Harijans desire the consolation of temple entry or not, whether, if temples are thrown open to them they will make us of them or not, caste Hindus have to perform their simple duty. They have to open their temples for Harijans to offer worship in, precisely on the same terms as for themselves. A debtor is not absolved from the duty of payment because his creditor does not care for the payment or has forgotten the debt altogether.

"And when temples are thrown open to Harijans, schools, wells and many similar facilities will be automatically open to Harijans. It is surely easy enough to realize that untouchability may subsist side by side with economic uplift. Many Ezhavas in Travancore and Namasudras in Bengal possess decent fortunes and are yet treated as pariahs of society. The bar sinister is all the more galling to them by reason of their flourishing condition. Dr. Ambedkar suffers from the curse in spite of his high educational attainments and his superior economic condition. He is naturally more sensitive to the insult of untouchability. But the reproach will be automatically removed, immediately caste Hindus proclaim the banishment of untouchability by admitting Harijans to their temples on term of absolute equality with themselves. It will not then become necessary for any Harijan individually to go to temples, if he does not desire to do so. The declaration of the opening of temples will cover him with the rest. It will be like the abolition of slavery. It will be a vast and glorious step in the much needed and overdue purification of Hinduism.

"Temple entry permission, to be of use, has naturally to be a voluntary act on the part of Hindus. It has to be, therefore, a genuine change of heart in the caste Hindus. Legislation is never the less necessary because of the fact that in law the entry of the Harijans into caste Hindu temples is said to be prohibited. Legislation will constitute the seal of approval of the vast mass of Hindus. I personally should not want that legislation in the teeth of universal caste Hindu opposition. My own belief is that caste Hindus as a whole do not oppose temple entry by Harijans. I should abide by the result of an honestly conducted referendum. Anyway, let the reformers realize that, whatever happens in the legislature at Delhi, the movement for temple entry and the necessary legislation must continue."

In an article published under the title "Temple Entry vs. Economic Uplift" in the *Harijan* issue of 16-3-1934 Gandhiji said: "One sees sometimes in the public criticism on the temple entry question. It is double-barrelled, being directed on the one hand by Harijans and on the other by sanatanists. Some of the Harijans say, 'We do not want temple entry; do not build temples, but use all you receive for economic uplift.' Some sanatanists say, 'Give up the temple entry question altogether. You are hurting our feeling by forcing Harijans into temples.' Both are we wrong in substance. Not one single piece out of the purse has been or will be spent for building temples. Attempt is being made only to have public temples opened to Harijans on the same terms on which they are open to the other Hindus. It is a matter of choice for Harijans to visit or not to visit them. Savarna Hindus have to lift the bar against Harijans. For these millions who regard temples as treasure-chests of spiritual wealth, they are living realities which they hold dear as life itself. If they are truly repentant towards Harijans they must share these treasures with the latter. I know what the opening of temples means to Harijans. Only last week, between Dharwar and Belgaum, I opened three temples to Harijans in the presence of crowds of Savarna Hindus and Harijans. If critics had been present at the opening and noticed the pleasure on the countenances of the Harijans present as they bowed before the image and received the Prasad, their criticism would have been silenced. Harijans critics would have realized that, apart from themselves, Harijans at large did desire temple entry. Sanatanist critics would have realized that temples, wherever they were opened, were being opened with the fullest concurrence of the temple goers concerned and in the presence of crowds of them. No hole and corner opening can do any good to Hinduism. To be of spiritual of any value at all, the opening has to be performed with due publicity, solemnity and the willing consent of the existing temple goers, and not of such self-styled reformers as have no faith or interest in temples and for whom temples may even be a superstition. Temple entry agitation requires no financial outlay, it does not lend itself to agitation except by a few workers who have faith in temples and whose words would command attention from the mass Savarna mind. It is, therefore, a question that can only be and is being gently and cautiously handled. The only insistence is on the right and the duty of the believing reformer advocating temple entry and showing that without it the reformation will not only be incomplete but fruitless. For, without temples being freely open to Harijans, untouchability could not be said to have been removed root and branch.

"As for the economic uplift, it is altogether wrong to put it in opposition to temple entry. Temple entry can only help such uplift. For, when Harijans are freely admitted to temples, all the avenues to economic betterment must be automatically open to Harijans as to others. So far as the monies received are concerned, they will all be used only for economic uplift, if it is admitted that educational uplift also means economic, in that it makes the educated Harijan fitter for running life's race. I am aware that education among the Savarnas has often rendered them less fit for the race. But that has been so, because their education has meant contempt for labour. There is not much danger of such a mishap with the general body of Harijans for sometime to come at least. And the danger can be averted altogether, if those who are in charge of the movement will take care to purge Harijan education of the evils of the current method, which ignores the technical side for the most part, if not altogether" (Sheshrao Chavan: *Gandhi and Ambedkar Saviours of Untouchables,* pp. 160-202).

Chapter 10

Gandhi and Ambedkar on the Word Harijan

In the *Harijan* issue of 11th February 1933, Gandhiji wrote, "Several correspondents have adopted the name *Harijan* for untouchables. Some English friends have asked me for its meaning. It is not a name of my coining. Some years ago, several untouchable correspondents complained that I used the word *Asprishya* in the pages of *Navajivan*. *Asprishya* means literally untouchable. I then invited them to suggest a better name and one of the untouchable correspondents suggested the adoption of the name *Harijan* on the strength of its having been used by the first known poet saint of Gujarat. Though the quotation he sent me did not exactly fit the cause he wanted to make out for the adoption, I thought that it was a good word. Harijan means a 'man of God'. All the religions of the world describe God preeminently as the friend of the friendless, help of the helpless, and protector of the weak. The rest of the world apart, in India who can be more friendless, helpless or weaker than the forty millions or more Hindus of India who are classified as untouchables? If therefore, anybody of people can be truly described as men of God, they are surely there helpless friendless and despised people. Hence, in the pages of *Navajivan*, since then I have always adopted "Harijan" as the name signifying untouchable. And, when God chose to entrust me with their service even whilst undergoing imprisonment, I could not use any other word for describing them. I recoil with horror from that word and all it implies. Not that change of name brings about any change of status, but one may at least be spared the use of term which is itself one of reproach. When caste Hindus have their own inner conviction and, therefore, voluntarily got rid of the present day untouchability, we shall all be called Harijans, for according to my humble opinion, caste Hindus will then have found favour with God and may, therefore, be fitly, described as His men."

A caste-Hindu correspondent in a letter to Gandhiji wrote, "If these depressed classes are finally to be merged in the Hindus, was it not better that instead of 'Harijans' they should have been given the name 'Hindus' which would have applied to both caste Hindus and the depressed classes? It is still time that the word 'Harijan' is given up in favour of the word 'Hindus' so that the caste Hindus and the Hindu depressed classes are known in common parley as well as in government papers as only Hindus."

Gandhiji replied to this correspondent through the column of *Harijan* issue of 11th March 1933 in which he said: "The correspondent is too late with his suggestion. If a separate register of untouchable classes had not come to stay, at least for the time being, the common name might have answered the purpose. But the separate register makes it absolutely necessary to know the untouchable classes by some name, and has no ill flavour about it? I regard 'Harijan' as a fitting name because the caste Hindus cannot be properly considered God's children, but the untouchables certainly can.

"I have suggested the real method of abolishing the distinction between caste Hindus and Harijans, namely, by caste Hindus performing the purification ceremony of ridding themselves of untouchability and becoming Harijans themselves. And if it is open to be classified as untouchables in the register for untouchables, I should most decidedly advise caste Hindus to declare themselves as such to live also as such. That will be a substantial and organic method of amalgamating the two into one body. This is the proper place for referring to the same suggestion made by a Harijan friend but from a different standpoint. He says that the best way of getting rid of untouchability is to advise Harijans to adopt name that will never signify an untouchable and to declare themselves also as mere Hindus or as mere Brahmins, Kshatriyas or Vaishyas. This suggestion was made to me even as early as 1915, when I began to crusade against untouchability. This Harijan had his own experience and told me that he had traveled from one end of India to other, that he had freely entered all the principal places of pilgrimage without let or hindrance and that he had taken with him a party.

"When he was introduced to me, I saw no mark about him of being a Harijan. He was dressed like a Brahmin, had a *tilak* on his forehead, a *mala* of *Tulsi* or *rudraksha*. He and his party took up their abode in Dharmashalas and never had the slightest difficulty, having unhesitatingly proclaimed themselves as belonging to one varna or the other.

"My visitor told me that this practice of untouchables hiding their identity was quite a common thing amongst them and that it was growing. He unfortunately received no encouragement from me. I told him that this practice might be convenient for him and the few who could afford the means and had sufficient training to be able to shed some of the habits which marked out an untouchable from the rest, but the practice of a few, apart from its being dishonest and therefore tending to deterioration of manhood, would make no impression upon the tens of thousands of untouchables who could not even stir out of their villages.

"The reply that I then gave applies with equal force even today. The straightest and the quickest method, therefore, is to conduct the movement openly, to know the untouchables as such and yet for caste Hindus to treat them of absolute equality with themselves and as movement has begun on a very large scale and the declaration was made on behalf of caste Hindus that untouchability was gone, it surely became necessary to know untouchables by an inoffensive name whilst the best name to know them by."

Someone sent a letter to Gandhiji in which he said: "You gave us the name Harijan. We feel therefore, as if we are a separate community to be known by giving us this name."

Gandhiji replied this letter through *Harijan* in its issue of 9th February 1934 which runs as follows: "I may be wounding the susceptibilities of half a dozen, but not of others. No other name has been received all round with so much approbation as this has. You should remember that it is not of my coining.

So long as they have to be separately designated, some name is necessary. Then why not one which is inoffensive?"

The C.P. government announced through its notification that the so-called depressed classes will be known as *Harijans*, and criminal tribes as wandering tribes. Gandhiji congratulated the C.P. government through the columns of *Harijan* and hoped that the other governments would copy the good example set by the C.P. government (*Harijan*, 15.6.1934).

Shri H.K. Mullick sent a letter in the name of the editor of the *Harijan* in which he said: "I was rather pained to find that the keen intellect of Mr. M.D. missed the real point involved in the representation made by some friends who met Gandhiji claiming to be the representatives of the Harijans or rather 'depressed classes' as they preferred to call them" (*Harijan*, 10.8.1934).

"The 'bad odour' attaching to the term depressed classes is a surety of its ultimate extinction and complete disappearance along with the development of consciousness consequent solidification of the general Hindu community at large, which we all know, is the aim of Gandhiji in his great and unique endeavour", continued Mullick. But the sweetness of the term 'Harijan' is likely to perpetuate the gulf between them and the Savarna Hindus, which is surely not desired by Gandhiji. The point should have been noticed by Mr. M.D. whose use of the adjective 'curious' appears to be remarkable and at the same time regrettable, coming as it does from one of the closet associates of the Mahatma.

"I myself feel interested in the matter as one belonging to this great class, but feel indifferent to the application that others may choose to give, excepting, of course, the result it is likely to have on the future position to the great community in the large Hindu fold. Will you kindly show this to Mr. M.D.?"

In reply to this letter Gandhiji wrote in *Harijan* in its issue of 14th September 1934, "M.D. has passed the foregoing to me. I know Sjt. Mullick, as I had the pleasure of meeting him in Calcutta during the recent visit. I can share his nervousness and his preference for an odious appellation so long as the stigma of untouchability persists. But I invite Sjt. Mullick to enter into the feeling of reformers who have no untouchability in them and who, therefore, have horror of using an odious name for those whom they love and are eager to serve to the best of their ability. Add to this the fact that tens of thousands of untouchables do not like the word *Achhut*, *Asprishya* and the like and that they do like the word *Harijan*. The aim of us all is the total extinction of untouchability. When that happy day arrives either the word *Harijan* will disappear or we shall all be proud to be called *Harijans*—devotees of God—deserving to be so described, having been free of the virus of high and low."

A part of a dialogue between Gandhiji and a number of Harijan sevaks of Delhi which appeared in a weekly letter by M.D. is given below.

"Q: But why should we be called Harijans and not Hindus?"

"A: I know that a small section of you resents the name but you may know the genesis of the name. You used to be called Depressed Classes or Asprishyas or Achhuts (untouchables).

"All these names the vast mass of you naturally resented. Some of you sent their protest to me and asked me to find out a better name. In English I had adopted better word than "depressed" viz., 'suppressed' but whilst I was casting about for a good Indian word a friend suggested the word 'Harijan' taken from the song of one of our saints. It appealed to me because it best described your condition and still had no bad odour about it. It means a devotee of God, and God is the Help of the Helpless, and as it is the helpless who naturally turn to God. I thought you deserved the name better than I, for instance. For whilst I have aspired to become a Harijan, you are Harijan in the very nature of things. But you will say, when your objective is to make Harijans Hindus why don't you start by calling them Hindus straightway? What am I to do until I have not succeeded in abolishing untouchability?" (*Harijan*, 4.4.1936).

The question and answers on the word 'Harijan' went on right up to 1946. In the year 1946 the following question was asked to Gandhiji.

From the psychological point of views, I think the name 'Harijan' instills into the minds of people to whom it is applied a feeling of inferiority, however sacred that name may be. This feeling is very difficult to wipe out from them—to whatever extent they are advanced—if they are always called 'Harijan'. Similarly, if a man in the street is asked about a "Harijan" the first thing he will speak of is 'Untouchability and the depressed classes'.

Would it not be possible to save the 'Harijan' from involuntarily acquiring such an inferiority feeling and other people from thinking about them without the 'Qualification' ascribed to them? Would it not be preferable to choose a name which could also bring in its fold people from other sects?

To this Gandhiji replied: "This subject was years ago dealt in the pages of *Young India*. The name 'Harijan' has sacred association. It was suggested by a Harijan as a substitute for *Asprishya* (untouchable), Dalit (Depressed) Mehtars, Chamars, Pariahs, etc. The government officers put them in schedule and therefore called them the scheduled classes, thus making confusion worse confounded. Those who were not untouchables were classes among the scheduled and the ones who could be so-called were excluded. We have now arrived at a stage, thanks to the government policy; when to be included among the scheduled classes is to be coveted. The government have created a separate electorate agitating for the seats in all elective institutions. I do not mind such ambition, if it carries honest merit with it. But it becomes positively mischievous, when seats are coveted irrespective of merit. The wish to be so educated as to be qualified for the highest post is to be appreciated and encouraged, the wish to be appointed to such a post on the basis of belonging to a caste or a class is essentially to be deprecated and discouraged.

"The real remedy has been suggested by me. The feeling of inferiority must go. It is going, but slowly. The process can be accelerated, if every Hindu would deliberately shed his superiority and in practice becomes a Harijan or, if you like, a Mahar, the lowest class among Harijans. Then we will become children of God as the word 'Harijan' means. Until this is done, no matter which word signifies untouchables, it will smell of inferiority. The process has to be carried thoroughly in every walk of life till the last trace of untouchability is removed. When that happy day arrives every quarter will be a Harijan quarter and cleanliness of the heart and home will be the order of the day" (*Harijan*, 14.4.1946).

Ambedkar expressed his feelings about the word 'Harijan' in the following words:

"The untouchables simply detest the name Harijan. Various grounds of objection are urged against the name. In the first place it had not bettered their position. It has not elevated them in the eyes of Hindus. The new name has become completely identified with the subject matter of the old. Every book knows that Harijans are simply not other than the old untouchables. The new name provides no escape to the untouchables from the curse of untouchability. With the new name they are damned as much as they were with the old. Secondly, the untouchables say that they prefer to be called untouchables. They argue that it is better that the wrong should be called by its known name. It is better for the patient to know what he is suffering from. It is better for the wrong doer that wrong is there still to be redressed. And concealment is a fraud upon the untouchables and a false absolution to the Hindu. Thirdly, there is also the feeling that the name Harijan is indicative of pity. If the name meant chosen people of God as the Jews claimed themselves to be it would have been different matter. But to call them children of God is to invite pity from their tyrants by pointing out their helplessness and their dependent condition. The more manly among the untouchables resent the degrading implications of this new name.

"How great was the resentment of the untouchables against this new name can be seen from the fact that the whole body of the representatives of the untouchables in Bombay Legislative Assembly walked out of House in protest when the Congress Government introduced a measure giving to the name Harijan the sanction of law?"

The following dialogue took place on the amendment with regard to the word Harijan during the debate held on 22 January 1939 in Bombay Legislative Assembly.

Dr. B.R. Ambedkar: I am very sorry, but I think I cannot help saying that this is a matter on which the wishes of this group ought to have prevailed with government. Nobody would have been hurt, the interest of the country would not have been injured if the amendment moved by my honourable friend. Mr. Gaikwad had been accepted in view of the fact that the government whishes to use its majority in a tyrannic dissatisfaction by walking out in a body and not participating further in the days proceedings.

B.G. Kher: I hope the honourable member (Dr. Ambedkar) will give me an opportunity of saying a few words. It is a very sad commentary that feeling in this country, where even the slightest question of caste or creed is concerned, is so even today. As the honourable leader of the Independent Labour Party knows, since a long time an attempt had been made to take away from currency in our language the word *Asprishya* because the idea is the reminder of the most painful associations of what has been universally now admitted to be a stain on Hinduism. I quite agree with honourable member Mr. Gaikwad that by merely changing the name will not achieve this object. The present section is an attempt in that direction. We tried an alternative expression, we wanted to say, 'Parishishta Varga'. But that is the translation of the English expression "Scheduled Classes" and we thought the 'Parishishta varga' would be a very inappropriate expression to introduce into the Marathi language, if instead of using the English for that expression. "Parishishta varga" and the only alternative to denote what class was meant. I can understand the feelings as they do, that they do not like any attempt to differentiate them from the rest of the Hindus, but even for the purpose of legislation, to achieve this result even for bettering the conditions of this class; we have to designate them as apart from the other Hindus—we may call them *Asprishya* or by any other name, and the fewer the expression we use to differentiate and classify as different such a large body of Hindus the better, but I know that since the last four or five years the word Harijan has now gained a currency if not in the whole of the country, at least in many parts of the country. This is an attempt to substitute a word for the expression 'Scheduled Classes' which ought to have met with the approval of the honourable member, the Leader of the Independent Labour Party. It is extremely unfortunate that he does not look at the question in that light, but he suggests as alternative which is suitable for the expression, 'Scheduled Classes'. I do expect it will be possible to speak his feelings. In the alternative, I do appeal to him, at any rate, to read into this section as no desire to hurt the feelings of a large class of people, who are unfortunately known as 'untouchables' but merely a desire to recognize an expression which has, for such a long time, gained currency would appeal to him not to see in the word 'Harijan' and in the definition, an attempt to cast any reflection on his community.

Dr. B.R. Ambedkar: Sir, as you have ruled that this is not an occasion for making speeches, I will not make any speech. All that I will say is this I am not in a position to suggest any better name but I must say that the name, 'Harijan' has now become practically equivalent to term 'Asprishya' beyond that there is nothing remaining in that name, and I would think that of honourable Prime Minister had felt in the same way in which we feel that the expression 'Scheduled Class' then it was his duty, for the moment, to have withdrawn that word and later on he would have discussed the matter with us with a view to find out some alternative term. His arguments, however, have not earned any conviction to us. I will therefore leave the Hall.

Dr. Ambedkar and other members of the Independent Labour Party then walked out of the House angrily.

At the Round Table Conference Dr. Ambedkar proposed that the untouchables be called 'protestant Hindus' or 'Non-conformist Hindus'. What emerged instead when the electorate award was made and eventually incorporated in the Government of India Act 1935 was the new official term 'Scheduled Classes'.

The controversy with regard to the word 'Harijan' has been kept alive and the motives are attributed to Gandhiji, for calling the untouchables Harijan.

Justice Chandrashekhar Dharmadhikari, a veteran Gandhian and an admirer of Ambedkar says: "It has nowadays become a fashion to criticize Mahatma Gandhi by taking shelter on one or the other pretext. Some political leaders have started giving public speeches and statements that Mahatma Gandhi was the enemy of the untouchables. The campaign is, needless to say, politically motivated with a view to grab power and not to build the Samaj.

"Mahatma Gandhi belonged to all. He did not belong to a particular caste, creed, language or province. In our country, one who belongs to all belongs to none and therefore everybody feels free to criticize Gandhiji. But history does not change by not reading it. It is unfortunate that the attack is being made on Gandhiji without understanding his life and message or his contribution for the independence of India."

Justice Dharmadhikar cited a poem composed by Kusumagraja, a well known Marathi poet and the recipient of Jnapeeth Award. In the said poem it is depicted that the portraits of the leaders themselves hold a meeting in Bombay on 'Chowpati' in the night after ten o'clock. First of all the portrait of Chatrapati Shivaji Maharaj comes forward and says: 'I laid the foundation of the Swaraj for the Rayat i.e., common masses. I was then a national figure, but now I have been confined to Maharashtra and that too of one caste. Mahatma Phule came and said: "I set up Satya Shodhak Samaj to abolish caste and creed, opened schools for the education of girls. In spite of this I have been given place in Maharashtra in the Vegetable markets only." Then came Babasaheb Ambedkar and said: "I have drafted the constitution to create democratic India, based on equality and fraternity and in which the untouchability will be abolished, but I have been confined to Neo-Buddhists only." After Ambedkar, Lokmanya Tilak came and expressed: "At least one caste is behind you, but I am acclaimed only by Chit Pawan, Sub Caste among Brahmins." Ultimately Mahatma Gandhi appeared with tears in his eyes and in his style of speaking in few words said: "There is at least one caste or sub-caste behind you, but behind me there are only walls of the government offices on which I have been hung."

"Nathuram Godse killed Gandhiji and the followers of Mahatma Gandhi have hung him (Gandhiji) on the walls of the government offices. Everybody takes pride in condemning Gandhiji and thinking that thereby he will be successful in his leadership.

"Those who want to understand Gandhiji must know that he advocated for 'Harijan Seva' and not for 'Harijan Uddhar'. Gandhiji constantly pleaded for Harijan Seva, i.e., service. In his view, unless the untouchability was removed from the minds and hearts of caste Hindus, it would not be abolished. Mahatma Gandhi who was a revolutionary adopted 'broom' with *charkha*, as symbols of revolution. He gave recognition to the dignity of labour, and the *charkha* was meant to bring economic equality and dignity of labour. In the same way he introduced the broom and collective cleanliness to abolish social injustice. He himself used to clean his latrine and made the residents of the Ashram clean the latrines. He thought that the status of man could not be measured from the work he did. He felt that the high and lowness of the caste would find no place in this country when the *Bhagavad Gita* would be in the hands of Bhangis and the broom in the hands of Brahmins. The programme undertaken by Gandhiji for 'Harijan Seva' was penance for Savarnas. He believed that the Sarvodaya is possible only through Antodaya. What he adopted was, in fact first brought into currency by a saint Narsi Mehta, who himself was a Nagar Brahmin.

"A question is now being raised that if Harijans are children of God, then who are other Hindus? Are they 'Durjan' or 'Dushta jan'?

"In the opinion of Mahatma, Harijans are really the children of God. Had they not been there, the Brahmins would not have been able to keep themselves clean. In spite of it the caste Hindus have been committing atrocities on them. And, therefore, Gandhiji believed that the caste Hindus have no right to call themselves 'Harijans'. With this view Gandhiji launched the movement for the abolition of untouchability. Had the Hindus not joined Gandhiji in this movement, it would not have been possible to put a clause in the constitution of India to abolish untouchability. He tried to change the hearts of caste Hindus and so he became the leader of the movement launched for the removal of untouchability.

"There was not single God who could represent the untouchables. Even a saint like 'Chokha Mela' did not have permission to take the darshan of Panduranga at Pandharpur. He could go only to the steps of the temple. It was again Gandhiji who started and led the movement for temple entry.

"Dr. Ambedkar aroused the feelings of untouchables for their own upliftment and led their movement. It may be said that Ambedkar worked for the upliftment of Harijans and Gandhiji strived for removing untouchability from the minds of caste Hindus. The programmes of both Gandhiji and Ambedkar, in fact, were supplementary and complementary to each other and not contradictory.

"Ambedkar's movement was against Brahminism and not against Brahmins. He believed that there could be Brahminism in untouchables too. There is a feeling of high and low in them also. Ambedkar congratulated and encouraged them to launch a movement against those untouchables who possess the spirit of Brahminism.

"It is the spirit of Brahminism that kept on exploiting. There have been saints and Mahatmas in India who tried to create sympathy and pity for the downtrodden but none of them came forward to lead the movement for the removal of untouchability. It was Mahatma Gandhi who came forward and led the movement. It must be borne in mind that had Mahatma Gandhi not been there, Ambedkar would not have been the Law Minister of this country. It was Gandhiji who prevailed upon Jawaharlal Nehru to have Ambedkar in his cabinet much against his vehement opposition. Not only this, but every intellectual knows that when Nehru and Sarojini Naidu went to Gandhiji to tell him that they are not finding a competent person to draft the constitution of India and they are thinking of inviting Sir Ivor Jennings who had prepared the draft constitutions of many countries, Gandhiji instantly suggested the name of Ambedkar for the purpose and relieved Nehru from his great worry. Of course Dr. Ambedkar deserved these honours in his own right.

"Today untouchable leaders are happy and people are most unhappy. Those who oppose Mahatma Gandhi do not speak about disparity. Nobody wants to speak about economic slavery which is at our doors. Political leaders are misleading the masses by creating the caste conflicts, instead of providing bread, clothes and jobs required for the millions of people of India. Leaders have become 'Dealers'. Today, 'Leaders are bidders at the auction of popularity.'

"Science has proved that to whatever caste, creed or religion, we belong, there are only four blood groups. There could be one and the same blood group of Brahmin and a Valmiki. It is a matter to think over seriously as to whether we want to maintain the caste and the class on the basis of the colour of the body. We are in a bad habit of throwing the dirt of our house either on the road or hide it under the carpet. Dirt cannot be removed by hiding it. A constructive programme is required to remove it. And this was the gift of Mahatma and Subhash Chandra Bose called him 'Rashtra Pita'. There is no need to plead for Gandhiji. We need only to understand his thought and preaching, so that the common men are not misled. And this is what we expect from knowledgeable, intellectual and educated citizens."

Justice Dharmadhikari reminds of what Gandhiji said, while addressing a conference of all castes, held in Prema Bai Hall of Ahmedabad, in 1916. Gandhiji had warned that if the untouchability and the feelings of high caste and low caste are not removed, the Hindus and Hinduism is bound to be doomed. After saying this, Gandhiji bowed before the audience and said, "This head is ever ready to make sacrifice for the removal of untouchability."

Gandhiji always encouraged inter-caste marriages. He had made it a point not to attend any marriage ceremony, where one of the party was not a Harijan. He also made it a point not to step into a temple which was not open for Harijans. When he was asked about his profession in the court of law, he replied, "I am a weaver, I am a labourer, I am a Bhangi, I am a kisan".

Gandhiji was really a weaver, a kisan and a bhangi. Where does the Varma remain now? In this sense every individual belongs to four Varnas.

Removal of untouchability had become a part of a Gandhiji's life. He was prepared to die for it. It was the ultimate object of his life. He brought in use the word 'Harijan' for all the castes and sub-castes in untouchables, as a result of which all castes and sub-castes people from amongst untouchables flocked together under one name 'Harijan' forgetting their sub-castes.

"Gandhiji wanted to see a 'Bhangi' as the head of the state. He said that he did not want to be reborn, but if at all there is a rebirth, he should be reborn as Bhangi, the lowest among the Harijans. Looked from this angle, Gandhiji became 'harijan' in his own right in the real sense."

Gandhiji said, "I have long since considered myself to be a Bhangi in my speech, in my action and above all in my mind and spirit. Anyone who looks upon them with contempt does the same to me. Indeed, I hold it an honour to be among the despised Harijans and among them with Bhangis."

While in Delhi, Gandhiji insisted on living in the Bhangi colony where all the dignitaries, British or Indian, had to go and meet him and where many momentous meetings of working committee of the congress were held.

From the writings and clarifications made by Gandhiji through the columns of the *Harijan*, it is beyond doubt that the word 'Harijan' was not the brainchild of Gandhiji. It was actually suggested by one of the untouchable correspondents, that too on the strength of its having been used by the first known saint poet of Gujarat, Narsi Mehta and since then Gandhiji adopted this new word in the pages of *Navajivan*. As a matter of fact Gandhiji had coined the word, 'Suppressed' for the word 'Depressed'. But while he was casting about for a good Indian word, the untouchable correspondent suggested the word 'Harijan'. It appealed to Gandhiji as it best described the conditions of untouchables and still had no bad odour about it. And therefore, Gandhiji cannot be blamed for the word 'Harijan'. If at all anybody is to be blamed it should be the untouchable correspondent who originally suggested the name and also the saint poet of Gujarat who used the word in his song and more than both, the blame should lay at he doors of sage Valmiki, who was the first to use the word 'Harijan'.

It is not that the politicians and those who oppose the "word" Harijan do not know the genesis of word Harijan, but they seem to be deliberately distorting the facts and criticizing Gandhiji for their political gain. They probably want to play the role of a shepherd to drive the untouchables, who are still so ignorant, that it is easy to play on their sentiments.

Gandhi and Ambedkar both knew that mere change in the name will not bring transformation in the status and condition of the untouchables. Gandhiji said that one may at least be spared the use of a term which is itself one of reproach. He insisted that if every Hindu would deliberately shed his superiority and in practice became a Harijan, then we would become true children of God, as the word Harijan means. Ambedkar was of the opinion that with the new name, the untouchables were damned as much as they were with old, and therefore it was better that the wrong should be called by its known name. It was better for the patient to know what he was suffering from. It was better further that the wrong was there still to be redressed. Therefore the followers of Ambedkar prefer the word *dalit* and not *harijan*.

Whatever the feelings of Ambedkar and his followers are it remains a reality that the word Harijan has become popular and it is freely used for all the castes and sub-castes among untouchables, without any disrespect to anybody (Sheshrao Chavan: *Gandhi and Ambedkar—Saviours of Untouchables*, pp. 236-51).

Chapter 11

True Faces of Gandhi and Ambedkar

Gandhi and Ambedkar were historic necessity—Gandhi for the independence of India and Ambedkar for social liberation of the untouchables. Gandhi represented the masses of India; Ambedkar represented untouchables of India. Both were quintessence of the conscious and sub-conscious will of the millions.

Gandhi softened the Hindu heart; Ambedkar awakened the self-respect and interest in politics among the untouchables. In fact, they are the only two persons in India who will rule on the hearts of the masses and untouchables.

Ambedkar's slogan, "Educate, agitate and organize worked like a magic on the untouchables and they rallied around him."

Historic Necessity

Whatever, the views Ambedkar held about Gandhi, it is a fact that Gandhi did more than any one else to change the hearts of Savarna Hindus for the eradication of untouchability. His impact was such that in the opinion of Eleanor Zellot:

"The viewpoints of Gandhi and Ambedkar were amalgamated in such a way that political and social measures which Ambedkar would have approved are taken in the name of Gandhi. Although the measure of legally abolishing untouchability was adopted in the Constituent Assembly with the slogans of Mahatma Gandhi-Ki-Jai, Gandhi never advocated legal measures, feeling as he did that all changes must come voluntarily from the heart;

yet such was his effect on the Hindu mind that the practice of untouchability is now considered as wrong and the upliftment of the untouchables to the level of others as good."

Gandhi and Ambedkar were conscious of each other's necessary place in any final solution of the problem of untouchability. While their paths often diverged, they ultimately converged, forcing on the Indian conscience the problem of untouchability as an issue of national concern. Gandhi's work was in fact, complementary to that of Ambedkar's work and vice versa, although owing to differences of approach they often came in conflict with each other.

Gandhi was a Vaishya (Bania) and still insisted on the eradication of untouchability. Ambedkar was a Mahar (Shudra) and indignantly insisted on the abolition of Varna structure, thereby leveling up all castes into one oceanic unity. Gandhi and Ambedkar were historic necessity—Gandhi for the independence of India and Ambedkar for emancipation of the untouchables.

Gandhi represented the masses of India, Ambedkar represented the untouchables of India. Both were quintessence of the conscious and subconscious will of the millions. They were the men of the keenest intellect, of fine feeling and good test, wide vision, very human and yet essentially the ascetics, who suppressed their passion and emotions, sublimated them and directed them in the spiritual channels. They were tremendous personalities, drawing people to themselves like a magnet.

Gandhi softened the Hindu heart. Ambedkar awakened self-respect and interest in politics among the untouchables and, therefore, both are considered as the saviours of untouchables.

Embodiment of Compassion

Gandhi and Ambedkar were the embodiment of compassion. And that is why Gandhi was placed in the majestic hierarchy of Buddha and Ambedkar to the rank of the Buddhist Pantheon as Bodhisattva.

In the words of S. Chandrashekhar: "Mahatma Gandhi, despite his anachronistic and quaint belief in Varnashrama Dharma, pioneered a myriad ways, more than anyone else since

Buddha, to awaken the conscience of Hindu India to ameliorate the lot of the Harijans."

"When the pre-independence saga of India comes to be written," observes Justice V.R. Krishna Iyer, "only prejudice can assign a higher role in the liberation of the backward-most brackets to anyone above Ambedkar. While both Gandhi and Ambedkar were symbols of revolt against the caste-conscious oppressors within the Hindu fold, they chose the different strategies and different ideologies. If Gandhi was a deliverer of Indians, including the weakest sector, from the British, Ambedkar was the spearhead of black power against Varna front. There were many issues on which the two militant giants would not agree for the obvious reason that Gandhi wanted to reform and end injustice, while Ambedkar demanded rebellion for the annihilation of the caste system itself."

Justice V.R. Krishna Iyer further says: "When we consider the stature and achievements of Ambedkar as an intrepid warrior for socio-economic liberation of the lowliest, the lost and the last, especially the dalits and the exploited tribals, there is no doubt that without diminishing the tremendous conscientisation of the Hindu community by Gandhi vis-à-vis untouchability and Harijan debasement Bhimrao Ramji Ambedkar's ceaseless war on behalf of the Panchama proletariat, in its widest connotation is incomparable. And yet, the irony of history is that as the house passed the provision abolishing untouchability on 29th November 1948, the hallowed walls resounded with shouts of 'Mahatma Gandhi-ki-jai' although present at the session as Chairman of the Drafting Committee was Ambedkar, an untouchable himself and Commander-in-Chief of the Untouchable Army which waged a war against the reactionary system which sustained the Social Status-Quo Ante."

Complementary and Supplementary

Gandhi and Ambedkar could be termed as revolutionary, though their paths and methods were distinct and different. Ambedkar wanted his men to live with dignity by their own efforts and not at the mercy of others. Gandhi wanted to change the hearts of Savarnas for the eradication of untouchability. He firmly believed that the problem of untouchability cannot be solved unless there is change in the attitude of Savarnas. He once said: "The freedom will be meaningless if the untouchability is not removed." He went to the extent of asserting that the Hindus would have no right to claim Swaraj, as long as freedom was not restored to the exploited class. Gandhi held that our political bondage was a well deserved punishment meted out to us for observing untouchability. That is why his Harijan upliftment movement was not intended for upliftment of Harijans, it was for the salvation of caste Hindus. It was primarily meant as penance for purification of their hearts, as a sequence to the crime they perpetrated against the Harijans. On the other hand, Ambedkar wanted untouchability to be banned by law and be made an offence.

Justice Chandrashekhar Dharmadhikari, a true follower of Gandhi and an ardent admirer of Ambedkar says: "The two movements, i.e. one of Gandhi and another of Ambedkar were complementary and supplementary to each other."

Justice Dharmadhikari further says: "Those who want to understand Gandhi must know that he advocated for 'Harijan Seva' and not for 'Harijan Uddhar'. In his view unless the untouchability was removed from the minds and hearts of caste Hindus, it would not be abolished. Gandhi adopted 'broom' and 'charkha' as symbols of revolution. Charkha was meant to bring economic equality and dignity of labour. He believed that the high and lowness of the caste would find no place in this country when the 'Bhagvat Gita' would be in the hands of Bhangis and the broom in the hands of upper classes. The constructive programs undertaken by Gandhi for Harijan Seva was penance for Savarnas."

Whatever differences existed between Gandhi and Ambedkar, both were agreed that the blot on society should be wiped out. Both of them linked untouchability to the religious sphere as a main lever. Viewed thus, the differences between them appear to be minor and marginal.

Similarities in Gandhi and Ambedkar

Gandhi's hold on the masses and Ambedkar's hold on the untouchables was tremendous. They were adored as well as worshipped. Gandhi repeatedly said: "The people are silent. I will be the advocate for this silence. I will speak for dumb. I will speak for the small to the great and of the feeble to the strong. I will speak for all the despairing and silent ones. I will interpret the grumblings, murmurs, the tumults of crowds, the complaints ill pronounced and all those cries of beasts that through ignorance and through sufferings, man is forced to utter. I will be the word of the people. I will say everything." Ambedkar thought of the untouchables exactly in the same way.

The people of India had unflinching faith in Gandhi and the untouchables of India implicitly believed in Ambedkar. They could get themselves believed in, for they fulfilled their historical necessity of the hour and actualized the need of the age.

The remarkable feature of the leadership of Gandhi and Ambedkar was that they were able to lead and direct their movements without lowering any of their standards even by hair's breadth. They were able to command the respectful obedience of millions. This influence can be said to have sprung from their strength and incessant sacrifice.

Gandhi and Ambedkar wanted to remove the economic disparity, because both firmly believed that unless the economic disparity was removed there could be neither social justice nor the downtrodden come up in life.

Though there was nothing divine about Gandhi and Ambedkar, yet they were spiritual leaders, emancipated saviours and Messiahs for the socially downtrodden and the victims of socio-economic exploitation.

Gandhi and Ambedkar were gifted with the superb capacity to write. Both have left behind a record of their thoughts and activities and dreams embodied in their voluminous writings, letters and speeches. In their writings and speeches there were no lies, no hypocrisy, no fear, no favour.

Opposed to Hero-worship

Gandhi and Ambedkar both hated hero-worship. They did not want their followers to do it either, for they were deeply conscious of the evils of hero-worship, and the havoc it played in the country down the centuries.

Ambedkar said: "Over regard for leaders saps self-confidence of masses, leaves them helpless, when left leaderless in the hour of trial or when led by unscrupulous leaders." While inaugurating the school of politics in Poona, Ambedkar declared that he did not wish to set up a school or creed of his own. He said that he would be sorry if such a school came into existence after his death. He further said that he knew of tragedies caused by the creation of political creeds. He wanted people to weigh his ideas and be satisfied that he was right before they decided to follow him.

On the occasion of the celebration of his Golden Jubilee, Ambedkar said: "You have been celebrating my birthday for fifteen years. I have never attended them. I have always been opposed to them. You have celebrated my Golden Jubilee now, let that be enough. Let there be no more celebrations."

Ambedkar did not like his people to celebrate his birthday, which he considered as an act of deifying an individual and warned them. Speaking in reply to the address of welcome presented to him at Bombay in the first week of March 1933, he said:

"The ideas of hero-worship will bring ruin on you, if you do not nip them in the bud. If you fall a victim to these ideas, your fate will be no better than logs of wood in the national stream of life. Your struggle will come to naught. I may add that these ideas of hero-worship, deification and neglect of duty have ruined the Hindu society and are responsible for the degradation of our country."

On the eve of his 55th birth day, while sending a message to "Jai Bhim" published from Madras for the special issue, Ambedkar said: "It is an unfortunate fact, that in India the political leader is placed on the same footing as the Prophet. Outside India, people celebrate the birthday of their Prophets. It is only in India that the birthdays of both the Prophet as well as the politicians are celebrated. It is a pity that it should be so. Personally I do not like the celebration of my birthday. I am too much of a democrat to relish man-worship which I regard as perversion of democracy. Admiration, love, regard and respect for a leader, if he deserves them, are permissible and should be enough for both the leader and the followers. But worship of the leader is certainly not permissible. It is demoralizing to both."

And now see what Gandhi said on the erection of his statue in Bombay in 1947: "I must dissent emphatically from any proposal to spend any money on preparing a statue of me, especially at a time when people do not have enough food and clothing. In Bombay the beautiful insanitation reigns. There is so much overcrowding that poor people are packed like sardines. Wise use of ten lakhs of rupees will consist in its being spent on some public utility. That would be the best statue."

Gandhi would happily forsake a thousand statues of himself for one man or woman or even a child who attempted to live according to his ideals. The last thing he wanted was to be put on a pedestal and worshipped. Ambedkar felt exactly on the same lines.

What a travesty of their ideal? Every town and city is flooded with the statues of Gandhi and Ambedkar.

In celebrating the birthday of Gandhi and Ambedkar we must not overlook what the critics and opponents say. The critics will ask what is the point in celebrating the birthday of Gandhi and Ambedkar. That the days of hero-worship are gone long past will be the line of their argument. True hero-worship is dying. Of that there is no doubt. It was dying even in the days of Carlyle who indignantly complained against his age saying—

"This is an age that as it were denies the existence of great men: denies the inevitableness of great men."

"Show our critics a great man", he said and "They begin to what they call 'account for him'; not to worship him but take the dimensions of him."

But hero-worship is certainly not dead in India. India is still par excellence the land of idolatry. There is idolatry in religion, there is idolatry in politics. Heroes and hero-worship is a hard fact in India's political life. The hero-worship is demoralizing for the devotee and is dangerous to the country. The criticism in so far as it conveys a caution that you must know that your man is really great before you start worshipping him. This unfortunately is not an easy task. For in these days, with the Press in hand, it is easy to manufacture great men. Carlyle used a happy phrase when he described the great men of history as so many Bank Notes. Like Bank Notes they represent gold. What we have to see is that they are not forged notes. We ought to be more cautious in our worship of great men. For in this country we have perhaps arrived at such a stage when alongside the notice boards saying "beware of pick-pockets" we need to have notice boards saying "beware of great men". Even Carlyle who defended the worship of great men warned his readers how:

"Multitudes of men have figured in history as great men who were false and selfish." He regretted deeply that "The World's wages (of homage) are pocketed (by these so-called great men), the World's work is not done. Heroes have gone out; quacks have come in."

Gandhi and Ambedkar never received the honours of apotheosis as these great men of India today are destined to receive. How could they? They did not come with a message hot from Senai. They performed no miracles and promised no speedy deliverance and splendour. They were not genius and they had no superhuman qualities. But there are compensations. If Gandhi and Ambedkar did not show splendour and dominance they brought us no catastrophe. If they had no superhuman qualities to use in the service of India, India was saved from ruin by its abuse. If they were not a genius, they did not display that perverse supersubtlety of intellect and a temper of mind which is fundamentally dishonest and which has sown the seeds of distrust and which has made settlement so difficult of achievement. There is nothing exuberant and extravagant in Gandhi and Ambedkar. They refused to reap cheap notoriety by playing the part of an extremist. They refused to mislead people by playing upon and exploiting the patriotic sentiments of the people. They refused to be a party to methods which are crude, which have volume but no effect and which are neither foolproof nor knave-proof and which break the back even of the most earnest and sincere servants of the country and disable them from further effort. Gandhi and Ambedkar were like the wise Captain who knows that his duty is not to play with his ship clever and masterful tricks, just for effect and show in the midst of the ocean but to take it safely to its appointed port. In short Gandhi and Ambedkar were not forged bank notes and in worshipping them there is no feeling of kneeling before anything that is false.

In the second place the celebration of the birthday of Gandhi and Ambedkar is not an act of hero-worship. Hero-worship in the sense of expressing our unbounded admiration is one thing. To obey the hero is a totally different kind of hero-worship. There is nothing wrong in the former while the latter is no doubt a most pernicious thing. The former is only man's respect for everything which is noble and of which the great man is only an embodiment. The latter is that villain's fealty to his lord. The former does not take away one's intelligence to think and independence to act. The latter makes one a perfect fool. The former involves no disaster to the State. The latter is the source of positive danger to it. In short in celebrating Gandhi and Ambedkar's birthday we are not worshipping a boss who is elected by no one, accountable to no one and removable by no one, but paying our tribute of admiration to leaders who led and did not drive people, who sought to give effect to their deliberate judgment and did not try to impose their own will upon them by trickery or by violence.

In the third place it is not hero-worship for which the gathering assembles. This is an occasion to remind ourselves of the political philosophy of Gandhi and Ambedkar. To my mind it has become necessary to remind ourselves of it from time to time. For their's is a philosophy which is safe and sound, sure if slow. Even if it does not glitter it is nonetheless gold. Do any have doubt? If they have let them ponder over the following utterances of Bismark, Balfour and Morley. Bismark the great German Statesman said:

"Politics is the game of the possible."

Balfour in his Introduction to Walter Bagehot's well-known book of the English Constitution says:

"If we would find the true basis of the long drawn process which has gradually converted medieval monarchy into a modern democracy the process by which so much has been changed and so little destroyed, we must study temperament and character rather than intellect and theory. This is a truth which those who recommend the wholesale adoption of British Institutions in strange lands might remember with advantage. Such an experiment can hardly be without its dangers. Constitutions easily copied; temperaments are not; and if it should happen that the borrowed constitution and the native temperament fail to correspond, the misfit may have serious results. It matters little what other gifts people may possess if they are wanting in these which, from this point of view, are of most importance. If, for example, they have no capacity for grading their loyalties as well as for being moved by them; If they have no natural inclination no liberty and no natural respect for law; If they lack good humour and tolerate foul play; If they know not how to compromise or when; If they have not that distrust of extreme conclusions which is sometimes misdescribed as want of logic; If corruption does not repel them; and if their divisions tend to the either too numerous or too profound, the successful working of British Institutions may be difficult or impossible. It may indeed be least possible where the art of Parliamentary persuasion and the dexterities of party management are brought to their highest perfection."

Morley has observed:

"To hurry on after logical perfection is to show one's self-ignorance of the material of that social structure with which the politician has to deal. To disdain anything short of an organic change in thought or institution is infatuation. To be willing to make such changes too frequently, even when they are possible, is fool-hardiness. That fatal French saying about small reforms being the worst enemies of great reforms is, in the sense in which it is commonly used, a formula of social ruin."

These are the principles on which success in Politics depends. Are they different from those which Gandhi and Ambedkar enunciated? It bespeaks greatness in Gandhi and Ambedkar that they should have propounded them years before Bismark, Balfour and Morley.

The generation which Gandhi and Ambedkar served was wise in taking them as its political guide, friend and philosopher.

Their greatness lies in the fact that they can be a guide, friend and philosopher to the present, nay even to future generations.

Posterity is always interested in the last words and last regrets of great men. The last words of great men are not always significant of their experience of his world or their vision of the next. For instance the last thoughts of Socrates were to call Crito and say, "We owe a cock to Aesculapius; discharge the debt, and by no means omit it." But their last regrets are always significant and worth pondering over. Take the case of Napoleon. Napoleon before his death at St. Helena showed evidence of being uneasy over three capital points which constituted his last regrets. They were: that he could not have died at some supreme moment of his career; that he left Egypt and gave up his Eastern ambitions; and last but by no means the least his defeat at Waterloo. Had Gandhi and Ambedkar any supreme regrets? One thing is certain that Gandhi and Ambedkar if they had any, could not have the same regrets such as those which disturbed the peace of mind of Napoleon. Gandhi and Ambedkar lived for service and not for glory. It mattered very little to them whether the moment of their death was glorious or inglorious or whether they died as a hero, as a conqueror or a master or whether they died as a common man sometimes does of common cold. As a matter of fact Gandhi and Ambedkar were not troubled by any regrets. So far as record goes Gandhi and Ambedkar do not seem to be conscious of any act or event about which they had any regrets. But it is worth-while asking could Gandhi and Ambedkar have any regrets if they came to life today? I am sure there is one matter over which they will feel extremely grieved. For Gandhi not to see India of his dream and for Ambedkar not to see his people a ruling class.

Corruption

Gandhi had come to realize that the Congress rank and file were as corrupt and greedy in power as they had been idealistic and self-sacrificing out of power. He said: "I know that if I survive the struggle for freedom, I might have to give non-violent battles to my own countrymen, which may be as stubborn as that in which I am now engaged."

He further said: "I can retain neither respect nor affection for a Government which has been moving from wrong to wrong to defend its immorality. Such a Government must be moved to repentance."

Ambedkar's feelings were equally strong on corruption. As a Labor Member of the Viceroy's Executive Council and as free India's Law Minister, he had one of his own men of his confidence, without anybody's knowledge posted on administrative side to keep a strict vigile and exercise control on the growing menace of corruption, favoritism and nepotism rampant in the department.

Gandhi on Ambedkar

Gandhi's opposition to Ambedkar was purely on principles and policies. Personally he paid Ambedkar glowing tributes even while expressing his disapproval of his role as a representative of untouchables at the Round Table Conference. He said: "I have the highest regard for Ambedkar. He has every right to be bitter. That he does not break our heads is an act of self-restraint on his part. He is today much saturated with suspicion that he cannot see anything else. He sees in every Hindu a determined opponent of the untouchables and it is quite natural."

On another occasion Gandhi said: "Intellectually Ambedkar is superior to the thousands of intelligent and educated caste Hindus. His personal cleanliness is as high as that of any of us. Today, he is an eminent lecturer in Law. Tomorrow, you may find him as Judge of the High Court. In other words there is no position in the government of this country to which he may not aspire and rise and to which an orthodox Brahmin can rise."

Gandhi described Ambedkar as a challenge to Hinduism. He observed: "Ambedkar is not alone in his disgust. He is its most uncompromising exponent and one of the ablest among them. Thank God, in the front rank of leaders, he is singularly alone and as yet but a representative of a very small minority. But what he says is voiced with more or less vehemence by many leaders belonging to the depressed classes."

On Mahad Satyagraha of Ambedkar, Gandhi said: "I cannot help thinking that Dr. Ambedkar was fully justified in putting to test the resolution of the Bombay Legislative Council and the

Mahad Municipality by advising the so-called untouchables to go to the tank to quench their thirst. No incident of this character should pass by unnoticed on the part of associations like the Hindu Mahasabha interested in this reform. Let them investigate the statements made by my correspondent and if they can be substantiated, let them condemn the action of the "touchables". There is nothing like the growth of enlightened public opinion for eradicating everything evil, which untouchability undoubtedly is."

The settlement arrived at the Poona Pact is, so far as I (Gandhi) can see, a generous gesture on all sides. It is a matter of hearts, and my Hindu gratitude is due to Dr. Ambedkar, Rao Bahadur Srinivasan and their party on the one hand and Rao Bahadur M.C. Rajah on the other. They could have taken up an uncompromising and defiant attitude by way of punishment to the so-called caste Hindus for the sins of generations. If they had done so, I at least could not have resented their attitude and my death would have been but a trifling price exacted for the torture that the outcastes of Hinduism have been going through for unknown generations. But they chose a nobler path and have thus shown that they have followed the precept of forgiveness enjoined by all religions. Let me hope that the caste Hindus will prove themselves worthy of this forgiveness and carry out to the letter and spirit every clause of the settlement with all its implications (Mahatma Gandhi: *Collected Works*, Vol. LI, pp. 143-45).

Let not Dr. Ambedkar's just wrath deject the reformer, let it spur him to greater effort. For whilst it is true that the number of workers against untouchability has greatly increased, there can be no doubt that the number is yet too small to overtake the prejudice of ages. Nevertheless, a movement which has attained the proportions that the anti-untouchability campaign has attained and in which the slightest untoward incident can attract worldwide attention cannot but be on its last legs. Humanity will not suffer it any longer.

Ambedkar on Gandhi

On the role of Gandhi in the Round Table Conference, Dr. Ambedkar said:

What shall I say about the Congress? What was its point of view? I am sure I am not exaggerating or misrepresenting facts when I say that the Congress point of view at the Round Table Conference was that the Congress was the only party in India and that no body else counted and that the British should settle with Congress only. This was the burden of Mr. Gandhi's song at the Round Table Conference. He was so busy in establishing his own claim to recognition by the British as the dictator of India that he forgot altogether that the important question was not, with whom the settlement should be made but what were to be terms of that settlement. As to the terms of the settlement, Mr. Gandhi was quite unequal to the task. When he went to London he had forgotten that he would have before him not those who go to him to obtain his advice and return with his blessing but persons who would treat him as a lawyer treats a witness in the box. Mr. Gandhi also forgot that he was going to a political conference. He went there as though he was going to a Vaishnava Shrine singing the Narsi Mehta's Songs. When I think of the whole affair I am wondering if any nation had ever sent a representative to negotiate the terms of a national settlement who was more unfit than Mr. Gandhi. How unfit Mr. Gandhi was to negotiate a settlement becomes evident when one realizes that this Ambassador of India was ready to return to India with only Provincial Autonomy when as a matter of fact he was sent to negotiate on the basis of Independence. No man has brought greater disasters to the interests of India than did Mr. Gandhi at the Round Table Conference. Less one speaks of him the better.

This is what Ambedkar said about Gandhi on other occasions:

We are standing today at the point of time where the old age ends and the new begins. The old age was the age of Ranade, Agarkar, Tilak, Gokhale, Wachha, Sir, Pherozeshah Mehta, Surendranath Bannerjee. The new age is the age of Mr. Gandhi and this generation is said to be Gandhi generation. As one who knows something of the old age and also something of the new I see some very definite marks of difference between the two. The type of leadership has undergone a profound change. In the age of Ranade the leaders struggled to modernize India. In the age of Gandhi the leaders are making her a living specimen of antiquity.

In the age of Ranade leaders depended upon experience as a corrective method of their thoughts and their deeds. The leaders of the present age depend upon their inner voice as their guide. Not only is there a difference in their mental make up there is a difference even in their viewpoint regarding external appearance. The leaders of the old age took care to be well clad while the leaders of the present age take pride in being half clad. The leaders of the Gandhi age are of course aware of these differences. But far from blushing for their views and their appearance they claim that the India of Gandhi is superior to India of Ranade. They say that the age of Mr. Gandhi is an agitated and a expectant age, which the age of Mr. Ranade was not.

To my mind there is no doubt that this Gandhi age is the dark age of India. It is an age in which people instead of looking for their ideals in the future are returning to antiquity. It is an age in which people have ceased to think for themselves and as they have ceased to think they have ceased to read and examine the facts of their lives.

"The age of Ranade, Gokhale, Agarkar and Tilak and the movements started by them were different from the Gandhi age. Their age was the age of knowledge. There is absolutely no doubt about it. Gandhi's age can be called the "Tamo Yug" of India. The politics of Agarkar and Tilak was based on honesty and truth. It was not hollow and noisy. But the politics of Gandhi is hollow and noisy. It is the most dishonest politics in the history of Indian polity. Gandhi was the man responsible for eliminating politics. Politics has been denuded of its virtue" (Dr. Babasaheb Ambedkar: *Writings and Speeches*, Vol. 17(II), p. 69).

"Everybody felt that Mr. Gandhi was the most determined enemy of the Untouchables. So much of his energy and attention did Mr. Gandhi concentrate on the question of the Untouchables that it would not be unfair if it was said that the main purpose for which Mr. Gandhi came to the Round Table Conference was to oppose the demands of the Untouchables....

The friends of Mr. Gandhi could not understand Mr. Gandhi's attitude to the demands of the Untouchables. To give recognition to the Muslims and the Sikhs and to refuse it to the Untouchables came to them as a surprise and a puzzle. Whenever they asked for an explanation, Mr. Gandhi did nothing except to get angry. Mr. Gandhi himself could not give a logical and consistent defence of his opposition to the Untouchables. Inside the Round Table Conference the defence was that the Hindus had seriously taken up the cause of Untouchables and that therefore there was no reason to give them political safeguards" (Dr. Babasaheb Ambedkar: *Writings and Speeches*, Vol. 9, p. 70).

"To Gandhi removal of untouchability was a platform and not a programme of action and so Gandhi was not the liberator or emancipator of the untouchables."

Mr. Bernard Shaw has said that the British do everything on principle. Similarly Mr. Gandhi says he does everything on the principle of morality and good faith.

Having been disgusted with the Round Table Conference where there were critics but no devotees, Mr. Gandhi was first to return to India.... Though in jail, not Swaraj, but the untouchables were on his brain.

Epic Fast

This is what Ambedkar remarked on Gandhi's Epic Fast:

Mr. Gandhi commenced his fast unto death on 20th September 1932 as a protest against the grant of separate electorates to the untouchables.... Suffice it to say that although Mr. Gandhi declared a fast unto death, he did not want to die. He wanted very much to live.... All eyes naturally turned to me as the man of the moment or rather as the villain of peace.... I responded to the call of humanity and saved the life of Mr. Gandhi by agreeing to alter the Communal Award in a manner satisfactory to Mr. Gandhi.

The Fast Unto Death of Mr. Gandhi was described as second crucifixion, as martyrdom, and as triumphal struggle. I described it as a political stunt. His utterances had to me always the ring of falsity and even insincerity.

Gandhi was pleading, "My life is in your hands, will you save me?" He had lost his courage and was anxious to save his face and any how save his life. There was nothing noble in the fast.

It was a foul and filthy act. It was a vile and wicked act. How can the untouchables regard such a man as honest and sincere?

Contrast

Gandhi was the symbol of the masses of India. Ambedkar was the symbol of the aristocracy.

Gandhi—A Symbol of Masses

Gandhi identified himself with the common people, just as they were. This was the reason why he insisted upon wearing the loin-cloth as a symbol of his faith and of his life. This was also the reason why he made himself property-less, stripping himself of practically every possession in the world. When he died Gandhi owned only two or three loin-clothes, and a shawl or two, a pair of spectacles, a one-dollar Ingersoll watch, a fountain pen, and a few sheets of paper. That was the all property he owned or wanted to own, just that he might be identified with the life of the Indian people. This was the reason he organized the Ashram, and for years lived with his followers in this Ashram. The Ashram was really nothing in the world but a kind of a duplicate of a typical Indian village. And since there were seven hundred thousand of these villages in India in which hundreds of millions of his fellow-countrymen lived, he would also live in such a place, that he might be more close to the people whom he loved and whom he sought to lead.

Gandhi said: "I have long since considered myself to be a 'bhangi' in my speech, in my action and above all in mind and spirit. If I lived apart from Harijans, what right had I to question the action of others who went further in their adherence to untouchability? If it was duty to reside in Harijan quarters, I must perform it irrespective of the reaction of the step on the others." And true to his words, while in Delhi, Gandhi insisted on living in the Bhangi Colony, where all the dignitaries, British or Indian, had to go to meet him and where many momentous meetings of the Working Committee of the Congress were held.

Ambedkar—A Symbol of Aristocracy

The house of Ambedkar, be it 22, Prithviraj Road, where he lived as Labour Member of the Viceroy's Executive Council; 1,

Hardinge Avenue, his official residence as the first Law Minister of Independent India; 26, Alipur Road where he spent the last days of his life and breathed his last in Delhi indicate his style and standard of living.

Rows and rows and scores of wooden almirahs and racks to house his huge library, steel almirahs to keep his nicely stitched woolen and cotton dresses, hats and caps, small boxes for keeping his costly fountain pens and pencils, beautiful extra-ordinary writing table, reclining tilting arm chairs, dinning table, radiogram, dressing table, crockery, wall clocks, watches and time-pieces, fridge, room cooler, sofa sets, countless big and small pieces of furniture and household articles indicated Ambedkar's style and standard of aristocratic living.

Judge's Chair

Ambedkar was provided Judge's chair while drafting the Constitution. He took so much liking for this chair that he got four more such chairs prepared from teak wood for his use at his residence.

It may be recollected that Ambedkar was offered Judgeship, which he had declined to remain in the service of untouchables for their uplift. Although he did not sit as a Judge on the chair of the Judge, he used them while drafting the constitution and thereafter in his house.

Clocks

Ambedkar had following clocks in his house:

A platinum coated round big clock in the front drawing room; another extra-ordinary size clock with wonderful carving on its wooden casement; yet another fine clock in a wooden case resting on four nicely carved wooden legs with pendulum.

Four time-pieces, out of which one was kept on the side table by the side of his bed; the second on his writing table; the third in the dining hall and the fourth in his another bed room.

Few wrist watches, pocket watches with beautiful strong straps. One or two golden ones were his priceless possession.

Fountain Pens

Ambedkar was fond of costly fountain pens. Among his best pens, were Parker, Sheffer and Waterman. Golden pen, presented to him on his birthday, which he kept very carefully under lock and key.

Spectacles

Ambedkar put on gold rimmed spectacles when in study and sun glasses when going out. He had lot of pair of spectacles with fine casings.

Cars

Ambedkar had two cars. One at Delhi and the other at Bombay.

Rajgriha

Ambedkar constructed a palatial house for himself in the Hindu Colony at Bombay, which was predominantly a Brahmin locality. This house was not built in a normal way. Like Thomas Jefferson, he bought books on architecture, and studied them. So fascinated was Ambedkar with the idea of raising a grand structure to his liking that he caused some parts of the house to be demolished after they were built, and got them reconstructed.

Looking to the strange ideas of Ambedkar, one of his colleagues remarked that if Ambedkar kept on insisting like this having a window after the model of one from the grand structure of the London Museum, a door after the model of the New York library, the dome and shape of a palace, the house will never see its completion.

The construction of the house was at long last completed. Ambedkar fondly named the house as Rajgriha after the glorious palace of Lord Gautama Buddha. Ambedkar, unfortunately was not destined to spend the evening of his life in the Rajgriha.

All this lifestyle would make one say that although Ambedkar dedicated his life for the emancipation of untouchables, he himself did not live their life.

After the death of his wife Kasturba, Gandhi did not marry. He said: "I cannot imagine life without Ba. Her passing has left a vacuum which will never be filled." He further said: "If I had to choose a companion for myself life after life, I would only choose Ba."

Ambedkar after the death of his first wife Ramabai, married and that too with a Brahmin woman by name Sharda Kabir. Ambedkar's views on Brahmins are too well known to be repeated.

Nobility of Gandhi

There was widespread belief that Gandhi wanted Ambedkar to become the President of India. This was supported by a write up in the "Illustrated Weekly of India" of 22nd January 1950 issue to the effect that if Gandhi had his way, Ambedkar-life-long opponent of Gandhi—would have been even the head of the State.

Gandhi suggested the name of Ambedkar for the Drafting Committee of the Constituent Assembly. It so happened that Jawaharlal Nehru and Mrs. Sarojini Naidu went to Gandhi to tell him that they were not finding a capable person to prepare the Draft Constitution of India, and they were thinking of inviting the constitutional expert like Ivor Jennings. On hearing this, Gandhi instantly suggested to make use of Ambedkar.

Gandhi also prevailed upon Nehru to have Ambedkar in his cabinet. Nehru frankly told Gandhi that he would not have Ambedkar in his cabinet, because he was a blockade in the freedom struggle. Gandhi told Nehru that freedom has come to India and not to him and therefore Ambedkar's talent and capabilities must be utilized for building up modern India. Nehru was thus left with no alternative but to induct Ambedkar in his cabinet. However, he made him Law Minister for which Ambedkar was not happy. This is evident from the statement of his resignation made by him on 10th of October 1951 in Parliament in which he said:

As a result of my being a member of Viceroy's Council, I knew the Law Ministry to be administratively of no importance. It gave no opportunity for shaping the policy of the Government of India. We used to call it an empty soap box only good for old lawyers to play with. When the Prime Minister made me the offer, I told him that besides being a lawyer by my education and experience,

I was competent to run any administrative Department and that in the old Viceroy's Executive Council I held two administrative portfolios, that of Labour and C.P.W.D., where a great deal of planning projects were dealt with by me and would like to have some administrative portfolio. The Prime Minister agreed and said he would give me in addition to Law the Planning Department which, he said, he was intending to create. Unfortunately the Planning Department came very late in the day and when it did come I was left out. During my time, there have been many transfers of portfolios from one Minister to another. I thought I might be considered for any one of them. But I have always been left out of consideration. Many ministers have been given two or three portfolios so that they have been overburdened. Others like me have been wanting more work. I have not even been considered for holding a portfolio temporarily when a Minister in charge has gone abroad for a few days. It is difficult to understand what principle is underlying the distribution of Government work among Ministers which the Prime Minister follows. Is it capacity? Is it trust? Is it friendship? Is it pliability? I was not even appointed to be a member of main Committees of the Cabinet such as the Foreign Affairs Committee or the Defense Committee. When the Economic Affairs Committee was formed, I expected, in view of the fact that I was primarily a student of Economics and Finance, to be appointed to this Committee. But I was left out. I was appointed to it by the Cabinet, when the Prime Minister had gone to England. But when he returned, in one of his many essays in the reconstruction of the Cabinet, he left me out. In a subsequent reconstruction my name was added to Committee, but that was as a result of my protest.

Ambedkar was surprised on his induction as Law Minister. In his words: "The offer came as a great surprise to me. I was in the opposite camp and had already been condemned as unworthy of association when the interim Government was formed in August 1946. I was left to speculate as to what could have happened to bring about this change in the attitude of the Prime Minister."

Ambedkar was equally surprised on his election to the Drafting Committee. He said: "...I had not the remotest idea that I would be called upon to undertake most responsible function.

I was, therefore, surprised when the Assembly elected me to the Drafting Committee. I was more than surprised when the Drafting Committee elected me to be its Chairman."

Gandhi opposed Ambedkar on principles, but never nursed any feeling of hate against him. This is the nobility of Gandhi.

Ambedkar on Congress

Revealing the attitude of Congress on free India's constitution, Ambedkar said: "As to the question of a Constitution for free India, the Congress simply does not look upon it as a problem. Asked, what about the constitution of free India? The Congress reply is that it would be democracy. What sort of democracy would it be? The Congress answer is that it would be based on adult franchise. Will there be any other safeguards, besides adult suffrage for preventing the tyranny of a Hindu communal majority? The Congress reply is emphatically in negative. Asked, why this opposition to safeguards? The Congress says that it is a vivisection of a nation—an argument the picturesqueness of which intended to cover its stupidity and which has its origin in the geniuses of Mr. Gandhi and for which the high class Hindus, who stand to loose by these safeguards feel so grateful to him."

Ambedkar further said: "Whatever the philosophic grounds advanced by the Congress in opposing the demand for constitutional guarantees is to keep the political field a free pasture for the Hindu majority. The Hindu communal majority is the backbone of the Congress. It is made up by the Hindus and is fed by the Hindus. It is the majority which constitutes the clientele of the Congress and the Congress, therefore, is bound to protect the rights of its clients. The Congress is deceiving the world by using nationalism as cloak for a free field for rank communalism. Nobody would have cared to bother about the representative character of the Congress and to inquire, whom it represents and whom it does not, if the Congress were not to arrogate itself the right to say what should be the Constitution of India" (Dr. Babasaheb Ambedkar: *Writings and Speeches*, Vol. 9, pp. 169-70, 172).

The Congress wants a free India with full, unrestricted freedom to the Hindus in a free India to dispose the untouchables in any way they liked.

The untouchables feel that the Congress is not honest in its dealings with them, but not even the country.

Not being radical party the Congress cannot be trusted to undertake a radical programme of social and economic reconstruction without which the untouchables can never succeed in improving their lot. For the untouchables to join such a party is futile and senseless thing. The Congress will not do anything for them but will only use them as they have done.

The untouchables who are in the Congress are at the end of the tail and the tail so lengthened that it cannot wag. Such are the disadvantages that are arisen from the untouchables having joined the Congress. They are not merely disadvantages. I call them dire consequences. All social movement has become dead. All political power has become migratory.

Some of the untouchables who stood on the Congress ticket were just careerist men on the make who wanted to climb in the legislature so as to be within call when the places of office or profit come for distribution. They did not care by whose ladder they climbed. Even these careerists would not have joined the Congress if it were possible for them to have got themselves elected independently of the Congress.

The representatives of the untouchables were supposed to be the watch-dogs of the untouchables, but by reason of having joined the Congress they are muzzled dogs. Far from biting they are not even able to bark.

The untouchable members are completely under the control of the Congress Party Executive. They have only such freedom as the Congress Executive may choose to allow them. The result is that though the tale of woes of the untouchables is ever increasing, the untouchable members of the legislature are unable even to ask a question about them. So pitiable has their condition become that the Congress party sometimes requires them to vote against a measure that may in the opinion of untouchable members of the legislature be beneficial to the untouchables.

The Congress might do something for the untouchables if it was compelled to do by force of circumstances. There is only one circumstance in which the Congress would feel such a compulsion, when the Congress finds itself dependent upon the representatives of the untouchables for its majority in the legislature.

It is my firm conviction that for the untouchables to merge in the Congress cannot but be fatal for them (Dr. Babasaheb Ambedkar: *Writings and Speeches*, Vol. 5, pp. 344-47).

Congress Rehabilitated Ambedkar

Ambedkar had ceased to be a member of the Constituent Assembly consequent upon the partition of Bengal. There was no hope of his getting re-elected even from his own Bombay Presidency, where he had already been defeated by the Congress. However, the same Congress came forward and sponsored his candidature.

Dr. Rajendra Prasad, the President of the Constituent Assembly in his letter of 30th June 1947 to B.G. Kher, who was then Prime Minister of Bombay Presidency wrote: "Apart from any other consideration, we have found Dr. Ambedkar's work both in the Constituent Assembly and the various committees to which he was appointed to be of such an order as to require that we should not be deprived of his services. As you know that he was elected from Bengal and after the division of the province he has ceased to be a member of the Constituent Assembly. I am anxious that he should attend the next session of the Constituent Assembly commencing from 14th July and it is therefore necessary that he should be elected immediately" (Dr. Babasaheb Ambedkar: *Writings and Speeches*, Vol. 13, pp. 24-26).

Sardar Patel also wrote a letter on 1st July 1947 to B.G. Kher, Prime Minister of Bombay Presidency in which he said: "Confirming my conversation with you last night, you have to make arrangements for Dr. Ambedkar's election, if possible before 14th. If the date for the nomination is the 4th, then there would be no difficulty, but if the nomination date is changed to the 11th, then the only way to finish the work before the 14th is to persuade other candidates to withdraw. Any way, you will do your best" (*Sardar Patel's Correspondence*, Vol. 5, p. 149).

The very Congress which Ambedkar called a burning house, made him the Chief Architect of the Indian Constitution. Had the Congress not got him re-elected, Ambedkar probably would have ended his political career as a roaring lion against Gandhi and the Congress.

Ambedkar seems to have realized this as is evident from what he said about Congress in his speech in the Constituent Assembly on 4th November 1948. He said: "There would have been nothing but chaos. This possibility of chaos was reduced to nil by the existence of the Congress party inside the Assembly, which brought into its proceedings a sense of order and discipline. It is because of the discipline of the Congress party that the Drafting Committee was able to pilot the Constitution in the Assembly with the sure knowledge as to the fate of each article and each amendment. The Congress party is, therefore, entitled to all the credit for the smooth sailing of the Draft Constitution in the Assembly."

Contradictions

There have been several contradictions in thinking and actions of Ambedkar, some of them are given below:

Poona Pact

Gandhi began his Fast Unto Death on 20th September 1932 in Yervada Jail of Poona against the Communal Award declared by Prime Minister Ramsay MacDonald.

Ambedkar issued his statement, the substance of which is given below:

"I cannot accept the assurances of the Mahatma that he and his Congress will do the needful. I cannot leave so important a question as the protection of my people to conventions and understandings. The Mahatma is not an immortal person and the Congress, assuming it is not a malevolent force, is not to have an abiding existence.

"If Mr. Gandhi wishes to have the Communal Award altered, it is for him to put forth his proposals and to prove that they give a better guarantee than has been given under the Award.

"Mahatma's act will result in nothing but terrorism by his followers against the depressed classes all over the country.

"Mahatma is releasing reactionary and uncontrollable forces, and is following the spirit of hatred between Hindu community and the depressed classes by resorting to this method and thereby widening the existing gulf between the two.

"Although I am entitled to say that I regard the matter as closed, I am prepared to consider the proposals of the Mahatma. I, however, trust that the Mahatma will not drive me to the necessity of making a choice between his life and the rights of my people. For I can never consent to deliver my people bound hand and foot to the caste Hindus for generations to come.

"I have not yet shown my full teeth. Do not imagine that we are staging a mock show at Poona. It is only a beginning of the struggle that would grow grimmer and fiercer day by day ultimately rocking the entire country."

Ambedkar expressed these views before meeting Gandhi in Yervada Jail. And now see what he said after meeting Gandhi.

"I must confess that I was immensely surprised when I met Mahatma Gandhi in the Yervada Jail—that there was so much common between him and me. I was astounded to see that the man who held such divergent views from mine at the Round Table Conference came to my rescue rather than to rescue the other side. I am very grateful to Mahatma Gandhi for having extricated from what might have been a very difficult situation.

"My only regret is, why did Mahatma not take this attitude at the Round Table Conference. If he had shown the same consideration to my point of view, it would not have been necessary for him to go through this ordeal. However, these are the things of the past. I am glad that I am here now to support the resolution.

"I believe it is no exaggeration for me to say that no man a few days ago was placed in a greater dilemma than I was. There was placed before me a difficult situation in which I had to make a choice between two difficult alternatives. There was the life of the greatest man in India to be saved. There was also before me the problem to try and safeguard the interests of the community which I was in my humble way trying to do at the Round Table Conference according to my light. I am happy to be able to say that it has become possible through the cooperation of all of us to find a solution so as to save the life of the Mahatma and at the same time consistent with such protection as is necessary for the interests of the depressed classes in future. I think in all these negotiations a large part of the credit must be attributed to the Mahatma."

U Turn

Ambedkar subsequently changed his mind and said that signing the Poona Pact was a sentimental blunder and he can never forgive himself for this blunder.

The Poona Pact was only the first blow inflicted upon the untouchables and that the Hindus who disliked were bent on inflicting on it other blows as and when circumstances gave them an occasion to do so. The two contentions, which the Hindus raised before the Hammond Committee, furnish the best evidence of the existence of a conspiracy by the Hindus the object of which was to make the Poona Pact as it could not be repudiated, of no benefit to the untouchables.

There was another and greater blow which the Congress indicted on the untouchables. It deprived them of any share in the Executive. The untouchables can never hope to get protection from the Police, justice from the Judiciary or the benefit of a Statutory Law from the administration, so long as the public services continued to be manned by the Hindus.

The Congress sucked the juice out of the Poona Pact and threw the rind in the face of the untouchables.

Mr. Gandhi is still on war path so far as the untouchables are concerned. He may start the trouble over again. The time to trust him has not arrived. The untouchables must still hold that the best way to safeguard themselves is to say, "Beware of Mr. Gandhi."

Constituent Assembly

Dr. Ambedkar had vehemently opposed the proposals for formation of the Constituent Assembly for the reasons narrated by him in his address at the Annual Session of the All India Scheduled Castes Federation held in Bombay on 6th May 1945. This is what Dr. Ambedkar said in his address:

".... Should there be a Constituent Assembly, charged with the function of making a Constitution? Constituent Assembly is on the lips of everybody. The Congress party in its resolutions, passed before the Congress ministries resigned, demanded that the Constitution for India should be made by a Constituent Assembly composed of Indians. A Constituent Assembly was included in the Cripps Proposals. The Sapru Committee has followed suit.

"I must state that I am wholly opposed to the proposals of a Constituent Assembly. It is absolutely superfluous. I regard it as a most dangerous project, which may involve this country in a civil war. In the first place, I do not see why a Constituent Assembly is at all necessary. Indians are not in the same position as the Fathers of the American Constitution were, when they framed the Constitution of the United States. They had to evolve ideas, suitable for the Constitution for a free people. They had no Constitutional patterns before them to draw upon. This cannot, however, be the case for the Indians. Constitutional ideas and Constitutional forms are ready at hand. Again, room for variety is very small. There are not more than two or three Constitutional patterns to choose from. Thirdly, there are hardly any big and purely Constitutional questions about which there can be said to be much dispute among Indians. It is agreed that the future Indian Constitution should be Federal. It is also more or less settled what subjects should go to the Centre and what to the Provinces. There is no quarrel over the division of Revenues between the Centre and Provinces, none on Franchise and none on the relation of the Judiciary to the Legislature and the Executive. The only point of dispute, which is outstanding centres round the question of the residuary powers—whether they should be with the Centre or with the Provinces. But that is hardly a matter worth bothering about. Indeed, the provision contained in the present Government of India Act could be adopted as the best compromise.

"Having agreed to this I cannot see why Constituent Assembly is necessary to incubate a Constitution. So much of the Constitution of India has already been written out in the Government of India Act 1935, that it seems to be an act of supererogation to appoint a Constituent Assembly to do the thing ever again. All that is necessary is to delete those sections of the Government of India Act 1935, which are inconsistent with Dominion Status.

"The only function which could be left to a Constituent Assembly is to find a solution of the communal problem. I am quite positive that whatever be the terms of reference of the Constituent Assembly, the Communal Question should not form a part of them. Consider the composition of the Constituent Assembly as suggested by the Sapru Committee. The total membership is fixed at 160. The election is by joint electorates by members of the Provincial Legislative Assemblies under a system of proportional representation and the decision is to be by three-fourths of the members present and voting. Can a minority accept this Constituent Assembly as a safe body, in the impartiality of which it can place implicit confidence? The answer to this question must depend upon what answer one can give to two other questions: Does it guarantee that the representatives of a minority elected to the Assembly will be its true representatives? Secondly, does it guarantee that the decision of the Assembly with regard to the claims of any particular minority will not in fact be an imposition on the minority? On neither of these two questions can I confidently say that a minority need have no cause for fear.

"There are many other arguments against the plan of a Constituent Assembly. I may mention one, which I confess has influenced me greatly. When I read the history of Union between Scotland and England, I was shocked the corruption and bribery that was practiced to win the consent of the Scottish Parliament. The whole of the Scottish Parliament was bought. The chances of corruption and bribery being used in the Indian Constituent Assembly to buy over members to support decisions desired by interested groups are very real. Their effects, I am sure, cannot be overlooked. If this happens, it will not only make mockery of the Constituent Assembly but I feel quite certain that any attempt, made to enforce its decisions will result in a civil war. It is my considered opinion that the proposal of Constituent Assembly is more dangerous than profitable and should not be entertained."

The next day, that is on 7th May 1945, the conference of the Scheduled Castes Federation passed the resolution which Ambedkar had drafted. It vehemently denounced the proposal for a Constituent Assembly which the Sapru Committee had put forward. It opposed the very idea of summoning a Constituent Assembly. And declared that the Assembly which was being sought placed the Scheduled Castes at the mercy of Hindus and Muslims without providing any safeguards for them.

That remained Ambedkar's considered view till the very eve of the formation of the Constituent Assembly.

Ambedkar was interviewed by the Cabinet Delegation on behalf of the Scheduled Castes Federation. In reply to an enquiry as to the method of representation of Scheduled Castes in the constituent assembly, he said that he did not want a constituent assembly at all. It would be dominated by the Caste Hindus, and the Scheduled Castes would be no more than a small minority which would always be outvoted. All the assurances of protection which His Majesty's Government had given to the minorities would go by the board. His own proposal was that the tasks envisaged for the constituent assembly should be divided into two classes, namely (a) constitutional questions properly so-called, e.g. the relations between the legislature and the executive and their respective composition and functions, and (b) communal questions. Matters under (a) should be referred to a commission presided over by an eminent constitutional lawyer from Great Britain or the USA. The other members should be two Indian experts and one representative each of the Hindu and Muslim communities. The terms of reference should be the Government of India Act of 1935 and the commission should be required to recommend what changes should be referred to a conference of the leaders of the different communities. If the conference failed to arrive at an agreed solution, His Majesty's Government should make an award.

Ambedkar claimed that, before they left, the British must ensure that the new constitution guaranteed to the Scheduled Castes the elementary human rights of life, liberty and the pursuit of happiness, and that it restored their separate electorates and gave them the other safeguards which they demanded. The Secretary of State suggested that Indian politics had been dominated by two issues, the question of winning independence from British rule and the Hindu-Muslim problem. Once these were out of the way, party divisions would probably be on economic issues. Surely the Scheduled Castes would have a better chance of securing their rights by allying themselves with the left wing than by relying on the British, who were about to hand over power. Ambedkar reiterated that so long as there were joint electorates. Scheduled Caste voters would be so few that Hindu candidates could safely ignore their wishes. Caste Hindus would never support Scheduled Caste candidates. Separate electorates were fundamental; without them the Scheduled Castes would never have their own representatives (V.P. Menon: *The Transfer of Power in India,* pp. 284-85).

This was what Ambedkar telling the Cabinet Delegation and the Viceroy in April 1946!

Even in November 1946—that is, even till just a fortnight before the Constituent Assembly was to begin its first session—there seemed to be every possibility that Ambedkar would do a "Deliverance Day" again, team up with the Muslim League and boycott the Assembly. In his Private and Secret dispatch of 27 November 1946 to the Secretary of State, the Viceroy, Lord Wavell, noted, "The All India Scheduled Castes Federation (Ambedkar's Body) have announced that they will shortly consider whether they should boycott the deliberations of the Constituent Assembly; their present tendency seems to be to do so, and if they do, it would mean that they have moved over to the Muslim League."

And these views and maneuvers were as well known to everyone who had been fighting for the country's Independence and who was to soon join the Constituent Assembly as the record of Ambedkar during the preceding quarter century (Arun Shourie: *Worshipping False Gods,* pp. 407-09).

In earlier part of his address at the All India Scheduled Castes Federation, published in Volume 1 of his *Writings and Speeches* on pages 358 to 360 under "Responsibility for Framing the Constitution," Dr. Ambedkar said: "Before I set out in concrete terms the Constitutional proposals I have in mind, I wish to raise two preliminary issues. First is: Who should frame a Constitution for India? It is necessary to raise this question because there are quite a lot of people in India who are hoping, if not asking, British Government to resolve the deadlock and frame a Constitution of India. I think there is a gross fallacy in such view, which needs to be exposed. A Constitution framed by the British Government and imposed upon Indians sufficed in the past. But if the nature of the future Constitution Indians are clamouring for, is born in mind it will be clear that an imposed Constitution will not do.

"The difference between the past Constitutions and the future Constitution of India is fundamental, and those, who still rely on the British for framing a Constitution for India, do not seem to have realized this difference. The difference lies in this that the past Constitutions contained a breakdown clause. But the future Constitution of India cannot contain such a breakdown clause. People in India decry the breakdown clause—by now the notorious Section 93 of the Government of India Act 1935. That is because they do not know the why and how of its place in the Act. Its importance will become apparent of two important considerations governing the political life of a community are born in mind. First of these considerations is that the Law and Order is the medicine of the body politic, and when the body politic goes sick the medicine must be administered. Indeed, so important is this consideration that failure to administer it must be deemed to be a crime against society civilization. The second consideration is that though it is true that no Government has a vested right to govern, it is equally true that there must always be a government to govern, which I mean maintain Law and Order, until it is displaced by a better Government. The breakdown clause serves these two purposes. As such, it is not the highest value for the peace and tranquility of the people. For, when Constitutional government fails, the breakdown clause has at least the merit of maintaining government.

"In the past this distinction between Constitutional government and government with provision for government stepping in when Constitutional government failed, was a feasible proposition. It was feasible because while the British Government to give the Indians the right to Constitutional government, and also to keep to itself the right to govern, in case there was a breakdown in the Constitutional government. The reason is quite obvious. The past Constitution of India did not treat India as a Dominion. The future Constitution will proceed on the assumption that India will be a Dominion. The breakdown clause or the possibility of the government stepping in, when Constitutional government has failed, can be reconciled in the case of a country, which had no Dominion Status. But the two are irreconcilable in the case of a Dominion. In the case of the Dominion or for the matter of that in the case of any free country, there is either a Constitutional government or a Rebellion.

What does this mean? It is impossible to frame a Constitution for an Indian Dominion with possibility of a breakdown. To put the same thing in a different language the Constitution must be so made that it will not only command the obedience but also the respect of all; and all or if not all, at any rate, all important elements in the national life the India shall be prepared to uphold it and to give it their support. This can happen only if the Constitution is framed by Indians for Indians and with the voluntary consent of Indians. If the Constitution is imposed by the British Government and is not accepted by one section and is opposed by another, there will arise in the country an element, hostile to the Constitution, and which will devote its energies not to working the Constitution but to breaking it. The anti-Constitution party may look upon destroying the Constitution as its only duty and may engage itself in pronouncing against a party working the Constitution in the real Latin American fashion.

It is useless for the British to frame a Constitution for India, which they will not remain to enforce. The same result will ensure if the Constitution is imposed by one powerful section or a combination of such sections on other sections. I am, therefore, firmly of opinion that if Indians want Dominion Status, they cannot escape the responsibility of framing their own Constitution (Dr. Babasaheb Ambedkar: *Writings and Speeches*, Vol. I, pp. 358-60).

It was ultimately decided to form the Constituent Assembly with members elected from various provinces. Ambedkar's party was totally wiped out. Of the 1585 seats in the various Assemblies, his Scheduled Caste Federation got only one. The worst of it was that even in the Bombay Presidency, Ambedkar and his party were trounced. Of the 175 candidates none of them was elected. Ambedkar himself was defeated from his own Bombay Presidency.

Dr. Ambedkar's fear that the formation of the Constituent Assembly will involve the country in a civil war and the chances of corruption and bribery being used in the Constituent Assembly to buy over members to support decisions desired by interested groups have been proved wrong.

Constitution

Before becoming a member of the Constituent Assembly, Ambedkar had said: ".... So much Constitution of India has already been written out in the Government of India Act 1935, that it seems to be an act of supererogation to appoint a Constituent Assembly to do the thing ever again. All that is necessary is to delete those sections of the Government of India Act 1935, which are inconsistent with the Dominion Status."

Subsequently, Ambedkar took sommersault, which is evident from what he said while presenting the Draft Constitution in the Constituent Assembly on 4th November 1948. He said: "The charge of producing a blind copy of the Constitution of other countries is based on an inadequate study of the Constitution. I have shown what is new in the Draft Constitution and I am sure those who have studied other constitutions and who are prepared to consider the matter dispassionately will agree that the Drafting Committee in performing its duty has not been guilty of such blind and slavish imitation as it is represented to be."

Ambedkar further said: "As to the accusation that the Drafting Committee has produced a good part of the provisions of the Government of India Act 1935, I make no apologies. There is nothing to be ashamed of in borrowing. It involves no plagiarism. Nobody holds any patent rights in the fundamental ideas of a constitution" (Dr. Babasaheb Ambedkar: *Writings and Speeches*, Vol. 13, pp. 49-70).

No Greater Lie

Ambedkar repudiated the charge made against him by some Congressmen that he had played a very insignificant part in drafting the constitution. He said that there can be no greater lie than this. He further said that he was prepared to prove by documentary evidence how his colleagues on the Drafting Committee had shown little interest in the drafting of the constitution. They rarely attended the meetings of the Drafting Committee and the whole burden fell on him and the Secretary of the Constitution (*Ambedkar and Social Justice*, Publication Division, Government of India, Vol. II, p. 277).

I was a Hack

And now see what Ambedkar said in Parliament on 2nd September 1953. Ambedkar said: "People always keep on saying to me, Oh. You are the maker of the constitution. My answer is I was a hack. What I was asked to do, I did much against my will."

During discussion, addressing the Speaker of the Lok Sabha, Ambedkar said: "Sir, my friends tell me that I have made the constitution. But I am quite prepared to say that I shall be the first person to burn it out. I do not want it. It does not suit anybody" (Dr. Babasaheb Ambedkar: *Writings and Speeches*, Vol. 15, pp. 860-64).

This was in 1953. And now see what Ambedkar said on 19th March 1955 in Parliament. He said: "...I say with certain amount of pride that the constitution which has been given to this country is a wonderful document. It has been said not by myself, but by many people, many other students of constitution. It is the simplest and the easiest. Many, many publishers have written to me to write a commentary on the constitution, promising a good sum. But I have always told them that to write a commentary on this constitution is to admit that the constitution is a bad one and an un-understandable one. It is not so.

The following dialogue took place in Parliament, when Ambedkar made the above statement:

Dr. Anup Singh (Punjab)

Last time when you spoke, you said that you would burn the constitution.

Dr. B.R. Ambedkar

Do you want reply to that? I will give it right now. The reason is this. We built the temple for God to come in and reside, but before the God could be installed, if the devil has taken the possession of it, what else could we do except destroy the temple? We did not intend that it should be occupied by Asuras. We intended it to be occupied by the Devas. That is the reason why I said I would rather like to burn it.

Dr. B.K.P. Sinha (Bihar)

Destroy the Devil rather than the temple.

Dr. B.R. Ambedkar

You cannot do it. We have not got the strength. If you will read the Brahamana, the Satha-Patha Brahamana, you will see that the Gods have always been defeated by the Asuras and that the Asuras had the Amrit with them, which the Gods had to take away in order to survive in the battle (Dr. Babasaheb Ambedkar: *Writings and Speeches*, Vol. 15, pp. 947-49).

Ambedkar did not explain who the Asuras were and who the Devas?

K.S. Hegde, a Member of Parliament from Madras, later Judge of the Supreme Court and later still the Speaker of the Lok Sabha) said:

".... It is astounding to have a person who was put Minister in charge of preparing the Constitution disown responsibility in the manner Ambedkar has done and to proclaim that he would burn the Constitution. "Is he setting a good political precedent?" Hegde asked, adding, "I am sorry Dr. Ambedkar only abused and got out of the House. If he abuses, he should be prepared to receive the reactions thereof." "It came with ill grace from Dr. Ambedkar when he said that his heart was not in the Constitution, that he was merely perpetuating a fraud, to put it in the mildest form." "His whole life has been one of a series of contradictions," Hegde pointed out. "First he tried to live in communalism and now probably it is too late in the day for him to get himself out of that past. I have nothing but pity for him...."

Hegde furher said: "I am not on Ambedkar's inconsistencies at the moment, but on his remarks about the authorship of the Constitution: was Ambedkar just palming off responsibility, or was he giving us a glimpse into what his role had actually been in regard to the drafting of the Constitution? That the remarks were not just an off-the-cuff outburst is evident from the fact that he repeated the description to the political scientist and biographer, Michael Brecher during an interview three years later, a few months before his death (Arun Shourie: *Worshipping False Gods,* pp. 377-88).

In the words of Michael Brecher:

"Speaking in Parliament in the autumn of 1953, he called for a complete repudiation of the Constitution. When reminded of his role, he said, 'I was a hack. I did what I was asked to do. I only carried out the wishes of the majority. The disillusioned Ambedkar reiterated this view in the spring of 1956, a few months before his death. By this he meant that decisions were first taken in the Congress party caucus and then translated into constitutional language by the Drafting Committee (Michael Brecher: *Nehru—A Political Biography,* p. 423).

Article Relating to Governor

The Provincial Constitution Committee of which Sardar Patel was the Chairman had recommended that while "for the most part, the Governor will act on advice of the Council of Ministers, but he is required to act on his discretion in the following matters: (1) the prevention of any grave menace to the peace and tranquility of the Province or any part thereof...; (2) the summoning and dissolving of the Provincial Legislature...; (3) the superintendence, direction and control of elections...;

(4) the appointment of the Chairman and the members of the Provincial Public Services Commission and of the Provincial Auditor-General...." "It is to be noted," the Committee had added, "that the Governor, under the proposed Constitution, is to be elected by the people, so that he is not likely to abuse his 'discretionary' powers."

That report had been finalized and submitted to the President of the Constituent Assembly on 27 June 1947. But a fortnight later when Sardar Patel rose to move the report of the Committee for consideration by the Constituent Assembly, he told the Assembly that the report of the Committee "is not the final draft of the Provincial Constitution". One by one he reversed the recommendations of the Committee in regard to three of the four items on which according to the report the Governor was to exercise his discretion. The only function in regard to which the Governor was now envisaged to act on his own was in summoning the Legislature.

The Constituent Assembly took up the draft of the relevant Articles for consideration on 31 May and 1 June 1949. The Drafting Committee had suggested two alternative provisions: one providing for a Governor who would be directly elected by the people, and the other for a Governor who would be appointed by the President. On the latter too there were two possibilities: that the Legislature forward a panel of names to the President and the latter appoint one of the persons without any panel being put up to him. The draft regarding the powers and functions of the Governor, that is Article 143, read: "There shall be a Council of Ministers with the Chief Minister at the head to aid and advise the Governor in the exercise of his functions except in so far as he is by or under this Constitution required to exercise his functions or any of them in his discretion."

Ambedkar explained, first, that in regard to the method of election or appointment of the Governor the Drafting Committee had had no choice but to furnish alternatives for the Constituent Assembly to consider: the Assembly had already accepted the principle that the Governor would be elected; as such, Ambedkar explained, "The Drafting Committee had no choice in the matter at all because according to the directions given to the

Drafting Committee it was bound to accept the principle which had been sanctioned by the House itself." But since then things had proceeded in a different direction, he went on to add: the view now was "that the Governor is not to have any kind of functions—to use a familiar phraseology, 'no functions which he is required to discharge either in his discretion or in his individual judgment'. According to the principles of the new Constitution he is required to follow the advice of his Ministry in all matters...." Ambedkar said that the Drafting Committee had made a provision for the alternative of the Governor being appointed by the President because "we felt that the powers of the Governor were so limited, so nominal, his position so ornamental that probably very few would come to stand for election". He was not bothered by the prospect that there might be a conflict or rivalry between an elected Chief Minister and an elected Governor, Ambedkar said: the Chief Minister was going to be elected on the basis of the policies and programme he proposed to implement while the Governor was going to be elected on the basis of his personality. He had been persuaded by the other consideration, Ambedkar said: as the Governor was not going to have any substantive functions, how justified would it be to subject the country to the enormous costs of an election for each of these ornamental posts? In fact, said Ambedkar, as "this functionary is going to be a purely ornamental functionary, how he comes into being, whether by nomination or by some other machinery, is a purely psychological question—what would appeal most to the people—a person nominated or a person in whose nomination the Legislature has in some way participated. Beyond that, it seems to me it has no consequence...."

As that is the position, H.V. Kamath and a number of other members argued, the words in the draft Article "except in so far as he is by or under this Constitution required to exercise his functions or any of them in his discretion" should be deleted. They tabled an amendment to the draft Article for this purpose. Ambedkar and other members of the Drafting Committee now argued the opposite. The words should not be deleted, they said, because the Assembly had not yet taken a view on other draft Articles of the Constitution which endowed some discretionary powers in the Governor. Vesting such powers in an appointed Governor is not in any way incompatible with responsible Government, Ambedkar said. As under other Articles on which the Assembly had yet to take a final view the Governor had been assigned functions which he was to discharge in his discretion, "the House cannot escape from mentioning in some manner that the Governor shall have discretion".

But does the Article relating to the President not require that he must in all matters act in accordance with the advice of the Council of Ministers? Isn't there a difference therefore between Articles relating to the President and those relating to the Governor, Kamath asked. "Of course there is," Ambedkar replied, "because we do not want to vest the President with any discretionary power. Because the Provincial Governments are required to work in subordination to the Central Government, and therefore in order to see that they do act in subordination to the Central Government the Governor will reserve certain things in order to give the President the opportunity to see that the rules under which the Provincial Governments are supposed to act according to the Constitution or in subordination to the Central Government are observes...."

Clearly the balance which Ambedkar was indicating on June 1 was very different from the balance he had spelled out on 31 May. B. Shiva Rao speaks to the result: "It is...worth noting that as the various Articles which conferred these discretionary functions came up for consideration, the Drafting Committee suggested amendments deleting the requirement that the Governor would act in his discretion. As a result, in the Constitution as adopted finally, full ministerial responsibility without any discretionary powers for the Governor was established over the whole field of State administration. The only matter in which the Governor could act independently of his Ministers was in relation to certain tribal areas in Assam where, for a transitional period, the administration was made a Central responsibility and the Governor was to act as the agent of the Central Government. But in spite of this radical change in the content of the powers of the Governor, no change was made in the draft Article 143 and the reference to the Governor exercising certain functions in his discretion still remains. At the revision the Article was renumbered 163.

Does a sequence such as this speak to the Article springing virginal and complete from the mind of one person—Ambedkar in this case—or to some other process? And does the sequence —one day the balance of Ambedkar's argument tilts one way, another day it tilts the other way—not indicate that he was only telling the truth when he told the Rajya Sabha, "We lawyers defend many things"? And the "Drafting" Committee: does it lay down what the Article shall be, or does it indicate two very dissimilar alternatives and wait upon the Assembly to choose? And the Assembly itself: does it settle the matter unambiguously and finally, or does it for the time being retain words which in fact go contrary to the direction in which its own decision is tending?

Relating to Property

The Article relating to the right to property went through several rounds, and was the subject of earnest discussion. It went through many versions: when it came up for consideration at the Premiers' Conference, Ambedkar narrated that the Article had caused the Drafting Committee "a lot of headache", so much so that he suggested that the Article be dropped altogether and in its stead an entry be provided in the Legislative Lists reproducing verbatim the relevant words from the Australian Constitution. Alladi Krishnaswami and others shot down that suggestion on the ground that it would not meet any of the problems which had come up. The drafts and redrafts continued to go to and fro. Eventually the draft of the Article that the Drafting Committee sent up closely followed Section 299 of the Government of India Act, 1935. It provided that no property would be acquired except for a public purpose, and that it would not be acquired without compensation and unless either the amount of compensation was fixed or the principles on which it was to be fixed were set out. When the draft came up for consideration in the Constituent Assembly, Pandit Nehru himself moved an amendment to replace the text wholesale. He told the Assembly that the new text was "the result of a great deal of consultation", that it reflected a compromise between various approaches.

Two years later, in 1952, the Supreme Court handed down judgments in which it held that the existence of a public purpose was a prerequisite for the exercise of the power of compulsory acquisition. The Government then brought in an amendment to the Constitution which provided, among other things, that "no such law [aimed at acquiring property] shall be called in question in any court on the ground that the compensation provided by that law is not adequate". The amendment also provided that where the law did not transfer the property to the State or a Corporation owned or controlled by the State "it shall not be deemed to provide for the compulsory acquisition or requisitioning of property, notwithstanding that it deprives any person of his property". In a word, there was no longer any need in such cases for either of the two conditions—the existence of a public purpose, or the payment of just compensation. This part of the matter was thus put beyond the reach of courts. Government asserted that the new text was in accord with what the Drafting Committee had intended.

Ambedkar refuted the suggestion. Here is what he told the Rajya Sabha on 19 March 1955: "Article 31 with which we are dealing now in this Bill is an Article for which I, and the Drafting Committee, can take no responsibility whatsoever. We do not take any responsibility for that. That is not our draft." He said that at the time this Article was being considered "the Congress Party...was so divided within itself that we did not know what to do, what to put and what not to put." Ambedkar said that there had been three points of view within the Congress on the question: a section led by Sardar Patel had wanted that the Constitution provide for compensation on the lines of the existing Land Acquisition Act, namely market price plus 15 per cent; Pandit Nehru wanted that no compensation should be provided for at all; Pandit Pant, who was the Chief Minister of Uttar Pradesh at the time, had been concerned mainly to safeguard the *zamindari*—abolition legislation he had got through. "There was thus this tripartite struggle," Ambedkar told the House, "and we left it to them to decide in any way they liked. And they merely embodied what their decision was in Article 31. This Article 31,

in my judgment, is a very ugly thing, something which I do not like to look at...."

Due Process Clause

Consider a third example. Few provisions gave rise to as much earnest debate as the "due process" clause in the Fundamental Rights part of the Constitution. The original drafts—of Sir B.N. Rau, of K.M. Munshi—had provided that no person shall be deprived of his life, liberty or property except by "due process of law". This expression, as is well known, had been taken over from what had become the keystone of American judgments on rights of the individual vis-à-vis the State. Through it the courts in the U.S.A. had held that the courts would inquire into not just whether the procedures prescribed by law had been adhered to in a formal sense, they would also ensure that the substance of the law under which the State had acted was just. Several persons, including Sir B.N. Rau, drew attention to the fact that this provision had occasioned endless litigation in American courts. They proposed that the words "due process of law" be replaced by words that would leave greater leeway for the Executive, namely "by procedure established by law". (Incidentally, the latter expression too was being taken verbatim from another Constitution, in this case the new Constitution of Japan.) Others argued that a change of this sort would leave the citizen at the mercy of the Executive and the Legislature—and in the system that was being adopted, the latter would be in the control of the Executive.

Ambedkar's position on the matter swung from one end to the other. When the Article came up for consideration in the Constituent Assembly, there was vigourous opposition to the change which had been made. Ambedkar proposed that consideration of the Article be postponed for a week so as to give the Drafting Committee more time to come up with a formulation which would harmonize the different concerns that the members were expressing. The Assembly resumed consideration of the draft Article on 13 December 1948. Recall what Ambedkar said as he moved the Article for the consideration of the Assembly:

There are two views on this point. One view is this: that the Legislature may be trusted not to make any law which would abrogate the Fundamental Rights of man, so to say, the Fundamental Rights which apply to every individual, and consequently there is no danger arising from the introduction of the phrase 'due process'. Another view is this: that it is not possible to trust the Legislature; the Legislature is likely to err, is likely to be led away by passion, by party prejudice, by party considerations, and the Legislature may make a law which may abrogate what may be regarded as the fundamental principles which safeguard the individual rights of a citizen. We are therefore placed in two difficult positions. One is to give the Judiciary the authority to sit in judgment over the will of the Legislature and to question the law made by the Legislature on the ground that it is not good law, in consonance with fundamental principles. Is that a desirable principle? The second position is that the Legislature ought to be trusted not to make bad laws. It is very difficult to come to any definite conclusion. There are dangers on both sides. For myself I cannot altogether omit the possibility of a Legislature packed by partymen making laws which may abrogate or violate what we regard as certain fundamental principles affecting the life and liberty of an individual. At the same time, I do not see how five or six gentlemen sitting in the Federal or Supreme Court examining laws made by the Legislature and by dint of their own individual conscience or their bias or prejudices [can] be trusted to determine which law is good and which law is bad. It is rather a case where a man has to sail between Charybdis and Scylla and I therefore would not say anything. I would leave it to the House to decide in any way it likes.

Are these the words of the author of a document who is informing an Assembly about his creation, or the words of a rapporteur so that he may record it?

A volume can be filled with examples of this kind. The point however will be obvious by now: in speaking as he did in the Rajya Sabha on Articles about the powers of the Governor or about the right to property was Ambedkar merely passing off responsibility or was he truthfully describing the role that he had actually played? Was he not giving us a glimpse into the way the Constitution was actually framed—by an iterative, collective effort, by the contribution of numerous persons, by numerous accommodation of many, many points of view? (Arun Shourie: *Worshipping False Gods*, pp. 388-95, 397-99).

Love-Hate Relationship

When Gandhi died, the Government of India received more than 3000 messages expressing condolences from foreign countries alone. They included tributes from King George, President Harry S. Truman, Prime Minister Clement Atlee, Mrs. Eleanor Roosewelt, Albert Einstein and scores of others. The Ministry of Information of the Government of India declared: "Perhaps no man in recorded history received such spontaneous tributes of universal praise, reverence and love as did Gandhi on his death. Never before such a flood of love and sympathy had been poured out as was poured on the death of Gandhi. People from every land poured out their affection.

The United Nations Organization took an unprecedented step of observing official mourning on the death of Gandhi. Such recognition is accorded only to the Head of State. Gandhi was not Head of the State.

In November 1968, the General Assembly of the UNESCO took the equally unprecedented step of passing unanimously and with acclamation a resolution to observe the period from 2nd October 1968 to 2nd October 1969 as Gandhi Centenary Year.

The United Nations declared a decade of Culture and Peace for the children of the world.

On 15th June 2007, the United Nations General Assembly unanimously resolved to observe 2nd October—the birth anniversary of Mahatma Gandhi as the International Day of Non-violence.

Jawaharlal Nehru, the first Prime Minister of India in his broadcast on 30th January 1948 said: ".... The light has gone out. The light that shone in this country was no ordinary light. The light that has illuminated this country for these many years will illumine this country for many more years and a thousand years later that light will still be seen in this country and the world will see it and it will give solace to innumerable hearts. For that represented something more than the immediate present; it represented the living truth...the eternal truth, reminding us of the right path, drawing us from error, taking this country to freedom."

Nehru concluded: "In the ages to come, centuries and may be millenniums after us people will think of this generation when this man of God trod the earth and will think of us, however small, could also follow his path and probably tread on that holy ground where his feet had been. Let us be worthy of him, let us always be so."

Mrs. Merry Bethune, American Negro leader said: "Gandhi cannot die, his spirit is free to stir men's souls in every corner of the earth. As we, mothers of earth, stand in awesome fear of the roar of Jetplanes, the crash of atom bombs, and the unknown horrors of germ warfare, we must turn our eyes in hope to East where the sun of Mahatma blazes."

Dr. Francis Neilson, in his book, *The Tragedy of Europe* writes: "Gandhi is unique. There is no record of a man of his position challenging a great empire. A Diogenes in action, a St. Francis in humility, a Socrates in wisdom, he reveals to the world utter paltriness of the methods of the statesman, who relies upon force to gain his end. In this context, spiritual, integrity triumphs over the physical opposition of the forces of state. That was Gandhi's triumph. That was his achievement. That marks his place in history."

Gandhi's life and position in the world history are memorably summed up by Albert Einstein: "The veneration in which Gandhi has been held throughout the world rests on the recognition, for the most part unconscious, that in our age of moral decay he was the only statesman who represented that higher conception of human relations in the political sphere to which we must aspire with all our powers. We must learn the difficult lesson that the future of mankind will only be tolerable when our course in world affairs, as in all other matters, is based upon justice and law rather than the threat of naked power. Generations to come

...scarce believe that such a one as this ever in flesh and blood walked upon this earth."

Chaster Bowles said: "Among all the revolutionaries who have dominated the political stage in our country—Lenin, Mussolini, Hitler, Stalin and Mao—Gandhi alone offered the prospect of reform without destruction. While his revolutionary contemporaries were feeding the flames of pernicious chaos, he saw in the innate dignity of the individual human being, no matter how humble or downtrodden, the key to orderly political and social progress."

Chester Bowles further said: "Yet because Gandhi showed tens of millions of individual citizens how to speak out for freedom, for peace and for individual dignity, I believe that mankind is on the right path and that our task is an easier one."

Pearl S. Buck said: "It was strangely fitting that Gandhi should have died suddenly one day at the hand of one of his own people. I am sure we often think of the great drama of that death. It usually happens that a man of such stature approaches heights intolerable to certain lost souls. Christ always has his Judas. The dualism of our universe manifests itself in many ways. Gandhi died when he was triumphant in leadership. He did not sicken and weaken as lesser men might do. He simply was sent on his way to what beyond we do not know."

In the opinion of R.R. Diwakar: "Gandhi wears a triple crown. He has earned it through incessant, loving action, dedication to truth and pursued through Ahimsa. The three Yogas or the synthesis of the three Yogas themselves thus found in Gandhi a living example, which otherwise would have been thought to be merely an idea. While textbooks on Yoga give us ideas, Gandhi gave a demonstration for which the world shall ever remain indebted."

James W. Douglass said: "Because he envisioned the face of God as Truth, Gandhi experimented with truth in a lifelong struggle to see God face to face. In the course of that struggle, which became in part the struggle of India and finally the British Empire and the world, Gandhi encountered God as suffering love. In realizing through his experiments that the God of Truth is found through the God of suffering love, Gandhi passed to the redeeming truth of the Incarnation."

Romain Rolland declared that he regarded Gandhi as "Christ who only lacked the Cross". We have now given him the Cross also. Gandhi's death was a classical ending to his life. He died with the name of God on his lips and love in his heart. Even as he received the bullet wounds he greeted his murderer and wished him well. He lived up to what he preached.

S. Radhakrishnan, the philosopher President of India said: "Such men are filled with spiritual poise and yet take upon themselves the burden of suffering humanity are born in the world at long intervals. We have killed Gandhi's body, but the spirit in him which a light from above will penetrate far into space and time and inspire countless generations for nobler living."

K. Santhanam said: "Under his inspiring leadership even common clay became often transmuted into pure gold. But the transformation of society is a terribly slow process. It may take decades and centuries before a sufficient number of persons may elect to adopt whole-heartedly Gandhiji's doctrine of truth, non-violence and satyagraha so that the life of the world may become directed towards his ideals. Now that he is dead, time is on his side."

Humayun Kabir said: "Evil struck at Gandhi and killed his mortal body, but his message it could not kill. Liberated from physical bonds, his spirit strode the world and achieved a power which in his life he had never enjoyed. His death vindicated his life, and in death he triumphed even as another who conquered the world by laying down his life two thousand years ago."

John Haynes Holmes said: "Gandhi was immortal and omnipotent conqueror for he possessed the hearts of men for ever. As long as there will be a human race upon this planet, he will be remembered and revered as the greatest Indian since Gautam Buddha and as the greatest man since Jesus Christ."

Holmes further said: "And not only all India but also the world, for the world was standing still and silent, in reverence of this one man, and his frail body was burned, and his mighty soul liberated into eternity. I say it advisedly, measuring my words, that the greatest statesman who ever lived, and the mightiest soldier, never received such a tribute as this, and I venture to prophecy never will. Gandhi had captured the heart of mankind. There was not any man anywhere who did not love him. And Gandhi had conquered as well not only the affection of our hearts, but also the conviction of our minds. As the world bowed in homage before this man, what was it but a confession of sin that he was right, and we knew it; and that all the dreadful ways of force and violence, which we had followed through the centuries, were not only wrong but criminal and wicked."

Fredrick John Fisher said: "I have known men to say, I hate him. I despise everything for which he stands. And then I have greeted them as they came away from Gandhi, murmuring. I was mistaken. Love him, or hate him, if you can. You cannot ignore him. He remains unique."

And now see what Ambedkar said on the assassination of Gandhi:

In his letter of 8th February 1948 to Sharda alias Laxmi Kabir, who later became his wife, Ambedkar wrote: "....My own view is that great men are of great service to their country, but they are also at certain times a great hindrance to the progress of their country. There is one incidence in Roman history which comes to my mind on this occasion. When Caesar was done to death and the matter was reported to Cicero, Cicero said to the messenger: "Tell the Romans, your hour of liberty has come." While one regrets the assassination of Mr. Gandhi, one cannot help finding in his heart the echo of sentiments expressed by Cicero on the assassination of Caesar. Mr. Gandhi had become a positive danger to this country. He had choked all the thoughts. He was holding together the Congress, which is a combination of all the bad and self-seeking elements in society who agreed on no social or moral principle governing the life of society except the one of praising and flattering Mr. Gandhi. Such a body is unfit to govern a country. As the 'Bible' says that sometimes good cometh out of evil, so also I think that good will come out of the death of Mr. Gandhi. It will release people from bondage to superman, it will make them think for themselves and it will compel them to stand on their own merits."

Ambedkar further wrote: "What is surprising is that those who feel wrath or those who feel grief for the assassination of Mr. Gandhi seem to be so few. Indeed, one of the most surprising thing I noticed about the funeral procession, which no doubt was very large, a majority of them were in a holiday mood as though they were going to Urs or Yatra" (Nanak Chand Rattu: *Little Known Facets of Dr. Ambedkar,* p. 197).

The above words are the height of Ambedkar's hatred for Gandhi. How would his followers react if the same comment is made by the followers of Gandhi on the funeral procession of Ambedkar.

The readers themselves may decide as to how far Ambedkar was justified in what he said after the death of Gandhi and earlier saying: "Good God! Is this man Gandhi our saviour?" and advising untouchables to Beware of Mr. Gandhi.

I can only say that the relations between Gandhi and Ambedkar were that of love and hate. Gandhi loved, respected and admired Ambedkar, whereas, Ambedkar missed no opportunity to criticize, condemn and humiliate Gandhi during his life and even after his death.

Gandhi firmly believed: "We can only win over the opponent by love, never by hate. Hate is the subtlest form of violence. Hatred injures the hater, never the hated." Buddha's message was: "For never in this world does hatred cease by hatred; hatred ceases by love." Gandhi meticulously followed Buddha's message in respect of all including Ambedkar. Gandhi believed that someday, he would convert Ambedkar to love him. But it remained his hope against hope. May be because of his sufferings as untouchable. In that sense, it could be termed as natural reaction.